J.G. FARRELL

BY THE SAME AUTHOR

Chink

J.G. FARRELL

The Making of a Writer

Lavinia Greacen

BLOOMSBURY

First published in Great Britain 1999

Copyright © 1999 by Lavinia Greacen

The moral right of the author has been asserted

Bloomsbury Publishing Plc, 38 Soho Square, London, W1V 5DF

A CIP catalogue record for this book
is available from the British Library

ISBN 0 7475 4463 8

10 9 8 7 6 5 4 3 2 1

Typeset by Hewer Text Ltd, Edinburgh
Printed in Great Britain by Clays Limited, St Ives plc

For Sophia Hope Greacen,
born 26 March 1997,
with my love

A lamp was burning in his study and in the glass of the book-cases he saw his own image, shadowy in detail . . . The face also in shadow, anonymous, the face of a man like other men, who in a few years would be lost to history, whose personality would be no more individual than the shadowy reflection in the glass.

The Siege of Krishnapur

'So I cure him, so what? So I postpone his death a few years . . . what difference does it make to him or to anyone else?'

The Lung

I don't mean to sound ironic, the characters have my sympathy. The human condition – we all have my sympathy.

J.G. Farrell, letter to Carol Drisko, 16 August 1968

Contents

Acknowledgments   xi
Foreword   xv
Prologue   1

Part One

1 At the Centre of a Vast Empire   9
2 The Vanished Comfort and Security of Earlier Days   21
3 Run Very Fast, Very Fast Indeed   35
4 The Yearning, the Boredom, the Heartache   53
5 A Ballistic Missile   67
6 In Human Affairs, Things Tend Inevitably
     to Go Wrong   81
7 The Beauty of the Cold Season   99
8 Water Becoming Hard Ice   119
9 This Is the Kind of Life I Want   135
10 The Slow, Dangerous Ascent   151
11 A Sea of Dark Feathers   171
12 A Nebulous Desire for Escape   187
13 The Extreme Outer Edge of Endeavour   205
14 A Traveller through Unmapped Country   227

Part Two

15 Out into the Open Sea   245
16 A Foot Wedged in the Door of Eternity   271

17 In the Right Place at the Right Time   *295*
18 At Large in the Minefields   *321*
19 A Tiny Bit World-weary   *355*
20 A Place to Breathe   *379*

Epilogue   401
'The World of J.G. Farrell' by Derek Mahon   401
Notes and References   403
Index   421

Acknowledgments

Jim Farrell's family have been supportive from the outset, while leaving me entirely free to form my own point of view. I would like to take this opportunity to wholeheartedly thank his brothers, Robert and Richard, and his late mother, Jo. With poignant timing, Mrs Josephine Farrell died in February 1999 in her ninetieth year, twenty years after her second son and ten years after her husband.

One of my strongest impressions is of the large number of friends who still miss Jim Farrell acutely. Among people who knew him personally, whether they live in England, Ireland, America or Europe, it was his gift for friendship that seems irreplaceable. I include their names with gratitude among the rollcall of all those who have kindly helped me, but cloaked – as Jim might, perhaps, have recommended – in the anonymity of alphabetical order. Sadly, a few names already bear out his conclusions about transience.

Tom Aitken, Brigid Allen, Angela Amos, Dr Major Vickram Anand, Ian Angus, Gary Arnott, Nicholas Back, Mrs Sheilah Baird, Vincent Banville, Paul Barker, Franz and Marlis Beer, Monika Beisner, Alan Bennett, Dr Lalloo Bhagwan, Andrew Bonar-Law, Mrs Jill Bond, Mrs Sue Bond, Mrs Pat Booth, Dr Michael Bott, Sue Bradbury, Dr A. Brading, Mrs Pamela Bradley, Alfred Brendel, Dr Colin Brooks, Julia Brown, Kenneth H. Brown, Kevin Brownlow, Felicity Bryan, Ralph Burrows, Tim Cadigan, Sir Michael Caine, David Caute, Shiv Chirimar, Susannah Clapp, Jonathan Clowes, Alastair Cooke, John Cooney, Mrs Jill Cox, Allan Cumming, Bob Cumming, Mrs Patricia Cumming, John Curtis, Geoffrey Davidson, Phillip and Jill

Davies, Mrs Beryl Dawson, Malcolm and Claire Dean, Robin
Denniston, Kay Dick, Norma di Marco, Diana and Robert
Ditchfield, Elsie Donald, Roger Donald, Sean and Clodagh
Dooney, Hans Dorflinger, Robert Downie, Mrs Kathleen Doyle,
Margaret Drabble, Carol Drisko, Geoffrey Drought, Maureen
Duffy, John D. Eadie, Maureen Erasmus, Liza Evans, Anthony
Farrell, Revd Tom Farrell, Erwin Fleissner, John B. Fox, Stephen
Frears, A.G. Fryer, Mrs Sandy Fuller, Bamber Gascoigne, An-
drew Gemill, Sir Martin Gilbert, Fay Godwin, Martyn Goff,
Tony Gould, Tom Gover, Miriam Gross, John Guare, Phillip
Haas, James Hale, Dr Elie Harar, Philippa Harrison, Jan Hart-
man, Joseph Hone, Hubert Hours, Paul Huxley, Norman Ilett,
Ruth Prawer Jhabvala, Terry and Gaye Johnson, Manog Ka-
poor, R.R.V. Kaufmann, Paul Keegan, J.P. Kennedy, Neo Ah
Kiat, Francis King, Jack Kirwan, Mrs Ann Kitz, Brian and Rose
Knox Peebles, Robert Kostrzewa, Rattan Kotwai, Tim Kuchna,
Dr Pranev Kumar, Rajesh Lal, Irving Lazar, Geoffrey Lee, Mrs
Jenifer Leech, Rosemary Legge, Jane Leonard, Michael Leonard,
Nadege Lepra, Suzanne Lowry, Garda Noel Lupton, Alison
Lurie, Mrs Ann McCaffrey, Dr James McCormick, Russell
McCormmach, Brian McMurry, Superintendent Maguire,
Mrs Doreen Mahon, Mrs Ann Mankowitz, Tom Maschler,
Russell Meek, Mrs Judy Miller, Karl Miller, Terence Mitchell,
Timothy Mo, Anil Mookim, H.E. Moore, Caroline Moorehead,
Patricia Moynagh, Rhona Murphy, Roger Murray, Kevin
Myers, V.S. Naipaul, Professor J.K.B. Nicholas, Foy Nissen,
James Nugent SC, Edna O'Brien, Barbara and Jack O'Connell,
Des O'Driscoll, Jerry and Mary O'Mahony, Liam O'Regan,
Rowan O'Sullivan, Mrs Alison Palmer-Carter, Roy Parker,
Robert and Kathleen Parrish, Stephanie and Michel Passebois,
Brian Pearce, Geoffrey and Jane Perrin, Nevill Phillips, Piers
Plowright, Dennis Potter, Anthony Powell, Hilary and Donald
Pratt, Christopher Pringle, S. Gorley Putt, Dr Colm Quigley,
Richard Rawlinson, Piers and Emily Read, Dr William Riding,
C.I. Robertson, Michael Roemer, Deborah Rogers, Kenneth
Rose, Catherine Rothwell, Anthony and Sally Sampson, André
Shiffrin, Claude and Anna Simha, Dyanne and Roger Simon,
David Simpson, Andrew Sinclair, Christopher Sinclair-Steven-
son, Alan Smith, Anthony Smith, G.D. Smith, Hilary and John

Spurling, Barrie Stead, David Stockton, Dermot and Molly Stokes, Catherine and Anthony Storr, Dr Robin Stott, Thomas Summersill, Amajit Singh Talwar, Dr Alf Tansey, Bertrand Tavernier, Paul Theroux, Roger Thompson, Harvey Thorp, Claire Tomalin, Lavinia Trevor, Calvin Trillin, Carole and Shelby Tucker, Mrs Sarah Uffelman, Maggie van Reenan, Tom Wakefield, Stephen and Yvonne Wall, Mrs Bridget Walsh, Marina Warner, Janet Watts, Arnold Weinstein, John Wells, Buckley Wickham, Revd J.R.I. Wikeley, Lacy Wright, Fred Zinnemann. Robert, Camille and Amanda Greacen gave precious moral and practical support. So did Namesh and Lottie Hansjee.

Jim Farrell's collected papers are held in the Manuscripts Department, Trinity College Library, Dublin, presided over by Dr Bernard Meehan. Other libraries and institutions where I have been given assistance in *Dublin* include the Berkeley and Lecky Library of Trinity College, Dundrum Public Library, the Gilbert Library, the National Library of Ireland. In *England*: the Bodleian Library, Oxford, Nuffield Orthopaedic Centre, Reading University Library, Rossall School, Royal College of Surgeons, Southport Library, Terra Nova School, Wellcome Museum of History of Medicine at the Science Museum. In *New York*: the Harkness Foundation. In *France*: l'Université de Paris, Lycée. In *India*, *Singapore* and *Vietnam*: fond memories of help at every turn.

I would like to thank A.M. Heath & Co Ltd on behalf of the Estate of the Late Sonia Brownell Orwell. And also Gallery Books for their kind permission to reproduce 'The World of J.G. Farrell' by Derek Mahon, from *The Yellow Book* (1997).

My salaams, as Jim liked to say, to Bruce Hunter, who conjured this book into existence, and to the most amiable and meticulous team of Anne Chisholm, Rosemary Davidson and Pascal Cariss at Bloomsbury. Also, harking back further, I do not forget the encouragement of Roland Philipps and Katie Owen; nor that of Laurence Cassidy of the (Irish) Arts Council, to whom I am indebted for a Travel Award to New York. Air France, similarly, enabled me to explore Jim's French years. Michael Shaw not only masterminded my trip to India, Singapore and Vietnam, but joined the quest, being a JGF fan. And for xiv J G Farrell

standing those absences, which inevitably led to so many

understanding those absences, which inevitably led to so many more (both physical and mental), I appreciate the generous nature of my inimitable husband, Walter.

Lastly, I salute the academic advance guard. In particular, Ralph J. Crane of the University of Waikato, New Zealand, Jennifer Livett of the University of Tasmania (joint authors of *Troubled Pleasures*, Four Courts Press, Dublin 1997), Lars Hartveit of the University of Bergen, and Daniel Lea, organiser of the conference, '(Re-)Constructing History: The Novels of J.G. Farrell', held at Royal Holloway College, University of London on 28 June 1997. Ronald Binns led the way in England with the Methuen monograph *J.G. Farrell* (1986). And to the swelling ranks of students worldwide who choose to interpret aspects of the Empire Trilogy for their Ph.D. degrees, there is challenge, as well as comfort, in *The Singapore Grip* in the final words: *Tomorrow is another day, as they say, as they say.*

Lavinia Greacen, Ticknock, Co. Dublin, March 1999

Foreword

L avinia Greacen begins and ends her dramatic and moving
narrative with a description of how Jim Farrell, the finest
novelist of recent times, drowned in Bantry Bay on Saturday 11
August 1979, at the age of forty-four. Two days later eighteen
more lives were lost when gale-force winds broke up the Fastnet
Race; but Jim wasn't sailing, he was fishing. He had bought a
house near Kilcrohane, County Cork, only five months before
and turned into the complete angler in a matter of weeks.
Though born in England, he spent much of his youth in Ireland
and returned constantly in his thoughts. Like Brendan Archer in
Troubles he had left the love of his life here and never quite
severed the umbilical cord.

He travelled a great deal, latterly in India and South-East Asia
to research *The Siege of Krishnapur* and *The Singapore Grip* –
though his research was singular in that he drafted the novels
first and made his field trips afterwards to confirm or revise the
background he had read up or imagined at home in London. He
travelled in time too, of course, and his evocation of the Raj at
the time of the Indian Mutiny must be one of the best there is.
One of the remarkable things about the work is his uncanny
sense of period, his eye for the clinching detail – an elephant's-
foot wastepaper basket in *Troubles*, or the contents of Prince
Hari's room in the *Siege*: 'Near a fireplace of marble inlaid with
garnets, lapis lazuli and agate, the Maharajah's son sat on a
chair constructed entirely of antlers, eating a boiled egg and
reading *Blackwood's Magazine*. Beside the chair a large cushion
on the floor still bore the impression of where he had been sitting
a moment earlier. He preferred squatting on the floor to the

discomfort of chairs but feared that his English visitors might regard this as backward.'

Out of context this reads, I realize, rather like a racist joke; but Jim was no racist. On the contrary, he is one of the few English (or Anglo-Irish) writers about the British Empire who can see events through the eyes of the colonized, certainly in the *Siege* and the *Grip*, where the submerged life of the Chinese community is explored sympathetically. The exception, curiously, is *Troubles*, where everything is seen through the eyes, or binoculars, of the Big House characters; and although the 'native Irish' are treated affectionately, they remain oddly baffling to the narrator, as to his protagonist: 'The Major raised the binoculars and gazed once more at the young man on the rock jetty, wondering what he was saying to the crowd. Behind him as he spoke great towering breakers would build up; a solid wall of water as big as a house would mount over his gesticulating arms, hang there above him for an instant as if about to engulf him, then crash around him in a torrent of foam. "He looks like a wild young fellow," the Major said as he handed the binoculars back. Before turning away he watched another wave tower over the young Irishman, hang for a moment, and at last topple to boil impotently around his feet. It was, after all, only the lack of perspective that made it seem he would be swept away.'

Re-reading that, I'm aware of an uncanny parallel between the 'wild young fellow', presumably a Sinn Féin organizer, who wouldn't be swept away, and his creator, who would; and I'm reminded of some remarks, in a piece Jim wrote on his early reading, about the 'hallucinating clarity of image' he admired in Conrad and Richard Hughes. He talks too about Loti's *Pêcheur d'Islande* which he read at school: 'I realised with surprise that I was becoming intensely interested in this story of Breton fishermen and their difficulties . . . So powerful an impression did this book make on me that even today there are certain phenomena for which an expression of Loti's will alone suffice. A certain wintry light over the sea, for example, still conjures up Loti's *lumière blafarde*. I had no idea then, nor have I now, of the precise meaning of *blafard*. In my own mind it bears such perfect witness as it is, that to find its accepted meaning might prove an inconvenience.' Well, the Oxford French Dictionary gives 'pale, pallid, wan, sallow, dull, leaden'. But of course Jim is perfectly right: none of them is sufficiently *blafard*, with its edge of wildness, insanity even.

There was nothing obviously wild, much less insane, about the man I knew. Eccentric, yes; outspoken too. Adopting John Berger's precedent, he continued the practice, now alas in abeyance, whereby the recipient of a Booker Prize should bite the feeding hand in no uncertain terms. Presented with his winning cheque for *The Siege of Krishnapur*, as Lavinia Greacen relates in Chapter 17 'In the Right Place at the Right Time', he made a short speech of thanks in his mild, wandering voice and took the opportunity to criticize conditions on the Booker McConnell plantations in the West Indies.

'We devote too much time to satisfying the ego, time which could be better spent in fruitful speculation or in the service of the senses; in any case, owning things one doesn't need for some primary purpose, and that includes almost everything, has gone clean out of fashion. I'm sorry to have to break this news of the death of materialism so bluntly; I'm afraid it will come as a shock to some of your readers.' Thus spake Jim when, an unlikely fashion journalist, I interviewed him for *Vogue* in 1974 (Chapter 17). Ascetic epicurean, gregarious solitary, aristocrat of the spirit, he was then entering upon the late, disinterested 'Marxist' phase (though he was never really a Marxist) which would issue in his most ambitious work, *The Singapore Grip*, with its clear-eyed depiction of economic imperialism at work in South-East Asia and the Far East.

But there's an intimation of something else too in his hip *Vogue* prophecy. When, at his mother's suggestion, my wife and I visited the Kilcrohane house in 1981, we found on his desk and bookshelves Japanese dictionaries and Buddhist texts which seemed to indicate the way his thoughts were tending during his last year, and even to reveal an important, if barely visible, aspect of his nature; for his early brush with death and subsequent singularity had developed in him a mystical strain, one which expressed itself in impatience with London and withdrawal to the silence of West Cork – there, in an old phrase, to make his soul. When the wise man grows weary of the world, said the Buddha, he becomes empty of desire; 'when he is empty of desire, he becomes free; when he is free he knows that he is free, that rebirth is at an end, that virtue is accomplished, that duty is done and that there is no more returning to this world; thus he knows.'

Derek Mahon, Dublin, 1999

Prologue

'*D*ublin Ireland. Aug. 14' began the 1979 Reuters report carried by newspapers worldwide. 'Author J.G. Farrell, 43, who won literary fame for his novels about the British Empire, is believed to have drowned off the southwest coast of Ireland, police said today. A vacationer told police he saw Mr Farrell slip and fall into the sea Saturday while fishing near his home in Bantry Bay. Police said the area was particularly dangerous because of strong currents. Divers searching the area have not found the body.'

> *The Major was floating in soft black water in a disused quarry. The depth of the water was so great that when he dropped a white pebble into it he could still see it minutes afterwards, winking in the darkness as it sank. Then he was sinking beside it, down and down. 'Death is the only peace on earth,' he thought as he was sinking.*

As soon as he was notified, the novelist's younger brother, Richard, flew over from England to join the search. From the public phone box in Kilcrohane he rang the Dublin solicitor Jack Kirwan, a friend from childhood. 'Died 11.8.79 at 6pm, Saturday', Jack jotted down. 'Aged 44 approx. Fell into sea – fishing on rocks near his house. Witnessed by a lady called Mrs Foley with 3 young children. Body not found – weather terrible. Could be days – weeks – months or never. Mrs F: she had taken her children fishing. Decided water was too rough. One of children said wave hit Jim. Child of 12 said: 'He is in the water.' She said 'Lie on back and I will get help.' Did not respond. Did not appear to attempt to swim. No visible efforts. Screams. She tried to reach down. 4–5 yards. Suddenly he was swept under and disappeared. Q. undercurrent. He was upright in water. Was wearing boots.'

The *Guardian* journalist Malcolm Dean set off within twenty-four hours to cover the story at his own request, and on arrival phoned David Simpson in London, who was known to have been a recent guest. Once again the call was written down verbatim. 'Collapsed. A tourist family told the police that his body slipped into the water and was swept out to sea without struggle. Fog has prevented coastguard planes from joining the search. Children aged 10 and 6 saw the collapse. Fell in water. Turbulent wild weather, though Jerry not . . .' At that point the line broke, so David managed to get through to Jerry O'Mahony, whom he recognised as the local contact. 'He fell to ground,' he scribbled on. 'No flailing, no swimming. Collapsed. Fell into water.'

Jim Farrell, that most elusive of twentieth-century novelists, was an early victim of the freak storm that two nights after his death ripped apart the Fastnet race, drowning eighteen crew members. One sailor who survived, Captain John Coote, publicly attributed his escape to having been born with a caul, part of a membrane from the womb, believed from Roman times to forestall a watery grave. Barometers plummeted as the centre of the depression roared up the Irish Sea and raged unabated for fourteen hours, blowing first from the south-west and switching around to a westerly direction, causing sixty-knot winds and towering fifty-foot waves called grey beards. It would become known as the worst night in history for the local Ballycotton, Dunmore East and Courtmacsherry lifeboats, necessitating the biggest joint air-sea rescue operation ever mounted. Five lifeboat stations, three Irish Air Corps helicopters, three British Nimrods, eight naval frigates, two tugs, a Dutch destroyer and the B & I car-ferry *St Killian*, as well as commercial freighters and private boats, came to the aid of the stricken yachts.

Mrs Foley, the only witness, had found herself that evening in the nightmare predicament of being unable to leave her children in such dangerous conditions and when she did succeed in raising the alarm there was no trace of a body. At first the identity of the lone fisherman was unclear, but Farrell's name was on a bag of tackle found carefully stowed near the scene of the accident, and when Gardai called at the house that the Booker Prize-winning author had bought not long before, they found his car in the garage, the doors unlocked and nobody inside. After taking the phone call, Richard Farrell had to break the news to his mother; it was, he would admit later, the hardest thing he had ever had to do. His father was too ill to be informed and his mother believed he did not know, but a week later he began to fret, saying, 'Something's happened to Jim.'

Richard and his uncle Harry Russell helped local men to comb the coastline, and in the water below the rocks and slipway a specialised Dutch company of divers came and went. Malcolm Dean covered the search from a helicopter, but had little to file back. Under the headline 'Fog Hits Hunt for Drowned Novelist' he reported that Irish coastguards were still checking the shore, but that the body was thought to have been swept out to sea and fog still prevented planes from joining in. However, at that point Bantry Bay was twelve miles wide, and even under good conditions locating a body from the air was said to be like looking for a needle in a haystack. When the weather allowed, Jerry O'Mahony and Peter Burgess, who were both experienced amateur divers, scoured the sea floor around the jutting smooth block from which they knew Jim liked to fish.

The playwright John Spurling was out of touch in a remote Welsh holiday cottage with his family when the telegram came from Terence Kilmartin of the *Observer* asking for an obituary by return. Shocked, John complied, telling himself that his old friend would have done the same for him. 'I hope you aren't alone in Paris when you hear it,' his wife, the biographer Hilary Spurling, wrote to Sonia Orwell, widow of the writer of *1984*. 'Jim is dead – he was drowned last Saturday . . . It has rained every day since. We wished you were here before, but doubly so now . . . I feel furiously jealous of all the people who have done nothing to get nowhere and go on living for ever . . . Ann [Colville] says she hopes they don't find his body, he would have preferred it lost – certainly there is something dramatic, enigmatic, even dashing, like himself about his death.'

Sonia had already seen the Reuters story in the *International*

Herald Tribune, and his death, she observed bleakly in reply, made everything seem sadder. 'I think I was having a pretty sad summer anyhow . . . There is something quite dreadful about old age, so I suppose there goes an argument for dying young, but I can't quite see which is the right age to die, as you can, as in Jim's case, be far too young.' By then the Sunday papers had carried obituaries of three writers, with Jim Farrell placed ahead of Nicholas Monsarrat and Jean Rhys. In one, significantly, his early novel *A Man from Elsewhere* was given as *A Man from the Sea*.

Among Jim's many friends the news of his death had the impact of Kennedy's assassination or Elvis Presley's death: most would remember where they were at the time. 'Even Jim in his most affected cynical mood', pointed out one, 'would have been moved.' The Spurlings were playing Mah Jong with their children; David Simpson was cycling with a friend, and he cycled on in tears. Edna O'Brien, who dreaded water, shuddered, and Elsie Donald, cut off on holiday on a Greek island, was so reminded of a helium balloon by the moon overhead that she wrote a postcard to Jim and tore it up, convinced all of a sudden that there was no point. Michael Frayn told the *New Yorker* writer Calvin 'Bud' Trillin over dinner in London. Furious with himself for having lost touch since a youthful meeting in Pamplona in 1960, Bud bought a copy of *The Siege of Krishnapur* next morning and read it right through that day in one sitting. Jim had, he realised, pulled it off.

Weidenfeld's chief fiction editor, John Curtis, returned from holiday abroad and opened the *Bookseller* on the way to work. 'Death of Distinguished Award-winning Novelist', he read with disbelief. 'Mr Farrell was well into his next novel at the time of the accident, of which Weidenfeld, his hardback publisher, expected delivery at the end of this year.' Margaret Drabble, similarly, was catching up with the newspapers over breakfast with her children. 'Good God,' she exclaimed, 'the other James Farrell is dead,' and, wondering at the unnatural silence, glanced up. 'Ours', they enlightened her, 'is dead, too.' That 'the other James Farrell', as Jim scathingly referred to the author of *Studs Lonigan* with whom he was so often confused, should hog that limelight too, was, perhaps, the final irony. 'On Thursday,'

Martha English, who administered the Harkness fellowships in New York, noted with exasperation 'a large obituary notice for James T. Farrell, novelist, *aged 75*. To check this I rang the *Sunday Observer*. Incredibly TWO James Farrells have died, within the space of a few days, both novelists.' Meanwhile, lyrically cheerful letters from Jim were daily dropping through door-flaps, as if he were saying goodbye.

The search was scaled down, although the dives continued, to a watch kept along both shores of Bantry Bay to allow for drift. Further up the coastline Lord Mountbatten, the dowager Lady Brabourne and two fifteen-year-olds, Nicholas Knatchbull and Paul Maxwell, were killed on 27 August when their boat was blown up by the IRA, and on the same day eighteen soldiers died in an explosion at Warrenpoint, beside Carlingford Lough. The waters of Bantry Bay mirrored the weather, enigmatic and opaque.

'I was hoping that we would have some luck in locating Jim's remains,' noted Jerry O'Mahony on 29 August. 'But so far the search has proved futile. However, right now the weather is excellent and maybe we will have more success. We have done about eight dives in the immediate area of the drowning but have so far recognised his fishing rod and what would appear to be his anorak, just the Sunday past. I was certain when we found the anorak that we'd find him, but Bantry Bay is a big place and if his body is not in the immediate area only the sea can wash it in.' Usually a body was located within two weeks, but a man who had drowned in the region two years before had not yet been found, and only ten days before the bodies of two local victims of the January Whiddy Island explosion had been washed up.

There was a more disturbing reason for why the body might never be found which Jerry chose not to share with the Farrell family. Among some of those whose livelihoods were bound up with the sea the superstition persisted, as it had when J.M. Synge wrote *The Aran Islands*, that it was unlucky to remove a body washed up on to a beach. If deprived the sea would snatch back a life, so a body might be left where it was to be retrieved by the waves, or buried beneath the tide-line without informing the authorities. 'What the sea has claimed,' as Synge had empathised, 'you should *never* take back.'

The discovery of the anorak, which Mrs Foley had seen being worn, ruled out strong currents, and the fishing rod, when recovered, was still set up. Jerry had called at the house with replacement fish-hooks the day before the apparent death and his anguish was tinged with self-blame; at the same time he was puzzled because he was sure Jim could swim well enough to get ashore.

'It was strange, as I don't think he would have panicked,' he said subsequently. 'I thought that finding the fully extended fishing rod was odd, too. It's highly unlikely he'd have thrown it in. I had this idea all the time I dived that maybe this guy was not dead, after all.'

Part One

CHAPTER ONE

At the Centre of a Vast Empire

Had it had not been for the sea, J.G. Farrell's parents would never have met. It was aboard the S.S. *Ranchi*, cruising the North Sea off Norway in 1929, that they were introduced, and they became unofficially engaged before the liner docked. Josephine Russell was nineteen, optimistic and decisive. William Farrell, nine years her senior, was on the lookout for a wife; his masculine round of a shared bachelor chummery in India had palled and domesticity attracted him. He had begun his six-month leave hoping to lay down foundations for a family life, and time was inexorably slipping past.

Jo, as she was known, was reaping her reward for having returned home to Portlaoise from Dublin at short notice to enable her parents to visit a seriously ill aunt in England. The cruise was recompense and holiday combined. She was the oldest of the family of four, and shared her father's zest for travel, if not yet his awareness of the need to offset provincialism; a subtle widening of horizons accounted for her presence aboard.

Jo's inveterate companion was her sister Sheilah, and Bill, as his friends called him, had a colleague along; all four, being competitive, were drawn to the games on deck. On the day they met Jo jibbed, for once, at taking part, but Sheilah overruled her and pointed to the two tanned, intriguing men. 'Very broad and very quiet,' she assessed as they got to know one another better. 'He didn't talk much, but he was very well read and he had a wonderful sense of humour – ironic and quick.' She thought him good-looking and was unworried by his receding hair, already showing signs of going grey. Her experience was limited to the

orbit of the widowed E.N.T. surgeon for whom she worked in
Fitzwilliam Square, Dublin, and close observation of medical
students at work and play made Bill's extra years an asset. It
impressed her to learn that at her age he had taken charge of his
life and joined the United Molasses Company in Java, deviating
only for an intensive language course in Holland on the way, and
that he had taken the unfamiliar in his stride, choosing a billet
with three Dutchmen to perfect his accent. His adventurous side
was buttressed by a reassuringly conservative bent and, having
trained as an accountant, he was currently managing a factory in
India, an indication of further promotion as that country contributed most to company profits. United Molasses dealt in
treacle throughout the Far East, but in India, where it was
mixed with tobacco before smoking, it was in such demand
that it was imported in bulk by tanker, to be pumped ashore,
stored and sold in cans. Bill's factory was in Chittagong, a
convenient port in northern Bengal, and fluency in Hindi as
well as Dutch backed up the impact of brown skin and sun-
bleached hair. For Jo, however, it was his mastery of English that
bridged the gap between them, although initially she set the pace.
What drew them together, she would always say afterwards,
was the fun they had in chatting.

As they played quoits together and took turns about the deck
it became plain that there was an inverse symmetry in their
family histories. In the swirling crosscurrents of the nineteenth
century the moves of the Farrells had directly counterbalanced
those of the Russells. The Quaker O'Farrells had emigrated via
Sligo by boat and dropped the prefix when settling in Liverpool,
where through industry and acumen they had thrived. Meanwhile the Russells had made a successful move in the opposite
direction, going first from London to Liverpool, and then on to
Ireland. Irony makes its first appearance here. The Russells, who
saw themselves as Irish and lived in Ireland, had an English
surname and mainly English antecedents, while the Farrells, who
saw themselves exclusively as English, had the Irish name and
distant family connections. Tangled attitudes and insights would
be an ideal preparation for novels about those potentially
troublesome intricacies, transposed on to a greater Empire scale.

Bill was born in 1900 and shaped by the red-bricked certainties of turn-of-the-century Liverpool, where his father, Thomas James Farrell, was a prominent wine and spirit merchant who had started out as a bookkeeper, and whose company, James Smith & Co., had recently opened a second branch in Manchester. Bill's father concentrated on the present and looked towards the future. Sentiment and the past exerted little pull, as his choice of wife bore out: Margaret was tiny, fiery and proudly Welsh. Her disapproval encompassed all things Irish, with Catholicism at the molten core.

Bill had grown up at 65 Kremlin Drive in Stoneycroft, a respectable suburb. He was one of three, born between an older sister, May, and a younger brother, Tom. The boys attended Liverpool Collegiate School, where their sporting talents burnished the feat of assimilation, and the muscular Farrell brothers captained the top rugger, soccer and athletic teams for three consecutive years. Sport was important to all the Farrells, with May's hockey reputation no less formidable; games existed to be played hard and to be won, within the rules. Bill was a natural athlete, as capable of accelerated bursts of speed as he was of stoical endurance, and quick analysis of an opponent's strengths and weaknesses shaped his outlook on and off the field.

Kremlin Drive was close enough to the docks for the pulse of an invisible empire to be felt. The beat of vigorous circulation was hard to miss for boys growing up in Liverpool before the First World War. Bill was at his most impressionable age in settled times, when commercial calculations stretched years ahead and opportunity was measured against predictable expansion, and at fourteen, on the outbreak of war, the shock was amplified by proximity to the rapidly adapting port. Early withdrawal from his mother's possessiveness was hastened by her frequent rush to judgement, and in turning to his father's world he warmed to its objective nature. When he was old enough to take part in the war himself, Bill sidestepped lethal glamour, personified by May's fiancé in the Royal Flying Corps, and trained as a telegrapher. At its end he again made a rational evaluation.

He had no real interest in the wine business, unlike Tom, and all around unemployment and discontent were rife. Beyond, where the port had always beckoned, lay fresh opportunity and less competition. Family tradition encouraged such a move. Language barriers were no deterrent after coming out top in French throughout his school career, and the prospect of loneliness held no real threat. Books had illuminated his reflective adolescence, and a well-furnished mind offset any shortage of comradeship and possessions. Bill was realistic, and aboard the S.S. *Ranchi* it stood out that nothing had caused him to change his attitude since.

Prudence Josephine Russell, as her passport described her, was, at first glance, little different from the other young female passengers. But her accent set her apart; it was a humorous, educated, but unmistakably Irish lilt, and her flair for anecdote and mimicry stemmed from experiences quite unlike Bill's own. In childhood she had come across the bloody results of an ambush while walking near her quiet home, with a car crushed under a partially sawn-through tree and the victim slumped dead inside, behind broken glass. The bridge over the canal on the way to Maryborough, was blown up so repeatedly that a time came when no further repairs were authorised, and makeshift planks became a lasting reminder of subversion. Bill had been brought up to take life at face value, but to Jo things were not necessarily as they might seem.

Despite her youth, she was of the same mould as her grandfather, after whom she had been named. Joseph Russell, whose adventures would help to inspire *The Singapore Grip*, had run away to sea in response to family pressure to become a doctor and risen to ship's captain. Based in Liverpool until retirement, he had sailed the great routes of the world. On one voyage Joseph carried out an appendectomy armed with a medical book and whiskey for anaesthetic; the coffin of one Chinese crewman buried at sea refused to sink, and in Far Eastern ports it was necessary to fight off copper thieves to save the hull. Three marriages produced two sons by each of his first two wives, and it had been Robert Gordon Hall Russell, the youngest, who made the move to Ireland. A distant uncle had done very well as a timber merchant in Tipperary, and Robert prudently studied forestry before taking the plunge. On arrival he persuaded his older stepbrother George to join him, and Russell Bros, Timber Merchants, opened in Templemore before expanding to larger premises fifty miles away in Maryborough, County Leix. Most of the stock was homegrown, and the regular supply of fine woods was due in great part to Bob Russell's popularity. Invitations to private shoots brought access to wooded cover that was frequently old and rare, and if a discreet sale was sought word quickly spread that he could be relied on to give a good price. Russell Bros soon exported to England, where fine woods were in demand, as well as selling to the Irish trade and, in partnership with Gray's of Cambridge, manufacturing the tennis rackets and cricket bats for which they became renowned.

In the early years the brothers married two sisters, and once again Robert made the running. Edith Miller was a gentle soprano from Queenstown in County Cork whom he met while taking singing lessons for his good baritone voice. A twin, like Edward Spencer's daughters in *Troubles*, Edith was quite unlike her wilful fictional counterparts, being ultra-feminine and con-ciliatory. The separation from home entailed by the marriage proposal – a drive of 130 miles, through Mallow, Buttevant and Thurles, across the Slieve Bloom mountains and up to the edge of the Bog of Allen – was less of a wrench once George began courting her older sister, Clara. But in 1909, for the birth of Jo, her first child, she made sure to return home.

One of Jo's earliest memories was of peeping from her grand-mother's house in Queenstown at the funeral for victims of the torpedoed *Lusitania* as the long melancholy cortège proceeded past on the way to the Protestant cemetery at the top of the hill. The house overlooked the harbour, where bright searchlights raked back and forth at night, and when she was old enough to understand about German submarines, she also learned that her grandmother's family had originally been named Müller, and that they had arrived from Germany themselves only fifty years before. Shaen, the comfortable old house outside Maryborough where Bob Russell would install his growing family after 4 Kellyville Terrace, became her security in a shifting world.

During the height of the Troubles, Jo was insulated from nationalist fervour. Her father mentioned 'the rebellion' with exasperation, and the birth in 1916 of her brother Harry stood out mainly for its sensation of danger far away. She was told her mother and new baby brother were in the Portobello Nursing

Home in Dublin and watched her father load up the car each day, before his afternoon visit, with as much bread to distribute as could be crammed inside; there was such rioting in the city, he explained, that food shops were closed. One night in 1921, however, without warning danger crossed the divide.

Jo had finished packing her school trunk for the start of term and gone to bed, when a group of men banged on the hall door and demanded weapons for the IRA, marching Bob Russell before them at gunpoint; sensibly, he had already handed his shotguns in to the Royal Irish Constabulary for safekeeping. The younger children stayed asleep, but the door of tomboy Jo's room was ajar. She listened to the voices and footsteps coming nearer, heading for the gunroom at the end of her corridor, and holding her breath heard rummaging in the open school trunk they had to pass. When the men had left, empty-handed, her father told her that he had asked them not to go into the children's rooms, and they had kept their word. Her conclusion was somewhat different. They had targeted her father because he was English; she would do her best to belong.

Identification with Ireland was made stronger by unhappy experiences at Dagfield, near Southport, her first English boarding school, where she was so homesick and in such conflict with the rigid discipline that she became ill and was moved to Lowther College in Wales; there she thrived. Ireland remained home, despite the narrowing of attitudes and opportunities after Independence. Maryborough might be renamed Portlaoise and Queenstown now known as Cobh, but during the school holidays things seemed much the same. Life in a comfortable house situated outside a county town, cushioned by the income from a profitable family business, was pleasant and companionable, and the reality that many Protestants were leaving was not apparent. Her mother continued to attend musical concerts, coming in to say goodnight beforehand with hair piled high and wearing her best dress, and her father's interests straddled the religious divide. He had become chairman of the Visitors' Committee of Portlaoise prison and carried out his duties with fair-mindedness, proud that a slate sundial was presented to him by the prisoners, with their signatures engraved. Cricket was his passion, and all likely players were invited to join the local team which he ran. The tenor John McCormack, a neighbour, de-clined for fear a ball would hit him and, as he said, 'damage my troat'. Jo, a born storyteller, listened and watched.

Precious interludes in Ireland, however, had always to give way to monochrome school elsewhere, and her ambition to read medicine at Trinity College was ruled out on grounds of ex-pense. She succeeded in returning to Dublin, but to a secretarial course at Alexandra College, off St Stephen's Green, and the subsequent compromise of a job with a widowed E.N.T. spe-cialist, Dr Graham, in Fitzwilliam Square. At nineteen she was capably acting as nanny to his three-year-old child, as well as running his consulting rooms as receptionist and secretary, and although her role had seemed fulfilling at first, it no longer counted as a challenge.

Bill proposed within the week, while they were still at sea, and when the cruise ended he kept up his pursuit. He was spending his leave with his parents in Liverpool, but there was a direct ferry service to Dublin and, synchronising trips with her day off, he began taking the boat over each Monday and returning on Tuesday evening. Bob Russell approved, and when she had to spend a fortnight on nanny duty at the doctor's holiday house, beside the sea in County Wexford, Bill followed, putting up at a guesthouse nearby. In both families the identical question was now raised. The Russells – circumspectly – enquired if Bill was Catholic, as his name implied; in Liverpool, Bill's mother tackled matters head on, but the assurance that Jo was Protestant made no dent in her implacable hostility. However, Bill's formality in asking for permission sealed his suitability in Russell family opinion, and on his last day in Ireland, with his leave up, they went to Weirs, the Grafton Street jewellers, to buy an engage-ment ring. They would next meet the day before their wedding, on the other side of the world.

Jo left her job that September and began the preparations for the journey, glad that her father was accompanying her as far as his business commitments would allow; to his regret he would not be able to give her away. Rangoon had been agreed as the port of arrival, and there Bill would meet the Bibby Line boat. Jo, her mother and Sheilah shopped in Dublin for the new clothes that would be needed, aware that high temperatures called for frequent changes, and being a deft needlewoman, Jo made several outfits herself. For the ceremony she chose a short blue matching dress and hat, because they could be worn again, and the finishing touches to her trousseau were accomplished in London, where the whole family came to see her and her father off.

It was a five-week journey which, as soon as she recovered from seasickness, would stand out as the time of her life. A pretty girl who loved dancing was in great demand among the predominently male passengers returning from home leave, and her engagement ring proved an incentive to flirtation. 'Nobody going out', she was assured, 'actually marries the man they've come to meet.' Her father was tolerant, and at Cairo he disembarked, leaving her under the wing of a suitable couple of his own age met aboard; Mr O'Dell, the husband, ran the Forestry Department in Burma, and friendship had ripened over a mutual interest in teak.

On a humid Sunday in Rangoon at the end of November, eight months after they had last met, Jo recognised Bill in the crowd at the foot of the gangway. Instantly she guessed that something was wrong. He greeted her warmly and there was no question about his delight at seeing her, but excited as she was she could sense his poorly disguised anxiety. As they tried to talk in the hubbub he had to strain to catch her words, and with a jolt she realised he could not hear. She forgot the heat and her irritation that nobody had warned her to buy a larger size in shoes, and disguised her shock. 'I knew there was one thing I couldn't do, and that was turn around and go back,' she said years later. 'You couldn't do that to any man.' She had no illusions about the outcome, because incurable deafness had accounted for Dr Graham's most poignant patients.

Subsequently she came to blame his mother for not telling her that deafness ran in the family and that he had, in fact, been showing the first signs at the time of their engagement. But Bill, significantly, had banished injury and illness from his letters: shades of Angela's obfuscation in *Troubles* when writing to her fiancé Brendan Archer at the front. Since his return he had suffered two bad accidents, either of which could account for the sudden deterioration. On the polo field, the sport he relished, he had been concussed in a crashing fall, and within a matter of days, in his Territorial Army capacity, he had been injured when the armoury of Chittagong barracks became the focus of an armed raid. With the Free India campaign gathering momentum, every European who could handle a gun was expected to join up, and he had been hit by 'a gunfull of buckshot' in the head and back; some pellets had lodged too near his spine to be removed, and temporarily paralysed his hands. She made him see a specialist there and then, who in her presence assured Bill that he would recover and wrote out a prescription for drops. The psychological effect was immediate, as she intended; subsequently the diagnosis would be tinnitus, characterised by incessant buzzing and ringing in the head, which could be aggravated by injury and was progressively disabling.

The wedding next day went ahead. Wearing her blue dress and hat, Jo married Bill on 1 December 1929 in the huge cantonment church dating from the heyday of the South Sea Company, with the youthful Bishop of Burma officiating. Bill had organised a special licence in advance and roped in a colleague from work as best man. Mr O'Dell, as promised, gave her away, and his wife was one witness, the other a passer-by. Jo had stayed at the O'Dells' house the night before, and visited the bishop with Bill after dark to swear the licence affidavit that certified there was no existing marriage.

Holding the arm of a man who was standing in for her father, beneath revolving fans that stretched up to the high vaulted roof, she negotiated 'miles' of dusty red carpet between empty pews, towards the few distant figures waiting by the chancel steps; nothing was as she had expected. The ceremony over, the bishop rushed across to the organ and hitched up the sleeves of his surplice in time to play the 'Wedding March' for the long walk back down the aisle. On Bill's arm this time, she glimpsed red and green lizards darting about on either side among the discarded prayer books and vacant stalls. The cool Bengal hill station of Kilaw was their honeymoon destination, a 24-hour train journey away, and during their first night there a minor earthquake shook the hotel. In the sudden confusion she became tangled in the mosquito net, never having slept beneath one before.

Jo wrote home each week, giving no hint about Bill's deafness. Their bungalow was easy to run, she made light of the quirks of the cook and servants, and Bill was relieved to be free of the household accounts; punctiliously he gave her half his pay. They were part of the mostly British commercial community in Bengal, made up of business and professional men and their families; boxwallahs, to old India hands. Most intended to remain only for as long as their contract specified, and looked down upon all Indians, whether Hindu or Muslim, much to Jo's disgust. She and Bill, she felt, were different. But when she became ill – bacillary as well as amoebic dysentery was part of every newcomer's experience – she was glad to be taken to the European hospital, although it had only four beds.

The Victorian pattern of her days was dictated by long Empire practice. 'We'd get up early and go out and play games while it was cool – tennis or nine holes of golf,' she would recall. 'Then back to change and have breakfast. Bill would go to the office. Then he'd return home for tiffin, which we'd have together. Back to the office often, or we'd play more sport in the afternoon, unless it was too hot. The monsoon pinned you down, of course. The social life was super. There were very few couples of our own age, but lots of young men living in chummeries, so lovely games. Tennis, golf, polo, skittles.' Fascination with that Imperial perspective would be the distant legacy of her second son.

Bill, however, was aware that things were about to change, because his deafness was making him more observant and introspective, as well as heightening his sensitivity to atmosphere. He had always been pragmatic, and exposure to Indian culture emphasised the fatalism that was a strong Farrell characteristic. He found increasing solace in his wife's family motto, '*Que sera, sera*'. The spirit of the times, that propelling force which infuses the Empire Trilogy, was a factor Bill picked up instinctively, and he knew that India in the early 1930s was not the carefree playground his young wife apparently believed it to be. He kept his feelings to himself, unaware that she considered unrest to be the natural state of affairs. 'There was a definite sense of British power unravelling,' she would elaborate, 'but I'd been living with it all my life. I was used to it.' That outlook, too, would be handed on.

The weapons stolen from the Chittagong armoury on the night of Bill's injury were suspected to be still in the vicinity, so within a few months of Jo's arrival a siege mentality had taken root. A Gurkha battalion was detailed to camp nearby and for a while the community felt safe, but civil disturbances continued to break out. In periods of tension women were no longer allowed to stay at home during the day; instead they were instructed to accompany their men to the office, where they had to kill time in the shade. To break the monotony, Bill planned a few days in Calcutta at the Great Eastern, Kipling's favourite hotel, which advertised newly installed air conditioning: with Farrellesque bathos, the management had not yet mastered the controls, and their room was so icy they had to cut short their stay. Most at ease in his day-to-day routine, where he could anticipate what people were saying, Bill took to showing Jo how much he valued her in little ways. During her lowest period in hospital she woke to find a copy of H.V. Morton's *In Search of Ireland* by her bed; he had kept it as a surprise for just such an occasion.

When her pregnancy was confirmed it meant she would have to return to England by herself for the birth. The doctor in Chittagong, an Irishman from Wexford, advised her 'to go home' in good time, and Bill backed him up, adamant that their children should be born in England to be sure of British nationality. She set out obediently on the long journey to Bombay, intending to come straight back. *The train puffed steadily . . . over dusty glaring plains of dried mud, with here and there a mud village, a well, a field of sugar-cane, a few palms, a pair of yoked water-buffalo, another mud village, a field of mustard improbably yellow, a temple, a few banyan or peepul trees and so on and on until . . . the young woman by the window who was so interested in everything eventually became hypnotized . . .* When the *Viceroy of India* docked in England, in chill grey weather, she took another train as far as Victoria, where her mother, who had travelled from Ireland to be with her, waited. In April 1932, at a nursing home in Reading, she gave birth to a son and named him Robert, after her father. 'Both well', noted the announcement in the *Daily Telegraph*, tempting fate.

Bill's letter of congratulation advised her to remain where she was, 'for the foreseeable future'. Publicly, she was to explain it was too hazardous for a young baby to be exposed to the unhealthy climate of a monsoon, but the real reason was that the Depression was blighting business throughout the Empire. He wrote regularly to warn her that his position was precarious: it made sense for her to wait on in England in case he had to return suddenly himself, in which case he would first auction their furniture. In the gloomy spring of 1934 that situation came about. Without a job, in a widening spiral of unemployment, Bill 'came home', and his mood was fatalistic and withdrawn. The further deterioration in his hearing was impossible to disguise, and his father had just been diagnosed with terminal cancer.

They moved to Liverpool to be nearby, renting a furnished 'semi' at 15 Hampton Court Road, West Derby. Money was a constant anxiety. Bill qualified for a small disability pension on a sliding scale of allowances for three years, but it was not enough to live on, and deafness now locked him out of the general business world. It was not simply a matter of missing amplified remarks: he could no longer use the telephone and, since he could not hear oncoming traffic, he could not get insurance to drive. A series of consultations in Dublin with Jo's ex-employer, Dr Graham, was the final hope, but the resulting course of vibro-massage had no effect, and Bill was told that no further treatment was possible. His father's death was protracted and painful, his mother was possessive and, beset by tribulation, his own health broke down. He became, in Jo's words, 'very bad with his nerves, terribly jumpy. His head noises were shattering.'

Imperceptibly, the balance within the marriage altered as Bill slipped into depression and despair. An accountancy job in the family wine business seemed like charity, but for want of an alternative he accepted and numbly reported back each day. Fatalism deepened as control slipped away. India and the Far East maintained their hold upon his thoughts, but the news that Jo was pregnant once more showed where the future actually lay.

CHAPTER TWO

The Vanished Comfort and Security of Earlier Days 1935–1947

J ames Gordon Farrell was born during the bleakest period of his parents' lives. The pregnancy was proceeding without complications, with a nursing home booked for the end of February, when on 25 January 1935 Jo heard that Bill's elderly uncle, who had been a cheerful guest at supper the night before, had died in his sleep. The news sent her into premature labour. Bill was at work, the doctor was out on his rounds and could not be contacted, and the nursing home said they had no room. Vera, who helped with housework, put clean sheets on the bed and rang for a taxi. Three cars sped to the door, causing the neighbours to stare. Bill's mother and the doctor's wife had both used their initiative, and the nursing home was prevailed upon to offer a room. A keen irony separates the public flurry of his entry into the world, and the invisibility of his exit.

Tipping the maternity scales at under 5 lbs, the newborn boy was a sorry sight. 'Wait a month and you won't know him,' reassured the doctor, possessor of an Irish cap for rugby. 'He has a good pair of lungs and a good heart.' Jo believed him: the huge hands cradling her baby reminded her of Russell Bros tennis rackets. When he had gone the nurse poked up the fire. The baby had been born with a caul, she explained, so that would have to be burned before word got around, because there was a ghoulish market for the good fortune it was said to bring. 'Your lucky baby will never drown,' she added over her shoulder, and Jo heard the hiss as it was consumed by flame. The chosen Christian names were even-handed – for a second son, the second name of each grandfather – and the christening took place on 3 March at St Mary the Virgin, West Derby in a font dated 1856, the year before the Indian Mutiny. Jo shook out the lacy Russell christening gown without a qualm; the caul had had a significance for her which she had not shared with the nurse, because the last boy to be christened in it had joined the Navy during the 1914–1918 war, and drowned when HMS *Hood* went down.

Jimmy, as the baby was called, quickly made up for his bad start. From being compared to a doll, so fragile that he had to be bathed in cod-liver oil, he gained weight rapidly and soon looked older than his age, with a sturdy build and blue-black hair. At nine months he was sitting up in the pram, dressed in grey jersey and flannels; Jo's sister Sheilah was reminded of a schoolboy. Walking came easily, but he was so slow to talk that his grandmother alluded to it pointedly. But when Vera had to have her appendix out, leaving Jo in sole charge, it became clear that Jim simply held out his hand if he wanted anything. 'I wouldn't give him a thing unless he asked for it,' she said later. 'By the time Vera came back my Lord could talk.' His nurse's affectionate indulgence would be repaid in *The Singapore Grip*. In a studio portrait of the brothers, taken when Jim was two, Robert – whom he called Oddie, because of the way he pronounced his name – smiles shyly at the camera and Jim upstages him, contriving to look both sunny and pugnacious. He was the family favourite, and he knew it.

War broke out when he was four, putting Liverpool in the forefront of naval and military upheaval, with added danger from the air. Bill's deafness precluded call-up but his mathematical skills were in demand, and he was drafted to an aircraft factory in Cumberland on 24-hour production, returning briefly every six weeks when it closed for maintenance. In the noisy factory his cocoon of silence was an asset, preventing loss of concentration, and the ability to make a useful contribution boosted his morale. He settled into a decaying hotel in Workington, and Jo and the boys escaped the threat of bombing by moving in with an elderly widowed relation who lived in style in Southport. The chauffeur and housekeeper of Alderman William Mawdsley JP – Uncle Will – had been called up, and Jo took on both roles. The old man was fond of children, having none himself, and he was easygoing with them both, especially Jimmy, his godson.

Boscobel, at the top of Preston Road, was named after the English Civil War novel by William Harrison Ainsworth. It had seven bedrooms and three drawing rooms, as well as a study, dining room and spacious kitchen quarters, with a warren of storage rooms at garden level. Dark oak panelling and thick walls spelled security, and the Bangor blue slated roof culminated in a fairytale turret. The boys shared a maid's attic on the top floor, and attended a kindergarten further along the wide, tree-lined road lit by Victorian cast-iron lamps after dark. Hesketh Park was nearby for afternoon walks, where a bandstand hosted concerts; the winding paths were thronged with pram-pushers and strollers, uniforms mingling with mufti. And beyond was the seafront, dominated by a gigantic statue of Queen Victoria. In summer there were the sands for buckets and spades and the sea for swimming, and in winter the covered walkways by shop windows offered snug protection from the rain.

Southport was a seaside holiday town, as driven by the seasons during war as it was during peace. Jim was an alert and sensitive child, and he absorbed seasonal change of pace – quickening in readiness for summer, falling back as days got shorter. In his mind's eye the resort would become *a giant plant that flowered and withered according to a natural cycle* with its residents as ephemeral and interchangeable as *insignificant petals*. The houses he passed on afternoon walks, the majority with discreet signs offering bed and breakfast, lodged in his mind. *What had happened to all the large, solid families who had once lived in these houses? They had been so sure that living in solid houses at the centre of a vast Empire they had a foot wedged in the door of Eternity.* Claims on permanence could be staked out in bricks and mortar, but these were flimsy defences against the unstoppable progression of the seasons.

Jim was an outgoing, energetic boy, drawn to challenge and to mischief, and when his brother was confined to bed for a year, due to an infection of the heart muscle, he was left to his own devices. At five he fell out of an apple tree and broke his nose; next he hurt his mouth when tumbling off his bicycle and an abscess developed in his cheek. Boscobel's windows took a pounding as soon as he received a Russell Bros cricket bat, and when caught in the act he was sent to apologise, only to return from Uncle Will with chocolate and a silver spoon. 'When he was older we told him that he wasn't born with a silver spoon in his mouth, but he grabbed one as soon as he could,' said his mother fondly. 'He could always get away with murder.' Stubbornness was a hallmark, the precursor to iron self-discipline.

In Croxton School, the kindergarten, Jim was as beguiling as he was wilful, according to Mary Roberts, who taught him from a wheelchair. She would let him off early to watch the soldiers drilling in Preston Road. Annoyed at being ignored whenever his brother was reading, he one day announced, '*I'd* like to read that,' and snatched the book, retreating out of reach. It was *Ivanhoe*, and he laboured over the first page, but by the next day he had finished a chapter and joined Robert's governess in the sickroom. Having been told to bring any book he liked, he produced a tome from Uncle Will's bookcase and proved that he understood it by answering questions. 'Very bright', an assessment noted. But Robert never felt usurped. They enjoyed the comics *Hotspur*, *Wizard* and *Rover* together, disdaining *Beano* and *Dandy*, their interdependency echoing their father's youthful relationship with his brother Tom.

When Bill was home he gave the boys undivided attention, and they often went to the cinema together. They would choose the cheapest seats in the front row to give Bill's damaged hearing every chance, and the sensation of sitting between his father's reassuring bulk and Robert's congenial presence in the half-light near the screen, where adventure unfolded a few feet away, started Jim's lifetime fascination with film. 'Bang, bang, bang, the Indians are coming . . .' began his first story, embarked upon with his father's encouragement. Both parents were good storytellers and each had their own approach. Jo's gift was her fund of childhood anecdotes enlivened by mimicry, and *Troubles* would be her reward. Bill's imagination was fired by India and Java, and he wove elaborate tales with an *Arabian Nights* perspective, while his few stories about himself had a self-mocking, whimsical air. The boys' favourite was a wry account of quenching a minor rebellion with a golf club and a soda syphon, saluted in the original dedication of *The Siege of Krishnapur*. There was a

vulnerable dignity about their father that precluded offhanded-
ness or answering back, and the boys hung on his words with
attention that might not have been given so freely if he had been
able to respond to interruptions. It made them patient and
protective at a spontaneous age, but the sense of exile from a
larger and more colourful world was being unwittingly absorbed.

Bill read aloud compellingly, taking pleasure in sharing the
books he loved and simultaneously escaping his own frustrations. When he was home they would have supper in the study
which faced the garden, and their mother would bring in her
mending and listen, too. Enrapt in the blacked-out room, Jim's
imagination soared. Bill believed that the one-dimensional English view had to be offset by books from around the world, and
their early favourite was *Uncle Billy Possum*, published by the
Bodley Head. 'Jim and I used to look at the title page,' revealed
his brother, 'and wonder how the Bodley Head got in touch with
such wonderful animals – animals we could never see in the
countryside around us. Blue Jay, Jimmy Skunk . . . Why no
possums around Southport?' Bill's own favourite, P.G. Wodehouse, was introduced, and they became so steeped in Blandings
Castle lore that he unbent and allowed himself to be snapped in
Lord Emsworth pose. 'Whenever I think of Daddy,' Robert
would say in adulthood to his mother, 'I always think of a
book or a newspaper, or of legs sticking out of an armchair,' and
they agreed that he had probably missed his librarian's vocation.

Jim's cheekiness was near the surface, but in check. 'Dear
Daddy, I'm sorry I could not get you a present as I am hard up
and I had'ent time to earn any money. I hope you get this letter in
time to wish you many happy returns. I wish you were home as I
am saving up for a book and I might be able to wangle it out [of]
you.' Twenty pencilled X's undid the jibe; their relationship was
at its most demonstrative on paper. Bill's abiding interest in
sport opened other doors, and in 1979, at an exhausting point of
change and stress, Jim would retreat back to the memory of
playing noisy family games of bat and ball.

The impact of war was becoming more evident, a factor that
would shape all three novels of the Empire Trilogy. Their mother
joined the Red Cross as a home visitor, gave First Aid classes,
and helped out in Southport Orthopaedic Hospital, which took

both military and civilian casualties. On their father's visits home they could hear the evening news by hanging over the landing banisters, knowing the wireless would be turned up to maximum volume. Until early 1942 air raids were relatively light, compared to the punishment Liverpool was taking, and the area round Hesketh Park remained unscathed. Suddenly, overnight, the war came directly to them. On 15 April that year a stick of incendiary bombs was dropped on Southport, followed by high-explosive bombs, and Preston Road took the full force. Four people were killed in the house next door but one, glass shattered in all Boscobel's windows and their hall door was blown halfway up the stairs.

'The whistle went, and there was no time to be frightened,' Jo recalled. 'I was a light sleeper so I was woken by the first bombs whistling down, and fortunately Bill was home. In the earlier raids we had slept in the cellars because he couldn't hear the air-raid warnings, but by this time we had decided that wasn't too healthy. We seized the boys and carried them downstairs, feeling our way in the dark in case there was damage, and I dumped Jim by the cellar steps. "Why can't we go down?" he asked, but I went first to see if it was safe. There was a tin of fancy biscuits down there that we had brought before the war and they had wanted for ages. It took those bombs to get them.' In *The Siege of Krishnapur* sugar biscuits would be given pride of place among the most popular hoarded items.

In daylight Bill took them for an inspection, explaining the effects of blast. One wall had been sucked out and the roof needed emergency tarpaulin cover, but their homebuilt playhouse, incongruously, was still standing. 'I don't see any dead bodies,' Jim complained. Within weeks the same area was blitzed by landmines, and one lodged in the branches of their best apple tree. The house was evacuated and cordoned off, and a soldier was put on guard until the arrival of the bomb-disposal officer. The conscript could be observed lying back at ease in a deckchair, puffing a cigarette and reading a lurid thriller: a lasting embodiment of the mock-heroics of war.

Evacuees arrived daily by train, some from as far away as London, but the majority from Liverpool's bombed dockside. In two days alone in September 1941 15,000 had poured into

Southport. Jo was a billeting officer, and a succession of disorientated families inhabited Boscobel's generous supply of
bedrooms. The shock to Jim and his brother was profound.
'This was our first glimpse of people less fortunate than ourselves,' as Robert pointed out. 'They came with rations – often
cream crackers, we noticed – and they were obviously frightened
and disturbed. Even their accents were different.'

The first evacuee was a young mother of two babies, one only
ten weeks old, but as the months wore on the rapid turnover
erased individuality. The trail of displaced people included a
group of London civil servants, a man from India, and a rich
widow who arrived with her housekeeper in tow. A barrister
whose stentorian snores rang out through the thick oak bedroom doors stayed on until the end of the war. There were
always pregnant young mothers from Bootle present, gossiping
or red-eyed, and rarely an empty bed. With the attics pressed
into service, the boys slept in the cellars which doubled as
communal air-raid shelters whenever bombers droned overhead.
Jim took everything in, round-eyed. 'I remember as a child . . .
how adults in pyjamas would assemble in our air-raid shelter
clutching the most extraordinary objects,' he singled out when
promoting *The Singapore Grip* thirty-five years later. The absurdity of being attached to possessions underpins the Empire
Trilogy; control, he would conclude, sprang from spartan self-
sufficiency.

Watching the larger-than-life procession provided the spark in
The Singapore Grip for Ehrendorf's Second Law: *In human
affairs things tend inevitably to go wrong. Things are slightly
worse at any given moment than at any preceding moment.*
Sights that Jim witnessed in close-up as a child admitted him to
the anguish of the dispossessed, and the stocky boy who bustled
about the house, cheerful and proprietorial, would become their
unlikely chronicler. In *The Siege of Krishnapur* the huddled
women and children at bay during the Indian Mutiny *stared
about them with that wide-eyed, alert look which people have
during emergencies but which is really the result of shock.* Jim
began to ask questions with no easy answers, and it began to be
said that he shouldn't be trusted with pocket money because he
was bound to give it away. As he would admit himself much

later, 'My tolerance for misery – other people's – is not all that high.'

When crying babies and loud voices got too much, he escaped into a book. The Biggles fan graduated to *Rupert of Hentzau* and *The Prisoner of Zenda*, his fictional companions during term time after Oddie's recovery and despatch to prep school. 'He was very independent in his thinking, and he could be quite cantankerous,' his mother observed. 'Nobody ever had Jim in their pocket. He had an independence that was outside everything, as if he had come from Barnardo's. He would say "I'm thinking of doing . . ." and you knew he had already done it.'

Jim was fortunate in having a father who illuminatingly compared the structure of English to the rules of a game – 'Thirteen split infinitives!' Bill would roar as they listened to a talk on the Home Service – and nothing was sacred about the construction of a classic book. Critical examination was compared to post-match analysis, and when reading *Treasure Island* aloud Bill took time to explain how and why the character of Jim Hawkins was designed to appeal. He had the gift of inviting detection while retaining the magic, and even meal times were used for word games, which they played to win.

In 1943 a younger brother, Richard, was born, and Jim was no longer the baby. He appeared to relinquish the position without distress, confident of remaining the favourite. Being the eldest in Robert's absence, he relished the authority: he had full responsibility for a blue-green budgie called Peter and a hive of bees, which was despatched to a farmer on the moors each summer for heather to enrich the honey. His inseparable chum was the family dog, a boisterous mongrel called Pat. Every morning was *full of freshness and hope irrespective of the weather*.

Danger, Jim would come to believe, lies in surrendering to the enjoyment of the moment; that is the time to be most on guard. The formative lesson came at the age of eight, when Pat was put down for biting the maternity nurse: in Jim's anguished opinion the dog had only been protecting the baby. And then in 1944 it was his turn to follow Robert – to be billeted and displaced himself – to Terra Nova school in Cheshire. After a few weeks he developed alopecia and horrified his mother by the extent of the bald patches in his hair. 'Don't worry,' the headmaster countered Jo's argument that it was a nervous condition. 'Lots of children get it.'

Jim was one of 75 pupils, the 851st boy to enrol. The school was situated at Jodrell Bank, a large estate near Chester, where it had moved when its buildings at Birkdale had been requisitioned by Somerset House on the outbreak of war. The name honoured Newfoundland in Canada, where the founder, Edward Owen, had been born in 1871 – the bell from a ship wrecked off that distant coast had struck the hours until recently – and old boys included the first flyer to perch an aeroplane on the summit of Helvellyn in the Lake District. 'A boy must enter heart and soul into everything connected with his school,' the founder's dictum laid down, 'to obtain the full benefit from his life here.'

Thomas Weildon Brown, the headmaster who succeeded Owen, was known as Whacker Brown, and the school was run on military lines. Fuss was anathema, the three 'houses' were named A, B and C, and Brown prided himself on never having made a speech to parents. His mission was to bring out the latent abilities of the 'ordinary boy', exemplified by the record number of Common Entrance passes, and all were expected to fit the mould. The regime aimed to give the average boy a square deal, and the divisive element in team games was anticipated, and guarded against. 'We don't award colours and we have very few cups,' Brown expounded. 'I have always felt that it is a mistake to exalt individual boys . . . They've got to realise that they are members of a community and that each one of them has a place in it. Another thing that is worth driving home is that if a boy is not a natural scholar or athlete but is, say, a good gardener, he deserves respect for that ability.' In *The Siege of Krishnapur* that outlook colours the hero, George Fleury, who believes *nobody is superior to anyone else, he may only be better at doing a specific thing.* Jim disliked Brown intensely at the time – 'He brought the teaching of Latin to a fine and cruel art,' he told his mother at one stage – but he was to be a formative influence. As Robert would muse many years after they left, it came as a shock to realise that the rest of the world was not like that.

The Georgian building, with stables dating back to the fifteenth century, was imposing, but it had not yet recovered from years of neglect, and the fifty-acre grounds were overgrown. Throughout Jim's time there, masters and boys joined in restoration – so much so that it was decided not to move back to Birkdale when the chance came – and Jim toiled as energetically as the rest. His child's perspective of house and untenanted outbuildings, encroached on by wilderness, imbues the scale and decay of the Majestic Hotel in *Troubles*.

Boys were known by surname, and Jim was Farrell II. Uniform was a Norfolk jacket and short trousers in herringbone tweed, with grey flannel shirts, black ties and black shoes. Green caps with a narrow white ribbon border added a touch of colour, and a navy blazer with a white TN monograph brightened summer terms. Two Sundays a term were allowed for a day leave-out, and there were no half-days. The only unpredictable element was the rumoured school ghost, Count Jodrell.

Each 'set' had twelve boys based in their own room, and lessons began at 9.30am, with the first two hours devoted to Latin and poetry. At 1pm the school assembled to fall in and march to the dining room, where the seating plan remained the same all term. Talking was not allowed while Brown and his wife served the main course and maids handed round the plates. If silence was needed instantly, the headmaster scraped his chair back on the floor, something unwary visitors sometimes achieved too, to their consternation. Games began at 2.30pm, followed by an hour of maths, and half an hour of prep after tea. In the evening hobbies took over, with stamp collecting, modelmaking, chess and board games encouraged. The time-table was the same every day of the school year. On Saturdays the highlight of the week, a black and white 16mm film, was shown. 'Please tell Miss Roberts I am in the 4th set for Maths, French, Latin, English and Modern', Jim wrote home. 'I am 9th in a class of about fifteen for maths and I've beaten all the new boys. It was the ~~flicks~~ pictures last night and there was a Laurel and Hardy one which was quite good.' . . . 'On ~~Wednesday~~ we had a match with Sandbatch and we won twelve nil. There were two good flicks last night.' Critical appraisal of that medium would never slacken.

'I think James likes school,' Robert reported to his parents towards the end of term, by which time the alopecia was clearing up. By the following year Jim was intent on capturing dialect; not quite the 'average boy' Brown had in mind. 'Dear Mum, it snowed on Saturday for about twenty minutes during french . . . I went to the party yesterday and I won a tanner ont Musical Chairs. I did an all. There's a house match tomorrow. B v C there . . . Be a good lass, love from James.'

The motto was *Labor et Ludus*, which made sense to Jim as soon as he began rugger. The small school had an illustrious reputation, based on its 1933 first XV which had boasted three future Public School captains and several 'other ranks', and Jim's solid build and bursts of speed were tailor-made for the game. He played at scrum-half, and at the age of eleven showed sufficient flair to be picked for the first team; within the year he was on the first XI cricket team as well.

Army drill with wooden dummy rifles took place each morning before prayers, and Sergeant-major A.E. Matthews of the Durham Light Infantry, a First World War regular and crack shot, was Jim's first blimpish example. In 1945 Sergeant P.W. Plant took over and contributed more up-to-date mannerisms, having been attached to the 4th Battalion Black Watch in the 51st Highland Division and seen service with the Eighth Army in the Middle East. Lessons from far-off trench life, meanwhile, pervaded the school, with Brown falling back on his experiences whenever a moral tale was needed in class.

It was Brown's contemporary, Clifton Mackenzie, known to boys as The Pie, whose war had most relevance for Jim, precisely because he had put it behind him. A university athlete, The Pie had lost a leg in France in 1918, but he ran junior rugby, played a tough game of tennis, and was Master in Charge of cricket. His gifts included a keen intellect, lit by an ironic turn of phrase. Middle French and Bottom Maths were the scene of their first encounters, and when Jim was promoted to scholarship sets in English and History he quickly came to appreciate the application of succint light verse. A time would come when he would draw strength from Mackenzie's other example, as the span of the Major's life in *Troubles* would delicately underline.

Jim progressed from the Analysis Book – a unique Terra Nova learning technique which laid down the foundations of English and Latin grammar – to the novels of Richard Hughes, and he took full advantage of the well-stocked library. All aspects of English came easily, and though his grasp of French was not of scholarship level he was told that he had inherited his father's aptitude for languages. He was appointed one of the three senior monitors, and on the rugger pitch he began to be spoken of as the next captain of the first XV.

A large and heavily built boy, who blushed easily and had a humorous glint, Jim gave the impression at the age of twelve of having duly entered 'heart and soul' into Terra Nova life. His antipathy towards Brown was well-disguised, and in his final year came the ultimate accolade with appointment to Head of School. It was a role for which the qualities of reliability, trustworthiness and strength of character were deemed essential, particularly when the postwar surge of pupils appeared likely to destabilise the school. Jim would often claim that he had always been an outsider, but in 1947 nothing seemed further from the truth.

Traditionally the head boy puts too much into the job to do himself full justice academically, but Jim succeeded in avoiding that trap, on top of captaining the first teams in rugby and cricket. In the Common Entrance he got 100 per cent for Latin, and did so well overall that he qualified to sit a separate paper for an exhibition to Rossall, which was Bill's first choice for public school. He was placed second, but the wealthy family of the winner released the financial scholarship to the next in line. His name was painted up on the school Honours board, and he left with a characteristic parting shot. 'It was one of my many extraneous duties to see the Farrell boys off at Crewe station,' noted Dr Kaufmann, the maths master. 'James amused me greatly at the station by handing me as a "leaving present" a copy, purchased at the station bookstall, of *Teach Yourself Geometry*, evidence of a subtle sense of humour in a 13 year old.'

Labor et Ludus personified, Jim had fitted the mould to perfection – but at a price. Terra Nova, in the manner of prep schools of its era, laid the foundations for three distinctive traits. Conformity would result in a lifelong struggle between convention and originality. Inhibition would make him suppress the needs of his emotions, and equate self-sufficiency with strength.

And the emphasis on study and analysis would lead to an unshakable belief that they alone ensured control. All had already resulted in success, and they would do so again. For a writer, however, they were a decidedly mixed blessing.

CHAPTER THREE

Run Very Fast, Very Fast Indeed
1947–1952

The sea, again; this time the Irish Sea. There was a re-alignment of family influence in the aftermath of the war, because when passage to Ireland was no longer hindered by U boats and military controls the Russells came into focus, exerting a persuasive pull. Bob Russell's aged appearance and ill health was a shock, and added an emotional argument to the economic one of moving to live in Ireland. At first Jim resisted spending his school holidays in Dublin, and he was allowed to choose for himself; within a short while he fell in line.

His father, who had most to lose, went along with the decision. On reflection, Bill accepted that there was nothing to keep him in England: his wartime work had ended, his mother lived with his brother's family in the house in Kremlin Drive, and the Southport move had served its purpose. Bill had no wish to return to the wine business, and the interconnecting Dublin business world promised better, as Bob Russell's contacts were legion. The wellbeing of his family was his whole life.

Jo had missed her parents acutely in the fifteen years of separation, understanding all that lay behind her father's teasing letters, with their tongue-in-cheek lamentation that it was 'a terrible sorrow' that she lived so far away. A trust fund he set up in recognition of Bill's disability would cover English school fees so the boys' education would not be disrupted, and he made no claim in return. With typical lightness of touch he proposed a house on the canal bank full of rat-holes, his way of saying that he would fund a home of their choice and lobby on Bill's behalf.

Crossing back over the Irish Sea, one family among so many in the postwar flux, would have wider implications for Jim than a change of house, but that jolt was at first the most profound. While househunting the Farrells took a year's lease on an upstairs flat at 16 Northumberland Road, Ballsbridge, a terraced street in a good quarter of Dublin where many of the Edwardian family houses were divided into flats. The winter of 1947 was a grim introduction. The roof leaked, and the only fuel was sodden turf, which they had to haul upstairs; fires smoked, and the acrid tang mingled with that of damp. The streetscape which Jo was having to relearn was camouflaged by hardpacked snow.

Northumberland Road was a literary neighbourhood, recognised by the opening of Parsons Bookshop at Baggot Street Bridge, and it would come to have a bookish reputation which Jim would prize. Patrick Kavanagh's digs were in Pembroke Road, the Behans were nearby in Herbert Street, and Frank O'Connor and Liam O'Flaherty lived in Wilton Place. But for the Farrells, in those early days, it had other connotations. Bob Russell pointed out that Northumberland Road was the route along which British soldiers had marched after disembarking at Kingstown to quell the rebellion in 1920. In *Troubles* Jim would set an assassination on the canal bridge a few yards from their flat. *An old man – white moustache, grey face spattered with scarlet – lay on his back, eyes rolled up beneath the lids so that only the whites were visible. A gold watch, linked by a chain to the top buttonhole of his waistcoat, still lay in the palm of his right hand encircled by long ivory fingernails.*

Before his final term at Terra Nova they had found a more rural setting. Bill was fixed up with an accountancy role at Atco Motors in Rathmines, and the family was installed in The Gwanda, built by a retired colonial from Rhodesia, in five acres in Shankill, to the south of the city. It was within easy commuting distance on the Harcourt Street railway line, and the short walk to the station absolved Jo from driving Bill to work.

Everything about The Gwanda pleased Jim. It was placed within the triangle of two converging lanes, and a tall ash tree stood guard. A solid-fuel Aga heated the kitchen, where an overhead rack solved the problem of airing clothes, and the walk-in larder had hooks for sides of bacon and sufficient shelves to withstand a siege. In the small drawing room a mahogany chimneypiece stretched up to the ceiling, and the dark woodwork recalled Boscobel; this time, however, the house was their own. There were five bedrooms, a tennis court, and, soon, an elderly gardener, Tom Carton, who came with the property. A small local shop sold newspapers, sweets and groceries, and the centre of Dublin was only fifteen minutes away by car.

Two pet dogs, an Alsatian and a dachshund, joined the family and hens were bought. It was planned to fatten piglets for profit and Bill cheerfully marked 'W.J.F. facit' in the wet concrete floor of a converted pigsty; twenty years afterwards the memory of the *asphyxiating, ammoniac stench* would evoke a nightmarish twist in *Troubles*. Fruit and vegetables could provide an extra source of income, so raspberries and strawberries were planted. The restaurant of the Green Cinema in St Stephen's Green, in which the Russells were major shareholders, provided a ready market, and resourcefulness was the order of the day. Ireland's glut of food was astounding to the family, used as they were to rationing, but petrol and electricity cost more and few had money to spare. Jo entered her produce in the Light Fruit class of the Dublin Horse Show, where Russell Bros traditionally took a stand, and holidays were possible. They went to Dooagh, near Westport in County Mayo, where they rowed a curragh and swam to an island. At Fanad Head in County Donegal, where they took a remote coastguard's cottage and lived on eggs, mackerel and lobster one summer, a farmer told Jim that it would make a man of him to drink a foaming glass of milk straight from the cow. *If that had been all that was needed*, he would comment from adult perspective.

With his capacity for listening, honed by attentiveness to Bill, the new influences were correspondingly vivid. He got about, to local shops for 'messages', listening from the back seat when his mother gave lifts, exploring Shankill lanes by bike, and making regular trips into Dublin, and absorbed much that he overheard. The wireless was as likely to be tuned to Radio Eireann now as to the Home Service, and he found an affinity with the humorous turn of phrase, the oblique put-down, the instant pounce on the absurd or bizarre, and the addiction shared by small communities everywhere to assembling dossiers of minor eccentricities. Along the way he picked up a discernment about larger-than-life reputations, and the mutation of reality into myth. It was an apprenticeship in fictional technique.

One of Jim's mentors was Tom Carton, who wove stories as he hand-scythed the bank, pruned apple trees, mucked out the pigs or salted surplus runner beans in crocks. Small, stooped and weatherbeaten, his oblique approach appealed to Jim. The theft of apples from a tree near the road was stopped by the ruse of hiding when the culprits were heard scrambling up the bank, and simultaneously barking like a dog and hooking a looped wire, which he happened to he holding, over the nearest arm. Mrs Doyle came in twice a week to help in the house, and poignant ballads accompanied her brushing and scrubbing; his favourite was 'The Wild Colonial Boy'. Not least of the major figures in Jim's landscape was his grandfather, Bob Russell, who was of the opinion that Mrs Doyle sang rebel songs. The *large and jovial figure* kept busy in retirement, emanating the sure touch of a man in the right place at the right time, which Jim already sensed he would never possess. The older two boys had first stayed at his house, Shaen, in 1942, flying from Speke to Collinstown in a seven-seater de Havilland Downie biplane with blacked-out windows that had fully matched their Sexton Blake expectations, and subsequent encounters enhanced his stature. In 1946 Jim was shown around Portlaoise prison during a hunger strike, at a time when one prisoner was under sentence of death. 'I have never forgotten the impression of sheer boredom and despair,' he would emphasise publicly in the mid–1970s, when English opinion demonised the IRA.

With Bob Russell's health failing, however, an extra burden fell on Jo, who had to look after her parents seventy miles away and simultaneously care for Bill, who relied on her as heavily as the three energetic boys. The demands of family life were not lost upon Jim, who saw that his father's family exerted pressure from a distance, which conversely inflicted guilt. Bill's brother, Tom, sent across his oldest son, also called Tom and three years senior to Jim, for a holiday so the cousins would not lose touch, a move which had the effect on Jim of flinging down a gauntlet. Not only was the more athletic Tom on the first XV, but his school was

Liverpool College, fount of the Farrell sporting triumphs. In *The Hill Station* he would get even.

As he grew more observant, Jim realised that it was his practical mother who took charge, and he grew to despise his father for being passive. The deafness became a cause for shame: he hated it if Bill was shouted at like a child by visitors, or ignored in preference to Jo, but judged him harshly for not standing up for himself. 'Weakness of character is common to all the men in my family,' he would claim at convenient moments ahead. But if men were weak, it followed that women were stronger and would instinctively seek to dominate.

In September 1948, accompanied by Bill, Jim took the boat to Liverpool for the first term at Rossall, situated at Fleetwood, near Blackpool. *His father was sitting at ease, humming softly to himself and stirring the coffee, as if unaware that his son was about to tumble over a precipice into unknown terror. Catching his eye, he winked . . . 'I don't suppose we'll recognise you the next time we see you.' And then, as if a hint of his son's agony had penetrated the wall of unconcern which separated them . . . 'It may seem a bit strange at first but you'll soon get used to the swing of things . . . Goodbye, old man. See you at Christmas.' . . . He did not know whether to cry, or to pretend to read a book, or to look out of the window . . . He sat there filled with misery and fear, but already aware, too, that there was a certain strength within himself, water becoming hard ice.*

The watery analogy was appropriate, because the low-lying marshy ground surrounding the coastal school became flooded whenever high tides coupled with westerly gales to breach the sea wall. 'A very desolate position,' Rossall's first headmaster had commented gloomily. Life within was bounded by the weather and the tides, with no escape from the ebb and flow of water, even in the infirmary. Winds blasted the quadrangle with such force in winter that boys held hands to keep their balance, contemptuous of the crude innuendo from other schools. Jim was glad of the dark blue blazer with RS emblazoned, not for the new identity it conferred, but for its warmth.

Founded for the sons of clergy in 1844, the school was in a low period when he arrived. Most pupils came from the north of England but, dating from the direct steamship route between

Fleetwood and Ireland, it retained a loyal Irish following. Patrick Campbell had been a contemporary of Jo's brother Harry, who had promptly instigated spitting matches, and Jim was similarly competitive in his first interview with the headmaster. 'My favourite holiday treat is a good thriller by him,' he retorted when asked what he knew about Beethoven.

Spread Eagle House was one of eight, each averaging fifty boys. Jim detested the housemaster, Harry McNair, from the start. 'He was a martinet when you first joined – a fierce disciplinarian,' a fellow pupil explained. 'He had favourites, and one of his quirks was that he was disinterested in younger brothers. As you got older he would ignore you – wouldn't speak to you at all. It didn't break Jim or me, but it did break others. If he took a dislike to you, you were damned.' It was useful preparation for withstanding critical neglect in future, however.

Balding, rubicund and wiry, McNair's presence emanated from his room about the entrance arch. He was in his fifties and a late starter as a schoolmaster, a man who made violins as a hobby and suppressed his own musical bent as sternly as he suppressed the boys in his care. Jim lampooned McNair's idiosyncrasies, earning applause for a barbed rendering of 'It's so nice to have Old Harry around the house' in a school concert, but instead of taking revenge in his future novels he chose to ignore him, as he himself had been ignored.

The headmaster, the Reverend Carl Young, held sway with the assistance of his wife, Dorothy, and their team approach might have been designed with Jim in mind. Young was an absent-minded scholar, not an administrator, but no-one held that against him. He would eat a meal and not know afterwards what had been on the plate, go upstairs to change for a function and be found asleep in bed, and his car was given a wide berth unless his wife was behind the wheel. Dorothy Young, daughter of a professor at Trinity College, Dublin, was grey-haired and dynamic. Years of administering to boys of mixed ability had not dimmed her ambition to foster literary talent – Leslie Charteris was a former pupil, Jim soon heard – and she was reported to approve of athletic boys. Shouldering his way around her drawing room, Jim's strapping build was as apparent as his consuming interest in books.

'Mrs Young took up the cause of those hounded by McNair,' noticed a contemporary. 'She would spot people she thought were being sat upon and engineer practical help, but with hindsight I would think that having her take such an interest in his victims exacerbated McNair's dislike, as he knew they could go above him to someone higher.' There was no recurrence of the alopecia, but Jim developed a stutter for a while and was given the nickname Larry the Lamb.

A bonus from being head boy at Terra Nova was the insider's view of boarding systems, and Jim mastered the Spread Eagle routine with minimum effort. But exeat weekends drew attention to his separateness, as without parents in the same country it was left to his housemaster to take him out. The wistful preoccupation with fitting in, which unites Major Brendan Archer in *Troubles*, Fleury in *The Siege of Krishnapur* and Matthew Webb in *The Singapore Grip*, was a feeling Jim knew well.

Under McNair, strong allegiances were formed, and Jim shared a study with Nevill Phillips, an affable boy from a fashionable prep school further south. 'In our different ways,' Phillips would muse, 'we were both loners.' Their ground-floor study, extended years earlier for Thomas Beecham and his grand piano, also set them apart. The temperature dropped and they did Prep with their feet on the single metal heating pipe, until the occupants of the study next door sent an electric current through. 'We were thought to be snobs,' Phillips said unapologetically. 'I often wondered what it would be like to go to a southern public school.' For Jim the displacement was more disturbing: he already felt Irish in England and English in Ireland, and now he was considered a southerner in the north, where he had grown up.

Many of Rossall's traditions, surrealistically reshaped, stud the Empire Trilogy. Its anthem, with the chorus '*Floreat Rossallia*', brings inspiration in *The Singapore Grip* to the Japanese officer Matsushita. *Moreover, he was surrounded by a little circle of poisonous snakes which had reared up around him as if to listen as he sang to them, conducting himself with his sabre . . . 'Floreat Sand . . . ha . . . haa . . . liaaaah!'* The portable book-shaped carved memorial to Old Rossallians killed in the 1914–18 war heightens Edward Spencer's allegiance to the

Crown in *Troubles. Edward had grasped each page . . . and folded it outward and back on concealed hinges, revealing row after row of photographs of young men . . . one or two . . . dazzled by the sun, looked to be already in agony.* The school had already been the setting for two Victorian novels by Clive Phillips Wolley, *Snap* and *The Queensbury Cup*, but the new Spread Eagle House boy with his stutter, scuffed black shoes and austere, late 1940s uniform was looking around, and his memory for detail would prove prodigious.

Rossall Hockey was a cross between hockey and rugby, a seaside variation of the Eton Field Game, and matches were played on the hard sand surface of a stretch of beach below the school. It was a tough game with its own rules and jargon, featuring eleven players a side. 'Down shore!' was shouted if the sea was on a player's right, 'Up shore!' if on the left, and the Full Back could stamp the ball into the sand. If the tide came up while a match was in progress play continued for as long as possible, so no boy was allowed to play until he could swim. The public swimming pool on the seafront was the Rossall Hockey training ground. Concentration on the nuance of tidal movement became second nature, its potential menace rubbed in by safety regulations resulting from past tragedies. Three boys had been drowned while playing, including two cousins from Ireland swept out to sea. 'My first view [of the sea] made a great impression on me,' Wolley had written in 1895. 'I used to watch the waves with delight from the old sea-wall . . . On one side was the long line of surf to the Blackpool Headland [but] in spite of the fair seeming of those glassy green waters, they were not altogether innocent.' The effect on Jim is evident in all his books, from the intended fate of the Major in *Troubles,* buried in sand up to his neck to drown when the tide comes up, to numerous drowning references. He began to have a regular nightmare in which he was being pulled down underwater, and the dream lay in wait when he was in his forties.

As at Terra Nova, few masters escaped scrutiny – *eminently normal bachelors who are so often pursued by some curious minor obsession, like wearing a golf glove while writing on the blackboard or opening all windows in the depths of winter* – and quirks were prized. The head of Modern Languages, G.M.

Arthursen, was memorable for his impenetrable handwriting, testiness and small moustache, but it was GMA, or Whisky Joe as he was known to the boys, who brought French alive and would be the one to keep in touch. When Jim subsequently saw the film *If*, he had no trouble identifying with the call to bloody revolt, and his sole quibble was that 'Ross' was less photogenic.

'He became a difficult person – not easy to live in a study with,' noticed Phillips. 'Impatient, sarcastic, rather saturnine. A morbid character, in many ways. We often played silly games then, and I remember him sitting in a corner and not wanting to enjoy it or join in. He gave the impression that the rest of us were really rather silly.' Angry black moods descended for no apparent reason; he had little patience with the slower-minded, and none with the pretentious or complacent. Small things that might pass over another boy's head affected Jim deeply, and he hated himself for brushing aside a beggar at the boat train after Bill remarked, 'I think he asked you because you have a kind face.' Crossing back and forth to Ireland each holiday by ferry via *the smoky savagery of Holyhead station*, he was offended by the travel-arrangement posters for their implication that Irish passengers were 'subhuman', although he could see how laughable stock 'Paddies' might appear. Imperceptibly, his accent reflected the double view. The English voice with its faint northern inflexion became a drawl which gently mocked each syllable, neither brogue nor twang.

Regular commuting showed up the psychological raw spots of each country. As Jim adjusted to *that dreadful lurching one feels as one first leaves the protection of the Howth peninsula and forges out into the open sea*, the approach of England loomed hugely, magnifying the greater population, power structures and potential for rapacity and manipulation, as well as the patronising inability to comprehend an alternative set of priorities. Ireland, behind, would dwindle in proportion, made smaller by ex-colonial obsessions, blinkered interests, preoccupation with England's opinion, commercial stagnation, religious narrowness and the lack of an international political view. Even after independence was won, it was clear the coloniser's influence continued, and tearful farewell scenes at both ports brought home the cost in human terms.

As his irritations mounted, Jim sought physical release in sport. Cricket appealed sufficiently for him to be selected for his house team, but rugger was his passion. In the first season he was put on the Under Fifteens as centre three-quarter, and the emphasis on endurance, acceleration and quick tactical judgement suited him as his weight built up. He could run very fast for 100 yards, but then lost speed; it was more than enough, however, for a try. In the showers and dormitory mirrors his body was a source of pride which he took good care to disguise, drawing attention instead to his boxer's nose, which was broken twice, adding a nasal tone. At 12 stone and 5 ft 10 ins he was put on the first XV, and seen as a good team player, sound and strong. 'Jim could do it all and was dependable,' assessed Norman Ilett, who took rugby practice. 'He didn't like being pushed about, and occasionally he got cross if you were rude to him. The game meant a great deal and he thought about it constantly.'

Most matches were against northern public schools, including Stonyhurst and Fettes; Sedburgh was said to field the most implacable side. Jim's contribution was vigorous, as Rossall match reports attest. 'For the first 20 minutes our weakened team pressed hard without luck and consequently with no result. But . . . just before half time Farrell, backing up, cut in the right, cleverly dribbled the ball down into the circle.' [and] 'Now they began to be more aggressive . . . and scored a try which they converted. After this they pressed hard but we managed to keep our line intact. Then [we] broke through to score which Farrell converted. There had been no further score when the whistle went.' 'At half-time the score was 8–3. Farrell J kicked the goal, then [we] kicked the ball over the line and fell on it . . . Farrell J converted these tries and also kicked a penalty goal. The final score was 26–6.' Long after his Booker Prize celebrity he cherished a yellowing cutting about a very different triumph, taken from the sports pages of the *Daily Telegraph*. 'Rossall School beat King William's College by five goals and a penalty goal to a try at Fleetwood yesterday,' it report began. 'For Rossall . . . J.G. Farrell converted all five tries, kicked the penalty goal, and was just short another penalty kick.'

In public Jim was flippant about his red-and-white rugby colours, but Tom Gover, a contemporary, saw behind the act.

'Jim wasn't gamesy in an arrogant way. There was a strange diffidence about him. He'd drink with all the hearties, but he wouldn't make their noise. He was a part of their group, but separate. He was a great observer, always slightly detached.' In 'The Memoirs of a Fragile Three-Quarter', which soon appeared in *The Rossallian* under the prophetic name 'J.G. Farrell', Gover's opinion was borne out.

> *'No thanks, quite alright,' I gasped. 'Sure?' he asked, a trifle disappointed. 'Quite thanks; it was just the way your boot got me: my knee felt a little numb.' This was a gross understatement; my knee cap felt as if it had been shattered. I limped painfully back to my position with what I hoped was a trace of an undaunted smile playing about my lips . . . The referee blew the whistle and we started again. Our opponents got it from the scrum. My opposite number, an ungainly creature with bristly hair, lumbered towards me, grasping the ball firmly in one massive paw. He gathered speed . . . Another scrum [and] the scrum-half passed the ball to the stand-off and thence to me; as if by magic my pain vanished and spotting a gap in our opponents' defence, I hurtled towards it with the musk and amber of revenge. I came to on the touch-line. As if from a great distance I heard a voice say resentfully, 'He should have passed out.' I did so.*

Regular appearances of his pen-name 'Seamus' (the Irish version of James), and J.G.F. in *The Rossallian* sealed the image of a cool character from whom others could learn. '*When my house-master came [in] unexpectedly the other day during Prep and found me dozing in front of the fire, I adjusted my tie and prepared to explain that I was imitating Descartes, who installed himself in a stove to work out his profound philosophical theories.*' . . . '*When asked why one has been doing something wrong, the standard answer is, of course, "I don't know". This, however, has two serious failings; it automatically gives the initiative to the opponent, and it is not original. However, it has the advantage that it has no real answer; whereas if you say "I thought we were allowed to", you immediately bring down crushing sarcasm on your intellectual ability and integrity. In the former, after thinking furiously for a minute or two, your opponent will be forced to give up the struggle and resort to the equally standard rejoinder, "What do you mean, you don't know?" hence implying a sketchy knowledge of spoken English.'*

Jim's attitude to religion was similarly worldly: he approached it as one more game with a public set of rules. In chapel he earmarked biblical passages for satire – *There was something very depressing about the way in which God, in any contest with Satan, always insisted on winning by a knockout* – and already considered that practical socialism won out over Church-of-England-rooted Conservatism, rebelling against the self-serving acceptance of a natural order. He continued to be generous to a fault when any of his friends were stuck for cash.

Physically, he was maturing faster than his age group, with stronger legs, broader shoulders and a bulkier frame. He began shaving at fourteen and hacked away with a safety razor each morning, only to feel the bristles of a five o'clock shadow before the start of Prep. 'What a pity I can't get electrolysis done on my beard,' he groaned to Gover. 'Shaving is a hell of a bore.' At fifteen, with a mop of black Brylcreemed hair, he agonised about the swarthiness of his appearance and grimaced at the hairs on the back of his hands. He was a heavy smoker, following the trend of the day, which helped to suppress appetite, but building up muscle and keeping fit burned up the calories, and he was hungrier than most. On Sundays, when boys made their own supper, he talked of training to be a chef and opening a restaurant in Dublin. He was beginning to form a secret ambition, however; each printed piece in *The Rossallian* was strengthening the self-image of himself as a writer.

The Korean War, Burgess and Maclean's defection, the Cold War, the death of Stalin . . . all might have been happening on another planet. In the enclosed miniature world of school he was as remote as Bill had felt in Bengal, and the tiniest detail stood out. At the Christmas Panto in 1952, Farrell, Phillips and a third boy put on a drag cabaret act serenading GMA to the tune of 'Wheel of Fortune', and the chorus, 'Kiss me quick, Kiss me simple, on my little pimple', brought the house down, because the master had developed one on his face. The debating club modelled itself on the Cambridge Union, and with his stutter outgrown Jim took increasing pleasure in demolishing the opposition. McNair's practice of leaving the day-to-day control of Spread Eagle House to the seniors was, in Phillips's words, 'arrogant-forming'; it was also a second invaluable lesson in taking an independent line.

Jim treated the RAF Combined Cadet Corps as a joke, and from the lofty rank of sergeant stored up cameos of bumbling parades, masters being saluted, identification classes on obsolete World War One airplanes, and an elderly flying trainer kept almost permanently in its cover. 'We had brass buttons and a belt buckle which we had to polish with Brasso,' according to Roger Donald, a fellow member. 'We had to take the buckle off to do that. Spit to shine the shoes. Jim *despised* that. He would come in and say to me, "Private Donald, we need you," and then we'd duck off and hide for two hours. We'd talk and read, smoking cigarettes. We'd poke fun at the whole thing.' Jim's disdain for the Corps, however, did not extend to the courage and self-sacrifice the Services could inspire, nor to possible personal benefit, and he toyed with applying for an RAF university scholarship, attracted by its generous financial grants.

Donald, an American, was on an English Speaking Union exchange year from Phillips Academy in Andover, Massachusetts. Ahead in sexual experience, he rated the rules petty-minded and the boys gauche and juvenile; instead of being overwhelmed intellectually, as he had anticipated, they were 'the dumbest lot' he had seen. Jim listened, and raised an eyebrow. 'He said, "Go off and read on your own. Don't let these people depress you." He didn't even condemn boys sleeping with boys. He had nothing to do with it himself, but he dismissed my revulsion by saying it was just the way life was. He thought my anger was amusing – that I didn't understand how the world worked. He stood out. He simultaneously succeeded at the place without endorsing it. The epitome of success for him was succeeding in a very small circle of people, without accepting the prevailing view.'

Sex was one sphere in which Roger Donald knew he was superior. Average Rossall experience stretched no further than dancing lessons at a nearby girls' boarding school – *to stand reluctantly in front of some mountainous, seated young beauty –* and Jim's raciest information came from the film *The Blue Lagoon*. And it was mainly due to Donald that the fame of his namesake, James T. Farrell, author of *Studs Lonigan* began to grate, because the impact of his slang brought books by Americans alive. Jim lost himself in Hemingway, Scott Fitzgerald, Faulkner and Wolfe, and when *The Catcher in the Rye* came out they devoured it together. Nevertheless, Jim hugged his growing writing aspirations to himself, except for the most oblique of clues. He had no real confidence, he murmured one day while blowing smoke rings, of being able to make a living from the literary world. 'He never said, "I want to be a writer",' Donald said later. 'But clearly it was his paramount interest.'

In the meantime, for want of a real alternative, Law was emerging as the best bet for university. His parents made no secret of their hope that he would follow the example of his older brother, Robert, who was studying for a Law degree at Trinity College, Dublin; and conveniently it was known that Rossall had 'a pipeline' to Law at Brasenose College, Oxford. His O-level passes were of sufficient grade, except in maths and biology, so as languages were a stronger point, German was added to Latin, Spanish and French. All aspects of English, as always, came so easily that he enjoyed mocking his own ability.

> *Good articles usually start off with a pithy quotation. But after much research the best I could find was 'Ghent, how I brought the Good News from Aix to' (or vice versa); which has . . . some severe weaknesses. The best I can do, to make it relevant, is to say that 'News (good, bad or indifferent) travels slowly in Ireland'. This may be the reason why, some weeks after I injured my ankle, the main flood of letters had not yet arrived . . .*

The ankle injury, however, had come as a catastrophe, and writing about it was a shrug in the face of disaster. 'I had them lined up in practice with forwards on one side and backs on the other,' explained Ilett, the master in charge. 'It was just for fun.

Jim caught the ball, he was tackled and knocked over, and he didn't get up again.' The painful ankle did not heal, leaving ample time for the ironic reflection that the tackle that had succeeded in putting him out of the game had come from the captain of his own side, Alf Tansey. Reduced to hobbling about, Jim transformed his handwriting, practising calligraphy as assiduously as he had kicked at goal, and a classical script evolved. But it was small consolation.

In the Easter term of Jim's final year at Rossall he discovered France, on an exchange arranged by GMA. École des Roches in Normandy was a boarding school like Rossall, but there all similarity ended, and as science lessons were not compulsory he spent those periods in a bar in town, where he eased his ankle and sipped Calvados. *On the whole life here is very pleasant, for the French are an understanding people who know exactly how to deal with foreigners*, he teased in *The Rossallian*. With fly-on-the-wall amusement he savoured the departure of another group of exchange boys, returning after a period spent cramming for their French exams. *The school stood to attention while the flag was hoisted, and then a choir sang a passably accurate rendering of 'God Save the Queen', and a French version of 'Auld Lang Syne', while the English boys were presented with a medal apiece. The latter then marched off in all their glory to the village station, where they missed the only train for the next four hours.*

When his own turn came to return to frugal England, things seemed flat. For the first time he detected grey in his hair, which indicated that he had inherited that dismal Farrell tendency and, with sport still out of the question, the run-up to A levels was depressing. When the French Oral was over, the examiner turned to GMA and remarked that Farrell had taken the trouble, unlike the other 150 candidates, to make it an enjoyable experience for them both.

More exams loomed, necessitating a further term. He abandoned the RAF scholarship idea and applied for the Arthur Jupp Exhibition to Brasenose, for which the quality most sought was leadership, judged in terms of games. He could not see himself as the eminent Dublin solicitor or barrister his parents envisaged, but Law would gain him three extra years to make up his mind, and was useful mental training. 'Law is my present choice,' he specified in his application, precise as always with the words he used.

'Dear Principal,' Young recommended:

> Farrell is a School Monitor, a boy of strong character who sets a very good example. He is a keen Christian and his influence over other boys is wholly good. He is a brilliant centre-three-quarter who uses his brains. He has real ability in Modern Languages and I believe that he may reach at least Exhibition standard. He has spent a term in a French school and I feel certain that he has benefited from rather a strange experience. His interests outside Modern Languages are quite wide; he debates very well and would be a stimulating and interesting member of the College.

In the event Jim did not win, but he was assured a Brasenose place on condition that he passèd maths and biology at Matriculation level. Entry was deferred for two years, in any case, due to the war backlog, and there was ample time to qualify because his Irish address spared him National Service.

Jim was not sad when the moment came to leave school in December 1953. Following his injury he had never got back into rugby, and his closest friends had gone the term before. Daydreaming about Oxford spires made Lancashire feel alien. *I . . . just wanted to get out of the bloody place . . . [Even] summer there used to smell of smoke like a charnel house. If you want to live in a place like that you've got to believe in God. How else can you live there when you're breathing in fish and chips and soot all the time, and every pub is full of little men with their hair parted in the middle?*

But there was another side to Jim, of which his older brother was well aware. 'The sight of poverty in Lancashire, as well as Ireland, had a great effect on Jim,' Robert pointed out. 'One – pinched with cold and shoeless, but with greenery; the other – smoky and greenless, but with clogs.' In his late teens Jim was poised on the edge of allegiance, and disgust battled with empathy. Already determined to vote Labour, separating him from majority allegiance to the Conservatives, the human condition drew him in one moment, and repelled him the next.

In that final term one incident showed up the inner divisions. An ill-assorted games team turned up from a lesser school, beside which Jim felt as superior as the rest. But then the circle of Rossall boys closed in and began to jeer, 'Brown shoes and blue suit, brown shoes and blue suit . . .' He turned menacingly around. 'And what is intrinsically wrong with that?'

CHAPTER FOUR

The Yearning, the Boredom,
the Heartache
1952–1955

'B lue eyes, light skin, thick dark hair, very white teeth and this lovely smile. You knew when Jim was having fun by the smile. I thought he was the handsomest man in the whole world and I was crazy about him. It was just too wonderful to touch his hand.' Jill Kirwan was sixteen when they met and danced together all evening at a private party held during the 1952 Christmas holidays in Portora, Oscar Wilde's old school. Jim was the same age, but at 5 ft 11 inches and so strongly built, he seemed older.

Jill was bubbly and pretty, with fair hair and a curvacious figure. On their dates he invariably took her to a film in central Dublin and a coffee bar afterwards, when she had to do the talking because he turned out to have nothing to say. 'I tried to chat about home things that were happening but he wasn't listening,' she concluded, disillusioned. 'He would look around him and just jerk out a word or two in a clipped way. I didn't enjoy his company and eventually decided this boy is fantastic-looking, but he's monosyllabic. I was shattered. I felt I could never reach him because he never spoke to me. He kept himself very private.' The follow-up letters were witty, but far too non-committal.

The hospitable Kirwan family, however, took an instant liking to him, and through them he became part of 'the group', consisting of friends of his own age at boarding school who returned to Dublin in the holidays. Dalkey Lodge, where Jill lived, was a Georgian house overlooking the sweep of Dublin

Bay, within cycling distance of The Gwanda, and it soon became a home from home. He admired her parents – Valentine Kirwan was a well-read and influential solicitor – and she was one of four, with a twin brother, Jack, who was as keen on rugby as he was himself. 'I was rather unhappy while living in Dublin,' he would tell an interviewer after his Booker win, 'because as a Protestant I felt somewhat cut off from the life of the country.' But the close-knit circle provided everything he needed at the time. There were sufficient young people from successful business and professional families to provide a round of socialising, and usually something was going on – the opportunity to sail, take a riding lesson, go for a swim, play tennis, croquet or a round of golf. The sea and the mountains were on their doorstep.

'He'd turn up most days and I don't think it mattered which one of us was in,' Jack Kirwan recalled. 'I was the exact opposite to Jim, a very late developer, yet I got on with him like a house on fire. His sense of humour appealed to me because it was full of fun, yet so cynical.' Their first meeting was before the ankle injury, and through Jack, who was a member of Palmerston Junior Rugby Club in the Christmas holidays, he joined Wanderers at Lansdowne Road, the oldest club after Trinity College. Jim saw it in a less hallowed light.

I arrived punctually at 12.30. A beautifully streamlined bus was standing outside the clubhouse. Any occupants, however, were hidden by a thick reef of smoke. I tapped on the window tentatively . . . As far as the gloom was concerned, it was like entering a cathedral, but that is where all similarity ended . . . They won the toss and while we were lining up the leader of their forwards bellowed 'Grab the ball and run like blazes!' 'That's right, shouted the vicar [captain of the opposition], 'Run very fast, very fast indeed.' Hardly were the words said when a thick Irish mist came down and I lost touch with the game . . . Nobody was very sure who won, although one of our side claimed that he had personally seen the vicar swear on oath that we had lost. This was confirmed by a line in the paper next morning which said 'the Wanderers arrived late, but this only postponed their defeat'.

Witnessing Jim's aptitude for the game, which Bill had hitherto only read about, was not enough to stop father and son drifting apart. The fault was Jim's; the Kirwans' gregarious outlook and higher standard of living showed up the isolation which Bill's invalidity imposed, and his job compared unfavourably. Asked what his father did, Jim pointed angrily to an Atco mower propped against the wall; to the same question twenty years later he retorted with scathing emphasis, 'My father was a *clerk*.' His reaction was to set up separate compartments. 'It was odd because we all knew the Kirwan parents, but the Farrells were shadowy figures,' one of the group remembered. 'Jim existed on the fringe, as a floating person. It was difficult thinking of him even having a home.' Jill Kirwan had little patience with his attitude, and found his behaviour baffling. 'I thought his house was lovely,' she would note. 'If he came in he was the one who mattered, he was the centre of attention with everything quiet and neat. At ours there were so many people it was hardly noticed if you didn't come to dinner. It felt like a railway station in comparison.'

His resentment had intensified in 1953 with the sale of The Gwanda, after a suspected heart condition was added to his mother's worries, aggravated by stairs. When the new purchasers called, Jim sat stubbornly outside, tinkering with a gramophone and refusing to speak, and the move to the smaller single-storied Balholm, in Saval Park Road, Dalkey, coincided with his final term at Rossall. 'A *bungalow*,' he described it with contempt, humiliation heightened by the proximity to Dalkey Lodge and the busy port of Dun Laoghaire.

In *A Girl in the Head*, the third of his novels, much of his rancour would go into the character of Count Boris Slattery. *From his window he could see a line of cars crawling along the coast road. He hated to think of the people . . . intent on enjoying themselves. He hated to see it in their faces, this fugitive belief that life was, against the evidence, to be enjoyed . . . What use is one day of escape in your rotten little lives? . . . One day at the sea isn't going to make any difference.* Jim shut himself away or prowled about, escaping Balholm, and disapproved of everything that had brought enchantment in Southport.

'It now seems to me that it rained ceaselessly, every day, throughout my Irish adolescence,' he would write from a future perspective. 'Reason tells me that this is impossible. My unlikely recollection is, nevertheless, that for five or six years I sat by a streaming windowpane reading Colette in a state which combined great lethargy and an acute sensitivity to the sensual world.' The games of bridge that his mother enjoyed aroused his scorn, Bill's regular foursomes on the nine-hole golf course up the road offended him, and Doris Day's top-ten hit 'Que Sera, Sera', the Russell family motto, was a personal affront. Like George Fleury, his hero in *The Siege of Krishnapur*, he felt himself to be *the victim of the beauty and sadness of the universe.*

His parents gravitated towards ex-colonials, and he turned a cold eye on nostalgia and reliance on routine; people who had spent time away, it was clear, could never fit in again. However, the crisscross patterns of that circle would proffer a fertile image for the tyranny exerted by possessions. More than twenty years after the Farrells' return from India, another local couple with a Chittagong connection were introduced, and an invitation extended. Jo was promptly shown round and her hostess opened a bedroom door with the caution, 'You're bound to recognise this . . .' There stood her precious matching suite of mahogany furniture – cupboard, chest of drawers and bedside locker – which Bill had auctioned off before leaving.

Jim's mood was not improved by the regular rejection of romantic short stories which he was beginning to write under the pseudonym of Dora Parke Saville, making ironic use of his new address. But his speciality was telling stories against himself, and at school, following suit, he was portraying 'Seamus' no longer as the suave know-all. *I bravely make conversation and try to pretend to be unaware that a six-year-old boy has taken a morbid interest in me and is flailing away at my ankle with a croquet mallet.'* In the early 1950s the Major's modest personality was already at work.

Jim hated sailing, but the Kirwans dragged him along; he refused to play golf, and declared that tennis, swimming and croquet were dull. The Phoenix Cricket Club, hockey at Three Rock Rovers, Kildare point-to-points, Leopardstown races and Fairyhouse . . . the traditional Protestant circuit was deplored at great length, but assiduously mapped out. Jack was both uneasy and impressed. 'He had a vicious, devastating, fatalistic sense of humour. And there was always that underlying feeling of the futility of things. 'What's the use?'

Jim's uncle was a director of the Green Cinema in St Stephen's Green, so he could often get all his friends in for nothing. 'Ignore the moss-covered seats,' he would warn, but the prudish censorship that made the others giggle raised Jim's hackles straight away. While they whispered and nudged he stared fixedly at the screen, detecting cuts by shifts in camera angle, and on the way home would offer surreal explanations for every gap, the more grotesque the better. Six hundred books a year, on average, were banned, and he regularly checked the listings in the *Irish Times*, rejoicing when *Under Milk Wood* slipped through via the air-waves of the BBC.

Jim's closest intellectual companion was his older brother. They bought the record of *A Child's Christmas in Wales* and together walked as far as Killiney Hill Road on clear evenings to look over at the Welsh hills. 'They shimmer,' Jim observed longingly, 'like a mysterious kingdom.' On a visit to the Gaiety to see Siobhan McKenna in Synge's *Playboy of the Western World*, it became evident that he was taking a great interest in technique. 'I could see Jim wracking his brains to see what made it tick with the audience,' Robert noted. 'He watched the stalls as closely as the stage.'

At seventeen, Jim turned his attention to Jill's friend Pat Rankin, another twin, and broke the group's unwritten rules. His phone call to her was soon common knowledge, and struck the girls as absolutely wrong. 'As far as we were concerned,' said Jill's younger sister, 'that was offside. First Jill, then Pat, we felt it could be anyone as long as she was pretty.' *Girls and the fresh sea wind that modelled their summer dresses to the shape of their bodies . . . slender nervous hands always ready to anchor their skirts against a particularly lecherous gust. But the smell of the sea! It [was] the purity of love itself while . . . silken hair streamed out on the wind, rich with salt and the sun and smiling faces.* A handwritten business card was pinned up in the Kirwans' hayloft advising 'Lovesick and/or woolly' clients to call at Balholm, Saval Park Road for 'advice and help, based on personal experience'. Stung, Jim invented a sophisticated alter-ego inspired by Charteris's The Saint, and the slogan 'Farrell was here' began appearing on the same wall. 'Farrell will know,' he would murmur if someone was at a loss, and the invisible Farrell achieved independent life. One day he scrawled 'J.G. Farrell'.

Puberty . . . It comes as something of a shock when an insignificant appendage which for years has seemed to be nothing but a water tap suddenly wakes up and starts slapping you around. Indiscriminate lust alarmed Jim as much as it did the gang, because the prospect of being manacled by desire to someone with whom he had nothing in common was the strongest incentive for keeping himself in check. *It was he who lent her all the qualities that disturbed his peace of mind. More precisely the source of the trouble was likely to be in his sexual organs. If he were to take a large pair of shears and clip them off he would be able to look at her objectively again.* He read *Ulysses* with increasing fellow feeling. As the group began to pair off his desperation only made matters worse. 'Nobody ever returned poor old Jim's infatuations,' one target remarked.

Filling out Bill's dinner jacket, or competitive in fancy dress, he was on the invitation list for private dances where chaperoning was unobtrusive and drinks soft: a glass of beer, at most, for boys. Until trusted with a car they depended on their parents to get home, and the same three-piece band played hits by Victor Sylvester and Nat King Cole. Impromptu hops in the Dalkey Lodge hayloft promised more, with 'Let's Boogie' painted on the door, jam jars for glasses, old school trunks to sit on and Guy Mitchell records. In great form they occasionally descended on the Top Hat Ballroom, and bought tickets.

He learned to drive, but the advantage was shortlived, and rolling up to a party in his mother's VW Beetle he would find Jack had beaten him to it in Mrs Kirwan's Morris Minor. The magic circle tightened, became oppressive. *It was all so unnatural, so bleeding unnatural. Fifty or sixty people crowded together into the room as if straphanging, travelling on the interminable journey towards the end of the evening, jostling, apologising and reading each other like newspapers. Home, he thought, before someone else nabs me.* Jim's discontent was palpable, and behind his back they called him a dark horse. 'He was very complicated,' concluded one girl. 'One of those people who was around in the background, never leading the group but always observing. He missed nothing.'

In rugby he relished a successful feint; the equivalent in conversation was getting a rise, and taunts considered outrageous were prepared in advance. Stalking into the Kirwan household, he was liable to go on the attack at once. 'What books are you reading? Do you read *any* books?' With unfortunate timing Roger Donald came for Christmas, Jim's least favourite season. *I can still see us all sitting around the table in paper hats, gloomy with drink [and] those endless infernal carols on the radio, endlessly repeated good wishes of people totally unconscious of your separate existence.* He faced it with an insincere grin, and Roger's sexual triumphs depressed him further. On Christmas Day he ridiculed the hypocrisy, and refused to sit down for the Queen's Speech, mimicking it instead. The following day at a drinks party he got into an argument with a retired colonel who claimed that the fox enjoyed the hunt. 'And how many conversations have you had with foxes?' Jim's sarcastic drawl rang out. A fox running across snow, luminous and vibrant, was his private image for the life force.

In May 1954, putting a good face on his reservations, he went along with family plans for filling the interval before Oxford and reported to Castlepark, Dublin's most prestigious prep school, as a junior master. 'He is a most respectable and reliable young man,' the Farrells's solicitor had backed up the application, 'and I have every confidence in recommending him to anyone seeking his services.' Jack Kirwan had been there, as had the majority of boys in the group, and two Russell cousins were current pupils. His contract was for a year and a term and his subject French, combined with the coaching of rugby and cricket. The pay was £200 a year plus board, and he had a half-day off a week.

Crenellated Castlepark – a glimmer of the Majestic Hotel – prepared Protestant boys of good family for public school, usually across the water. The syllabus was regulation Common Entrance, but the atmosphere was unique. Castlepark was not, Jim would say judiciously, run with the Prussian precision of Terra Nova. Elsewhere the world was moving on – Roger Bannister broke the four-minute mile, food rationing ended,

Russia exploded a nuclear bomb and the IRA raided Armagh barracks. In Castlepark the clock was stopped at 1904, the passage of time suspended by the presence of W.P. Toone, its original owner and ex-headmaster.

In retirement Toone continued to be driven up each day in his pre-war black Austin, erect and silver-haired behind his chauffeur, Sayer; Sayer's name would be appropriated for the hero of *A Man from Elsewhere*. Toone's allegiances were Edwardian – to the Crown, the Services and to cricket, and not necessarily in that order. His priorities stamped the school, as they would stamp the character of Edward Spencer in *Troubles*. St Patrick's Day was marked by a performance of a play set in a prep school, with a plot that featured a good boy and a chap going astray who at the last minute would be brought back to the light; the dialogue was so antiquated that boys baulked at saying it on stage. Sitting on a shooting stick, Toone still umpired cricket, prodding anyone he considered too slow and marking overs by dropping an old-fashioned florin, which hit the ground with a clink.

Pupils, in Toone's view, were still the sons of landed gentry, and the school song put across his philosophy.

> Let us play the game
> In the fields and in the classes
> So that each boy as he passes
> May leave a worthy name . . .

Standing behind the other masters, a quizzical smile would flit across Jim's face as it was sung. In the entrance hall a framed photograph dating from the Troubles showed a platoon of ten-year-olds in short trousers snapped to attention, dummy rifles at the ready to defend the Empire, and the latest Coronation had been a cause of celebration. Classrooms were bedecked with Union Jacks and the school given a day's holiday for a picnic on Killiney beach, which had taken place defiantly in lashing rain.

Jim was equally fascinated by Toone's successor, Donald Pringle. Pringle ran the school with total dedication, for which he was respected by the masters – to whom he was generous and fair – and judged a martinet by the boys. Brisk and forceful, his contribution to Spencer's personality in *Troubles* would be his concentrated energy – he even cut the large expanse of grass in front of the school himself – and the explosive temper, manner of speech, personal code and masculine pursuits; Pringle was an expert fly-fisherman. 'A frightful snob but he admitted it, so you could tease him,' one master testified. 'Between ourselves we would discuss things which we had observed, anything outrageous or Anglo-Irish.' At first Jim was intrigued but soon he grew exasperated, and his feelings would be passed on to the Major – *These days the mere sight of [him] was enough to set him grinding his teeth. Everything about him . . . his overbearing manner; the way he always insisted on being right* – and off duty he put into practice a technique that he would subsequently recommend. 'One way of keeping his insensitive claws from scratching your inner meat,' he advised a friend, 'would be to spare time [to write] about him. In this way you could harness all his gross egotism to a purpose of your own, and use your interviews as periods of clinical observation.'

Although Balholm was within several hundred yards of the main entrance, it was necessary to live in. His accommodation was in The Cottage, converted stabling behind The Castle, in a single bedroom leading off a central Common Room which had a log-fire, dim lights and elderly wiring. 'Jim was very good company, and he hid his discontent,' recalled Roy Parker, a contemporary. 'There were three of us resident, and we got on very well so we used to sit up chatting after midnight. We were all young and all bachelors, and it was a very pleasant life.' Jim mulled wine with a red-hot poker for Parker and Geoffrey Drought, whose sardonic humour he shared, and pay stretched to eating out locally and drinking pints of stout. As French master he had a fairly free hand – 'As long as there isn't a riot,' he was told, 'you can go about it pretty much as you like' – and he opted for stories of life at Les Roches to lighten set-course grammar. The extra chores of correcting Prep and taking tables at mealtimes held the occasional anecdotal bonus, and Pringle's breakfast rendering of grace – '*Benedictus, benedicat . . .*' – and the Lord's Prayer would find a lasting place in *Troubles*. Days began early and finished late, with little let-up at weekends; even on Sunday it was necessary to supervise the morning 'crocodile'

to church and the 45-minute afternoon walk. The boys' favourite route took in the Forty Foot beside Joyce's Martello Tower in
Sandycove in the hope of spotting goosepimpled naked men
entering or leaving the icy sea.

Almost immediately Jim got into Pringle's bad books; as
Parker said in absolution, 'Jim was not an early-morning person.' The billiards table was sacrosanct, and senior boys were
only allowed to use it for half an hour after Prep if they dutifully
replaced its heavy cover. 'Donald Pringle came in at breakfast
time in a great shouting match,' noted Parker. ' "Who left the
top of the billiard table off?" No-one owned up. Suddenly Jim
woke up and said, "I was playing billiards last night." Donald
glared.' He would take his revenge, but in his own way and his
own time. The younger masters regularly swapped stories about
Pringle's lack of taste buds, attributed to the pipe that was rarely
out of his mouth, and if a meal was especially bad they would
catch each other's eye. In Jim's presence one day the stew was
judged to be putrid, and Pringle astounded him by calling for a
second helping. In *Troubles* Edward Spencer shows a visitor a
reeking cauldron of dogs' food, and confides, '*You know, it
smells so good I shouldn't mind eating it myself.*'

At the time Jim held his fire, and watched. Duped by a boy who
had covered himself in red ink and lay on the floor motionless, he
consigned to memory the words of the friend in league who raised
the alarm. 'Please Sir, Carruthers is dead' became his catchphrase
for mocking the stiff-upper-lip. He studied the few boys with
titles, who slept between monogrammed sheets, and identified
accents and topics with gathering purpose. A gaunt and evange-
lical spinster taught the youngest boys in a junior schoolroom
divided by glass doors, and Jim's description went the rounds.
'She's like a vulture,' he had gasped, after catching sight of her
accidentally. 'She perches on top of her desk.' Colleagues in the
Common Room were surprised to be shown a thick wad of pages
and told that it was the first part of a novel; his enthusiasm for
Russian writers, however, was already a byword. 'He's either
reading Oblomov by Goncharov,' they joked between themselves, 'or Goncharov by Oblomov.'

Behind the banter lay a recognition that he was enduring,
rather than enjoying, teaching. 'Inevitably [he] found the in-

tellectual stimulus of the Common Room rather thin,' noted Drought drily. 'I think it fair to say that he tolerated CP, and had a love-hate relationship with the value systems which under-pinned the school. The acuteness of his observation was hilar-ious, but he sometimes plunged into moods of black despair.' The experience of living all year round in Dublin was showing Jim how *very foreign, after all, Ireland was! Fires were lit not so much against the chill in the air as against the melancholy; everyone was touched by it.* He, like the Major, could be found *transfixed by sadness, slumped in an armchair.* The prospect of a lifetime in such confines was abhorrent, and the smallness of the city grated on his nerves.

> *Almost twenty past five. The Old Stand would be filling up with cheerful red-faced men wearing Trinity ties and Pal-merston ties and Wanderers ties and Lansdowne ties, dipping their gleaming faces into pints of stout, dazzling with their imbecile virility the girls with too much make-up and clashing clothes . . . What in hell would [I] find to do in a place like that? . . . And then that granite mass of grey depression they call the Bank of Ireland. The sour smell of the sea on O'Connell Bridge. The dirty neon misery of O'Connell Street. You can't go home again as Thomas Wolfe, whose book I never finished, so rightly said. Dublin is the friendliest and most insensitive city in the world.*

To his dismay, his older brother Robert was taking up a job in Canada after Trinity College, heightening claustrophobia.

Jim still had to matriculate in biology and maths, however, and Jack Kirwan, who was studying Law at Trinity College, Dublin lent his cast-off textbooks. Jack was a living example of the fate Jim longed to avoid, and he observed how instinctively his friend fitted in and doubted whether he himself would ever be capable of doing so. But he succeeded in passing biology when, grudgingly, he put his mind to it, and it would bear sarcastic fruit in Spencer's experiment of firing a shotgun at his butler to measure fright by the quantity of saliva. *D'you realise that he could only produce four c.c.? It's incredible!* Maths was harder work; in the event he managed to get through.

Hilary Kirwan, two years younger than the twins, now became the object of his attentions. It was her year off, between school and university, and the stormy relationship was to prove an education in itself. 'I can remember some appalling nights,' she would eventually say. 'I didn't want anything to do with Jim physically because he had an intensity which repelled me at that age. I knew instinctively that he was a sensual person – his type of dancing was never to sling me around, he always liked the slow, smooochy style. There was one horrible evening at a party after the Trinity Ball with Eartha Kitt singing "Birds do it, Bees do it", and Jim just clenching his teeth and groaning; another when he suddenly said, "I'm going home." There were always meaningful silences between dances, and in black moods he would slam the door behind him.' On his next off-duty period, though, he would turn up as if nothing had happened, and as she was popular with boys she wisely guessed her chief attraction was that of the unattainable. *Why do other men always have the girls I want? It never fails. The bastards. But then for the first time in his life another thought occurred to him. Why did he always want the girls other men had? This thought disturbed him for a moment and then he put it out of his mind.*

He took her to the local Astoria cinema, relishing the *sweet and smoky* darkness, and coming out, hand in hand, the anti-climax was a shock. *[He] had somehow imagined that the foyer outside would be as black as ravens' feathers. He was astonished to be greeted by pallid daylight [which soon began] to open small chinks in the wall of his mind through which a bitter reality was already leaking.* Hilary could never understand why his mood changed without warning; he could only explain at third hand, on the printed page. *That slight shock one experiences on finding that the streets and faces outside are just a little greyer than they should be. There's nobody to blame for it, of course. A small, transparent bubble of desperation forms in your brain as you look around and become accustomed to the greyness once more.*

By the time Jim's contract neared its end the greyness had swept up from sea level, blotting out the Forty Foot and the Joyce Tower, the cinemas and the Top Hat Ballroom – 'No Jive, Creep or Dancing Cheek to Cheek' – and rolled in over the ramparts of Castlepark. His mood was grim. Out for a stroll with Drought, he slowed to allow a young mother pushing a pram to cross the road. 'Lady, you've had your fun,' he taunted. 'Now push it.' He took his frustrations out on Hilary, and she fought back. 'He would constantly say how hopeless everything was, making me feel worthless. "Oh my God," I would think, "I must get away from this." ' Jim knew that he was being destructive, but he could not stop. A mild party discussion about socialism resulted in him stalking out, leaving a boiling wake. On a weekend trip to Cork with Hilary and two of her friends he alternated between sulking and sarcasm. Passing a church, he said they should stop and get married, couple by couple, brushing aside their reminder that the other two were brother and sister. 'You could try,' he said derisively, lapsing back into silence. After one too many rows with Hilary he did not call back.

Another year of marking time before Oxford lay ahead, and he made up his mind to spend it in Canada, from where Robert sent good reports. In Castlepark he began painting word pictures of eating flapjacks and corn on the cob with the Rockies in the distance, saying nothing of his real ambition, which was to emulate Hemingway, and wrote off to Bill's cousin, Frank Farrell, who ran a Montreal advertising agency, in the hope of a job. The decision taken, he made his peace with Hilary and restored her to the asexual role of friend. To the beat of Bill Haley's 'Rock Around the Clock' plans rapidly took shape, and even Donald Pringle came up trumps.

> Mr J.G. Farrell was on my staff for four terms. I was completely satisfied with his work in class, and his enthusiasm and energy on the sports field did much to help the boys in their games. I found Mr Farrell to be a conscientious and loyal colleague who was very easy to work with. I am very sorry that his stay here was so short.

Twenty-six years after his parents met on nearby waters under similar circumstances, Jim sailed out of Liverpool on Cunard's R.M.S. *Saxonia*, bound for Quebec. He was one among 842 Tourist Class passengers, and excitedly aware of stepping into 'the watery sunlight of the real world'. At table he was drawn into guarded conversation with a Scottish couple named McNab, and their surname – retrieved for *The Siege of Krishnapur* and *The Hill Station* – would be the sole souvenir of the crossing. He spent most of the passage standing at the rail, *peering down at the water and thinking of nothing at all, completely hypnotised by the symmetry of the waves.*

CHAPTER FIVE

A Ballistic Missile
1955–1956

The small plane owned by the Foundation Company of Canada headed for Baffin Bay in the northern arctic, and crossed the tree line: the point of no return. Inside, Jim was squeezed in with the latest intake of migrant workers, and musing with silent irony on the link between his prep school Terra Nova and Newfoundland, off to the right below. In the bag at his feet were books to keep him sane, and P.G. Wodehouse and the *World of Blandings* mischievously led the way; in those pages Lord Emsworth had recommended flight to Canada whenever scandal threatened. 'So you are going to the Canadian arctic,' began the introductory booklet in his pocket ambiguously. 'It is an experience that [you] are not likely to forget.'

Montreal had been a disappointment. He had lasted two weeks as a clerk in Frank Farrell's Advertising Agency, and a day in a stockbroker's office, and by the end of the first month his money was running out. With his first paycheck he had treated himself to a long-promised Zeiss Contaflex camera to record impressions, but he could buy no extra rolls of film, and passing the Hotel Mount Royal he had to content himself with memorising the brassy blondes and hardfaced men knocking back whisky sours in the red-plush bar. The papers were full of the recent death of James Dean, and *Rebel Without a Cause* was showing, but he could not afford a ticket. A temporary dishwashing job or a long cigarette butt took on 'a providential glamour', and it had been discouraging to find there was nothing 'intrinsically romantic' about having all the time in the world to write. 'This kind of life', he filed away for future reference, 'is just terribly tiring, demoralizing and a constant strain.' His lucky break had been a chance encounter with an Old Rossallian working in the city, who tipped him off that huge money was to be made up in the Arctic on the Distant Early Warning radar system, and told him where to sign on. He had his muscular build, not his reference, to thank for the prompt seven-month contract.

The DEW Line was the West's defence against Russian H Bomb attack, composed of a chain of radar stations from Greenland to Alaska that hosted massive dishes tilted back to scan the skies; each wheeled imperceptibly, on hair-trigger alert for danger coming over the pole. The emergency Strategic Air Command had been launched on signals subsequently found to be as innocuous as moon echoes and flocks of geese, and the recent Bikini Atoll tests had heightened international tension, as well as fear of further error. Jim had debated the nuclear deterrent fervently at Rossall three years before, following America's entry in the H Bomb stakes, and during the final term at Castlepark much attention had been paid to the mass petition by Nobel Prize-winners which stated that radioactivity could wipe out entire nations. Bertrand Russell's new manifesto – 'Shall we put an end to the human race; or shall mankind renounce war?' – had dramatically been endorsed by Einstein two days before he died, and news broadcasts had been leading with Russia's offer to abolish 75 per cent of nuclear stocks. It was an interesting time to arrive. *An atomic war . . . and yet it could not happen. Or could it?*

On the ground, blurred by snow and sombre skies, the Arctic stretched monotonously for hundreds of thousands of square miles. Usually the sun was below the horizon and it was searingly cold, with a wind that never abated and numbed the nerves, peeling away unprotected skin. Insulating layers of clothes were vital, and the minimum clothing allowed indoors was wool underwear, tweed trousers, and a heavyweight sweater over a jersey shirt. An arctic suit and triple mitts were compulsory out of doors, and feet were protected by double pairs of woollen socks, followed by densely woven cloth duffles and Mukluk boots with two insoles, one of felt and the other of wire mesh, to avoid picking up frost crystals. As soon as Jim was in funds he bought a genuine Eskimo parka in Frobisher Bay, reporting to Robert by post that it was very cold but warm in the bank balance.

It was a physical, tough life, and before going to bed at night everything worn that day had first to be dried out; the leather mitts, infuriatingly, needed interminable massage to keep them supple. 'Think of your body as a furnace constantly giving off moist heat', notices throughout the Big Igloo preached. 'The food you eat is the fuel. The furnace has a built-in heat regulating mechanism trying to keep you evenly balanced in keeping with the air temperature [and] since you must wear heavier clothing there is a penalty: perspiration.' Accommodation was in bunks, equipped with waterfowl-down sleeping bags, and comic-strips and pin-ups abounded on all sides. Jim treated it like the Common Room, installing works by Joyce, Tolstoy, Louis MacNeice and D.H. Lawrence, alongside *The Decline and Fall of the Roman Empire*, and backed up by *The Oxford Book of English Verse* and *Ur of the Chaldia* by Leonard Woolley. An easygoing Irishman named Dick Delaney explained the subtleties of the system, and revealed an encyclopaedic knowledge of the cinema.

Every day presented the danger of frostbite. A first-degree case, newcomers were taught, was signalled by a tingling sensation or stiffening of the muscles; next a grey spot would appear and, unless one hand was quickly freed to press until circulation was restored, that spot would turn white and spread. Second-degree was more serious, because circulation had been 'arrested in the flesh', needing immediate medical treatment, and third-degree frostbite threatened the loss of a finger, toe or limb, depending on the extent of gangrene. Rubbing those areas with snow was condemned as an old wives' tale, and anyone who recognised symptoms was told to get straight to heated quarters, where a doctor would be summoned. 'Don't panic,' their instructor added, matter-of-factly. 'Remember that the damage has already been done.'

Armed with a snow knife for emergencies and his fully loaded camera, Jim explored the deceptive vistas of grey skies, ice and snow whenever he had the chance. Lessons in survival techniques drilled in the risk of getting lost in the sudden storms that blew up over the pole, and taught the skills of marking a trail by

staining snow and cutting a water-hole in thick ice. With so
much exercise and liberal helpings of high-protein food his
weight and strength rapidly built up, and he took pride in
hefting girders and crates of stores along with the rest of the
iron-hard labour force. As soon as he reported for duty as a
general labourer, however, his education and fluent French set
him apart.

'Secretarial duties' was a sinecure; the post of Camp Fire
Warden was not. Combustible material littered the site, and his
attempt at improving the amateur practice of sounding alarms
by 'hollering' was an instructive exercise in the uphill task of
changing established custom. The large metal triangle he rigged
up in the centre of camp proved an irresistible target to most men
who passed, and his scheme for catching culprits in the act was
foiled when he was snatched up from behind in vice-like arms
and dangled with both feet off the ground. 'So what are you
going to do about it, eh?' He stored it as an anecdote, to be told
against himself.

The urge to catch a fire on film – flames silhouetted against
snow – was compelling, and Jim rarely responded to an alarm
without his camera tucked in his parka. 'Come on, Mac!'
indignant voices bellowed the first time. 'You should be putting
water on it!' Acute observation, however, stored up images with
a fictional potential far beyond the scope of one-dimensional
photographs, however good.

*Streams of fire the size of oak trees blossomed out of the
windows of the upper storeys. Caterpillars of flame
wriggled their way down the worn and threadbare carpets
and sucked at the banisters and panelling until all the public
rooms were ablaze. The heat grew so intense that the
spectators were driven back with flushed faces . . . gazing
with shaded eyes at the blinding magnificence of the burning Majestic. . . . Now the fire, like some inadequately
chained-up oriental demon, was roaring and raging on
his left, occasionally making sudden darts forward as if
to seize him by the leg, and drag him back to its lair . . .
Suddenly Matthew realised that this fire had a personality
of its own. It was not just a fire, in fact, it was a living*

creature [with] a restless and cunning disposition, con-
stantly sending out rivulets of flame like outstretched claws
to surround and seize the men fighting it and squeeze them
to its fiery heart.

The local Eskimos were seen as a useful asset to be exploited, a
point made in print to all incoming workers. 'You can be kind to
them without spoiling them, and do not feel that you have to
give away your employer's food to make them happy. They are
perfectly willing and capable to work for what they get.' It was,
as Jim would come to see, the authentic voice of Empire.
Determined to treat the Eskimos he met as individuals, he
persuaded Delaney to teach him a few conversational gambits
in their own language, from 'Hello' to 'It is cold outside'. The
characteristics of an inward-looking, provincial community living on the edge fascinated him, and on visits to Frobisher Bay he
studied Hudson Bay employees and Northern Mounted Police,
and practised picking out long-term residents from the migrant
workers like himself, appalled by the proselytising of mission-
aries glimpsed in action.

Risk was as welcome as the regular paypacket. On one short
plane hop the engine cut out and was restarted just in time; from
then on he would cross his fingers during every flight. In the
supposedly 'dry' camp, where fights were frequent, men drank
aftershave and sucked anti-freeze through loaves of bread, a
method believed to filter out toxicity. He would later claim to
have seen two men die and accurately describe the final stages of
blindness and dementia, and say that Boxing Day was spent
alone with a corpse awaiting collection by an incoming plane for
burial. Lust could be as inflammatory as drink, and a near-riot
broke out when an air-hostess from a grounded plane was
believed to be staying overnight. In comparison, Jim's own
pursuits were schoolboyish. He sent a bundle of fake £500
notes to the Kirwans – 'I can't send you a present, but I'm
sending you money – and waited hopefully for his twenty-first
birthday. At the end of January a parcel containing a home-
made cake arrived, sewn by his mother into unbleached calico as
had been the practice in India. Opening the package, he found a
wreck of crumbs.

With the approach of spring and the imminent completion of his contract, strong sunlight brought the risk of eye-damage from ultraviolet rays reflected back from the snow: snowglasses were added to the armoury of protective items. It heralded a plague of biting flies which incubated just above the permafrost – sandflies, blackflies, mosquitoes and bulldogs. The day-to-day monotony of the job was hard to square with newspaper insistence on mounting nuclear tension and headlines generated by international political rhetoric. The ability to get to the verge without getting into the war was a necessary art, according to John Foster Dulles, US Secretary of State – 'If you are scared to go to the brink you are lost' – but the words bore little relation to the claustrophobic boredom of the bunk room, with its interminable discomfort and stale sweat. The double view was a discovery.

On 9 April Jim collected his backpay and headed down to civilisation, his good references accumulating. 'In the performance of both actual fire prevention and secretarial duties,' ran the latest, 'he has shown unusual intelligence, conscientiousness and integrity. We [can] unreservedly recommend him to anyone needing the services of a young man possessing [these] qualities.' But Jim had other plans in mind. He bought a second-hand blue two-door Chrysler and began the long drive for a reunion first with his brother Robert in British Columbia, calling in to see Frank Farrell on the way. The rough outdoor months had made no impression on his polite demeanour, but physically he had filled out and his sideburns were greying.

Behind the wheel, he crossed the American border, mesmerised by redwood forests and exultant at being master of his own fate. The long-standing arrangement was to stay with Roger Donald in Connecticut, and, loth to end the solitude after so many months of cramped conditions, he spun out the trip, pulling in to take photographs at whim. When some were developed they turned out to be blank, a mirror of his reaction to America. 'Nastily surprised', he noted in Cleveland, Ohio, and the higher standard of living compared to England and Ireland struck him as crass and materialistic, the impression rubbed in by the cars he passed which bristled with tail fins and yards of shining chrome. By the time he reached Roger's house he understood that he was more comfortable with resourceful-ness and restraint.

To Roger, he admitted feeling '*infinitely* superior', dragging out the word, and in holiday spirits at last he could find no fault with the assembled WASP friends, who had been portrayed in advance as left-wing, interested in literature and the Arts, and all – 'to some extent' – outsiders. Since the break-up with Hilary there had been no opportunity to meet girls, and when remem-bering her birthday he had been teasing and impersonal, signal-ling a void waiting to be filled. 'We would take a couple of girls to a bar,' noted Roger:

> and Jim's conversation was more erudite than you'd expect from such a big, athletic man. Women saw him as a poet, and God knows he could recite, throwing a line of poetry into conversation, light and witty. I'd get him dates and you could see girls being attracted to him. But he was no good at closing with a girl, and he would always go for the ones who were impossible.

Jim set his sights on Roger's girlfriend Barbara, a sculptor, and in her company became as tongue-tied as on his early dates with Jill. His frustration was compounded by Roger's lack of jeal-ousy, and in the Empire Trilogy Major Brendan Archer, George Fleury and Matthew Webb would each do battle with similar pangs.

Elvis Presley's pouting face was on billboards and magazine covers, and the stream of Presley hits had a record for every mood, from 'Don't Be Cruel' to 'Hound Dog', as time ran out and Jim's resentment of Roger's complacency built up. The news that Presley's twenty-first birthday had coincided with his own pressed home his lack of achievement in comparison; James Dean, as the papers let no-one forget, had won star-status before the age of twenty-four. At that point he himself would still be stuck with law books, a dusty prospect, and his old intolerance seeped back. 'Anybody not wearing a fraternity tie-pin (not to mention a tie)', he now sniped, 'runs the risk of instant crucifix-ion, by the Rotary Club of course.'

One grand gesture remained: to return in style. He confirmed his passage on the *Queen Elizabeth*, taking pleasure in counting out the dollars, and aimed the Chrysler at New York. He had bought it in the belief that he would have no problem getting his money back at the last minute from shady dealers at the docks, and he drove straight there, arriving less than twenty-four hours before sailing. No offer was forthcoming, and at night he locked the doors and slept on the back seat. As boarding time approached, in desperation, he stopped a stranger walking by, and was advised to drive it to a wide street and leave it there. In jaundiced mood he endured the crossing, and pondered on the mystery of why people were happy to pay good money for 'such nonsense'.

Within a matter of weeks, in October 1956, the time came around to report to Oxford. He did so with decidedly mixed feelings, conscious of having to brace himself for the 'constricting embrace' of the formal educational system. *The town had been pitch dark and utterly strange. The railway station had been crowded with returning undergraduates cheerfully greeting each other, and taxis had been scarce.* Hefting his bags as if they weighed nothing, he shared a taxi with a pretty girl heading for Lady Margaret Hall; unnoticed in the gloom near the station exit was a Victorian iron arch cast from the foundry mould for the Great Exhibition, and out of sight, stacked in the storeroom behind, was a windowless frame from Paxton's original design. Lonely, but long accustomed to making his way in new societies, Jim made light conversation, euphoric at being free again of family claims. Oxford counted as more than a necessary transition: for the first time his own choices would define him.

Although his reception at home had been gratifying, with exclamations over his weight gain to 13 stone 8 lbs, and he had taken his thirteen-year-old younger brother Richard over to Rossall for the start of his first term, he had felt more disconnected than ever. During his time away his cousin Tom Farrell had been selected to represent Great Britain in the 400 metres hurdles in the Olympics, which were to be held in Australia that December, an irritating revival of boyhood rivalry from Gwanda days. It was no easier in the present to hear Tom's praises sung, exacerbated by the news that his cousin was combining Physical

Education with Divinity at college, and intended to use his Olympic prestige to bring young people to Christianity.

In a city of intellectuals, Brasenose was the sporting college, which, aching to play rugby again, Jim viewed as a bonus. It was renowned for Blues as celebrated as William Webb Ellis, the originator of the game, and the cricketer Colin Cowdrey had gone down only five years before. The college took its name, shortened familiarly to BNC, from the brass nose of a mediaeval door knocker which hung in the Hall behind the Principal's chair, and Jim came to enjoy nodding his own broken nose at the sixteenth-century carved-stone version over the main college gate. John Buchan, Charles Morgan and John Middleton Murry had also studied there, and a more recent graduate was William Golding, one of the writers he most admired. The intimate Tudor proportions of Old Quad set the inward-looking tone, and the smallness of scale filled him with sudden confidence. *When I was an undergraduate, I used to think I was going to launch myself on the world like a ballistic missile.*

The library on the east side housed a collection of BNC authors stretching back over the past 150 years, and next door was the chapel, once attributed to Wren. Beyond, through the miniature quad known as the Deer Park, lay New Quad, which fronted on to High Street, and contained the seventeenth-century Stallybrass Law Library. Jim's rooms were opposite, reached through a low archway known as Amsterdam, and the warren of eighteenth-century accommodation was newly christened the Arab Quarter, after the influx of ex-servicemen from the Middle East. 'You know, the men with brown knees . . .' someone explained.

Jim was allotted 14b on Staircase XV, a set of unevenly matched rooms on the second floor, with one other occupant, Brian Pearce. There was a bedsitter at the back, overlooking the old Bath House, and a much larger room in front above the shops on High Street, with a postage-stamp-sized bedroom to one side. 'We launched into discussions at once about who had what,' Pearce said later. 'It transpired that I had the big room and bedroom and he had the bedsitter. I ended up spending more time in his. We didn't spend much time there because we were both roaring about, but late in the evening we'd have coffee together in Jim's well-lit, heated room.' Pearce had also been at school in the north, and his father was a schoolmaster who shared many traits with Bill. He had done his National Service in the RAF, and was reading Modern History, with reservations. Fair-haired and gregarious, he possessed a spiritual bent that his boisterous manner belied, and Jim found him congenial.

There were twelve new Law students, a dominant proportion among the hundred new faces in college, and the masterful Professor Ronald Mawdsley, a double Blue, held court at a long table in tutorials. Professor Barry Nicholas, in his thirties, preferred smaller and more cerebral sessions in his first-floor rooms above the Law Library. Both were steeped in Law but pragmatic about the fact that half their students were using the subject as a general training for the mind. Experience had taught them that not everyone would prosper. 'To do well, you need an analytical mind because lawyers have to make such precise distinctions,' Nicholas believed. 'On the whole, it doesn't appeal to those with an imaginative or literary bent, and they can be very frustrated.'

Jim was no exception. He faced into Elementary Roman Law – the Institutes of Gaius and the Institutes of Justinian – and English Constitutional and Criminal Law without excitement. 'He found it dead,' said Ralph Burrows, a fellow Rossallian who lived on the same staircase. 'He said it wasn't a living facet of life, which tends to develop as civilisation develops. This was bureaucratic gobbledegook and he was generally unhappy and disliked it. He didn't find the work arduous, rather it was that his heart was not in it.'

Cynical about power, Jim had been debating capital punishment since fifth form, and scrutiny of the machinery of the law served to reinforce his opinion. 'We were not permitted to get away with the vague idea that he was a a brutish animal,' he would submit when Caryl Chessman was executed in America after a twelve-year delay. 'So how can it be denied that others who are finished off more promptly are also human beings?' Law, justice and humanity were not, to reach for legal casuistry, necessarily synonymous.

He was unimpressed by having to be in by 11pm, jibbed at the wearing of gowns for lectures and tutorials, and considered himself a cut above those coming in from National Service, stamped to pattern by regimentation. 'He thought us rather juvenile,' according to Burrows. 'His humour – always very dry at Rossall – was dryer, and he was disdainful of typical undergraduate behaviour. His criticism of people who couldn't hold their drink was that they ought to be able to handle themselves better.' Jim soon became a familiar figure in the Buttery, sitting and talking on the edge of large groups, included but apart, serious and broad-shouldered with a smoke ring floating overhead.

His overwhelming impression was of anticlimax and smallness of scale. He had been counting on making up for lost time with girls, but the five women's colleges were overpoweringly outnumbered, and sexual frustration was the more intense for his being in peak physical condition. *Small muscles in his back awaken and glint, the deltoids in his shoulder and the thick heavy pectoral muscles across his chest harden slightly. His shoulders are broad and his chest powerful, long arms, thick biceps . . . The swirling water makes his body gleam and shimmer as if it were oiled.* Potent masculinity was one of the first impressions that he made.

Only rugger, at which Oxford regularly outshone Cambridge, did not disappoint. As soon as details of trials for college teams were posted up, he sent his name and record in to the BNC club secretary, and on the appointed day at the Abingdon Road grounds was one of the first to be selected. In the colours of black shirt and yellow-banded black socks, playing at his old position of centre three-quarter, he turned out twice a week for fixtures in the College League, pitted against heavyweight opponents as varied as the Royal Military College of Science at Shrivenham and the Honourable Artillery Company in London. 'He fitted in perfectly – one of the boys,' according to another freshman, Roger Murray. 'I was the ultimate hearty, the jock, and he was too. There were changing rooms in college, so we cycled back and jumped in the communal bath. Tea would be beer, beer and more beer.' Tom Farrell's celebrated Olympic coup still rankled, and to stand a chance of being picked for the annual varsity game at Twickenham, Jim realised he would have to raise his game by a phenomenal degree. As a stepping stone he resolved to get into Vincents, the élite sporting club. 'I used to consider myself very tough, almost aggressively so,' he would later tell an interviewer. 'Rugger was pretty well my life.' But, of course, there is a world of difference between 'pretty well' and 'entire'.

Having such a clearcut goal, and steadily advancing towards it through extra practice and daily sessions in the public pool, meant that life took on a positive aspect. Jim liked Murray, who had spent time in Canada after National Service, and respected their captain, Andrew Gemill, for his co-ordination and complete lack of fear. In the Turl Tavern and the King's Arms comradeship was immediate and uncomplicated, and winding his large frame around a bus-stop on the way back – *I'm a python . . . or do I mean a boa-constrictor?* – he lived entirely, for once, in the present.

Those in one compartment did not suspect his intimacy with those in another, and the burly jock at the Rugby Club Dinner toasting the big piss-up in store bore little relation to the preoccupied intellectual in the Buttery, whose concerns were the Hungarian uprising, the deepening crisis in Suez, and Colin Wilson's *The Outsider*. Jack Kirwan, in a more distant compartment, was surprised to get a letter out of the blue, having never had one from Jim before. 'He wrote to say he was playing rugby three or four times a week and better than ever in his life,' he noted. 'He spoke of it more enthusiastically than I can ever remember him being about anything.' When Norman Ilett travelled down from Fleetwood to attend the Old Rossallian dinner at Oxford he was shown the fulfilled sportsman, not the dissenting law student or burdened intellectual.

By the middle of November Jim was finding a balance. He stepped up work in the Law Library to comply with coming end-of-term exams and concentrated in lectures and tutorials. Rugby camaraderie showed that the life of a successful barrister or solicitor might have compensations, not least the high fees and the opportunities for sport. Anecdotal wit and the law were tailor-made for one another, and his preoccupation with human nature at times of crisis could be sustained. The potential to right wrongs, as well, was undeniable. As the start of his exams came nearer, which would coincide with Tom Farrell's trial of strength in Melbourne, he pressed on harder, suddenly anxious about failure.

The greater the mental pressure, the greater the need for physical release, and Jim swam more lengths and hurled himself around the pitch. On 28 November he injured his right shoulder badly in a tackle. It was such a predictable rugby knock that he had to be persuaded to see the college doctor, and afterwards he ignored medical advice to rest. That Saturday, for the third time in a week, he was back in action, intent on making up for lost tackling practice. Afterwards he lingered on in the changing room, oddly disorientated.

With some difficulty he arranged his legs underneath himself feeling as sick as death and enormously tired . . . A feeling of unspeakable desperation washed over him and he sat down abruptly with a bump on the hard wooden seat . . . [He] sighed deeply and felt a little better. 'Really, I just feel like going to bed,' he said aloud to no-one in particular. 'I really must see a doctor,' he thought. 'This can't be all due to hangover.' . . . He walked down the corridor clumsily like an old man. He was sweating . . .

Cutting the usual drinking session by saying that he wasn't up to it and might turn up later, he took a bus back to college and crawled as he was into bed, knowing that Pearce and Burrows were away. Burrows returned first, on Sunday night, and casually put his head around the open door. 'Jim was just very poorly,' he said afterwards, 'and his condition was not assisted by some party going on in the Arab Quarter.' Alarmed by the description of violent headache and severe pain in the back and shoulders, he got a college porter to call the doctor. On Monday a feverish temperature was added to the symptoms, and the following morning a pronounced weakness in the shoulders and rigidity of neck. By lunchtime Jim was on his way by ambulance to hospital, unable to stop his self-taught reflex of observation and impassively aware of being about to suffocate.

Trees were drifting across the square of darkened glass and they were beautiful in a way, blurred by vibration, soft as feathers drifting in a high wind . . . Then he had dipped under the dark glass and was among the trees. They were all around him and floating away into the air like a thousand spires, his remembered redwoods . . . Later again he was in a darker part of the forest and the air was full of incessant thunder, one shattering note melting into another until the sound became too painful to be endured and he was running over the soft ground and the trees became increasingly dense until he was forced to squeeze between their swollen trunks and then, at last, there were trees all around him, so close that he could no longer move nor breathe, captured and crushed. [The] picture began to move jerkily once more but this time he closed his eyes and saw nothing but angry flashes of light. 'How much longer?' 'An hour or so. Don't worry. We'll get you there in time.' 'I wasn't worried . . . Simply curious.'

CHAPTER SIX

In Human Affairs, Things Tend Inevitably to Go Wrong 1956–1957

T he telegram – 'Your son James Farrell is in the Slade Hospital with polio and is going tonight into an Iron Lung' – was on the mat at Balholm when Jo got home on 3 December from a tiring day of Christmas shopping. All flights had left, tickets for the 8.45pm mailboat were sold only for cash, the banks were shut and her purse was almost empty. Never had the sea seemed such a barrier. But friends rallied round, and she and Bill caught the ferry just in time, driving on from Holyhead throughout the night. At the Slade they were told that it would not be known for a fortnight if he would live and, masked and gowned, all they could do was stroke his curly hair. The next time they were allowed in, his head was shaved.

He was trapped, alone, inside the ultimate compartment, with his mind the solitary lever of control. The habit of observing and committing to memory would be a providential resource, and record an ordeal beyond the measurement of temperature chart or attentive hospital note. *The nurse was standing, watch in hand, looking at him carefully . . . Then the truth exploded in the room like a firework and drenched the darkness with fear. She was counting the rate of his breathing . . . He was hurtling into a sea of dark feathers which were slowly arresting him, softly smothering him. Death was saying to him: je te plumerai, mon petit, je te plumerai bien, tu vas voir . . . Time passed [and he] weakly tried to penetrate with his intelligence . . . Now let's get organised. I'm in hospital, hospital . . . he sailed on . . . an old, tired ship foundering in the darkness . . . It seemed only a minute before [her] hand was on his wrist again and she was watching the rise and fall of his chest. This time he knew for certain that he was breathing faster.* Between paroxysms of coughing and bright flashes against his eyes, his old nightmare returned of being swept down through bottomless dark waters.

When admitted, Jim's oxygen intake was reduced by three-quarters, and low muscle-power, linked to lack of oxygen, was whittling away at his ability to breathe. *A touch of panic stole over him . . . by this time [he] was gasping like a stranded fish and desperately struggling to hold the immense volume of blind, heavy, invisible water away from his mouth and nose . . . He had already astonished himself by maintaining his inwardly threshing body so relatively near the surface for so long, had told himself what seemed hours ago that he could only hang on for another 30 seconds.* All afternoon the struggle had continued, prolonged by his athletic fitness, and as the muscles of his larynx became affected he could no longer speak or swallow. He could, however hear. His case was freely discussed around the bed, with polio described for the benefit of junior nurses as a neurotropic virus. *He pictured himself sitting under a palm tree, chainsmoking nervously and grinding his teeth . . . It meant that an army of viruses was now . . . marching on the nerve-centres of his spinal column. He saw huge ant-like creatures . . . crunching away with bared teeth on succulent nerves . . . 'You must try to relax, you know, because contracted muscles are more easily affected.' . . . In that case I'm done for, he thought.*

Survival time without oxygen was a matter of minutes, and the one piece of good fortune was that Oxford was the national centre of polio treatment, equipped with an iron lung to take over when his own lungs were about to fail. Towards evening the news was broken by a doctor who stood with one arm around a coffin-shaped white metal box attached to a large rubber concertina, as if being photographed with a big-game trophy.

A man in overalls . . . was tinkering with its underneath in the region of what would have been, had it been a tiger, its genitals. As he worked he moved the machine slightly, revealing its flank which contained three circular portholes . . . 'Try that for size,' somebody said with hideous casual-

*ness as if offering a tentatively mixed drink. The sister . . .
moved to a switch on the wall. The concertina began to rise
and fall rhythmically. A nurse approached him with a wide
pad of gauze, heavily smeared in grease. 'We'll have to put
this round your neck to stop it getting sore. I'm afraid it's a
bit messy. No pyjama trousers either . . .' The doctor
unfastened a clamp and lifted one end of the box on vertical
rails, securing it there. Then he slid a narrow stretcher from
the interior . . . In dull throbbing torment [he was] carried
over with one of the nurses supporting his head and slid
into it feet first. A pad of sponge rubber with a hole in it for
his neck was placed in position and the metal blade which
had a similar crescent . . . brought down till it virtually
touched his neck and clamped there . . . 'Now let the
machine do the work. Don't fight it'.*

Immured in Cubicle 2 on the second floor, the iron lung was a
tomb and he the effigy, *as horizontal and as petrified as a stone
crusader.* A long white cabinet enclosed him up to his neck, and
a separate pump unit drove powerful bellows beneath: when air
was sucked out the fall in cabinet pressure caused his chest to
expand, drawing air into his lungs, and when the bellows
collapsed the process was reversed, at a rate set between 13
and 25 pulses per minute with hissing regularity. If the hospital
had a power cut, he was assured, it could be operated by hand,
but claustrophobia and panic were less than a breath away.
*'Nurse . . . for the love of God get me out of this bloody thing!'
. . . [She] was at his side in an instant, pressing her hand down
firmly on his forehead and calling loudly for the doctor . . . Then
the doctor was at his side, calm and competent . . . 'Take it easy,
old chap . . . We're going to give you something to calm you
down a bit . . .'*
Everything had to be synchronised with the overpowering
rhythm, and a sip of milk could snatch him down into *crimson,
flashing darkness, mercilessly battered by the pressure of the
machine. It seemed an age before he recovered the timing. For
my next trick ladies and gentlemen . . . I shall die.* At every
exhalation air leaked through the whistling rubber seal around
his neck; when that was finally rectified it started to vibrate, like

closed moistened lips. Illogically he craved a cigarette and to ease
the aching muscles of his back by turning over, even fractionally;
a feeding tube was forced up his right nostril, instead. *He began
to sweat, swallowing involuntarily with tears starting in his eyes
. . . The room was full of an icy white wind and there was no
horizon any more. With an effort he forced the perspectives to
reassert themselves.* Cataloguing detail was a help, momentarily
bringing the illusion of control. A bell was placed by his right
hand and a small mirror slotted above his head, angled to show
the door through which he could not go. With a flicker of wry
solace, he superimposed the set of a television hospital drama. If
a competent scriptwriter was pulling the strings, *a sad ending
[would be] unthinkable.*

His life was no longer considered to be in immediate danger
when his fluctuating temperature eventually settled and a faint
improvement in respiratory power was measurable. Bill, isolated
within his own infirmity, went back to Ireland to continue his
job, and Jo stayed on for a while, grateful for her wartime
medical experience. Immobile in the lung, aware that some
permanent paralysis was taking remorseless shape, Jim fought
against the conviction every night that he would be dead by
morning. Medication and the hallucinations of broken sleep
ushered in a terrifying world in which he was tortured by people
he could no longer recall, *among them a man, naked, his body
streaming with water, cartwheeling interminably and perfectly
over an immense tiled square.* He learned to abandon himself to
the dizzying spirals – *a prey to half-submerged fears that drifted
in the moving waters of his mind, unable to summon enough
concentration to evaluate them* – and wait for dawn and gradual
light, the only proof that he was still alive. Holding out against
the magnetic pull of lassitude would evoke the uncharacteristically theatrical self-image of clawing his way back to life with
numb and bleeding fingers.

The smallest irritation was magnified to unendurable dimensions. Overhead the glaring white globe of the ceiling light
pierced his eyes, and the alternative of a table lamp was little
better. *His mind wearily attacked the new arrangement of
shadows on the ceiling . . . with something of the despair a
mountaineer might experience on seeing another peak rising*

above what he had taken to be the final summit . . . The
shadows were long and sharp. Dark, immaterial spikes, they
scraped the skin of his brain. By day his eyes would smart and
water from the needle of escaping air at his neck, until the nurse
on duty dabbed with a pad of cotton-wool and added to the
futility of anger. At the stock phrase, 'What's up with you, then?'
he had to play along mutely with the shame of being patronised,
and in his second novel, *The Lung*, he would take his revenge.
'Nurse, I need an amanuensis.' 'I'm sure the doctor would have
told me if you need something like that.' Jim stored up examples
of gross insensitivity, from the disdainful intern who said it was
possible to get used to anything, to the Parthian shot of the
clergyman bearing a chalice of communion wine who reproved,
'I must tell you, you may die,' and on the printed page he took
care to even the score.

    'I'm afraid the wine is only Australian burgundy but it's the
best we could do. Anyway, it's conscecrated.' 'No thanks, I'd
rather not.' 'You're a Protestant, aren't you . . . or at any rate a
Christian?' 'I really don't want communion, thanks very much.'
'It's my painful duty to point out that you're gravely ill and
could die at any moment.' 'No . . . In any case, I can't swallow. I
have this tube.' Drifting in from the corridor, the chance ex-
clamation, 'Good God, you must be joking!' fermented into
'*Good* God, you *must* be joking,' the nearest he came to a
prayer. Towards evening, when the shadowy fears crowded
forward, he summoned up 'Abide with Me' from Rossall ennui;
as before, it proved ineffectual.

    Ominipotence, he had ample time to speculate, lay elsewhere.
Medical prognosis was more credible than prophecy, and
laboratory research transcended religious quest. The most
rousing sermon was untenable compared to the message of
the registrar, Dr Ironside, who said that if the lower muscles
remained strong there was every possibility of making a good
functional recovery, and scientific explanations alone had the
force of revelation. The degree of paralysis depended not upon
prayer, but upon the timing of the viral invasion of cells in the
spinal cord, so his extra rugby practice, ironically, had ensured
that his upper body and shoulders would bear the brunt of
damage. He studied the expressions and tested out the logic of

those who bent over him, and in doctors found the conviction
that he sought.

Floating towards apathy, sensing that much was being withheld for his own good, he envisioned himself as a corpse in a
coffin and craved for silence, but the ward radio played on. *One
record programme followed another. Disc-jockeys chattered
away to him as if he were an imbecile . . . His despair mounted.
He had nothing in common with these people. They belonged to
another race.* He swore to himself that if he escaped he would
never listen to a radio again, subsequently modified to allow
news and current affairs. The radio gibbered on during broadcasting hours, week in and week out, although his parents had
ordered a record player and a selection of his favourite classical
records. At his mother's departure he waved a mental goodbye,
powerless to express his feelings.

Strangers, gowned and masked, leaned over and looked
down, and there was no alternative to gazing unflinchingly
back. He felt *like a rare moth pinned to a board in a museum.*
The long-awaited day came when he was given a book to read,
propped open in the stand, but it was too juvenile to be of
interest and he could have read twenty pages in the time it took
for one to be turned. Dark glasses shielded his eyes from the
glare overhead, and he hid behind them, seeking privacy. As a
distraction, a recuperating child was wheeled into his room and
he was told to ring his bell whenever she cried.

Jim taught himself to block out the present by letting his mind
fix on random points of speculation, which he would embellish
from a surreal perspective. He used his imagination deliberately
as a distancing technique, in the way that long-term prisoners
build mental strategies to withstand torture or solitary confine-
ment. 'No pain or humiliation can touch you,' he would subsequently recommend, 'if you know the art of abstracting
yourself.' When being fed through the stomach tube as the iron
lung kneaded his chest without pause, the combination he most
dreaded, he absented himself. Sometimes he was a tiger – *striped,
dripping-fanged . . . loping away through the jungle looking for
a delicate virgin antelope to sink his snarling masculine teeth into*
– and sometimes a killer shark – *gliding through the bottle-green
glades of twilight passing shoals of tiny fish that wheeled and*

drilled like soldiers. When glucose was poured into the tube he closed his eyes and interpreted the delayed icy sensation in his stomach as the swallowing of a passing fish. *Swimming under the hull of a ship he could hear the beat of its engines, could feel them throbbing through his throbbing body; like raindrops, like moon craters he could see the barnacles on the ship's bottom in the cloudy lustre of the water.* In Cubicle 2 of the Slade Isolation Hospital he sharpened his senses by listening intently, applying the concentration previously used to observe, and examined each sound over and above the clamour of the radio, envisioning his mind as a film camera.

> *Outside . . . the early sunshine has given way to a soft greyish light that casts no shadows. The entire bowl of the sky is clouded but here and there a splash of darker grey suggests an individual cloud . . . The warmth and stillness give an impression of timelessness [and] a normally insignificant event (a small grey bird fluttering from one grey tree to another, for example) takes on a disturbing significance.*
>
> *At the rear of the hospital the man who has been delivering bread at the kitchen door emerges whistling with an enormous empty basket. He opens the rear door of his van, throws the basket inside, and then slams it again. [Now he] pauses at the door of the van and removes a pencil from behind his ear with which he makes a mark in a notebook before swinging himself up into the driving seat. Without troubling to close the sliding door he puts the van in gear and it moves slowly away with a high-pitched whine from its electric motor.*

Word had spread quickly in college, and he dreaded visiting hours. The iron lung was behind a wall of glass, putting him on shop-window display. It was harrowing to see him there with only his head protruding, agreed colleagues from the rugby team. 'He was utterly pathetic,' said Roger Marhall. 'One was conscious of seeing a fellow who was physically in the prime of his life laid low.' Others took a more impersonal view. 'You heard as you were wandering round the Quad that this chap had been taken ill, so you went to see him,' one such comment ran. 'I thought, he's a BNC man too, so I'll go along – poor chap.' Brian Pearce, rather to his own surprise, did not go very often. 'There was an element of guilt,' he admitted. 'But I reasoned that I was not his closest friend.' The news had filtered through to the Rossall network, making him the object of widespread pity. 'Rob has just told us of your bad luck,' wrote two Spread Eagle contemporaries. 'May we just say how very, very sorry we both are. We've agreed that if anyone can overcome such a setback, it will be you.' Phrases meant to comfort achieved the opposite result by confirming the low caste of invalid – 'I will make every effort to get over and see you next Vac,' encouraged one old chum, clearly horrified by the prospect – and Jim listened out for every nuance when cards and letters were read aloud. Those who stayed out of range were identified and not forgiven.

Professor Barry Nicholas made a point of visiting, and unconsciously increased the pressure. The sight of his tutor was a reminder of exams, and Jim was seized by anxiety to such an extent that exam stress was written up in his hospital notes. Anxiety was succeeded by apathy, and escape was in one direction only, down into the labyrinths of the mind. '*You know, it's difficult to cure someone who doesn't want to be cured.*' '*Most people think life's wonderful. I think it's a little pointless . . . 'Life isn't only wonderful. It's all there is.' 'Well, it doesn't seem enough.*'

At regular intervals he was taken out for a back rub to prevent bedsores, a near-death experience of invisible strangulation. A breathing mask was fitted over his face, the machine switched off, one of the cabinet portholes opened for the pressure to drop, the blade around his neck unclamped and lifted, and he was pulled out in one swift movement, inert upon the stretcher. *It seemed as if both his lungs were packed solid with cement. And the silence, the utter immobility of everything inside him . . . The absence of air . . . left him to face the facts again: suffocation was only on the other side of the steel skin around him.* The dizzy relief when it was over was tempered by dread of the next occasion, and the certain knowledge that as soon as he was considered strong enough he would have to endure a whole minute without air.

Nothing at all was moving in his chest except his accel-
erating heart. 'You may not feel much happening at first but
it's important to will yourself to breathe even if you don't
feel any response. First in and then out. You mustn't try to
breathe in the whole time.' . . . His head was beginning to
spin and his fists were clenched. After an eternity the doctor
closed the porthole and looked at his watch . . . Every day
he lay a little longer, drilled by headaches, in that lifeless
silence that stretched away towards the borders of suffoca-
tion. He knew that he would never cross the border and
topple over the brink into death, but somehow he could
never stop himself fearing that he would . . . While he lay
there in his private silence all his attention was given to the
intercostal muscles labouring desperately in his chest like
mice on a hillside.

For fourteen days, until the end of December, Jim was consumed
by the superhuman interior effort needed to breathe independently of the iron lung. *People drifted round the outskirts of the*
silence in another world. Microscopically he lengthened the
periods at liberty, and reached the stage where a shield-shaped
cuirass could be placed on his chest to help, but for it to be
effective he had to learn to frog-breathe, gulping and swallowing
sufficient air by using his tongue as a pump. On Christmas Eve
he succeeded in staying out until evening, and five days later the
whole night, too. On New Year's Eve his stomach tube was
removed – *one scarlet streak of pain* – and he celebrated the early
hours of 1957 in a standard hospital bed. *It was wonderful to*
find himself floating in a nest of pillows with the weight of all his
limbs supported . . . He lay motionless [like] *some debauched*
and indolent emperor. Instantaneously, the room that he had
grown to loathe was transformed into a magic forest. *All the*
objects in it, although he had seen them before, appeared new
and exciting . . . He had known that life was full of wonderful
things if one took the trouble to look for them . . . He was warm
in bed with a miracle of beauty being performed beside him.
On discharge from the isolation unit he was taken by ambulance, equipped with emergency breathing equipment, to the
Wingfield Morris Orthopaedic Hospital in nearby Headington,

and put under the care of Professor Trueta, reputed to be the top polio specialist in the country. The mainly single-storey pre-war buildings were linked by covered walkways, and the four-bedded Girdleston Ward was at the rear, facing a winter-bare square of garden. Winds gusted down the open-sided corridors, draughts billowed from windowless TB wards, and his euphoria evaporated. He was *an elderly butterfly trying to fly into the teeth of a gale.* In bed his arms lay at his side – *as dead as cooked hams* – and his shoulders seemed as immovable as his chest, forcing over-reliance on the cuirass.

His nights were disturbed by the heartstoppingly erratic breathing of the others, and the mechanical thump of a venti-lator which kept one patient alive. When he did briefly doze, nightmares jerked him awake – sweating, trembling and terrify-ingly short of breath – and nurses chided that he shouted in his sleep. But was he dreaming or hallucinating? *The room was filling up with that hard white despair from the window. Black clouds rushed up over the mountain and started to hail stones of frozen blood. The stones changed to blood flakes suffocating the white sky . . . There was a deep booming explosion . . . The door had been thrown open and a nurse was standing there with the tea-trolley.*

In Girdleston Ward Jim was at his lowest ebb. Likening all four of them to bodies on a battlefield, he remembered Napo-leon's comment, after Leipzig, that a single Paris night would replenish the dead; no-one, therefore, was indispensable or unique. In the iron lung he had not looked beyond survival, but during January the realisation of human transience con-sumed him: he had postponed death, not escaped it. The tune of 'Auld Lang Syne' was still on his brain, planted there by radio requests, and he fitted more appropriate words. *We'll take a cup of anguish yet for the sake of. Who indeed?*

Sipping from a tilted cup exhausted him, but his neck muscles were too weak to support his head. Trying to pull himself up without the use of his arms tangled him helplessly in the sheets. 'Keep your pecker up and leave the nurses alone, won't you!' exhorted a Rossall wag by post, and on the day the letter arrived he was shown what he actually looked like in a mirror. A concentration-camp victim gazed back, *with startled, sunken eyes, hollow cheeks and wildly matted hair. Every bone stood out clearly and between the higher ribs he could see a regular, tremulous flutter from the beating of his heart, while his lower ribs expanded like opening fingers with each breath he took. The muscles that stretched over his collar bone from neck to shoulder might have been taut pieces of string.* The notion of chasing the nurses was absurd.

During the first two months, Professor Trueta was assisted by Dr Harley, a fellow pioneer in the field of rigorous therapy; and the gymnasium was run by Mrs Agerholm, a well-known campaigner for polio vaccine. Each patient had their own physiotherapist, and to Jim the fine line between therapeutic challenge and medical sadism was not always apparent. Still bristling at the rebuke that it was possible to get used to anything, he began by asking why he had been switched to a ward of moribund cases. 'This is to show you', he was told briskly, 'how bad it really can be.' Deltoids, pectorals and triceps began to assume personal identities, and the exhausting two-day muscle tests to evaluate damage were promoted as a chance to show his mettle.

Results were depressing in the extreme. His neck muscles were very poor, his right shoulder totally paralysed, reflecting the earlier injury, and his left extremely weak; little response could be measured in the deltoid, the crucial lifting muscles from which his body hung, like a coathanger. The flex of his fingers was badly hampered, and the muscles on the back of his hands could not help to compensate because his thumb muscles were too damaged to work against the pull of gravity. The grim news of the second test was that physiotherapy was making little headway, despite the searing cramps it caused. Doubled up in bed – *locked tight, as immovably bent as a steel hook* – and determined to improve upon his efforts, he counted silently until they passed.

Close proximity to physiotherapists, occupational therapists and nurses, meanwhile, was admitting him to the previously secret world of women. In the scientific hothouse, without the filter of sexuality, everything he saw took on evolutionary purpose, and what began as an escapist game soon became a plausible theory. Women were programmed to achieve their ends, he deduced, through a range of biologically predetermined behaviour. Some bullied him into compliance, some cajoled and some used humour, but the purpose in each case was the same – to get their own way.

His physiotherapist with the face of an angel turned out to be tougher than a senior sports coach. *She . . . raised his arm again and pressed it sharply back and up. He gave a cry of pain and surprise. 'That hurts!' 'We call that spasm . . . More on Monday.'* The occupational therapist – *less attractive but furiously optimistic* – sidestepped his sneers at the hand-strengthening use of basket-weaving by substituting an electric typewriter; he added manipulation to the list of inherent female stratagems. Sitting futilely in a chair for an hour each morning, each useless arm propped upon a perilous cairn of unopened books, observation helped to pass the time.

But there were days when no distraction was possible, and in those moods his lists were personal, and composed entirely of loss. Privacy had always been important, and now he had none; he was back imprisoned in the dependent childhood role. After being wheeled from the X-ray department by a porter whose well-judged kicks to open the double doors conjured up his own lost expertise, he closed his eyes in bed and murmured the '*Dies Irae*'. In Mayfair, the blue-tiled hydrotherapy pool in the private wing, he watched bleakly as the overweight female patient in front of him was winched up out of the water, seeing her as a whale about to be clubbed with a mallet and himself as a living skeleton. In the water he was given two floating plastic ducks to hold: *the return to childhood was now complete*. Waking with a start one afternoon, he found his first love, Jill Kirwan, beside the bed. She was holding a bunch of daffodils and looking glamorous in a tight-waisted, pencil-slim green suit with black epaulettes, set off by a yellow stole. Humiliation was total.

'It was terribly dark, although it was daytime,' she described their mutual ordeal. 'I couldn't see Jimmy properly because I think he didn't want me to, but he didn't look like the guy I knew at all. His face was grey and his hair was different and I so desperately didn't want him to look like that. He was so ashamed of his own physical difference, I could tell. It was hard to talk. I felt embarrassed and unsure if I had done the right thing in coming, and I was vividly aware of all the previous flames and knew that I would only ever feel sorry for him now. I kept thinking, 'Golly, I'll have to extricate myself because someone so low could get the wrong impression very easily.' She escaped before the time was up, and caught an early train back to London, where she was on holiday.

Flooded by self-disgust and horror at her pity, Jim was left with a fierce desire to hurt her back, and in *The Lung* would do so. He lampooned her appearance – '*You look like the vamp in a low-budget film*' – and reversed the dynamics so that she was the one to be dismissed, but he also read her mind accurately. *She would have been thinking that he was lonely in hospital and that it was her duty to see him. Suddenly it was clear to him that she would never love him again as a woman loves a man. She would feel sorry for him* . . . Despair was not improved by a visit soon afterwards from Roger Donald, who found him in a wheelchair, frog-breathing with the aid of his chest respirator; the American paid him scant attention, and instead flirted with the nurses.

John Chisholm, the polio victim on the ventilator, was not expected to live, and when Jim learned that one of the prettiest nurses was about to marry him, her probable motivation became an obsession. Impressed as he was by anyone who rose to the challenge of an unexpected raw deal, he was unable to comprehend voluntary self-sacrifice, and he complained to Roger Donald that women preyed on illness, like vampires.

It's all an illusion. Life seems to offer everything, but the plain truth is that it offers almost nothing at all. He became engrossed by First World War poetry, and identified with the maimed. Passing the open door of the next ward on outings to the pool, he came to recognise a don's young wife who had caught polio while pregnant, and made a point of turning his head to smile each time and deliver a quip. One day her bed was empty and it became known that she had died in childbirth. *He thought of her growing up for nothing. Her body developing into a woman's body for nothing. All her desires and dreams and personality conceived for nothing* . . . 'There's a war poem, I remember . . . Something about: *Why should he die when cruel old campaigners win safe through?*' In the circumstances the only available method of suicide came down to the straight choice between hoarding the night-time sleeping pills or cutting his wrists with a knife secreted from a meal tray, *bleeding slowly and peacefully away into nothingness.* The knowledge that the bolthole was there, however, made continuation on present terms possible. *He knew that if he really wanted to kill himself, he could find a way.*

At first the young man of around his own age in the next bed, Stephen Wall, made little impression. The fact that he had been in hospital for over a year indicated a vista Jim dared not contemplate, but once they began to communicate he found himself focusing on Wall's achievements instead. The graduate with a rapier academic mind had been taken ill while writing his thesis on Victorian fiction, and although severely paralysed he was hard at work again. Books by Trollope littered his bed, and in his locker he kept a set of Conrad which he was keen to lend. The conclusion of *Heart of Darkness* – 'The horror, the horror' – struck a mutual chord. 'Jim could hardly talk at first, and nor could I,' Wall would recall, 'but when we did we had an immediate rapport. I felt the same as he did about the need to distance it all, to make it ridiculous.' In truncated sentences, punctuated by pauses to breathe, they escaped into cinematic technique, and discovered that Wall knew more than Jim about European directors. Dublin had fourteen cinemas, Jim would retaliate, to Oxford's five. Their favourite books were discussed in minute detail, and they agreed that the ghastly situation they were in was compounded of crisis, irony and black humour.

'But I felt, as another man, that real intimacy with Jim was very difficult,' Wall pointed out. 'You would approach so far and no farther. I was reminded of the Wordsworth couplet, "I approach the hiding places of my past, they seem open then they close". I always felt that you were getting close and then a shutter came down.' January 25th passed with no mention of a birthday, and when Jim moved on from Girdleston Ward at the end of the month he had to leave Wall there. He got himself wheeled back whenever possible.

Burrows Ward, with thirty-two beds, was in practice a tough assault course. It taught ambulant patients how to re-learn to walk and to become sufficiently independent to be allowed home, an agonising conveyor belt from present to future with no agreeable features. Jim reacted to the abrupt change of pace by hating Burrows, and despising those in positions of power within it. He felt that he was doubly imprisoned, trapped not only in his own body, but locked up in a punitive regime – *The ward was cleaned, tidied and polished under the acid eye of the sister, with a thoroughness and pointlessness that verged on the pathological* – and his by now customary cold temper exploded without apparent warning. The sign of returning vitality was logged with approval, however, by the staff, because the short-tempered atmosphere that prevailed deliberately encouraged a therapeutic head of steam.

'They were fighting for their life and individuality, and we understood,' according to Jim's physiotherapist, Barbara Yvonne Rouse. 'To be a good rehabilitator you need to be a bad patient, or your identity may go under. He was irritable but he didn't seem violently aggressive, unlike another patient in his group whom we were all scared to treat. But, of course, the articulate and educated patient can voice his complaint, and he certainly used black sarcasm on bungling nurses.' Jim glared at the portions of hospital food – *boeuf à l'angoisse, pommes tourmentées, oeuf dur inquiet* – and took his anger out on the nearest person, sourly aware that his frustration lay with himself. Thrown an orange or a packet of cigarettes, he still made to catch it with his right hand but his arm would not move, and the missile hit him on the chest or landed on the floor.

The lasting sensation was of being helpless. He resented the *immense grey jungle of useless or impossible effort. How could he possibly cut his way through it with any sense of purpose? I've got to assert myself through the inertia and mediocrity of other people and try and find an open place, a place to breathe.* If an ugly incident flared up among the other patients he relished the common exhalation of tension. Roger Donald visited again, and lectured him on the sins of behaving badly. 'There were some wonderfully pretty nurses there and they adored Jim. He was *terrible* to them, and it was very painful to watch.' Roger's shock was exacerbated by having always admired Jim's natural gallantry, and he had never imagined him to be capable of ridiculing a woman to her face. But Jim was keeping Roger at arm's length, too, and he brought down the shutters with sarcastic force. Losing his temper usually lowered his spirits further, by reminding him that the previous recourse of squaring up to someone physically was gone. Retaliation had to be verbal from now on, and that was one more loss. The hospital almoner began including him in her casebook, and her ability to listen was the greatest single help in coming to terms with being a cripple, as he insisted on referring to himself. He read *Don Quixote* with bitter appreciation. Gallows humour was endemic in Burrows Ward, and when visitors had gone nothing was sacrosanct; the darker the joke, the broader the laugh.

Jim borrowed Scott Moncrieff's translations of Proust from Stephen, and the shading of debility was there, too. His precarious breathing eerily conveyed Proust's asthma, and Swann's alienation matched his own. But there was a new element of apprenticeship in the attention that he was paying to the style, and under Wall's guidance he began to analyse and experiment. Both resisted renewed moves for their attendance at basket-making classes – 'It was humiliating to have to say so over and over,' Stephen would point out, 'and they should have realised we were neither of us basket-making people' – and Jim substituted his typewriter during occupational therapy, sitting propped up against the pillows. Each time he used up a sheet of paper he had to summon a nurse to put in another, and the laborious process was complicated further by having to locate each key and then apply enough force. Cursing his feeble fingers and aching arms, he soldiered on. 'It was during my long stay in hospital', he would acknowledge tersely later, 'that I started writing and doing some new thinking.'

Awareness of the world that was waiting grew more insistent as the exercises gathered momentum. No illusions survived the gym. When Jim first surveyed the large room with its familiar school wallbars and high decibel level, he thought of Dante's inferno when he saw the number of wheelchairs and crutches around the sides and the waiting steel beds, parked in ranks. Patients lay on the raised stage at the mercy of their physiotherapists, and tottered between parallel bars, sweating with the effort. He, too, *staggered . . . with loose, swaying puppet-strides, his head held stiffly forward by the locked, aching muscles of his neck.*

One recurrent image was of a snakes and ladders board: he had landed on a snake and slithered down to the tip of the tail, and the squares stretched ahead without a ladder in sight. *He was neither happy nor unhappy. He merely felt empty and tired. He performed his exercises mechanically and then, one day, abandoned them altogether. 'I've reached the end of the line, doctor. I'm bushed.'* In Burrows Ward such a statement was trumped at once. In that case, they were told, it was time they were getting out.

The objective was independence, with which he thoroughly agreed. He practised putting on his jacket by first manoeuvring his most damaged arm into the sleeve by the trick of holding the jacket low and bending sideways before pulling it up over the inert arm, and whisking it around to the other shoulder. *It was as if [his clothes] had belonged to another person, as, in a way, they had.* He was taught to clasp his hands together whenever he was standing, which eased his shoulders, and how to boost the effectiveness of his wasted right arm by supporting it with his left. Hospital policy was to rehabilitate patients by allowing them out for extending periods, accompanied by their physiotherapists in case of panic or collapse, and towards the end of February he ventured out for the first time with the agreeable Miss Rouse. *She took his overcoated arm and he had to smother a cry of pain. 'Other arm, please. That's the bad one.' 'Sorry, I forgot.' There was a high wind, fresh and exhilarating, that whistled in the trees and made the branches creak . . . 'I'm about all in. I think we should turn back.'*

The final medical picture gave no quarter, but he expected none. The top of his trunk had been severely affected but not his legs, so the separate poles would not become synchronised for a long time, upsetting balance. There would always be pain in his back and neck, and his habit of bending his head when reading would aggravate that. His writing, which was illegible, would only improve if he took every opportunity to exercise his hands, and since he was right-handed, the side most affected, the ache when doing so would diminish but never entirely go away. Continuation of physiotherapy was vital, because there was a possibility of further gain for two more years. Sexually there would be no permanent impairment, but he would have to make allowances for the lack of upper body strength and difficulty in breathing.

Lassitude was the result of taking in too little oxygen and this rate would not pick up, so it would be always like living at a very high altitude; he was advised to pace himself when speaking and to break sentences, to fit in an extra breath. The loss of inter-costal muscles and the damage to his diaphragm added threat to minor colds and coughs, so he should keep warm, protect his neck in winter, and avoid bad weather, especially rain. If he did develop a cold, he was to rest, and monitor his temperature and any chest infection. His heart, the matter-of-fact briefing con-cluded, had been under severe strain, and he must not try to do too much. Afterwards he would tell selected people that his heart was weak and he did not think he would live to be sixty, and in his third novel, *A Girl in the Head*, the hero, Boris Slattery, would suffer the heart attack that now became Jim's secret dread. The heart was only a muscle, after all, and he lived with permanent examples of how fallible muscles could be.

'You've been sick,' Professor Trueta advised when the time came for Jim to go home. 'Don't ask too much of yourself. It takes time learning to live again.' The words would imbue the philosophy of Dr McNab – *'the best of us all'* – in *The Siege of Krishnapur* and *The Hill Station*. On 22 February, markedly grey-haired and 4 stone lighter, Jim was discharged from hos-pital to travel home in the care of Peter Browne, a friend of the family who was a Fellow of All Souls. On the way he was surprised to notice that there were Easter eggs on sale in the shops, instead of the expected Christmas trees and holly. In Dublin his parents were waiting with the car, as they had always waited at the end of term at school.

But nothing else was the same. *His past he now saw as a long, perfectly familiar, perfectly straight road leading back to the distant horizon of his childhood . . . The familiar road had ended and the future was a jungle through which he had to cut his way.*

CHAPTER SEVEN

The Beauty of the Cold Season
1957–1958

The spring of 1957 was exceptionally overcast, and the heavy weight of sky imposed a mood of greyness and gloom. It was the most depressing climate for a fightback, but Jim began as he meant to go on. Brushing aside help, he worked out a method of sitting up, sliding across the bed and swivelling his legs; to cough, he turned over on his chest and hung his head over the side. Since he could not hold a cup in his right hand, he held it in his left and, though buttons continued to defeat him, he succeeded in brushing his hair by lowering his head down to the brush. It was imperative to break free, to relive adolescence, all over again.

Physiotherapy had been set up in advance at the Central Remedial Clinic on the other side of Dublin, putting him literally in the passenger seat. His mother did the daily chauffering and gave the staff a hand while waiting, which recalled her Red Cross work at Boscobel and his total dependency then. At home a pulley was rigged up over his bed for the incessant shoulder exercises, and he modelled himself upon The Pie at Terra Nova, who had not allowed the loss of a leg to curtail an energetic life. Holding the racket in alternate hands, he hit tennis balls against the pebble-dashed wall at the back of the bungalow, and in school holidays roped in his younger brother, Richard, as partner. If the weather was bad enough to keep him indoors, he used the palms of his hands to bounce the balls up and down. He walked beside his mother when she went shopping and carried her parcels, flexing his fingers against handle or string, and if a heavy suitcase needed to be picked up he was the first to

volunteer. Apprehension about falling over was difficult to
eradicate, and he dusted off his favourite Wodehouse catchphrase, 'Have you ever had that feeling you're going to die in ten
minutes' time?'

He was annoyed with himself but for a while found improve-
ment difficult . . . He declined to visit any of his former friends.
The company of people he knew had become abhorrent to him
. . . [Meals] became lugubrious and interminable, even [though]
in hospital he had explored the very depths of boredom. Alf
Tansey and Frank Taylor came to call: the two hefty Rossallians
were over studying medicine at the College of Surgeons in Dublin,
and it had been Tansey's impulsive tackle that had sabotaged the
final rugby season. Their news, after sincere commiserations, was
that Tansey was about to captain Lansdowne, up the road. The
small, quiet room magnified the physical imbalance, as well as the
fact that, unlike them, he was stuck at home. It was both a relief
and a rejection when they did not call back.

There was a crueller image which Jim had constantly to block
out. Tom Farrell's good performance in the Melbourne Olympics had coincided with the early horrors of the iron lung, and
his cousin's continued sporting triumphs made a mockery now
of his own efforts. Beating thirteen-year-old Richard at knock-
up tennis was pathetic when Tom was breaking the British
record in the 400 metres hurdles, and that September Tom
would defeat the world champion at White City, putting in
the best performance of the popular Britain versus Russia games.
Jim had to make do with the mild consolation of a newspaper
headline – 'Is it a coincidence that he lives in Kremlin Drive?' –
but twenty-two years later, in *The Hill Station*, amiable Tom
would assume the character of the ambitious Bishop of Simla,
for whom athletic prowess is an aggressive means to an end in
the advancement of his career.

As the weather began to pick up, Jim spent time in the garden.
His father was in charge of lawns and hedges, involving noisy
mowing and clipping, and his mother's latest interest was her
collection of old roses, many of which she had inherited from her
parents. *Eternal Youth, First Love, Peace. The wistful names*
spoke volumes about the poor, defeated rose-growers who had
christened them.

As Jim sat alone with aching neck and back in the bright garden, situated high over the sweep of Dublin Bay, pleasure in the moment – *How beautiful . . . the glimmering colours of his friends the roses* – would be wrecked by anguish at the oppression of time. Even his mother's best sunflower with its golden face was doomed, as surely as he was himself. *The blades of its petals [would be] bent inwards, dulled . . . The green leaves . . . paralysed and withered. I'm not dead, of course, but I'm dying. I know that much, I'm dying. Slowly but surely as the season advances. Who will help me now? . . . Nobody will help you because the seasons are remorseless. There's no difference between being magnificently golden and lifelessly withered. The circle chases itself eternally.*

Ultra-sensitive to doom and loss, he became engrossed by the continuing Suez Crisis, having been preoccupied by rugger and exam fever at its height the previous November. The lifeline of Empire, as they had always referred to the canal at Rossall, had been a subject often under discussion at Castlepark at the time when British troops were being withdrawn to placate Egyptian nationalism, but at the emotive moment of the last regiment's removal he had been driving through America, insulated from European news. The US decision to stop the loan for the Aswan Dam, justified as punishment for Nasser's links with Russia, had been a faint noise offstage, and Egypt's annexation of the canal to pay for the dam out of its dues had taken place while he was absorbed in settling into Brasenose. Britain, France and Israel had been banding together for a decisive counter-move when his own world fell apart, but while he had been in hospital, apparently, the supremacy had swung around. British troops had humiliatingly been pulled out and Anthony Eden compelled to resign as Prime Minister.

Jim busied himself with working out why, analysing the developments during his absence. Anti-government feeling had reached pre-war heights among the general public in reaction to a transparently sham pretext for military intervention, and the United Nations had called an emergency debate. In a sudden about-turn America had become an outspoken critic of colonial force, exposing Britain's inability to withstand American disapproval. Imperial conceit had been at work. The combination of pride, complacency and possessiveness had resulted in poor judgement, bedevilled by personality clashes, and the cyclic rise and fall of nations appeared as inevitable as the fading of the sunflower. Transience, once more.

The British national shock after Suez, overflowing into letters columns and radio discussions, affected Jim profoundly, and his own predicament emphasised the historical shift. The red on the map, commentators forecast, was going to shrink at accelerated speed, a point confirmed by Ghana's independence and the proposal of a European Common Market, signalled by the Treaty of Rome. The abrupt downturn in British power coincided with his personal lost ground.

In June Jim sat the papers for his deferred exam in Oxford, attending the Wingfield Morris hospital during the brief stay, and failed; his marks were rated very poor. Professor Nicholas wrote to point out that he would find it 'difficult' to manage in a legal setting, and advised an alternative degree for the next academic year. His unexpected choice was Modern Languages, rather than the more predictable English or History, on the grounds that French had been such a strong subject at school, and he spoke determinedly of reading Proust in the original. Translations were interpretations by the mind of someone else, and he was now opposed to dependency of any sort.

His mother had the Morris adapted, and he began to drive; changing gear, the most awkward manoeuvre, turned out to be less stressful than facing old friends in the Dalkey set. Jack Kirwan was visibly taken aback. 'Instead of the full, fat face I knew, he was drawn. His whole upper body was withered from the previously big, well-built frame. He was so decimated, so frail, and he could do so little, moving one hand with the other, and he looked much older because the grey in his hair was accentuated.' 'He was very self-conscious about his arm and dreadfully morose,' observed a former admirer. 'The diminishment sexually was what really distressed me. He had been so very physically attractive, big and strong. And then this shrivelled image – I couldn't believe it. He was so conscious of it, too; that was the terrible thing.' Shame was compounded by fresh injustice. Jim had kept to the rules of the sexual code, and now through no fault of his own lost out. Alert to pity, unable to disguise his wasted shoulders, which he overheard one girl describe woundingly as floppy, he turned up at dances and parties, but left early.

Away into the night and silence. But that was half the trouble. The night was O.K. but what of the silence? The silence against which in slow motion he was unable to avoid seeing the endlessly repeated film strip of his own sad, sour thoughts. Pat Rankin, who had turned him down in their teens for being too pushy, now found him too withdrawn. 'He just felt life had hit him a terrible blow,' said Pamela Caldicott, a quiet newcomer to the group in whom he felt able to confide. 'It had hit him sideways when he least expected it and taken away his potential.' At a picnic on Portmarnock Strand on a boiling hot day he kept his jacket on when everyone else stripped off, and as the temperature built up he rolled his trousers to his knees. If a camera was taken out he tried to take immediate avoiding action. *'This isn't me!'* . . . *'Yes it is. Look at the clothes.'* . . . *It showed a gaunt man with receding hair who was wearing one of his own shirts. Two deep, descending wrinkles were cut into the cheeks, compressing them into a wild grimace that might have denoted either pain or a kind of insane amusement. Moreover, the man's shoulders were stooped and his neck twisted.*

The Saint-like Farrell was gone, replaced by the Grim Reaper, complete with well-mimed hood and sickle, and he polished his impersonation of Richard III, too, winning plaudits for his efforts. 'He *was* Richard, all hunched and twisted,' noted Hilary Kirwan, who, to his relief, was about to spend the summer in Italy. 'And he had that nasal Olivier voice exactly right. We were so young and flippant, so wrapped up in ourselves, that we had no idea what he was really going through.' *He was isolated. He was looking down on the room from above. He saw the criss-cross threads of emotion with which, like mountaineers, the people in the room were trying to rope themselves together for the slow dangerous ascent of their lives. The descent, I mean, from youth and strength. The descent from dreams. I know all about that, he thought* . . . That speculation would propel the characterisation in all his future novels. How did people handle the descent from dreams? And how might they cope in a real crisis, like the one confronting him? He felt he had earned the right to guess.

The group had graduated to pubs around Trinity College, favouring Jammet's, O'Neill's and the Lincoln. Jack introduced Jim to the upstairs back bar of the Lincoln, which was scruffy and dark and smelled of Guinness. He held his pint of stout with difficulty in his left hand, bracing himself against a table or wall for balance, and felt that he belonged nowhere, envious of Jack's transparent sense of place. The outsider sensation was driven home by studying one of the regulars, Brendan Behan, in action. 'He loved to get us arguing,' said one of the Trinity circle, 'and he would slap down that day's leader in the *Irish Times* and challenge, "What do you lads think of that?" But he used to treat his wife Beatrice abominably. He would sit her in a dark corner and just say occasionally, "Send the mussus over a jar." ' Jim listened intently, his expatriate void exposed.

When Hilary returned from Italy she noticed how much progress he was making. 'There are only three intelligent people I know in this town,' he greeted her, and named two students she knew. 'The other, of course, is myself.' She snatched back the initiative by telling him that she had matched him with her best college friend, Judy Mitchell, for the October Trinity Commencement Ball, and he turned up obediently in Bill's now far too large dinner jacket at the Hibernian Hotel, deeply ashamed of the figure he cut.

Judy was a twenty-year-old blonde, with a stunning figure and cornflower-blue eyes, but it was her vitality that transfixed Jim. 'She eats daffodils at parties!' he exclaimed. The sudden death of her father, a dedicated doctor who never pressed his patients for payment and consequently left his family in dire financial straits, had interrupted her brilliant academic career, but she had passed his test of courage. Unable to afford the fees of Trinity College, Dublin, she had gone 'off books' in Economics the previous year, for which she had qualified at fifteen, taken a secretarial course and then an office job at the Guinness Brewery, and saved rigorously, enabling her to return. She danced and laughed that evening as if she had no cares in the world but, as she admitted when he got to know her better, she needed to win the top scholarship if she was to complete her degree.

'Miss Judy Mitchell', tipped the celebrity profile in *TCD*, the college magazine, 'could with equal ease play the languishing princess or swap mud pies with Huckleberry Finn . . . Stepping on high amongst the cream of the Economics School she is not beneath watching soccer matches or even boxing. Though she has dabbled (metaphorically) in the workings of Messrs. Guinness, she nevertheless has a strong liking for champagne – especially in the afternoon. This delightful mixture of queen and playboy goes with a firm strongmindness. The terrors of Schol. next April are hardly likely to disturb her equilibrium.' Shortly after they met she was elected Auditor of the Commerce and Economics Society, the first female Auditor in Trinity's long history.

Jim was as impressed as he was enchanted; before he realised it, his customary guard was down, and he found himself exhilaratingly in love. 'He was besotted with her,' said a male confidante. 'He was always very interested in women, but no-one meant as much to him as Judy. He was absolutely bowled over by her.' In blazer, flannels and the suede brothel creepers he favoured for formal occasions, he took her to films, met her family and regularly brought her home to spend time with his parents, for once holding nothing back. 'He was mad on her,' according to Pat Rankin. 'She was utterly beautiful, bright and vivacious, and she helped him.'

Uniquely, she could ease him out of depressions, because her view of his priorities matched his own. 'I can never imagine him being *anything* except a writer,' she rebuked anyone who dared to pour scorn, and she was as deft at teasing him down from arrogant heights as she was at coping with his misery. Pretending to ignore one black patch, she drove him to Wicklow where she had traced a Siamese kitten for sale, and the tiny creature's magnetism and intelligence broke through his self-preoccupation. He named it Tiffany, after the New York store, and, with his emotions so freshly re-awakened, the kitten's 'indescribable grace', as it basked on his bed or sprang in a single flowing movement on to the back of his chair, brought tears to his eyes.

The Mitchell family, however, were united in disquiet. 'I feel Jimmy *uses* Judy a little too much,' her brother Terence sighed to Molly, the oldest, and they agreed that he was going to make her unhappy in the end. Judy's brother-in-law made no secret of the fact that he disliked him. 'We never took to him,' he said flatly. 'He was carrying a chip from the polio and she was so open and lively. We just thought he simply wasn't her type at all.'

Starting at Oxford all over again, a year after his vigorous first entry, Jim self-effacingly reported back in October 1957, acutely sensitive to potential slights. Awaiting him in 5b, off Staircase XII on the panelled first floor overlooking New Quad, was a letter from Rossall advising that to be entitled to his Exhibition funds his Law tutor would have to certify that 'Mr J.G. Farrell has kept Term as required by the Statutes of the University, has conducted himself steadily in College and has pursued his studies with industry'. Nothing about polio, paralysis and absence; he left it as it was, unsigned. His Rossall study companion Nevill Phillips put in a brisk appearance, fresh from National Service, and found him sitting in the half-light with a blanket draped over the window. 'Come on, Jimmy,' he chivied. 'Don't just sit around.' Ignoring the implication of self-pity, Jim made no attempt to explain that the blanket helped to block out distraction whenever he was trying to write. The eventual completion of a novel, however long it took, had in the months since polio become his principal objective.

Oxford was *a city of effete embryo Hitlers*, and things that had irritated him before goaded him almost beyond endurance. He saw no point in *sitting behind these same crumbling walls and listening to a two-hour lecture on Punctuation [which] works up to a thrilling climax with the semi-colon* and made no secret of his general disdain. *I have heard every possible vacation job*, he would snipe in *Isis* when he had got back his bearings:

> *I know every inch of every military base from here to Cyprus to Hong Kong and back again to Salisbury Plain – if I hear the word Mons just once again I will strangle the person who utters it. I have had every wretched promiscuous girl . . . described to me a dozen times in every possible position [and am bored listening] to what the adjutant said to the captain [and] how we got off with those nurses without underwear and those typists with flats*

of their own and those receptionists [who] turned out to be
nymphomaniacs.

In contrast to the bracing coastal air of Dalkey, Oxford's damp
low-lying situation sapped the little energy he possessed, and he
was conscious of having to take an extra breath more frequently.
His first visit was to Stephen Wall, who in the interval had been
discharged and married Yvonne, the physiotherapist, and the
couple had set up home in Oxford to enable Stephen to resume
his academic career. Jim was shocked to find him confined to a
wheelchair for life, and Stephen, in turn, was saddened by how
alone Jim appeared. Both the Slade Isolation Unit and the
William Morris hospital were situated near Brasenose, and it
was impossible to forget that hedonistic student life co-existed
with a hellish underworld, equipped with instruments of exquisite torture.

He kept a copy of Gray's *Anatomy* to hand and talked of
Beckett's *Malone Dies*; his choice of records, too, betrayed his
cast of mind. 'Rien de Rien' by Jacques Brel was interspersed
with Vivaldi's Mandolin Concertos, and in desolation nothing
would do but Gregorian plain-chant. Death *was something*
which had happened, age after age, to these harassed cowled
figures who had somehow understood it . . . The strength of
their voices had comforted other people; not the strength of
religion, but the strength of the men themselves . . . Their voices
made death not only inevitable but eternal, not only tragic, but
right. With his blanket covering the window and light from a
low-wattage bulb in his desk lamp by the typewriter, day merged
into night.

Modern Languages, French and Spanish, turned out to be as
frustrating as Law. Straight across from his window, on the
opposite side of New Quad, was the window of his French tutor,
Professor Robert Shackleton, to whom he at once took a dislike.
As Senior Dean, a Fellow of Brasenose for twenty years and
Librarian for ten, as well as the Lecturer in French at Oxford
University and an honorary member of the Académie de Bordeaux and the Académie Montesquieu, Shackleton was a pillar
of college and accustomed to respect. He picked up Jim's
antipathy and responded in kind. Tall and balding, with a

ponderous manner beyond his years, he had recently been awarded the Prix Montesquieu and was said to take pains only with those destined for a First.

'Shackleton', Jim dismissed him openly, 'is a failure as a human being.' It was impossible to have a true dialogue, he elaborated, so there had to be something missing in 'the essential core' of the man. Unknown to him, the grammar-school-educated don was insecure enough to consider himself an outsider, too, as one of Jim's contemporaries subsequently pointed out. 'He probably greatly minded being mocked and was always ready to suspect it. Jim, of course, was contemptuous of him, but not for that reason, which he, above all, would have abhorred. The irony was that because Jim felt rejected and underestimated, he concluded that Shackleton was lazy, vain and privileged, and guilty of abusing his advantage.'

Mutual goading rapidly heightened the hostility. In tutorials Shackleton sat enthroned in a wingchair, and Jim had to take up humble station and await his turn to read his essay aloud for merciless dismemberment. Launched into full flight one day – 'Is there such a thing as the baroque in French literature?' – he noticed Shackleton's eyes on an open book that lay conveniently to hand. 'Is what you're reading interesting?' he drawled, after a suggestive pause. He despised the rational approach to the Enlightenment which valued proven fact alone and the insistence on establishing where a particular image came from. 'Nothing is original,' he would mimic the pedantic voice. 'There is a source for everything and the academic duty is to track it down. We are here to dissect construction, not to overvalue the imagination behind it.'

It became obvious to everyone in the joint tutorials that Shackleton considered Jim to be a poor fish in his response to polio, and privately rated him a quitter. As the acerbic don leaned back to hold forth on Montesquieu he habitually slipped one hand with supple dexterity behind his neck, an unconsciously provocative gesture to someone of limited shoulder movement and aching upper spine. Jim's retaliation was delayed until the writing of *The Siege of Krishnapur*, and followed Shackleton's instructions to the letter. *[The] Magistrate's judgements were invariably pitiless, and even, at times, when he*

*became excited, verged on the insulting . . . [He] suffered from
the disability of a free-thinking turn of mind and from a life that
was barren and dreary to match.*

The aspect of the language he preferred was to be found in the
Maison Française in the Woodstock Road, and on weekdays he
walked there and back to monitor French contemporary thinking through the cross-section of up-to-date newspapers and
magazines. Spanish, too, was studied out of college, which
helped to fill the spaces in his day which had previously been
taken up with sport.

The rhythm and isolation of walking solved two problems
simultaneously, by providing the necessary daily exercise and
the freedom of mind to think. When his balance felt steady
enough he bought a second-hand black bicycle for greater
freedom of movement, and its defect would give rise to an
appropriate analogy. *Have you ever ridden a bicycle that has
a tendency to slip out of gear from time to time? That's how I feel
sometimes. My mind is pedalling peacefully down the same
street of thoughts and then – whizz! It has jumped out of gear
and there's no resistance to my spinning feet.* His precariousness
was so marked that Roger Donald accused him of turning into
an old lady. 'Yes, but if you fall you can save yourself,' Jim
snapped back. 'I can't.' Eight years later he would portray his
fear of falling more lyrically. *He was unable to stop himself.
Faster and faster until his impetus became too great and he fell
forward. Hurled forward by his speed, bouncing and cartwheeling over those sharp stone teeth . . . He saw his skull with a dark
crack running across it. And as he watched, the crack began to
bulge . . . until a white liquid oozed out of it . . . and collected in
a white pool and the pool became a white bird, a dove, which
flew away into the sky with a glitter of white wings.*

Solitarily he crisscrossed The High or pedalled up Cornmar-
ket, identifying as he went with sad men with thin faces, the
beggars and street buskers. As he patrolled his circumscribed
stretch he often brooded upon the physical triumphs of his
cousin Tom, who that year competed in the European Cham-
pionships, captained the British team in Stockholm and reached
the semi-final at the Commonwealth Games. 'He had changed,'
Ralph Burrows noticed. 'His cynicism was more accentuated

and he wouldn't ever let you help him. He was very determined to overcome everything himself. "No, I've *got* to do it," he would say.'

In college he cultivated *a screen of cheerful irony*, later ascribed to Luc in *A Man From Elsewhere*, and began holding court for a favoured few in his rooms after lunch, with a touch of Brendan Behan about his approach. 'He would demand that we called,' said Phillip Davies, one of the new friends. 'He used to read out small pieces he'd written, and we'd start to argue. "What do you think of that," he'd ask. The debate was never finished, and there would be equal points on either side. Jim's wit and mine were very acerbic, and he talked incessantly out of the side of his mouth. It was a game to adopt attitudes and we all drank a bit of brandy. He had a way of putting his head back and looking at you down his nose, his head slightly to one side. Every conversation was a bit of a battle, and not so gentle, either.'

Members of Vincents were now anathema – *What he could never do was smile and wink at people and call barmen by their first names . . . act always in the sure knowledge that he had been born in the right place at the right time* – and he prized the attitude that questioned. The witty and epicurean Gary Arnott, a recent graduate who often returned from the City at weekends and made no secret of his homosexuality, took Roger Marshall's place, and a trio of American Rhodes scholars, Erwin Fleissner, Bob Cumming and Russell McCormmach, soon stood in for the team.

Jim first met Erwin in the Buttery lunch queue, over an idle remark about Ronald Firbank; the name was new to Erwin, a physicist from Yale, but he was struck by the sensitivity of Jim's face, and behind his own Ivy League conformity lay a strong resistance to tradition for tradition's sake. 'The place justified rebellion,' he said subsequently. 'It seemed as if we were locked in, and it wasn't even very interesting intellectually.' He introduced Jim to his schoolfriend Bob Cumming, who on the first day had sent over a one-line note from Christchurch, protesting 'What shall we *do* with this place?' The students Bob was encountering fell into two distinct types: those who overrated their own importance and that of Oxford, and the Beats, who were in wholesale rebellion. 'Jim was neither,' he analysed later. 'He was not taking Oxford, his own destiny or the destiny of the English-speaking world seriously. On the other hand, he wasn't beat, nor connected with Michael Horowitz and Co. He was rather cynical and detached, as if to say, "It's odd that we are here and that things are the somewhat absurd way they are." All of us had read French definitions of absurdity, but he more than anyone saw the world through those glasses.'

Erwin played tennis and rowed in his spare time; in contrast Bob had already invited Allen Ginsberg and Gregory Corso to give a reading in his rooms, and talked familiarly of William Burroughs. At Harvard he had edited *The Advocate*, the literary magazine, and he would be appointed literary editor of *Isis* within the year. 'You know how much I admire him,' Jim would later admit. 'But I used to feel about Bob that he was a 220-volt plug and I was a 110-volt light-bulb. I never felt things personally enough or intensely enough to be able to have an entirely satisfactory relationship with him. Which, of course, did not prevent me wanting to.'

The last to be introduced, Russell McCormmach, was at Christchurch with Bob and had trained as a physicist with Erwin, but it would be his immediate rapport with Jim that bound the four most closely. They met for the first time at Cambridge when Jim happened to be visiting Roger, who roomed with New Yorker André Shiffrin, at a time when Erwin called in to see Shiffrin, and brought Russell in tow. Roger and André were running *Granta*, and in the exclusively literary atmosphere that day Jim and Russell agreed that *The Great Gatsby* was a work of perfection. Back at Oxford, mutual approval flourished. Russell's self-effacing manner masked a penetrating intellect, and he was not only more widely read than anyone Jim had yet met, but he possessed a scientific grasp that Erwin insisted was extraordinary. Temporarily disgusted with science, he was reading Politics, Philosophy and Economics, and in disillusioned tune with Erwin, Bob and Jim.

That year and the next, when Jim roomed around the corner at Frewin Hall, he spent most of his leisure with the three Americans, meeting in each other's rooms, cheap restaurants like the Town and Gown or the Taj Mahal, or their favourite

pub, White's, which was out of bounds because it was so
popular with GIs from the nearby US airbase.

His need for solitude, however, was undiminished, and best
answered by the cinema. He haunted the Scala, which specialised
in foreign films; Europe and Japan, he was now prepared to
admit, led the field. At the Electra he cheered with the audience
when Robert Mitchum or James Stewart rode on screen, and the
Regal and the Super put on second showings of recent films,
enabling him to catch up on those he had missed while he was ill.
The Ritz showed the latest West End releases: he sat twice
through *Room at the Top*. Unobtrusively joining the queues
on his own, scarf muffled around thin neck and hands clasped in
front for balance, he saw himself as a damp squib; not a spent
force by any means, but by no possible stretch of imagination the
ballistic missile of his previous Oxford incarnation. In an era
that would draw early attention to the names of Brian Walden,
Patrick Garland, Alan Coren, Dudley Moore, Bernard Bergonzi,
Paul Johnson, Grey Gowrie, Ferdinand Mount, Paul Foot,
Richard Ingrams, Ved Mehta and Auberon Waugh, his role
was that of spectator. 'What a pity', Dennis Potter would
comment when he came across *The Siege of Krishnapur*, 'that
ships do not always pass in the day.'

Typing was becoming less of a chore as his hand and finger
muscles strengthened, but his arms and neck continued to ache,
and the classic writer's posture was as uncomfortable as he had
been warned. His writing was becoming decipherable, and he
had taken up sketching, both remedial and a fresh challenge.
Every day he worked at his portable typewriter, relying increasingly on routine, and the blacked-out window occasionally
conjured up the wartime evenings in Boscobel, and the spell
of his father's voice. He had a horror of literary poseurs – [The
bore] *had been told that he had the talent of a Great Writer [and]
he was writing a novel . . . A bearded friend of his appeared
opportunely* – and promptly went on the defensive if questioners
persisted. 'It's about people who are going away,' he would
hedge. Erwin, the least critical of the Americans, was shown a
few pages and gently pronounced the style too mannered, and
Jim came around to judging it harshly enough for no trace to
remain. Recollections of the plot vary, from an early draft of *The*

Lung to a doomed desert-island love idyll; both share the theme of transience and loss.

He did the bare minimum of work for French and Spanish, and instead read voraciously, supporting his head with his left hand. 'Jim takes up for Humbert in Nabokov's *Lolita*,' Bob Cumming jotted in his diary. 'In the end Humbert sacrifices himself to his love by acting completely in its terms. His self-indulgence was a product of his ideas and intellectual milieu.' But it was with Malcolm Lowry's alcoholic Consul in *Under the Volcano*, introduced to him by Russell, with whom he most completely identified, drawn to the fragmented vision which so resembled the after-effects of traumatic shock. Entranced by the cinematic perspective of the writing, he did some detective work and was surprised by the similarities between Lowry's life and his own. Both early childhoods had been spent near Liverpool, both fathers had an Empire background, and at public school both excelled at sport while simultaneously longing to become writers. Lowry had spent a year at sea before going up to Cambridge, a clear parallel with the Arctic, and most significantly Lowry, too, had not escaped. Between the ages of nine and thirteen he had been blind, through sudden ulceration of the corneas: the affinity drew on experience, as well as image.

The undertow of illness was also evident in Thomas Mann's *The Magic Mountain*. After polio, the setting of a Swiss sanatorium was hypnotic, and he read with such recognition – the all-encompassing world in which personalities expanded and pre-occupations narrowed down, where doctors were omnipotent and death and decay too tangible to ignore – that the experiences of the narrator Hans Castorp blended with his own. The sanatorium became a personal retreat, to which he would return at times of loneliness or stress and always with a sense of homecoming. Meeting Jim for the first time in New York in 1974, the young American writer Jan Hartman was taken aback by the resemblance to Castorp.

Externally, Jim now appeared more integrated, and attractively free of convention. He began to hold small informal lunches in his rooms, doing everything himself, which struck girls as rather exotic. Judy could not afford to visit, but the Kirwan girls arrived, and he smoothly laid on introductions, lunch and drinks. Unease was carefully disguised. When Sally Bentlif, the most glamorous of her year at Lady Margaret Hall, invited him to her twenty-first, he spent the evening with her stepfather, prompting his memories of being a Japanese prisoner of war. At the Blue Angel nightclub, on a London jaunt, he set the pace by exclaiming, 'I'll blow next week's rent!' but in fact sat alone, hunched and frail, as the others danced. 'So good-looking and so cadaverous and vulnerable, one's heart went out to him,' noticed Miriam May, who was reading English at St Anne's. 'He never gave the impression of being happy, but he was the last person to whine or moan. He was inured to not being happy – he didn't expect it to be any different. He bore unhappiness rather well.' So greatly outnumbered at Oxford that they were either the focus of unwanted attention or pain-fully in love, girls found it a relief to be with Jim. As they said between themselves, he made no demands at all, even of an indirect kind. In his own room, solitary and yearning, he sketched slim Cranach-style nudes.

By 1958 he was sufficiently confident to bring Judy to the Commem Ball, and to pick up the gauntlet flung down by Roger's Cambridge cronies to join them at the San Fermin festival at Pamplona during the Long Vac, before the Spanish holiday that he and Judy were planning that summer. The rough idea was to re-enact *The Sun Also Rises* and take part in the bull-running, and Jim's part was tailor-made as the impotent Jake; brilliant casting, they agreed raucously, at which he looked away to hide the prompt flush of anger. As well as Roger, André and himself, the cast included Jonathan Spence, who was also on a Paul Mellon scholarship to Clare, and Andrew Sinclair, a fellow Englishman and Jim's personal *bête noire*. Sinclair's novel *The Breaking of Bumbo* had made him Faber's second bestselling novelist after William Golding, and the arrogant Etonian liked to boast that he had written it in thirteen days. Jim often fulminated against him to Phillip Davies – 'Jim stumped around *furious* about Sinclair's publicity. He would have liked those accolades himself' – and, nursing his grievance, he put on a good face when the final details were hammered out. 'We were all laughing,' noted Roger of the planning stage, 'all believing this wonderful life would never end, and all interested in getting rich

by writing a really trashy novel.' Roger, Andrew, Jonathan and a
Polish countess named Ita Shabinska – who was a friend, of
course, of Andrew – arranged to drive down to Pamplona in
Roger's beige Morris Minor, where they would all link up.

Jim set off a month in advance, going via Cordoba where he
had a short holiday job teaching at a language school, and Sally
Bentlif promised to visit. In the event she never turned up. 'Isn't
the mosque in Cordoba wonderful?' she asked when she next
saw him. 'I never went to see it,' he replied, pulling the shutters
down.

The long train journey was intoxicating, and he gazed out of
the carriage window in search of Hemingwayesque details,
jotting down notes about yellow-ochre parasols in a café outside
Atocha and the circumference of circular metal tables. But
another type of detail stood out more plainly and, assessing
the exact blue of the sea beyond a fragrant wall of white jasmine,
he found himself focusing instead on a gaunt flower-seller with a
paralysed arm. Morbid thoughts were impossible to shake off.
He had chosen ultramarine espadrilles in deference to Lowry's
first book, *Ultramarine*, and in the crowded compartment it
occurred to him wryly that he could always unravel the soles and
hang himself.

On 7 July, his teaching stint completed, he set out to join the
others in Pamplona, taking wing *down a long sunlit valley in the
evening on an ancient train that stopped at every village, riding
on an open platform and drinking in the cool air and the
peaceful beauty of the cornfields glowing in the oblique rays
of the sun*. Three more Yale contemporaries had been co-opted,
and on arrival he faced the scrutiny of Ed Korn, Jay van Allen,
and Calvin 'Bud' Trillin. 'Ah, the other James Farrell,' Bud did
the honours, getting things off to an auspicious start. But though
placards   advertising   'Damn   Fine   Fiesta   –   Hemingway'
were flyposted around the Plaza, the inspiration for their pilgrimage turned out to be conspicuous by his absence; it was the
year that Hemingway stayed in Cuba, working on sketches that
would become *A Moveable Feast* and revising *The Garden of
Eden*.

The atmosphere was competitive, though Sinclair under-
played the car journey down as tedious and constipated, and

Jim found most in common with the academic-minded Spence and with Bud Trillin, who was witty and relaxed. They spoke in Hemingway lingo – 'With sweat and grit, treading in the tracks of the Master', as Andrew put it – and took pride in lack of sleep, drunkenness and discomfort, shouting over the ear-splitting riau-riau music which they compared to a gale blowing through wrapping paper on steel mesh, or a mob of fingernails scratching at wallpaper. It was, Jim volunteered, a very rude sound. Fundador brandy was cheap but he stuck to rough red wine, and saving money brought a vestige of control. They adopted the outdoor Café Kutz in the Plaza, choosing it for its Republican sympathies in the Spanish Civil War – 'Hemingway would have gone with us' – and Jim listened and watched and smiled his cryptic smile, summoning all his stamina. Making himself heard was exhausting over the repetitive fiesta song of the crowds who packed the square, with its thunderous climax '*Siete de Julio – San Fermin!*'.

Intrigue built up, aided by a mysterious girl in a chauffeur-driven white Rolls whom, following the Hemingway script, they christened Lady Brett – 'a beautiful pug on long legs', as Andrew, the victor, gloated – and rivalry in the early-morning bullrunning, which Jim had to content himself with watching. 'Anger. Mutual envy', jotted Sinclair in his notebook, where Jim was classified as 'incapacitated writer'. Rising to the occasion, he hammed up his breathing, coughed into his handkerchief and sagged in his café chair. 'We were reliving *Sun* consciously, all showing off,' Sinclair recorded with satisfaction.

Afternoons were devoted to the bullfight. In good seats in the shade, beside billboards for '*Valdespino – la marca de Jerez de siempre*', they watched each programme of seven corridas, featuring Antonio Ordonez, Gregorio Sanchez, El Trianero and Sanchez Chamaco, and bulls from Seville, Salamanca and El Escorial. 'Nobody hit a heart or a head,' summed up Sinclair. 'It was butchery all week. The great Ordonez failed – a stick here, a twitch there, *no direct* kill. Only El Chamaco, the gypsy hero, won. He killed the bull.' Jim was invariably silent on the way to the Café Kutz, horrified by the degradation of the bulls and of himself, as witness. *[As] a bull in a bull-ring with its wonderful muscles distracts the attention from the drops of its*

valuable blood on the sand, the drops becoming a trickle, the
trickle becoming a stream, the stream becoming a scarlet river
until, in the end, it wearily kneels and vomits the illusion by the
bucketful on to the yellow-grey sand.

A series of miniature corridas of his own took shape, in a
water-filled gravel pit where they repaired on the recommendation of 'the good book' when the morning sun was hottest. The
others would tear off their clothes and jump in, swimming back
and forth and around the perimeter, treading water to shout
insults. Jim could not even make it all the way across. 'He had
great difficulty and he obviously did envy the rude health of
people like Roger and myself,' Andrew realised. 'He always
swam with his shirt on, and he wouldn't stop trying. He was in
bad form.' Jim's *coup de grâce* would have been Sinclair's pity,
and he forced himself too far; for two days running he failed to
show up at the café, and when he did reappear, visibly wan, he
metaphorically lowered his horns at once. 'It's amazing how
cheap holidaying in Europe is,' he announced, pouring a glass of
wine with his left hand. 'You just have to lie in the dark in a
cheap room and eat nothing.' They pressed him for his symptoms, and he hooked to the right. 'My pee's turned a dark shade
of vino clarete.'

Verbal dexterity was Jim's chosen arena. In the blistering heat
he trotted out his Eskimo greeting, 'It is very cold outside,' and
proposed a Basque–Eskimo dictionary to Bud Trillin. Whenever
the conversation reverted to the skills of writing he took the
initiative, infected by the general high spirits. 'The feeling was
that we would all get what we wanted,' Roger described the last
few days. 'That we *were* breaking through. We knew we were a
fortunate and gifted lot.' It was collectively agreed that Jim was
going to be the greatest writer of them all, and clear that he
believed it, too. Eyes assessing their reaction and head tilted
back, he began one session with the definition that a publisher
was a flea dancing on the body of a larger corpus, and there was
a round of applause. 'I liked the man he represented,' decided
Andrew. 'Glum, withdrawn, obviously witty and apparently
suffering.'

When it was time to break up, Bud offered Jim a lift to Madrid
on his second-hand scooter, bought for the round trip on the

spur of the moment in Paris, where he was working with Time Inc. while waiting for the draft. As they threaded their way through a busy village market they bumped into a local woman, and in quick succession the bike fell over and they were surrounded by an angry mob. '*Mas espesio, per fervor!*' Bud pleaded, and inexplicably the crowd fell back and they got away. Delighted with Bud's panic-stricken misuse of the language, which had unintentionally seized the initiative by telling the Spaniards to speak more quickly, not less, Jim held on tight as they sped along and dared to live in the moment. The Pamplona experience had proved that he was perfectly capable of asserting himself among the only competitors who mattered, and narrow escape was the final euphoric touch. The sun burned the back of his neck, banishing pain, and the open road, paved with opportunity, stretched out ahead.

As a bestselling novel published the following year put it, 'We reckoned we were the top people, if you estimate big noises by the wind they make. We were the publicity boys, the golden kids of our year. We were different and said so. Maybe we didn't get much out of [university]; or maybe we got too much. But we *did* the things that were talked about, because we found them easy to do.'

The successful author was Andrew Sinclair, who dashed off another book after Pamplona in his customary fortnight. But it was the conclusion of *My Friend Judas* that would hurt Jim most, because by then the bleak theory that would evolve into Ehrendorf's Law had proved itself twice over. 'Yes, we *did* things,' rounded off Sinclair's hero, Ben Birt, prophetically. 'And we did ourselves, too, good and proper. Do, and what you've done will do you.'

CHAPTER EIGHT

Water Becoming Hard Ice
1959–1960

As Bud's scooter neared Madrid from the north-east, a Saxe blue soft-top convertible Morris Minor was accelerating past Perpignan, heading in the same direction. Inside were Phillip Davies from Oxford and his girlfriend Jill and, at Jim's invitation, Judy Mitchell. Judy's toenails were stained pink from standing in a strawberry-canning factory in Wisbech, earning money to augment her twenty-first birthday present of the holiday ahead, which they were all to share with Jim. The drive through France had been great fun, but the fact that they were a day late for the rendezvous niggled at the back of everyone's mind.

Although in his typed letters from Oxford Jim was as light and affectionate as ever, the previous Christmas had marked a change in his relationship with Judy. 'I find I'm very dissatisfied with you,' he had remarked at the start of a trip to Killarney in front of Hilary Kirwan and Roger Donald, who were in the car, and he continued to needle without let-up, sneering, 'Oh God, the ould sod! Let's make a postcard of it,' if she made the mistake of admiring a view. Hilary had whispered that he wanted to demoralise her because she refused to be subservient, and Roger had accused him of being psychologically sick. When criticised by friends for being too good to him, Judy insisted that he was the sort of person whom one liked to help to be happy, but as his health picked up he could unleash a destructive venom that was outside her experience. Physically she was as attracted to him as he now was to her – 'I don't feel sorry for him in *any* way,' she corrected people stoutly – but he twisted the Groucho Marx quip about not wanting to join any club that would have him, unable to believe her.

In Madrid he was sitting on the steps of the cathedral where they had arranged to meet, beneath a pyramid of cigarette smoke and surrounded by butts. His pleasure at seeing Judy was undisguised and all went well until that evening, when she jibbed at the plan for each couple to share a room. 'We were very innocent,' she explained later, 'and it just wasn't on the cards, certainly for me.' For a month they toured around the coast, from Torremolinos to Gibraltar, staying in pensions which nightly threw them into angry proximity, and he found fault with everything. Phillip's tolerance evaporated, and Jill kept quiet, afraid of making the situation worse. 'Have you ever had a subconscious drive to start a row which will wreck everything so that one's emotional landscape in turn becomes barren and tidy once more?' Jim would admit to another woman, when he was older and wiser. 'I have it all the time.'

Sexual frustration was not the only cause, the other two agreed: it was obvious that Jim suspected pity, and that he was fiercely unhappy with himself. On the beach the contrast was stark, with Judy golden brown and the centre of male attention, and Jim glowering, stubbornly keeping on his shirt. The day she set out to buy sweetcorn and, unable to speak Spanish, returned with a bag of carrots stood out for its serenity, allowing him sufficient advantage to be kind. Jim watched himself from a distance, powerless to be any different. *[The] strongest emotion I had ever experienced came from the refusal of love . . . the sensation of hurting and being hurt.* On the final leg of the return journey, crawling along the Embankment in dense London traffic, the car symbolically broke down.

Back at Oxford he continued to talk of marriage, telling friends that it was definitely on the cards. Phillip tried to put his reservations aside. 'Judy was his number-one girl, no shadow of doubt about it. All during that autumn term after Spain he'd talk about her all the time.' Once again Roger was invited over for Christmas, and the brawny American accepted on condition that he could bring his girlfriend; for the second year running, Jim arranged to escape to a seaside cottage at County Wexford, bringing Judy with them, as soon as they could decently get away from the festivities he loathed. It was the end of the two-year recovery period, which wiped out all hope of further physical improvement, and his writing was not going well. After Pamplona the pressure to achieve had intensified, and he longed instead to be alone.

The spartan Brittas Bay cottage was wooden, with bunks for beds and sand in the sleeping bags. Draughts swept through and the single driftwood fire was situated in the uncarpeted central room. The thin-walled bedrooms opening off it were unheated, and at night-time warfare was resumed. *[She] would cram on the brakes . . . in case she should skid too far and crash into a spontaneous expression of passion. Unfortunately it never came to that. Her brakes always had the better of me.* 'There were just the four of us,' recalled Roger in middle age. 'My girlfriend shared the same bedroom as me and naturally we slept together. Jim and Judy had the other bedroom and I took it for granted they were sleeping together too. But they weren't, and they would fight like mad. When I met that girlfriend many years later the first thing she said was, "Don't you remember those terrible rows in the middle of the night?" '

Judy returned early to Dublin to study for exams, and Jim reneged on his promise to take her to her cousin's twenty-first in Greystones, County Wicklow on 3 January, buckling thankfully down to work. Roger took the hint and they went for a last walk along the beach, discussing film-making and collecting drift-wood, and everything took on a cinematic perspective, *coarse-grained in black and white under the hurrying sky.* Abruptly they were brought up short by a sight which Jim had already focused upon before he recoiled. A drowned sheep lay *half buried in the sand, glass-eyed, fleece matted with sand and salt water, legs spread as if it had died in the act of beautifully moving,* and death and transience, recently somewhat over-looked, were reduced to a single lasting image.

There was no phone in the cottage, which was one of the reasons he so liked to be there, safe from disturbance. So when the call came through on 4 January, it was to Staunton's, the local shop where he bought groceries. He was handed a message telling him to ring Hilary urgently, and she broke the news over the public phone that Judy had been gravely injured in a car crash while taking a lift with friends to the party. She had been in the front passenger seat and taken the full force of the impact, and was not expected to live. 'He came up at once,' she described his reaction, 'and he came over to me in a desperate state. He said, "The whole way up I was debating whether you told me the truth, and whether she was really dead and you were breaking it gently to me." '

Judy was on a life-support machine in Loughlinstown Hospital on the city's southern outskirts, and when she was moved by ambulance to the central Richmond Hospital, which specialised in head injuries, he followed in his car. The staff let him stay beside her bed, ejecting him only when the nurses needed to attend to her, and at such times he wandered the streets or called around to her mother's flat, where her distraught family could scarcely bear to put up with him. The dark underworld had once more opened up. Head shaved, as his had been, on a breathing machine and fed through a nasal tube – that same red streak of pain – Judy lay in a coma without the flicker of an eye or a groan. The only sound was the unforgettable stertorous, mechanical breathing, the only smells were the old claustrophobic ones, and the only difference between past and present was the jagged tracheotomy in her throat. Pneumonia was mentioned, ice baths failed to bring down her temperature, and her skull was trepanned to relieve pressure on the brain. She remained on the danger list, deeply unresponsive, and he kept up his vigil, ignoring his twenty-fourth birthday and the start of term. Her family came to resent the sight of him possessively in place, with the implication that anything less was betrayal; willing her to regain consciousness, he could not let himself off the hook.

Judy's accident reverberates throughout the Farrell novels, darkening the Empire Trilogy, and is scrutinised obsessively in the first three semi-autobiographical books. '*But of course it was an accident,*' the central character of *A Girl in the Head* tries to convince himself. '*The sort of thing you can't do anything about.*' '*It's all my fault,*' a patient in *The Lung* mourns. '*I know that much. I shouldn't have . . .*' *Nobody contradicted him.* For Jim imagination would fuse permanently with the dreadful awakenings – *He scrambled hastily through a woolly, stifling dream and then sat up suddenly with the feeling that something terrible was going to happen, had happened. The room was in darkness and he was sweating* – to his seething antagonism which glints through *A Man From Elsewhere* towards Judy's family. *Nobody else seemed to pay any attention to it. They just went on eating, sleeping, drinking coffee and inviting people to stay, as if a death in the house was nothing more than a cold in the head.* Sitting for hours in silence, re-examining his behaviour, he was haunted by the succession of rows he had provoked. *'What's the matter?' 'How do you mean?' . . . 'You know perfectly well. Why don't you talk to me any more?' 'Well, I'm so busy.' 'That's not the reason. Is it because I'm a cripple?' 'Of course not . . . It's because I don't want to be unhappy.'* Bumping into Hilary on the hospital steps one morning, he told her that he intended to stay by Judy for the rest of his life, and promised never to leave her. 'I'll mind her,' he repeated. 'I'll bring her back.'

Six weeks after the crash Judy opened her eyes, and her brother Terence gave credit where credit was due. 'Jim was the first person who got a smile from her,' he said subsequently. 'He asked her if she remembered trying to buy sweetcorn in Spain, and I'm pretty certain he got a chuckle from her. My mother resented that greatly, because she would have liked to have been the one, but Judy wasn't so conscious that it was obvious.' Exhilaration was shortlived. When the tracheotomy was removed it was clear that she would have to learn again how to talk, and the overwhelming medical routine continued, merely shifting gear; the prognosis was that recovery would be protracted. One day towards the end of February Jim was not in his usual chair by the bed, and her family's initial relief dipped into apprehension at the sight of Judy's distress.

Back at Oxford he confided only in Phillip Davies, Brian Pearce, and a new friend made the previous year, Brian Knox Peebles; after each Dublin visit he would pick up where he had left off, without comment. At the Richmond Hospital Judy's recovery was suspended in slow motion. Her blonde hair had grown back and her face was unmarked, but her progress otherwise was forlorn, and she was having to be taught how to walk, as well as talk. His involuntary recoil from everything to do with hospital was impossible to conceal. The head injuries had left her with no short-term memory, and her ability to concentrate, which he had so admired, was gone.

Her pleasure at seeing him each time twisted the knife. 'I

sometimes wondered whether Judy would have gone on loving him if she hadn't had that accident,' commented her older sister, Molly. 'But she certainly did, after.' Her convalescence began at Molly's house, and the geographical imperatives meant that he monopolised her one moment, and abandoned her the next. Molly's protectiveness mounted. 'I would go to bed and leave them up, feeling cross because he wouldn't go. They wanted to be on their own, and I didn't want to leave them.'

The gaps between his visits lengthened, and Knox Peebles put the situation starkly one day, asking if he was going to 'go through with it', and marry her. 'He told me, "Oh, I don't know, Brian." Later when I asked him again he said he couldn't take on such problems, and he was very, very guilty about it. He was so fond of her, but the thought of looking after someone else as well as himself was too much.' He deduced that Jim was single-minded about becoming a writer, however poorly paid, and was convincing himself that it was better for Judy not to be subjected to his moods. Brian Pearce, with compassion, watched as he visibly wrestled with his conscience.

Jim shut his parents out of the decision, aware that they sympathised less with his literary ambitions than with his chronic ill health, and that their anxiety was as much for him as for Judy. But he was unable to keep up his customary guard. 'It put him into a great moral dilemma,' Phillip realised. 'He began saying to me, "I don't think I'm going to go on seeing her," and I disapproved of that. I didn't think it was morally right. We had endless discussions, with him saying, "What shall I do?" and he was terribly anxious.' Erwin spent a brief holiday at Balholm, and found himself involved without explanation. 'I sensed a bond but there was also a sense of tragedy,' he noted. 'Judy was a very sweet girl, very beautiful and very damaged, and there was that oscillation between them.'

With the exception of Bob Cumming and Brian Knox Peebles, all Jim's closest Oxford friends were about to go down. He threw himself into preparations for a farewell lunch, stipulating a bourbon and icecream punch. On the night of the Commem Ball, however, he was nowhere to be seen, and at the garden party he was unduly melancholy, which they attributed to unease about the coming year.

That summer Jim stayed in Oxford, intent on working without distraction. He shared a flat at 210 Woodstock Road with Brian Knox Peebles, on the first floor of a redbrick Victorian house owned by Major Blunt, a retired Indian army officer related to the poet Wilfred Scawen Blunt; the major was in his early seventies, comfortingly blimpish with a white moustache, and Brian would make an immediate connection as soon as he read *Troubles*. 'He was embarrassingly kind and Jim took it all to heart,' he conjectured. 'Don't pay the rent,' he would say, and he would bring him food and show him his favourite books.' When Brian left, Jim stayed on; in terms of need, it was like a spiritual retreat, providing a solace he could accept.

Another burst of concentrated writing followed, this time with Russell McCormmach in Dublin, where they rented a room for two weeks to collaborate on a filmscript, following the Hollywood example of Lowry and a contemporary from Cambridge. At first they toyed with a potboiler – 'ice clinking in glasses, that sort of thing' – but settled on a spoof about the English class system, writing alternate scenes and in between decamping to O'Neill's on the corner of Suffolk Street. The plot was set around a painter of pets to the aristocracy, and they called it *The Animal Urge*. 'It came naturally to us,' noted Russell, 'and we each improved one another's scenes. It was the first time I'd written in collaboration, and it was a lark. Jim had high hopes of it, seeing it as a means of supporting him while he wrote.' When the fortnight was up and it was time for Russell to return to America, they anticipated a sequel, but when Russell got around eventually to enquiring about progress, he was informed it had been 'flushed down the MCA toilet'.

Writing at full stretch blocked out the long-term decision about Judy, while simultaneously edging towards it. Erwin's final sight of the short doomed love story, in which, as he would subsequently recall, the hero reluctantly abandoned his girlfriend and returned to his authoritarian family, only to develop polio, hinted at the struggle between fulfilment and duty. But Erwin, too, was mutating in Jim's imagination, and in *The Singapore Grip* a novella would be included as Ehrendorf's juvenilia about *a gifted young American [who] goes to Oxford on a scholarship and there, having fallen in love with an English girl who surrounds herself with cynical sophisticated people, goes to the dogs, forgetting the sincere 'warm-hearted girl whose virginity he had made away with while crossing the Atlantic on a Cunard liner . . .'* Erwin's spell in England, as both were well aware, had been practically monastic.

In the autumn, when Jim returned to Oxford, the clash between duty and self-fulfilment remained unresolved. His digs in the final year were in a rabbit warren of a building at 65 The High, practically opposite Brasenose, where his room was next to that of Magdalen undergraduate Martin Gilbert, on the top floor. Greasy cooking fumes filtered up from the landlord's kitchen and the view from his window at the back swept from the tranquillity of Magdalen gardens, towards a distant outline of rolling hills. Martin Gilbert, subsequently to become Churchill's official biographer, was reading history, and a routine soon evolved of regularly chatting together over a drink in Jim's room as the light drained out of the sky. Expansive and intellectually voracious, Martin swiftly made up for the missing friends.

The two appeared unlikely companions at the obscure club lectures they mutually appreciated, or browsing absorbedly around Blackwell's laden second-hand shelves, one languid and gaunt, set apart by a remote and quizzical expression, the other stocky and voluble, with quick gestures, heavy glasses and thick hair; in practice, their interests and personalities dovetailed. Martin had travelled as far afield as India and Poland and already published papers on his conclusions; he was erudite about the interweave of politics and history, and keenly aware of the vagaries of human nature. He, in turn, was convinced that Jim had much to teach him. 'I, in my innocence, still thought the path forward was to be accepted, and Jim somehow knew it wasn't,' he would reflect. 'Nothing fooled him. He realised that the ruthless and ambitious would remain ruthless and ambitious, but he was always witty about it. He never put me down, but he often left me wondering why I'd accepted a certain thing, or taken a certain point of view.'

Although Jim was the older by as little as eighteen months, he took a paternal approach. Supporting Martin back up The High from The Cape of Good Hope one evening, he had to flag down a passing car when his charge fell over and his own strength proved too puny to haul him up. Six years later in *The Lung* the incident would resurface. *'For God's sake get up off the road, you fool . . . If you want to sit down, sit down in the bloody ditch.' . . . 'My head is beginning to feel like a plate of scrambled eggs.'*

Sitting high in their eyrie, they were similarly indignant about colour prejudice, snobbishness, and the types who jockeyed for student power, as well as the way that history was taught. 'So many things Oxford *ought* to contain,' one or the other invariably groaned. Less amazed by affectation than by the unjustified arrogance of people their own age who considered themselves socially superior, they built their case against complacency. Jim already voted Labour at every opportunity and would be a lifelong supporter, chivying his friends to do likewise. 'Group morality equals class morality,' jotted Martin. 'But society makes us selfconscious. We can stand apart and criticise only the society that created us.' He saw Jim as an athletic person brought low who continued to give out a strong physical presence, and in his company Jim shared that invigorating view. In recompense, Martin's warmth and questing mind – 'I was essentially an optimist,' he said of himself at that age, 'rather naïve and always an element of bumptiousness' – would mould George Fleury in *The Siege of Krishnapur*.

It was a wet, freezing winter, continually threatening snow, and the old buildings exuded damp. Out of doors Jim shivered, despite his scarf and extra layers, and indoors he blew on his hands and typed on, impressing Martin with his self-discipline. Interruption was unwelcome but occasionally he was glad of light relief, and Bob Cumming was his most frequent visitor. '7.11.59. Jim alone, making jokes and hoping for some communication,' Bob's diary entry ran on a day when everyone seemed 'tired, detached from each other'. Jim was accustomed to fatigue but sufficiently disturbed by his own detachment to examine his 'colossal indifference' microscopically in the character of Martin Sands, now taking embryo shape. 'The difference between people is mainly chemistry,' he propounded to Bob one evening, who attributed it to genuine nihilism.

His relationship with Shackleton had not improved, and with Finals in the offing he was fortunate to be introduced by Martin to Janet Dawson, who was reading French at St Hilda's; one-sided chemistry of a different order was the result. Unlike his own 'stagnant backwater', Janet was studying the interplay of European politics in turn-of-the-century French novels and she conveyed her enthusiasms with zeal. She was tiny and impetuous, with a limp from childhood polio and dark hair cut in a Parisian bob; her mannerisms were French, she spoke with bilingual flair, and she was fascinated by film technique. Unlike Jim, however, she wore her heart on her sleeve; he was masterly at sidestepping intimacy. She was one of the female students who had vowed publicly not to have sex until Britain banned the bomb, christened by Martin the Lysistrata Group; warily Jim included her as a threesome in their sessions, rather than breaking away as a couple, as she hoped. For an *Isis* interview with David Caute at All Souls, whose first novel, *At Fever Pitch*, was shortlisted for the John Llewellyn Rhys Prize, he took along Sally Bentlif instead. Reporter's role apart, there were the more insistent questions. How had Caute come to write it while so young? And how on earth had he got it published?

Jim wrote his first short story for an Oxford literary magazine on the subject of student suicide, prompted in part by the separate deaths of two contemporaries, relayed with anguish by Martin Gilbert; in his second novel he would look back at it scathingly. *Letter for Carola* describes the last day of an Oxford student who gasses himself and he added the twist of insufficient money for the meter. Although in future he would refer casually to one-way trips off Magdalen tower and dismiss suicide as 'merely like leaving a cinema before the end when the film had ceased to interest you', his observation of depression was clinically accurate, exposing his own despair. *The fact is, I am tired of myself . . . tired to death.* He also took the opportunity for two vignettes, one negative and one positive, and in went a recognisable caricature of Shackleton.

When he had read his essay, his tutor was silent for a while, looking out of the window into the College quadrangle. 'I don't really think . . . that it is very much use talking about this subject on the basis of what information your essay contains, if you care to overlook the semantic origins of the word "essay" and call it such . . . Well, do you think [it] is a valuable piece of scholarship? Perhaps you do. In that case I would be obliged to disagree with you.' 'I'm sick . . . I can't concentrate.' . . . 'Well, if you should happen to be able to do a little work, perhaps you would be so kind as to write an essay for next week.' . . . The bastard. What a bastard that man is!

The plaudit was for Janet, whose generous help with his exam preparation was invaluable, and she was the model for Carola, in whom the suicidal student confides. A more lasting trace of her personality would infuse Sarah in *Troubles*, along with the image of her limp.

Dreading the first anniversary of Judy's crash, he brought Bob Cumming and an Indian girl home that Christmas, and evaded his dilemma by focusing almost exclusively on university topics. 'Part of the sense of identity I have with Jim comes from the fact that he does *not* have the idea of himself as belonging to an aristocratic society which a number of the people I know at Oxford have,' commended Bob on Christmas Eve. 'Jim does not have any of this sense that fate or good breeding or any other factor has given him special privileges; in this way he's more like Americans who were my friends before coming to England.' But Bob was being kept at bay, and when they returned to Oxford Jim was no further along with his moral quandary.

His detachment from Oxford pressures made his room a sanctuary for Bob, so when word came that his brother had died unexpectedly in America he turned at once to Jim. 'Faced with my brother's death,' he wrote that night with anguish, 'I feel that Jim is *too* fatalistic. I want more help in fighting off this blow.' The gap between Jim's method of coping, through the damping-down of emotion, and that of the rest of their age-group was a disturbing glimpse, and in his grief Bob saw through the detachment to its core. 'I feel that Jim hasn't enough trust in life, has surrendered too easily,' he concluded, disillusioned.

Oblivious and single-minded, Jim concentrated on getting more work in print and prolonging the present. *My own imagined future*, he taunted those scrambling for job interviews in a new column in *Oxford Opinion*, has been limited to *a vague notion of smuggling gold bullion into, or out of, Switzerland (whichever is more profitable). In fact, I never passed beyond a picture of myself strolling along Copacabana Beach, dressed in a white dinner-jacket, smoking a black and gold cigarette in a long cigarette-holder, listening to the whisper of the surf in the velvet dusk, with the lights of Rio like glistening jewels behind me and, perhaps, a white sports-car back on the road.* When Brian Knox Peebles suggested joining a circus, he pounced on it as a splendid idea. It was depressing to have to commit yourself to forty years in an office, he conceded to his readers, but added significantly, *very few of us are stubborn enough or strong enough to say: this is the kind of life I want, I will not settle for less.*

While arguments in the Buttery centred on the most lucrative career move, he slipped away to Paris for Easter, Orwell's *Inside the Whale* under his arm, to attend a publicity launch for *Minutes To Go* by William Burroughs and Sinclair Beiles in Shakespeare and Company, wearing his *Oxford Opinion* hat. Walking by the towpath on his return, he turned to follow the flight of a bird and propitiously the low sun was like a blood orange, framed by clusters of white blossom. Only one obstacle remained.

Judy finally forced his hand, by planning a visit to Oxford during her first trip out of Ireland since the accident. He booked accommodation, promised to meet her train, and in preparation resorted to the cinema, the reliable panacea. The continental film being shown reminded him of *Les Liaisons Dangereuses*, which he had made a point of watching intently in Paris because of François Mauriac's claim that the recent sudden death of the actor Gérard Philippe, who played de Valmont, was foreshadowed in his face. Did Judy, perhaps, resemble Madame de Tourvel, famous for her strict morals? And could de Valmont's self-justification be his? 'I cannot bring myself to regret leaving you – it's beyond my control.' Jim made his arrangements and, when the time came, met the train.

As Judy made her way on his arm slowly into his digs, she discovered they were not going to be alone. Seated around the table in voluble discussion were four undergraduates, who carried on talking as if she was invisible. Jim made no effort to introduce her; on the contrary, he abandoned her at the door and joined them, taking the only free chair. 'I felt really snubbed and humiliated,' she admitted later. 'My strong feeling was that it was awful to be so crowded in, with that pretentious group being so rude to me. I was unable to contribute, and realised quite clearly that I wasn't the person for Jimmy with his friends. It was deliberate, to show me that I wasn't of the mettle required. It was his way of saying, "This is the life I lead and you don't fit in. These are the people I want." It was desperately shaming, and yet at the same time I was glad. It's a very good thing to see someone in his real setting. Jimmy in Dublin was fine, but Jimmy in Oxford was not the same person, and it was the Oxford side of him that he was really like.' Before taking her back to the station when she could take no more – 'Oh, must you go?' he said politely when he eventually acknowledged her misery – he made a point of showing her the backnumbers of *Oxford Opinion* and pointing out his name.

Afterwards de Valmont's self-hatred became Jim's own. There was no escape from psychological pre-programming, as existentialism argued and he believed, so any attempt at change was futile. The revelation of his own heartlessness was the final piece of the jigsaw, and throughout his novels he would rework the theme, seeking absolution and finding none. The title of his first book, *A Man From Elsewhere*, would be taken from the saying 'A man from elsewhere is a man without a soul'.

Peering into the pale, tortured face under its shining cloud of fair hair [he] longed to take her in his arms and make wild promises, but he was powerless to do so. Turning, he began to walk away, repeating senselessly to himself that if he could keep on going the scars would heal themselves. . . . He had stood looking at her coldly and then, without a word, he had opened the door for her to leave. My God, he thought, staring sightlessly . . . Thank God it's a dream . . . But slowly he realised with horror that it had not been a dream . . . He had sent her away without a word. In the morning he felt more utterly defeated than at any other time in his life that he could remember.

Judy's lack of recrimination made remorse the greater, as did other people's capacity for self-sacrifice. He had kept loosely in touch with John Chisholm after leaving hospital, whose nurse was now his wife and cared full-time for him at home, and he continued to visit Stephen and Yvonne: they had passed the test and so of course had Judy, because when the circumstances were reversed she had stood by him. He alone had failed. 'Remember', he copied into a pocket notebook, 'that all our failures are ultimately failures in love.' The sole justification for the damage he had inflicted was not to deviate now from his goal of becoming a novelist.

Many years later Erwin Fleissner met up with Jim in New York, and was saddened. 'I got a strong impression of desolateness,' he said afterwards. 'There was always something so courtly and distinguished about Jim. But there was also some question that he had about existence that he hadn't answered to his satisfaction. I would have thought worldly success would have made him pleased. But eventually the capacity to love and be loved is the most important thing.' *I sometimes feel that I'm made up of a whole series of antechambers with interconnecting doors leading by stages towards my real self*, he would seek to explain:

> *You deal with almost everyone you meet in the first antechamber, the people you know well in the second or third . . . But something has gone wrong. I've never been able to find the person who can unlock those final doors and enter the room where I really am – the real me, sitting and waiting in utter silence for someone to get to know me at last after all these futile years . . . Or could it be, I sometimes wonder, that it's up to me to unlock those final doors? Because to be frank I don't see how I can. Without the key, I mean.*

Permission was obtained for him to type his papers in front of a separate invigilator during 'Schools', and he hired the requisite gown and mortar board, impatient with tradition. His typing speed was slow and he failed to complete one section within the allotted time, resulting in a Third. He described it as undistinguished and would have preferred a Fourth, which implied razor-sharp judgement about work and play.

In *The Singapore Grip* Matthew Webb and Jim Ehrendorf

stroll by the Cherwell, as in real life Jim and Bob did in the summer of 1960. *The knowledge that they would soon be coming to the end of this phase of their life, saying goodbye to friends and launching out into careers that were still barely imaginable, had cast an air of melancholy over them . . . Ehrendorf had been saying how he felt he had changed . . . how difficult he believed he would find it returning to his home town in America . . . Poor Ehrendorf. Thanks to the Rhodes Scholarship . . . the poor fellow had split in half like an amoeba.* For Jim, however, the period at Oxford had the opposite effect, since it confirmed him in his purpose. Bob had by now come around to re-evaluating him again, and a closing diary entry assessed him as one of the four strongest personal influences at university. 'Why?' Bob analysed before packing up. 'His detachment, ability to free himself from demands of Oxford – any outside demands – and to follow his own sense of what he wants to do.'

Jim did not come back for the conferring of his degree; that compartment, too, was closed. Within a month of going down he was joining in a debate on censorship in the letters page of the *Irish Times*, attacking the novelist Monk Gibbon for daring to criticise Sean O'Casey and James Joyce, and already set, like O'Casey, Joyce and Beckett, upon exile. Life, as he claimed in his shortlived *Oxford Opinion* 'Notebook' column, was an experience that had to be personally created. *There is always a distinction*, he had notified his intention then, *between those who believe what they do, and those who do what they believe.* Meanwhile, Tom Farrell had set a new British record for the 400 metres hurdles and was in training for the forthcoming Rome Olympics. It marked out a natural span.

The decision was to take a post teaching English at a school in France to free several months a year in that country for writing, and he stayed around only for as long as it took for his visa to come through. On 25 September 1960 he set out in the specially adapted 1948 red Morris Minor – registration number NI 7031 – by ferry, via England and the Hook of Holland, travelling light. He had a letter of reference from Lord Moyne, better known to him as the writer Bryan Guinness, £58 in traveller's cheques and £10 cash, his portable typewriter, a few favourite books and the bare minimum of possessions. Tucked in his wallet were fifteen miniature photographs of Judy, laughing and trusting in the winter of 1957.

He was taking control, and any criticism would get short shrift. 'My starting point for the way I live or try to live my life, which I take it you're attacking,' he would retort to a friend within eighteen months, 'isn't logical but emotional, anyway.' The years at Oxford had succeeded in teaching him only one thing: conventional rules no longer applied.

CHAPTER NINE

This Is the Kind of Life I Want
1960–1962

The Lycée d'État Chaptal was in the provincial town of Mende, high in the Lozère region of the Massif Central. A river ran between the school and the town, and the large sandstone building faced outwards, down the road to Le Puys. The impression was of a barracks, with thick walls and regimented windows, but inside the rooms were bright and airy, staving off the oppressive phalanx of pine-forested peaks. Unlike Terra Nova, Rossall and Castlepark, it reflected back the identity of the region, rather than a widely distributed social class. Since its foundation in 1554 it had provided sound day-school education, and the brightest pupils looked no further than the universities of Montpellier or Clermont Ferrand. The statue of Mende's most famous son, Jean-Antoine Chaptal – Senateur et Ministre, Précurseur de l'Industrie Chimique – set a wider perspective from the previous century, but few heeded the purposeful figure in high-collared frock coat and stock.

A bare light-bulb dangled from the ceiling of Jim's lodging house in the town centre and the water in the single tap was cold, but he had a narrow bed, a wooden chair, a primus stove and a small table for his typewriter; it was precisely what he sought, cheap and pared to the bone. The morning walk to school was along streets lined with plane-trees, past a plaque to the local Resistance heroes '*mort en déportation*', with Chaptal as his imaginary companion; a strong impression of that brisk scientific and administrative bent would inhabit the Collector in *The Siege of Krishnapur*. Burnished chestnuts were scattered on the ground when he arrived, but rapidly the cool air sharpened to match the chill of Mann's territory in *The Magic Mountain*. Auspiciously the song of the moment was Edith Piaf's 'Je ne Regrette Rien'.

In class his mischievous approach ensured that frail Monsieur Farrell became a popular figure, and he fitted back instinctively into the schoolmaster's strict tempo; he was as close to the rhythm of the seasons, he sometimes mused, as a gardener or gamekeeper. His hours were short because his contract was part-time, and off duty he headed for one of Mende's many eating-houses, where over a café noir he extended his own education by enquiring in detail about the day's specialities. Elderly proprietors were pleased to talk, and when his mother came to stay she found him thoroughly at home. In the fervent rugby-playing region, photographs of the international teams of Ireland, England, Wales and Scotland, as well as France, were on display in bars, and mutual love of the game drew him to Monsieur Hours, a congenial master at the Lycée who taught English and had the build of a prop forward. Television reception in Mende was poor because of the surrounding crags, and to watch the Five Nations Championship matches they drove higher, to a crowded village bar ten kilometres away.

Jim felt most alive on his own, in the company of Proust, Rimbaud, Goncourt, Malraux, Gide, Sartre and Loti, whose *Pêcheurs d'Islande* had lit the touchpaper at Terra Nova. For warmth he climbed into bed to read, and he rated frugality a bonus: his choices were defining him, the essence of existentialism. The Communist paper *l'Humanité* disappointed with its support for Russian H Bomb tests – 'It dodged *all* the real issues' – but the impact of a major international news story was intensified by semi-isolation. During the censorship controversy in the *Irish Times* he had taken to reading the paper from cover to cover, and two days before his letter was printed, the departure of the first Irish Army battalion for UN duty in the newly independent Congo had been prominently featured, complete with photographic coverage. On 9 November French papers reported that ten of an eleven-man patrol drawn from those troops had been killed in an ambush at Niemba and, in the absence of anyone from Ireland to talk it over with, he brooded obsessively on the massacre. The ill-fated soldiers would continue to spark thoughts of rural barrack life and raw local lads embarking on a role beyond their comprehension, and the horror in the Congo would become the eventual key to *Troubles*, opening the way to his major theme.

The tender clarinet of Sidney Bechet teasing out 'Petite Fleur' accompanied France's tribulations in the Algerian War, relayed by portable radio to his room as atrocity followed atrocity. *The explosions, the detention camps, the torture to extract confessions*. In divided loyalties, tit-for-tat retaliation, opposing justifications for brutality, misjudgements and sheer bad luck, as well as political manoeuvring and the loss of stabilising certainties, magnified by a natural reluctance to accept change – Algeria reminded him of Ireland. Colonial disengagement everywhere, apparently, had the same ugly pattern. By December, when a group of Green Berets wiped out a dozen Algerian villages in reprisal for the killing of two truckloads of police, evoking the Black and Tans, his conclusions about cause and effect were in place.

Limits to acceptable public expenditure and political expediency made a mockery of posters claiming de Gaulle's support for French Algeria, a point rubbed in by every press photograph of the dispossessed *pieds noirs*. Jim soon learned to read between the lines of newspaper accounts, like the terse report shortly before Christmas of twenty-two conscripts found dead beside their truck. In the bars where he sipped a glass of pils and listened, it was common knowledge that the bodies would have been arranged to face Mecca, their genitals stuffed in their mouths and their bellies slashed open and filled with stones. The power of the Viceroy had suddenly become negotiable in Ireland and in India, and France was clearly on a similar track.

As an outsider, he was emotionally uninvolved – *He wanted desperately to feel real anger and real sympathy as an expiation for his pettiness, but he could not* – and he studied local people, deducing that many who felt the visceral response he lacked kept going by concentrating on minutiae. Within a year he was standing aside from Algerian tension himself, and creating a fictional scene involving an Arab around a farcical misunderstanding. *How was he to know?*

Irony was a solitary pleasure and, as anecdotes accumulated,

the wistful punchline 'How was I to know?' was a perfect
finishing touch. The exemplary headmaster and his wife were
reinvented in anecdotes as cuckold and sexual predator after a
Sunday spent with them searching for mushrooms in the woods,
and his landlady would later be portrayed as drifting into his
room in her dishabille upon the flimsiest excuse. In fact as the
months went on his letters out bristled with complaints about
the climate and the lack of girls, as the old rancour – for the old
reasons – gathered force. He had set the draft of his polio
experiences aside in favour of completing a commercially viable
novel before he returned, and his inability to find a starting point
brought on stomach cramps, even in class. He had been telling
people for years that he was a writer; was it possible that he had
been deluding himself all along?

It was thanks to the sympathy and encouragement of the
Lycée headmaster, he acknowledged years later, that he made his
first serious attempt at producing a book. The approach of
Professeur Jean Thibault-Chambault was the exact opposite of
Oxford's Professor Shackleton, and the headmaster's smiling
assertion that Jim would produce an excellent book was backed
by Sunday lunches *en famille* and the advice to get started
without further ado. During the second term Jim responded,
deciding that the setting would be France and the theme that of
identity, as the topic of first novels had always to address.

He had boasted to Oxford friends that he was going to write a
potboiler, but instead a tale of attrition and loss – of letting go –
took hold, heavily influenced by Sartre and the contemporary
French cinema. Sayer, the young hero of *A Man From Elsewhere*, emerged as a Communist journalist assigned by his editor
to blacken the reputation of a dying novelist and erstwhile fellow
traveller, Sinclair Regan, with the aim of avoiding the bad
publicity for the Party which would result from Catholic honours on his death. Acting on rumours of wartime collaboration,
Sayer's brief was to dig up details while accepting Regan's
hospitality, but his encounter with the mentally alert writer
and his daughter Gretchen would wipe out his own convictions.

Jim wrote with none of the ironic humour of his later work,
but the intended action-packed narrative soon changed focus,
moulded by his own experiences instead of issues of the day. As

he sought to take hold of the plot, the tug of war between the Soviet bloc and the West gave way to the struggle between compassion and the need for distance from those who laid too constricting a claim. And he equipped Regan with his personal credo, that *the whole object of a man's life should be to transcend himself by living at the extreme outer edge of endeavour, by will-power going beyond his capacities, creating more out of himself than the component parts.*

Exhaustion steadily accumulated, in tandem with a new craving for affection. Despite his protests about the lack of girls, he saw something of Marguerite, a placid teacher who introduced him to the bal musette, and got to know her friends, who included Albert, another master, and two sisters, the Bouloir girls. One of Marguerite's initial attractions was her self-sufficiency, which put him under no obligation, but superficial exchanges could not fill the sudden void, and the imminent prospect of leaving Mende to take up his post for the next academic year in Toulon, far from Thibault-Chambault's moral support, was grim.

Toulon was a sprawling naval port on the Mediterranean, massive, hectic and alien in comparison to Mende, as was the Interidant du Lycée in the Boulevard de Strasbourg. The vitriolic racialism behind graffiti and everyday street confrontations was a shock, and he had trouble understanding the flat southern accent. Only when it was too late to change accommodation did he comprehend the mental strain attached to Chalet Amélie, 35 Avenue Vert-Coteau, a modest nineteenth-century house of character towards the rear of the town, within easy walking distance of the school. Avenue Vert-Coteau, belying its rural name, ran right beside the busy mainline railway tracks.

'I live here in a strange little house', he noted before his spirits plummeted, 'with an old lady whose husband was a *cheminot* and who recites to me poetically the names of the trains that thunder past the house all the time. "Celui-la vient de Strasbourg, Vintimille, Beziers, Marseille, Bordeaux . . ." She even tells the time by them. I have a kitchen and a bedroom with a giant bed, as vast as Asia, from which I find it virtually impossible to rise in the mornings. Outside my window there's a palm-tree and a capricious tortoise wanders about the garden . . . Towards the end of the month it will be hard to resist the temptation of whipping it into a saucepan and making some mock turtle soup.'

At first the glare of sun and shimmering sea was mesmerising, intensified by re-reading Camus, and responding to the sensory pull he yearned to put his slow-moving novel aside for a story about 'the black side' of the sun, going so far as to sketch out the plot. But the need to produce a saleable book was too strong to ignore for long, and he sat at his typewriter in the small kitchen – 'bathed in blue, orange or plain sunlight from the extraordinary window-wall – baroque lavatory school of architecture' – wondering if he would ever be able to write anything worthwhile. The train timetable played havoc with the work routine he had established in Mende, and so indelible would be its impact that in his third book, *A Girl in the Head*, the hero similarly flinches from each *cataclysm of the express*.

'Sometime in the early hours of this morning,' he wrote in early November, 'I woke up and told myself that I must get out of the habit of thinking of myself as "becoming" and think of myself instead as "being". It is so hard to drop the idea that a big future is in store when life will begin and that the present is, so to speak, all the future we can expect – with variations, of course.' Within a couple of hours he developed a feverish cold, resulting in another unproductive day. 'I am more inclined', he added dejectedly, 'to think of myself as "having been".'

His rapidly approaching birthday held double reproach, because not only did he have too little to show for a man of twenty-seven, but an alarming new hair loss was emphasising the youthfulness of the *étudiantes* he taught. 'I must face the fact that I no longer have any claims on the sort of girls one sees,' he mourned late at night in the privacy of his kitchen, narrow shoulders and grey hair reflected back by the shiny glass wall. 'Beautiful shapely brown legs and chic hairstyles and smartly dressed, often in suits (the fashion of halfpleated skirts I like very much) but now too *young* for me . . . I may not have had my share of that age-group, but I just have to pass on.' He watched girls longingly in the cafés he frequented, tantalised by gamine sensuality, large sensitive eyes and hair that was long and fine – 'very, very beautiful'. One girl stood out from the crowd for her slenderness and her vitality, but despite his loneliness he made no move. 'I think that any relationship with me would be something of a disaster for her in much the same way as it was for Judy (whom she resembles quite a lot in some respects)' he speculated glumly. 'Perhaps she is simply a Judy returned to health for me? But at what age can a leopard still change its spots?' On 26 November, after a week of torpor, he inched up to page 56 of a projected 200-page first draft, and it marked the turning of a corner. 'I can no longer go along in the same unchanged manner,' he resolved.

Classes at La Rode, as the huge lycée was known, were a distraction, and his exasperation showed. In the staffroom his barbed anecdotes created fellow feeling with temporary teachers of both sexes from America, Australia, Italy and England; in his notebook not one, however, emerged well from scrutiny. 'Low intellectual force', 'naive', 'smug', 'manipulative', 'self-absorbed', 'hypochondriacal', 'plain', 'predictable' . . . After school hours he widened his field of study to include the student Communist leader and a mixed bunch of disciples, and seized every opportunity to examine his collection of human frailties at closer quarters. The cold analysis of those private conclusions ran counter to his mild and reassuring manner.

'Dull in a sinister kind of way', one couple was dismissed, while a quiet student won mention for 'the vapidity with which her parents procreated themselves after the war'. Another girl, 'permanently dissatisfied', was scorned for being 'a competent mimic of the lower classes', although one grandmother incurred his wrath for being a 'stupid, fat peasant'. Jim had always prompted confidences and now he sat in judgement, stirring the conversational pot. The female characters in his novel were the hardest to envisage, and he took a particular interest in feminine attitudes to sex and power. 'She said with obvious pleasure that she could twist [her boyfriend] about her little finger, that he was crazy about her and boasted twice that he had gone on the bottle when he thought she was being unfaithful. I pointed out that most girls would prefer a man they could not twist around their little fingers and she backpedalled lightly, but the damage was done.' Head tipped back, a little to one side, in the way that made even good friends want to pass muster, he looked for poseurs and found them everywhere. 'Really quite depressing,' he scribbled after one fruitful session. 'It made me think, although God knows I had a low opinion of the place, how much more mature their counterparts in Oxford seemed.'

But out of their company the tables were turned. He felt so oppressed that existence in Toulon 'did not add up to a life', and over-identification with Luc – Gretchen's discontented film-director admirer in the book – whose role he was enlarging, sapped him further. 'Luc has got so used to seeing everything in camera-shots that he has lost contact with reality', he noted despondently at one point. 'There's a lot of the Farrell syndrome in this character.' As Christmas and New Year's Eve came round again, hedged about with awful anniversaries, he identified with the character completely. 'Really my situation is basically the same,' he analysed, prepared to judge himself as harshly as he did others. 'I have become hypnotised by the externals to such an extent that I have become completely impotent.'

It was as if he had been firmly sealed in his skin once and for all and the last chance of . . . escaping from himself had been withdrawn. Later Jim would refer to this season as a flirtation with darkness, made bleaker by a brief relationship in January – 'le mois de Françoise' – with one of the Communist coterie which ended in recrimination on both sides. 'She described me as a "larve", herself as a "chrysalide, qui devient papillon",' he summed it up at the time. 'She believed that I had a fixation about myself and needed only a passive admiring audience to reflect myself back. This may have been disturbingly near the truth. But from the way she talked with contempt about other people of all kinds I could not help thinking that she shared my egomania with me.'

Repelled by solitary blank days at his typewriter, he took up a general invitation to drinks at the Cercle Naval, which led to cocktail parties aboard visiting American aircraft carriers, the *Centaur* and the *Tidesurge*. Paradise it was to be aboard, surrounded by lovely French girls and buckets of whiskey. 'When I was already well lit-up, I had two long and over-earnest conversations with a couple of mildly misfitting officers who had been seduced by the fact that I had said I was a writer.' After the hangover came accentuated reality: it was dishonest to make such a claim if he was incapable of producing a book. *And the unbearable knowledge of how everything must end, that there was only one way in which everything could end – and all the other things I'd known, that people are contemptible, that hope is a lie, that life is a sordid charade . . .*

During January Jim thought seriously about giving up the book he was working on, and blocked out a replacement. *Letters to My Keeper* would be more tenuous and 'infinitely more wild', being set around the Dostoyevskian nightmare of a sane prisoner in an asylum musing on the diverse scenarios that might have led to his committal. But with concentration wrecked by introspection and the racket of the trains, he put that outline, too, aside. 'The trouble, as I see it, is that I really have no fixed personality when I'm alone by myself (as opposed to when I'm talking to someone face to face – then I can be the person that the other person expects me to be),' he pondered wearily. 'Somerset Maugham says somewhere that he understands why the Church refused to bury actors in consecrated ground up to the 18th century: the actors he knew gave him the impression of having no soul offstage. I think this is just as true of writers. And Fitzgerald says, too, "A writer has got to be too many people if he's going to be any good." '

The hair loss was leading to patches of baldness which added to his misery, and when he remembered something similar during the homesick start at Terra Nova he saw one practical move, at least. The surgery sign of a doctor was on his daily route, and snapping shut *À la recherche du temps perdu* when his turn came, he was shown in. 'Une malade sévère!' his second French benefactor exclaimed.

Dr Delbos, a devotee of Proust, explained that alopecia areata was caused by stress, and would clear up of its own accord once the noise of the trains was removed. He prescribed two tickets for the opera, taking them out of his wallet with a shrug that indicated he had no need of them himself, and *The Leopard* by Lampedusa, a French edition of which was promptly handed across. Settling down to matters of greater interest, Delbos leaned back in his chair and Jim followed suit. 'He has intelligent views on the need for unified Europe,' he approved in his journal, charmed by the doctor's greying Errol Flynn moustache. 'His father fought in 1914 and he in '40, and later was in the

Resistance. But he insists that the war must be forgotten in the common interest. He said, not too convincingly, that for him racialism is merely a matter of aesthetics – that black and white don't go together but can live side by side; he also said that when young, if he had been offered a belle négresse he would willingly have slept with her.'

One visit led to another, at which medical anecdotes were varied by incidents from Delbos's skirmishes as a Conseilleur Municipal of Toulon, and as the alopecia slowly improved Jim became intrigued by the role of intuition and psychology in healing. The influence of Dr Delbos would stretch far into the future, from the shaping of Jim's style through his admiration for Lampedusa, to the development of Dr McNab's medical outlook in *The Siege of Krishnapur* and its intended culmination in *The Hill Station*.

'I had a mild "crise de dépression nerveuse" around Christmas,' he excused his silence in a letter on 21 February. 'So I've been lurking in a darkened room talking to phantoms and juggling with imaginary thunderbolts for the last few weeks – or is it months? Anyway, I've now decided that my old widow and her dog (called Pussy) have been getting on my nerves long enough and have decided to go and live elsewhere. Just where, I haven't yet decided . . . Physically I have been feeling quite rickety, a new and disagreeable sensation for me. The temptation to crawl away into a hole and wait for eternity is very strong.' In March the mistral hit Toulon, distorting concentration further, but halfway through the month he moved into a cheap room in the Hotel Sainte Hélène, on the Boulevard St Hélène which was far from passing trains and down near the old town and the port, and dared to believe that he might complete the first draft by Easter. The spidery scrawl of his recent handwriting was replaced by the clear lettering regained in Mende.

Coinciding with the move, the Algerian War was officially ended with the signing of a ceasefire, and Jim's interest was whetted by Delbos's keen dislike of de Gaulle and his own attendance at a recent presidential visit to Toulon. Despite the crowds in the square there had been little applause that day and de Gaulle, looking old and grey, had sung 'La Marseillaise' off-key. 'It was rather pathetic,' he had jotted down. 'For those who like, as I do, big men trying to roll boulders up mountain slopes the whole event was full of sadness.' With the ceasefire in place he again scanned the oblivious faces of passers-by, and as control passed to the rebel Algerian Liberation Army as soon as the French were committed to pulling out, the continuing parallel with Ireland was plain. In Toulon an increase in the numbers of unemployed army veterans matched the newspaper photographs of dispossessed colonists with crying children clinging to their arms; he knew all too well about having to cope with change on diminished resources.

Exercise was important, and now that his daily quota of words was at last consistent, so, more than ever, he needed the momentum of routine. One afternoon, as he emerged from the doorway of the hotel for his daily walk in the teeth of the mistral, which blew even harder so near the sea, there was a screech of brakes and he saw an old lady knocked down by a motorbike, which accelerated away. 'She collapsed in the road like a stranded whale', he recorded, 'and I had to struggle with her to the nearby pharmacie with blood streaming down her face and all the time this fiendish wind digging at our clothes.' The encounter would be pivotal four years later for the structure of *A Girl in the Head*, but it ruined his day's output at the time, a setback he blamed squarely on the mistral. 'Curiously enough, whichever direction I walk in I always seem to have it full in my face. But this may be sheer imagination – a definition of myself, so to speak.'

As his Easter deadline neared and the wind – 'I don't think I know anything more chilling or demoralising' – showed no sign of abating, he felt he could stand Toulon no longer, 'novel or no novel'. But a bulky package with American stamps unexpectedly arrived in the post, and inside was a lengthy manuscript by Russell. He read it enviously – 'a modern Faust – marvellous!' – and sent it back with praise, redoubling his own efforts. Bob Cumming, too, had made contact by airmail, urging him to call on his brother's young widow, Patricia, a talented poet who had moved with her two small daughters to Paris in the aftermath of her husband's sudden death. Reflecting that it was a long time since he had been with the kind of people he liked to be with, he set up an Easter Paris visit as incentive. In early April, without warning, the mistral dropped, and confidence that he would be able to finish in time surged back. He had arranged to stay with Patricia – Patsy – on 13 April but at the last minute postponed the trip by four days, and worked round the clock. After typing the last sentence he found it impossible to relax, and set off anxiously, promising himself that the breathing space would enable him to look freshly at the book as a whole as soon as he got back.

Patsy Cumming turned out to be as creatively driven as he was, but her continuing grief over her husband's death was painful to see. Taking to her at once, Jim made a mental resolution never to let a woman invest her entire happiness in him. At night he slept on the floor of her small apartment in rue Bouilloux-Lafont and he did his best to help, waking early to buy fresh croissants for breakfast, reading aloud to her daughters, winning over their cat Minou, and teasing Patsy about her impulsive driving from the front passenger seat of her Citroën deux-chevaux. At the bookshop Shakespeare and Company, the scene two years earlier of his interview with William Burroughs, the owner failed to recognise him and she was indignant on his behalf, a sign that he was helping her to forget her loss. 'I imagine he knew me but suspected I was a fake or a hanger-on', he said, pretending to take offence, and they agreed the book-shop was only interested in the derrière-garde.

Briefly Patsy's world became his, and he met Alan Cumming, a young cousin just down from university who was torn between divinity and art as a career. Through her, too, he got to know Franz Beer, a forceful Austrian artist who, with his German wife Claire and their children, welcomed guests to his studio-apartment with a carafe of good wine on the table, whatever the hour. Franz and Claire were rumoured to have been tortured by the Gestapo, a dark layer that led straight to the collaboration twist of *A Man From Elsewhere*. Together they all spent a day in the Bois de Meudon, and everything took on a literary gloss. Lying back contentedly in the spring sunshine, Jim pictured them as characters out of *The Alexandria Quartet* – 'As with Durrell's books I think there's something a bit voulu about us. We all take ourselves very seriously' – and instructed Patsy to take her children to the Luxembourg Gardens to play, in the footsteps of literary geniuses of the last two centuries. That night he wrote a short poem about transience, and at once his good humour drained away. The happy moment was already sealed off, irretrievably, and the next day he was impervious to everyone's feelings but his own.

Back in Toulon, he began rewriting straight away, and at long distance apologised to Patsy for his behaviour. 'These periods of "feeling strange" are a fairly frequent occurrence with me and can make me hard to get along with,' he said, attempting to restore the light touch. 'In any case, it all makes for a better display of a cross-section of my character if that should interest you at all Racine-wise or Alexander Korda-wise – god forbid.' He slipped the address of her flat into the first page as he retyped, one of many coded salutes to friends that recur throughout his books, and as La Rode was closed for the holidays he worked on without interruption in a state of rising exhilaration. By the end of the third week of May the manuscript was honed to his satisfaction, and he typed *James Farrell* beneath *A Man from Elsewhere*, dedicated it to his parents, and posted it off to Chatto and Windus in London that same day. He had equipped himself with the publisher's address before setting out for France, little realising that it would be almost two years before he used it.

In the swirl of anticlimax that immediately possessed him, Patsy's reply arrived in the form of a parcel. Inside was an expensive copy of Joyce's *Collected Letters* that he had admired in Shakespeare and Company, accompanied by a letter taking him to task point by point and rejecting his apology. He dashed off a long retort – 'And who's racked? I find myself very balanced and normal. And was there something I should have apologised to Franz and Claire for? How alarming . . .' – and within two hours was aghast, swept along by a current of emotion he had never experienced before. 'A word of apology for the silly letter,' he wrote hastily. 'I'm sure you divined that it was more motivated by panic than by anything else, but I could have merely said that I didn't want to talk about Life as it pertained to myself without being so tortuously facetious about it . . . The fact is that my mind goes blank when trying to recall conversations in which I have been put, however indirectly, on trial . . .' 'This is ridiculous,' he tried again later. 'I never [meant] to get mixed up in a wrangle with you over – over what, exactly? Or to hurt you in any way.' Long after Patsy had forgiven him, his super-sensitivity in the wake of intensive writing would continue to take him by surprise.

Now that his book was about to come under professional scrutiny, his own assessment swung around to rating it fairly competent, but not very good. Plots for a follow-up were discouragingly elusive, and to be in a vacuum was an odd sensation after two years of single-mindedness. 'I'm rather bored at the moment,' he deduced, 'as I don't seem to be able to sort out how I want to write my next book. I do know that I want it to be funny though, and at the moment the author himself isn't feeling very funny. Perhaps as time goes on I'll feel funnier, as opposed to strange, which I feel more and more.' On edge for the reply, he found Toulon parochial and unbearably hot – 'beastly town for weather' – and fired off applications for teaching posts in several European capitals with the intention of renting somewhere in Paris for the summer. But as the weeks drifted by and no publisher's acknowledgement came, he realised that there was no alternative to returning to England to monitor progress – or lack of it – at first hand.

'I'm feeling extremely nervous and restless and (yes) racked again', he said, outlining the new plan to Patsy. 'I feel that a change of countries immediately is required to maintain my mental equilibrium. I can say with pride that I don't know anyone who shows more indulgence to his mental equilibrium than myself. That will have to stop too. Somewhere in my novel one of the more racked and sympathetic (to me) characters says that he would just like to crawl back into a nice warm womb somewhere, preferably with lots of tinsel and fairy lights . . . My physicist friend Russell McCormmach once commented that he thought that in the long run over-sensitive, over-artistic people would fail to reproduce themselves, becoming impotent, and be cast aside by the life force.'

Worn down by the lack of response from Chatto and Windus, Jim anonymously pulled out of Toulon at the end of term. His period there had proved that there could be no let-up in the frugal and solitary way of life, and confirmed that he was right to be responsible only for himself. The punishing effort involved in completing his book had come as a shock, and he now understood why he was drawn to big men pushing boulders up mountain slopes. Asked many years later to define the human experience, he replied without hesitation that it was hostility all around, with the individual in a rather temporary shelter. But writing to Patsy when he had made the transition, he put a brave face on what might be in store. 'Next year,' he toasted defiantly, 'as I say every year, may be *our* year.'

CHAPTER TEN

The Slow, Dangerous Ascent
1963

Gary Arnott, bespectacled economist, had a good memory for faces. In the summer of 1962 he was with Rothschild's Bank, and weekend visits back to Oxford were a relaxation of the past. He blended in with the bowler hats and rolled umbrellas of the Square Mile, the archetypal City gent, but one clue to his singularity was his choice of a scooter, for speed in traffic, instead of the expensive car he could so easily afford. He was weaving along the inside lane by Victoria Station on his Vespa one June day when his attention was caught by a gaunt, tanned figure emerging slowly from the station. Pulling up at once, he shouted, 'Jim!'

Meeting Gary was fortuitous, because he had nowhere to stay and no clear plan in mind. He gladly let Arnott take charge and accepted a lift to his large flat in Bayswater, relieved to find a bed in London so effortlessly. They knew each other well enough to rule out any sexual misunderstanding, and when occasional future gossip misinterpreted Jim's solitary lifestyle and limp mannerisms as homosexuality, Gary was highly amused. 'If Jim had been in any way susceptible,' he always put the record straight with scorn, 'I would have known *all* about it.'

Set apart even more now by his Gallic shrug, his use of phrases like '*Sans blague*', and his fondness for Gauloises and wearing existentialist black, Jim's most pressing need was to find a source of income. The fact that his parents were still subsidising him, underwriting travel and providing a small allowance, was a sore and complex subject. With the idea that journalism might provide a solution, he went to stay with Brian Knox Peebles, who had moved to Sussex with his young bride, Rose, and was a cub reporter on the *Kent & Essex Courier*; Jim had been an usher at their wedding, along with David Caute. He accompanied Brian on his rounds for several days, and hastily abandoned the idea. 'My final decision,' he confided by post to Russell, 'was that 95% is utterly futile and that the 5% which isn't is done by people who are probably not professional journalists anyway. [It] is boring and petty and leaves a nasty taste in your mouth.'

Journalism was not the only prospect to prove illusory. He had looked foward to remeeting old friends, but though he found Brian as congenial as ever, the fact that he was married made a difference. Jim was so curt with Rose that Brian had to leap to her defence on one occasion, pointing out furiously that she was only nineteen. Jim apologised and employed his charm, but mentally re-arranged the perimeters of the relationship. Brian Pearce had married while working in America – 'Remember Burgoyne and colonise the easy way', Jim had cabled at the time – and at the sight of his contentment he felt excluded. But that was quickly followed by relief.

In July a noncommital letter from Chatto and Windus invited him to tea, and he arrived punctually, conscious of being inside a publishing house for the first time. 'It was a near miss, apparently,' he noted afterwards. 'Of the three directors who read it, two were in favour including Cecil Day Lewis. The third, although he didn't manage to make himself very clear, seemed to think it was technically OK but hollow inside . . . He got me on a sensitive nerve there. This thought has been haunting me for 3 or 4 years now. Anyway when I was finally ushered out of the holy of holies . . . clutching my manuscript in one hand, my raincoat in the other and trying to shake hands with them all, they paid me the dubious compliment of wishing me bad luck with other publishers so that they could see my next one.'

All was not lost, though, as someone at Chatto had sent the book on to Secker and Warburg – 'paradoxical in the circumstances'. Five weeks passed without hearing anything further, however, and by September Jim was prepared to lower his sights. 'My feeling', he noted glumly, 'is that I should find some lesser publisher to take it. This may be a hallucination though. I've long since given up placing any faith in this sort of deduction

[but] I could certainly use a hundred quid.' Nothing had come up in the way of a 'reasonable' job by then and he had camped out in a succession of uncomfortable flats, not wishing to sponge off Gary indefinitely. 'September Song' always moved him with its cadences of transience; that year the words took on added poignancy.

In the same week, however, both problems were solved. He found a bargain-priced basement flat at 48 Redcliffe Square, and a job teaching English in a Berlitz school. 'Fairly dull', he groaned to Russell, 'although it has its moments. The main trouble with it is that I'm so exhausted after doing a straight 3 hours in the morning and another 3 in the afternoon that I can't see myself being able to write a line. I'm just beginning to realise how ideal was the job in France as far as the work-money-time relationship goes.'

But there was a side to teaching languages that appealed to his competitive spirit, and on good days he thought of it as fencing, using his wits as a foil. Translation provided a useful intellectual workout – 'which I need to convince myself I'm doing something' – and he took up German once again, motivated after two years of stilted correspondence with a German penfriend, Gabrielle. He had met her originally while she was au-pairing in Dublin and re-met her towards the end of his stay in France, finding her much prettier than he remembered. 'A little more successful than these things usually are with me,' he wrote after she came to England for a visit. Intent on mastering the language more quickly than another Berlitz teacher, he began by comparing Maigret stories in the English, French and German translations; detective work indeed.

A few students came to his flat for extra-mural lessons, but run-of-the-mill work meant facing a mixed age-group from a wide range of countries. A pedantic German philology professor with glinting steel-rimmed glasses rarely missed a lesson, and each time his hand was raised Jim braced himself. 'Which are the six English words with a silent "H"?' he was asked one day. The subtle asides that were his stock in trade drew no response, but it was not time wasted, as the quirks of foreign speech in his novels would show.

Chips with Everything was on in the West End, and as he

bought his supper in Charlie's Place, an Earls Court workers' cafe around the corner from his flat, he mordantly compared the menu. 'Oh England, as D.H. Lawrence would have said, meaning something or other,' he made notes for typed letters to Russell McCormmach, moving aside the sauce bottles to write more easily at the plastic-covered table. Hating the autumn damp, he gulped down hot sweet tea with the ubiquitous chips, and lingered on in the fuggy cafe among the other regulars, mentally elsewhere.

'I found *Henderson the Rain King* by Saul Bellow very good and it started a few interesting trains of thought for my own stuff.' . . . 'I've got hold of Lowry's book of oddments *Hear Us O Lord from Heaven Thy Dwelling Place* which turned out to be disappointing.' In place of the stained menu he propped his latest favourite, and the Penguin paperback of *Under the Volcano* was usually near to hand. Deaf to cheerful banter and the clatter of plates, he tuned in to Lowry's 'infectious atmosphere of despair' and scribbled on. How about, he suggested to his old collaborator, a play about Pétain? 'I think we both stand a better chance of getting [it] through the indifference-barrier *together* than separately. I long to be working hard at something again with somebody. The thought of getting up early in the morning and working at something I *like* is just unbelievably good . . . Do think seriously about this. It might mean a measure of salvation for both of us if you can get together the fare.' Pétain was an uncommercial subject, but the lack of response from any publisher about *A Man from Elsewhere* had not trimmed Jim's attitude to compromise. 'I don't want to be known as a trash writer', he would counter to well-meant suggestions.

Oxford contemporaries who were moving ahead 'as if on strings' got a similarly curt dismissal, and the constant topic of ski parties set his teeth on edge. He considered himself to be on one side of the great divide and everyone else on the other, but knew exactly how he must appear himself. 'They have been inviting me (I suspect in order to add a little off-beat colour) to their dinner parties,' he let off steam. 'I sit, tieless, scruffy and speechless, while the other guests take it in turns to relate with delicate wit and breeding their various machinations in the world of endeavour. One speaks, the others sit with an interested smile clipped to their lips and inwardly rehearse while waiting their turns.' Jim would smile back and prompt and slip off early, envisaging himself as a performing bear and pondering the mutual exploitation throughout history of patron and artist.

In Gary's flat, conversely, parties fielded 'all kinds of eccentrics and illuminati and fallen angels', making him feel part of the Establishment in comparison. Juggling both extremes became a game and he relished the juxtaposition, with its extra frisson of hiding each world from the other. He took pride in having escaped English conditioning – 'I've lived the greater part of my life among non-English people, unless you count the Irish as English', he ticked off one foreigner who took him at face value – and the French interval now threw into stark relief the separate characteristics of the English as a race.

Secker and Warburg wrote to say they were turning down *A Man from Elsewhere*. With appropriate timing, the letter arrived as dense smog clamped down outside. Unaffected by traffic brought to a standstill, the closure of London airport and the cancellation of trains, Jim brooded in his basement room on the likelihood that his book had been rejected not on grounds of merit, which he could have understood, but because its profit margins would be too low. 'I don't think I'm being unjust,' he commented angrily, and made a foray with his scarf wrapped over his nose and mouth to post off the manuscript again. This time he chose Hutchinson, in the second rank, and his outlook was more fatalistic.

'One hopeful sign has been emerging from the general degradation of the last months,' he wrote to Russell from Dublin, where he dutifully returned for Christmas. 'And that is that I'm caring less and less about the public success of what I write, and more and more about my own opinion of its quality. One day I may even give up sending things to publishers or, rather, not care whether I send them or not . . . Like you, I have also come to the conclusion that my personal hard times have exhausted their usefulness as literary material and have become very much more interested in the possibility of creating a (possibly fantastic) world of my own for my novels.'

The temperature fell further, and in the New Year his morale followed suit. In spite of the brave words, his confidence was at rock bottom, and with it had gone the will to work which he had always taken for granted. On 23 January he bought a fresh typewriter ribbon and tried yet another start on a new book, but after half an hour of staring at the popping gas fire he was no further on. 'At the moment I'm caught between the belief that novels aren't for giving information (whatever else they may be for) and the belief that the only way out of the problem is by artificial tinkering with style', he wrote, reaching out to Russell. 'Perhaps the only way out of it is to abandon novel-writing . . . the above lines give off the musty odour of those dull ravings that a lot of minor writers are given to . . . Teaching seems increasingly futile. I can't remember ever spending so long without attempting something positive.'

Insomnia magnified the deadlock, and he took to walking all night in the bitter cold, as far afield as Putney and Notting Hill *tasting his own destruction*. Shop windows reflected back an unshaven, hollow-eyed failure, so he kept where possible to residential streets. Although realistic enough to agree that emotions were conditioned by books and films – *You reached a stage where you were no longer sure whether you were having the ideas or whether the ideas were having you* – he was pulled irresistibly towards pessimism and despair. Emerging from Ingmar Bergman's *Through a Glass, Darkly*, convinced it was in a class of its own for awakening neurotic impulses, he headed straight back to his icy room to finish reading *The Tin Drum*. 'Monumentally depressing.'

The arctic spell had notched up thirty consecutive days by the start of February and, unlike the Baffin Bay experience, Jim was ill-equipped to cope. By day he largely led an interior existence, reading newspapers when not teaching and finding 'trivia' compelling. He noted reports of birds frozen upside-down in ditches and the discovery of the body of a middle-aged woman who had died of exposure in her living room; then came the news of the suicide of Sylvia Plath. It was the bleakest, longest winter he could remember.

Patsy had returned to America with her daughters; Bob Cumming was in Thailand as an aid volunteer, and Gabrielle was in Munich. Jim half-heartedly followed up advertisments for jobs in Germany and Sweden, and the idea of living on a shoestring on a Greek island became enormously appealing. 'I detest life in England,' he wrote to Patsy Cumming. 'This is largely because all the people I knew at Oxford and Cambridge have moved straight to lucrative fascinating jobs on the *Observer, Sunday Times* etc. They invite me to parties to give me useless advice and tell me to get jobs like theirs, because that is where true happiness lies – as if I didn't know. I couldn't stand another winter [here]. This one has been unbelievably terrible for me and is still going on regardless, and the English I find increasingly hard to take.'

Overnight, miraculously, everything changed. A letter arrived from Hutchinson to say that *A Man from Elsewhere* had been accepted for publication in the New Authors series, and that £50 was due on the signing of the contract, with a further £100 on publication in September. The letter was signed by Graham Nicol, and Jim immediately rang and made an appointment to see him in the company offices in Great Portland Street. At 6pm, when the cheap rates came into effect, he rang his parents from a callbox. 'Mum,' he shouted excitedly as soon as the phone was picked up at the other end, 'I've got a taker!'

Hutchinson's New Authors imprint specialised in discovering unknown writers, rejecting 99 per cent of manuscripts submitted. 'He or she must speak with a fresh voice and show promise of further work', the chairman Robert Lusty was on record as saying. 'The one-book writer is too common a phenomenon. Nowadays what the literary scene needs is young writers who are talented, not willing to follow the well-trodden paths, and who have something to say.' Graham Nicol turned out to be in his early thirties, puckish and impatient. The New Authors imprint was his own creation and, despite the chairman's public support, there had been intense opposition internally to the list and that hostility continued. Undaunted, Nicol chivied and nurtured his authors with the aim of getting them next into Hutchinson's main stream. 'I could see right away that *A Man from Elsewhere* was out of the ordinary run of first novels,' was his explanation for including Jim. 'It was, in the best sense of the word, a highly professional piece of work, without a trace of the self-indulgence that one normally associates with young writers.'

The contact was drawn up on 19 February and signed within a week, opening up the prospect of pooled annual royalties at 10 per cent up to 5,000 copies sold, and Jim impulsively gave notice to the Berlitz college. 'It helps me to think of myself as "a writer" rather than a naïve idiot,' he excused himself. He gloried in being, as he put it, through the publication barrier at last, and then reaction kicked in. 'I spent about two weeks in steadily decreasing euphoria and by last weekend I was as tense and wretched as I had ever been', he confided to Russell in March. 'I would feel better about my book if I thought it was really good but, as I think I said to you before, I don't. Besides, it doesn't really seem to belong to me any more.' Other people's reservations, however, were dealt with sharply. Brian Knox Peebles seemed unimpressed after being allowed to see the typescript, and Rose compounded matters by venturing that she had not understood the ending. 'You don't deserve to read it,' he said, dismissing their opinions with contempt.

Informal meetings for everyone connected with the imprint were held every Monday evening in The Albany, a pub adjacent to Hutchinson's pre-war building. Jim would call in around 6pm, when the session was already in progress in the right-hand bar, and he left early, knowing that many would still be there at closing time with Fred the landlord's blessing. 'It was a time of poverty and loneliness, so we talked life and literature, not business, and drank a great deal, mainly beer,' another of Nicol's protégés, Maureen Duffy, recalled. 'Jim didn't drink as much as the rest of us. He was very quiet and I was fond of him, as far as that is possible without actually knowing someone, and he would have known that I was gay, which perhaps to him was a relief. We were both passionate about our writing and in some ways I felt we were alike – both having an English/Irish background and starting off together.'

Under Nicol's tutelage, everyone was writing experimentally, and consciously trying to outstrip the stereotypical Hampstead novel. Maureen, for instance, had recently been persuaded to switch from plays to novels. Those in funds bought the rounds, and Jim found the companionship stimulating, glad to be in the same boat, for once, as everyone else. Two evening classes a week for London County Council paid his way, and he was laconically investigating summer courier work for American tourists – 'a deadly job, I believe' – when the Albany meetings threw up a better idea. The names of literary agents were regularly bandied about, and taking Nicol's tip he made an appointment with Jonathan Clowes, who represented Len Deighton and Doris Lessing. Nicol advised that Clowes was always interested in new names, and pointed out that he had signed up Maureen Duffy.

Jim expected a middle-aged wheeler-dealer, but Jonathan Clowes was unassuming, reflective and impressively well-read. He was not much older than Jim himself, and made no secret of having left school at fifteen and worked as a house painter till the age of thirty, claiming that he had only survived his first year as an agent by taking on occasional decorating jobs and setting up a rota of his authors to run the office in his absence. He promoted books hard, preferred film options as a package deal, and at a static time in publishing had identified the extra earning potential from scripts for television and film. His reputation was for ruthlessness, and Jim approached his office in Upper Brook Street warily.

'He was quite worried when he first came to see me,' Clowes confirmed. 'He'd heard I gave a lot of editorial advice and also that I involved authors in promotion and interfered generally. Agents weren't expected to meddle with jackets or promotion – that was bad form. As for me, I thought Jim showed great potential, and that's why I took him on.' Authors were expected to do well enough to justify the investment of time and expense, and Jim viewed the 10 per cent levy on his earnings in the same light, anticipating an increased dividend in return. Since *A Man from Elsewhere* was already in the pipeline their working relationship would not start properly until the next book, but the thorny subject of editorial advice was raised and Clowes got the impression that Jim was keen for him to be involved. Promotion was also mentioned, and guardedly Jim agreed.

Shortly before publication a single interview took place. 'A girl with spots asked me if I wrote with a typewriter or in longhand, and said she knew that Sayer wasn't really a communist,' he related, owning up to his tongue-in-cheek approach. ' "You mean that you knew he was one of us," I said. "That's right," she said.' His remark that he did not think teaching

English to foreign students was quite his vocation was reported
in all seriousness, proving that irony was a hazardous commodity, but the interview was his first objective glimpse of himself in
his chosen role. 'Iron grey hair, thin fingers moving restlessly,
sensitive – almost delicate features, many nervous "You knows"
. . .' The photo on the book's dustjacket was more to his liking,
showing him as a young French intellectual. Gazing sideways, in
dark jacket, blue shirt and string tie, the impression he gave was
of a neat and ambitious academic, criticising the system from
within.

A Man from Elsewhere came out on 16 September, without
advertising and listed simply in the *Bookseller* under 'Publications of the Week'. Established authors with simultaneous new
books included Clowes's star client Len Deighton, as well as
Brendan Behan, Bernard Levin, Simon Raven, David Storey and
Iris Murdoch. Sensitive as Jim was to potential confusion with
Studs Lonigan's James T. Farrell, a matter he had taken care to
set straight in his interview, it was galling to find that Michael
Farrell was in posthumous contention with *Thy Tears Might
Cease*, which was being extensively advertised as 'an Irish
masterpiece' in advance. Having dreaded reviews, he began to
wonder if his book would be noticed at all, as it was vying with
the annual major titles aimed at the Christmas market, which
included the BBC bestseller *That Was The Week That Was* and
the brilliantly promoted *Beyond the Fringe*.

But when reviewers did turn their attention towards him, the
experience was excruciating. Some, like the *Daily Telegraph,*
were patronising – 'this first book augurs well for Mr Farrell' –
and others quibbled where they praised. The *Observer* began
well, then said the novel had the stamp of puppetry – 'though
puppetry of a fair order', and the *New Statesman* hit a raw spot
by condemning it as 'unreal and cerebral . . . dreamed up out of
literature and the current French cinema'. 'The novel's chief
weakness', proclaimed *The Times Literary Supplement*, while
allowing that the tale was well told, 'is shared with others which
include a "great writer" among the characters . . . The general
idea is that the only way a twentieth-century man can fulfil
himself is by rigorous individualism in the face of mass ideas,
mass culture . . . but we are not told how one practises rigorous

individualism and survives.'

Jim accepted the verdict gloomily. 'This is, of course, what makes *Elsewhere* finally a failure,' he agreed, 'that I merely described a situation that we all already knew existed without really having anything new to say about it.' But overall he had come out well. 'The extraordinary thing was that the reactions as to its virtues and faults seemed to be entirely haphazard and changing from one review to the next,' he reflected when the ordeal was over. 'I understand now why writers don't read reviews.' Hutchinson viewed the book as a critical success, but no words of praise from Graham Nicol could convince Jim that his first book had not been an outright failure. 'In itself', commented Nicol privately, 'a most unusual attitude for a young writer to take about his own work.'

Painfully self-conscious, Jim walked to each bookshop within his radius to double-check if the familiar cover was on display. He posted off the first of his six free copies to his parents, the second to his brother Robert and the third to Russell, accompanied by a disclaimer. 'For years I've been gloating to myself about the thrill of sending copies to all my friends and enemies, but now that I have some to send I can't be bothered. I don't think it's very good myself, though I think there are some successful pages.' By the time old friends asked him to sign copies, however, he had found a measure of protective colouring. 'Next time give me the 18s and I'll *tell* you the story', he inscribed one for Jack Kirwan, with a flourish.

While discussing the original contract Jim had assured Nicol, and in due course Clowes, that *Elsewhere* would not be his 'last word' on the novel. 'For the moment it's too nebulous for me to describe without talking it to pieces,' he fenced in October, and neither man pressed him. Russell probed at longer distance, and was similarly thrown off the scent. 'The one I'm working on now', Jim eventually answered, 'is still a shapeless salad of ideas and images and obstinately refuses all my attempts to explain to myself what it is all about.' He was buying time, but not for the reason all three presumed. Eroticism, laced with intrigue, was displacing the embryo book.

'If I say I love you, do you mind?/Make an idol of you, do you mind?' London was in the grip of pop music and the Profumo scandal throughout 1963; risk and hedonism were in the air. Jim had monitored the latest rumours through *Private Eye*, listened to gossip in The Albany, and begun attending the impromptu get-togethers thrown by Jonathan Clowes for agency authors, held at the office or his flat in Camden Town. The format of cheap wine, hot soup and the sharing of grouses and ideas paid off in terms of output, and producers and publishers were encouraged to call in as well.

At one of the first evenings there Jim had been introduced to a lanky Etonian named Robin Cook who wrote in rougher guise under the pseudonym Derek Raymond. Cook was charming and elegantly mannered, but he absorbed the red wine like a sponge and talked knowledgeably of drunks and conmen, prostitutes and pornographers. He had renounced Eton at seventeen – 'a den of vice, my dear fellow' – for seedy Soho clubs, and Jim was urged to come on to a party. Clowes, nearby, made a mental note of their rapport. 'Jim was fascinated by all that. He greatly admired the way Robin was able to mix in that milieu.'

As a direct result, Jim met his own callgirl – or part-time whore, as she referred to herself – in the same week that John Profumo, Secretary of State for War, made his first statement to a crowded House of Commons, flanked by Harold Macmillan, the Prime Minister, and Ian Macleod, the Leader of the House. 'The one thing of interest I have to report to you', Jim informed Russell as early as 4 April, 'is that I have been adopted by a couple of pleasant and (relatively) sweet-natured callgirls . . . At the beginning there was a vague idea that I should write their story, but I never really took this seriously as it isn't my line. Anyway, we are now good friends and they have provided me with something of an entrée into the underworld, not to mention first-hand accounts of some of the most unbelievable perversions.'

By the June opening of the trial of Stephen Ward, on the charge of living on the immoral earnings of Christine Keeler and Mandy Rice-Davies, he was ahead on slang and unsurprised by any of the evidence. Some of those on the fringes belonged to his zone of the underworld, and Profumo's resignation four days afterwards had a personal relevance that maximised every detail of the political freefall. By then the confidant had become the sexual partner, and Jim possessed a secret life of his own.

'Anyone I fancied I slept with, and I fancied Jim,' said the callgirl in question many years afterwards. 'I think we were both drunk the first time we went to bed, quite soon after we met.' Lucy, as she was to appear – transformed – in *The Siege of Krishnapur*, was cheerful and uncomplicated, and her common sense made an appealing counterpoint to her uninhibited approach to sex. One image always summed her up for Jim, blended into Botticelli's Venus for *A Girl in the Head* by a visit to the Uffizi.

[She] was standing naked and motionless at the water's edge, with a serene half-smile on her lips as if at the recollection of some pleasant memory. Her slender right hand was raised to cover her breasts . . . The lower part of her body vanished into . . . shimmering vapour [and] when she emerged again it appeared that some of the golden mist had become adhesive and was clinging to the cleft of her thighs. [He] groaned. He had never seen a girl of such beauty.

According to Jim, he came across her standing in the bath one day, looking at herself in a mirror, and glancing up she caught sight of him. 'I've got the prettiest pussy', she called out, 'in the world.'

She was about his own age, with long hair, a neat, well-rounded figure and reassuring regional accent. She laughed easily and was quick on the uptake, claiming that the callgirl set-up suited her 'down to the ground'. She had left school at fourteen and later headed to London against family advice, and after a succession of dull, low-paid jobs had followed a friend's example and set herself up with a flat and a phone. One girl operating from her own premises was not strictly illegal, as it did not qualify as a brothel, and she had no pimp or madam dictating terms; she set tremendous store, as he did, by independence. She read the *Daily Telegraph*, wore lambswool jumpers and modest, well-cut skirts or dresses, and kept her flat in housewifely order. The contrasts in her life had a great appeal for Jim.

'I was very amateurish really,' she said once. 'I'd go at it hell for leather and make money, and then do nothing for a while or spend it all on presents. Another girl would give my phone number, and I never had to advertise. I saw the same punters all the time, because they'd go round the same six or seven girls. Most were solicitors, barristers, a judge or two, rich Jews in the rag trade and some Tory politicians – always Tory, we joked about that. They'd say, "Didn't you think I gave a good speech today? Wasn't it wonderful?" Never mind about how the country was being run.' Her clients also included a duke, some elderly members of the House of Lords, and a few film and television celebrities, and her bills were generally taken care of by a businessman who paid up whether she saw him or not.

The ambience fascinated Jim, and in *A Girl in the Head* the callgirl's stock-in-trade takes surrealistic shape, with *magnificently baroque objects* of syringes, tubes, nozzles and foaming agents, rounded out by *extraordinarily luxurious French letters made of leopard-skin* and *a mink Dutch cap*. He would add his own twist to her anecdotes there, culminating in a farcical encounter in a freshly varnished rowboat. *He could visualize a nightmare prosecution in which the boat was shown as evidence against him. 'The marks of the girl's bottom, my Lord, after seduction. They will be seen to fit the buttocks of the defendant's young victim.'*

The grim standard of pornography, replete with clichés and devoid of any originality, challenged him to do better – 'I do believe I understand what works and what doesn't' – but he would never get around to setting the 'superb example' he envisaged. The bizarre sexual images which characterise his books show that separating the satirical from the erotic became no easier with age, and the insider's view did not help.

One eminent judge paid to be undressed and put to bed as a baby, complete with nappy and dummy, and left alone for a couple of hours, before being reclothed in pinstripe suit and club tie, handed his bowler, briefcase, mackintosh and umbrella, and escorted back to his train. One day the ritual was performed slightly out of sequence, and the judge departed in high dudgeon. 'My God,' she exclaimed to Jim over lunch, 'to think he might give someone thirty years this afternoon.' 'Oh no,' Jim's reply said as much about himself. 'His life is far too separated for that.'

Through her, he knew who was so perverted that he was blacklisted for being too 'hot', and who was popular for being kind. He knew who liked organising the callgirls domestic shopping lists, writing them out himself, and not only who needed to be blatantly aroused, but how. The underside of power and respectability was illuminating – 'They're all crooks, politicians . . .' he muttered so often that she felt right-wing in comparison – and the Establishment of every era took on added comic potential.

Her flat was in Park West, off the Edgware Road, and sometimes Jim moved in with her for a while from his temporary quarters at 35 Pembridge Road in Notting Hill. When the phone rang then he would take the calls – 'They would often know him and say "Oh Jim . . ." and he was a good friend, he would lie and lie for me' – but the drawback was having to make himself scarce, often at short notice. Told that someone was due in ten minutes, he would groan 'Oh God', and retreat to his front basement room. At other times she would pay off her taxi in the small hours, climb over the Pembridge Road railings and squeeze in through the half-open window, knowing he enjoyed being taken by surprise. 'Sex got better sometimes and we'd just stay together all day and night for a week. He was so very sensual. I wouldn't go to work – have clients, I should say. Then we'd have a row and I wouldn't see him for a while.'

In Gary Arnott's opinion, meeting her was the best thing that could have happened to Jim. She dealt with the bitter Groucho Marx quip with gusto, and the transformation could be seen in little ways. He stopped drawing nudes inspired by Cranach – 'expressing but not satiating occasional lusts' – and no longer bothered to wear a shirt when he sunbathed or swam. When she told him the effects of polio were scarcely noticeable he reasoned that she had no ulterior motive, since she was not out to make money from him or stake an emotional claim. Mentioning her to his mother, he described her wickedly as a teacher, but the impression of sexual subordination was genuine, and in *Troubles* would inhabit the Major, too. *She was sometimes impatient with him . . . laughed at him as if she found him ridiculous . . . She enjoyed teasing him but she enjoyed flirting with him too sometimes . . . It was clear that he was a traveller through*

unmapped country . . . 'Why are you so polite the whole time?'
she would ask derisively, while the Major, appalled, wondered
what was wrong with being polite . . . He was learning slowly,
by experience . . .

The comfort to be found in domesticity without strings was a
mutual discovery. On quiet, wet days they stayed indoors and
read, listened to the radio or watched her television, without
needing to talk; and in good weather they walked for miles. 'He
was so easy, so sensitive,' she approved, accustomed to male
selfishness. 'I manicured his hands and pedicured his feet for him
and he used to paint my toenails. I cut his hair – he worried
about his receding hairline – and sewed the odd button on. He
took the washing to the launderette. I'd cook for him and he'd
cook for me.' With *My Fair Lady* on at Drury Lane Jim saw
himself as Professor Henry Higgins to her Eliza, and he introduced her to European films and pinned up lists of books for her
to read. 'He'd say, "My God, you're intelligent. What a shame
you're so uneducated." I used to lap it up. I must have asked so
many questions, and he was never patronising. He talked about
packing everything in sometimes and paying for me to go back
to school.'

She was happy to be moulded. His first words on waking
were, 'How do you feel? Are you neurotic?' and she knew he
wanted her to answer, 'Yes.' He took her to Paris by ferry for
the weekend and watched her reactions; down that path, too,
would go the Major – *amused, paternal, indulgent, and a tiny
bit world-weary.* When she rang in tears in the middle of the
night after finding a dead cat in the street, he went straight
round, unperturbed by the reason for her late return. 'She was
just like a frightened child and terrifically moving,' he noted
down the next day. 'When I got there she was still sobbing
and had to be undressed and put to bed. She kept on saying
that she wanted to go home . . . She had had her hair cut as
short as a boy's and her skin was very smooth and brown . . .
Outside in the yellow street light it looked as if it was snowing
cornflakes.' She had never heard of the legend of Leda and the
Swan, yet she had a recurrent dream in which she was being
raped by a white swan.

Sexually, Jim did not mind sharing her, but it infuriated him that she continued to think of herself as a free agent while he was making plans for them as a pair. The difference between their outlooks was driven home when he bought theatre tickets as a treat, only to be told that she would not cancel the client already booked for that evening and accompany him unless he made up the money she would lose as well. He constantly urged her to get a better job – even stripping, he pointed out, would be an improvement – but she liked things the way they were. 'Oh, what a life,' he sighed to Brian Knox Peebles once. 'How is she ever going to get out of it?'

She had been drawn to him in the first place because he was a writer, and she liked watching him at work as she lay on his bed smoking and pretending to read, until without comment he would get up from the typewriter and lead the way to the Bunch of Grapes in the Brompton Road or the Onslow in South Kensington for the unwinding ritual of a drink. As time went by, however, she became increasingly uneasy. 'I didn't trust what he was writing down. He had a spiteful sense of humour, and I thought if he was so vicious about other people he was bound to be vicious about me behind my back.' When he came to write about her, though, it would be in kinder vein. In *The Siege of Krishnapur*, in the character of Lucy Hughes, the fallen woman, he would salute her sensuousness and practicality, touched by her capacity for survival. Several years later a girlfriend asked if he had ever minded her being a prostitute. 'It was different in those days,' he cut her short, leaving her to wonder if the times or he himself had changed. To opt for unmapped territory took courage, and his condemnation was reserved for those who chose to play safe.

It was her world he wanted, dissected, sharpened and satirised. Through her, he was accepted by two Corsican croupiers, widely believed to be on loan from the Mafia, and a convicted burglar who chainsmoked Capstan cigarettes and held forth about jobs he had done and the crookedness of the police. He learned that many callgirls were lesbian or bisexual, and became an observant regular in homosexual and transvestite pubs. He was present whenever the £200 in used notes for a detective in the Flying Squad was dropped off in a Queensway pub, and took lifts in the succession of allegedly stolen new Jaguars smelling of leather favoured by one of her more shadowy clients. Ten years on, in the 1970s, Jim would become a byword for his spare and dedicated way of life: guaranteed to slip away from dinner parties by 10.30pm, to treat Sundays as any other working day, and to get around London by bicycle or bus. Occasionally he would trot out a vignette about armed Corsicans or inept burglars, and enjoy his listeners' puzzled expressions. Already in the 1960s the certainty that nobody would believe what he was up to made the Jekyll and Hyde existence all the sweeter.

'I like my comforts,' became one of his stock phrases in 1963, announced with zest except when socialism was under discussion, when it would be proffered as wistful disqualification. He flagged down taxis, enjoyed smoke-filled nightclubs where his favourite dancing partner was a bunny girl, and spun evenings out late with whiskey and Gauloises cigarettes. A cheque from his parents meant for clothes was blown on a single night out with her on the town. But he was taking it all in, and in that respect his behaviour never varied. Warming up for the ball in *Troubles*, the Major is apprehensive – '*Hm, I told you I wasn't frightfully good at this sort of thing*' – only to discover, with identical understatement, that *dancing could really be quite enjoyable*.

Jim forgot very little, and that included the bad as well as the good. One of the girls in the ring was notorious for trying to seduce boyfriends, fiancés and husbands, and Jim's turn came, as he was warned it would, on a night when he was alone. He was not interested, the knowledge filtered out, after his prompt visit to Park West, equipped with cruel and clinical detail. In *Troubles* Jim would bestow his repugnance – *he had only to close his eyes to see glittering-ringed fingers parting thick white curtains of fat to invite him into some appalling darkness* – on the young Auxiliary Mortimer, and his personal legacy would be grotesque images of sex. At the time he recovered his external aplomb sufficiently to invite both girls to Paris within a few months, where all three, to save money, shared a large double bed.

The rows grew more frequent, erupting out of nowhere. The day came when she wanted to travel by taxi and he, reverting to type, preferred the bus: in the physical fight that resulted his strength took her by surprise. 'Sometimes he would say something cruel so casually that it would knock me for six,' she recounted. 'Once when we were walking in Hyde Park I said "Can we go abroad?" "You stupid cow," he snapped. "We *are* abroad." He meant we were out and about.' She accused him of being vicious, tired of watching him reduce her friends to tears, but escape routes were there on both sides and they did not split up. On one occasion she left him cooking lunch to fit in a quick hairdresser's appointment and, several weeks later, swept back in with a suntan and the explanation that she had been on the Riviera. 'You said, "Put the potatoes on at 12.45," ' he observed mildly. 'I waited a few hours and by 10pm I realised you were not coming back at all.'

They would continue to see each other down the years – to meet and gossip and usually sleep together – but the balance had already shifted. He continued to have access to her world and she knew less and less about his. Having her in the background made him feel, in one subsequent girlfriend's opinion, like a nineteenth-century man of letters; another was sure that he was proud of being 'well in with a tart'. But long after the Profumo scandal had faded in the public mind, she continued to influence Jim's life. She vetted his women, refused to take him seriously and remained consistently herself, which acted as a reminder of something it would have been better for him to forget. 'You're quite wrong about me thinking it's always men who choose (wish it were),' he corrected another girlfriend in a bleak aside once. 'In my experience it's *always* women who choose.'

Along with a fund of anecdotes and a subterranean glimpse of human behaviour, his enduring perception would be of how exploitative women were in their fundamental attitude to men. 'He didn't have a relaxed attitude to sex in any way,' one of his closest male friends would comment later. 'On the surface of it, he had a better chance with women than I had, but he actually found it more difficult.' The irony was that her outlook had freed Jim, at the cost of setting him uncompromisingly on guard.

His decision to leave London for Paris, in the hope of forcing a book out of the 'shapeless salad' of ideas and images before the middle of 1964, raised no objections from her; nor did he expect any. All that remained, if the gamble was to stand a chance, was to set up the work-money-time ratio that had paid off before.

CHAPTER ELEVEN

A *Sea of Dark Feathers*
1964–1965

'My biggest cause for dissatisfaction [with *Elsewhere*] is that I find something artificial about it and I don't think this is simply because I was present while it was being put together. Part of the trouble is stylistic. Sometimes the cadence of sentences becomes sonorous to the point of meaninglessness.' The working notebook was always kept in the inside pocket of his jacket so he could jot down thoughts as they occurred – on a bench in the small park off the Boulevard Jourdain, waiting for the Métro, sitting alone at an uneven café table. Grey hair combed straight back, pale raincoat highlighting the dark shirt and darker tie, he fitted naturally into the background, and the London year shrank down to a 'grisly mistake'.

Eleven hours a week of taking conversation classes in a suburban girls' school just about paid the bills, and the freedom from preparation and correction that had eaten into his free time in Mende and Toulon made up for the necessary ten hours of commuting on the Métro, 'crushed and gasping' in the morning rush hour. Without much difficulty he had got an official pass to stay for the academic year, a room shared with a shy Lebanese in the subsidised Cité Université, out in the Fourteenth arrondissement, and occasional work at the British Institute in the rue de la Sorbonne. 'I've begun another, very different [book],' he confided to Patsy Cumming within six weeks of arrival, 'about which I won't talk for the moment as there are things that are still not clear to me.'

At the Cité Université – 'an international students' doss house' – he was installed in the Fondation des États-Unis, a featureless

American-funded 1930s building overlooking the multi-laned
highway of the Boulevard Jourdain. Its main attractions for Jim,
apart from the student rates, were the swimming pool in the
basement and the Métro station opposite, because taking exercise and saving time were absolute priorities. Brakes screeched
and horns blared outside, day and night, and noisy young
Americans crowded the lobby, the stairs and the cafeteria. 'This
freezes me to the marrow,' he shuddered in the first few days. But
in the sanctuary of his room his typewriter was in position on the
table, and once the door was shut the annoyances drifted away.

The book proving so elusive was drawn from his polio
experiences; he had been tinkering with an approach, off
and on, for over six years. Now the succession of hateful
anniversaries immediately ahead added a rhythm to progress,
and he set an initial deadline to coincide with the month, eight
years earlier, of his release from hospital. Nothing, not even the
impact of President Kennedy's assassination on the stunned
students in the corridors, was allowed to get in the way.
Summoning up the nightmare, sensation by claustrophobic
sensation, he wrote with a fluency that surprised him, breaking
off at intervals to rest his aching arms or to refresh his stamina
and sensory memory in the chlorine atmosphere of the pool.
The experience was cathartic, leaving him drained and lonely as
he made his way about the big institutional building, but that,
too, had symmetry with the unfolding hospital life of his central
character, Martin Sands.

In *The Lung* Sands's ordeal echoes Jim's own, reshaped but
not exaggerated: he develops polio, spends weeks in an iron
lung, and is eventually discharged, transformed in outlook and
appearance. Horror is diffused by satire and black gallows
humour, and for the first time Jim allowed his wit and imagination full rein as he created a surreal world of patients and
hospital staff, where only doctors escape the scalpel of incisive
caricature. But writing from the polio victim's standpoint risked
a self-exposure he had not allowed himself before, and despite
his attempts to distance himself by making Sands twenty years
older and a hardened drinker and womaniser, his personal
anguish slipped through. Comedy would be the flesh; the bones
of the book were shock and anger, betrayal and remorse, and

exploitation and loss of trust. His yearning for the lost game of rugby was channelled into the emotions of the former champion cricketer 'Hurricane' Higgins.

Freed of the constraint of attempting to write to formula, Jim drew the curtains against the Paris skyline, blocked out the noise of traffic on the autoroute outside, and let his imagination range. *The park sloped away gently to a wooded valley in the distance where a cluster of tiny black trees seemed to have been pencilled on the snow. Beyond the trees the ground rose steeply again, sprinkled at first with toy houses and a church steeple, then rising once more to the broad spine and jagged crests of a small mountain that glistened peacefully in the last light of the winter afternoon* . . . The book was his, to do with as he liked. He conjured up a sexual tryst beside the therapy pool in which the paralysed but ingenious Sands undresses his nurse with surgical scissors. He hung a *beautiful abstract painting by Franz Beer* on an interior wall.

But bursts of satisfaction – occasionally elation – were short-lived, and even a letter from Hutchinson with the news that sales of *A Man from Elsewhere* were nearing 2,000 failed to lift a growing pessimism. 'I doubt if there is the vaguest chance of them reprinting,' he sniped, 'even if they sell all they have.' He badly needed to sustain his daily writing output and knew that one warning sign of a period of low vitality was the urge to get away from people and cities, and the magnetic pull of a Greek island in December signalled trouble ahead. A biography of Tolstoy – 'What a man! What energy! He really had the talent I most admire – that of playing everything for keeps' – showed up his own weariness in contrast, and to combat it he allowed himself a short break over Christmas, taking up a language student's long-standing invitation to visit her in Munich. Boarding the train at the Gare de l'Est for the ten-hour journey, however, he found it full of drunken Germans returning for Christmas, and after a while snapped his book shut and caught the eye of a young man sitting opposite, whom he had noticed was engrossed in Proust. Raising a humorous black eyebrow, the other murmured conspiratorially, 'We are the only two civilised ones on this train.'

His soulmate was Claude Simha, a Moroccan-Jewish paediatrician working in Montparnasse, and before the journey ended they knew they shared more than a love of Proust. 'Claude is one of the few doctors I know,' Jim would say warmly, 'who really reads books.' It was a potent combination. One of the first things he noticed were the meticulously clean hands and nails, in tune with every doctor glimpsed from the iron lung, and the black hair was neatly combed, the dark eyes twinkled behind heavy glasses, and the olive skin was set off by a neat suit and tie. They quickly established that Claude had qualified the year Jim left Oxford, was recovering from an unhappy love affair and hoped to find a new girl in Germany. By the time the train pulled into Munich they had arranged to explore the city together. United in mounting dislike of everything German, they stalked about in the bitter cold, commiserating with each over over the food – 'Horrible sausage!' pronounced Claude the gourmet – and exclaiming over street names like Dachau Strasse and Buchenwald Strasse. Back in Paris they were equally compatible, a factor that was to boost Jim's staying power more effectively than any change of scene.

When not engrossed in the book or teaching, Jim began to spend his free time with Claude. His new friend's room overlooked the Closerie des Lilas, the one-time haven of Hemingway and Fitzgerald. Passing the windows of La Palette on the main boulevard they made a point of glancing in to see if Sartre was at his usual table with Simone de Beauvoir; to Jim's disquiet Sartre looked quarrelsome, old and ill. Peering into the tiny Chez Rosalie in rue Campagne, he was pleased by Claude's tip that they still served hareng par l'huile there, as they had to Modigliani, and heading for the return Métro at Vavin he acknowledged Balzac, sculpted there by Rodin. But he jibbed at paying 1f 20c for a tiny cup of espresso at the Select and the Dôme when he could get a four-course meal for the same amount in the États-Unis, and he avoided the Dôme altogether after recognising the large figure of Andrew Sinclair at a table inside, holding forth in a way he knew all too well.

Jim and Claude patronised the Café Wadja in the nearby rue de la Grande Chaumière. The small café's real charm was its cheapness, but they felt great affection for the steamy windows, rough tiled floor and the cramped communal tables covered with oilcloth, and after a while rarely noticed the penance of hard wooden seats. The daily menu was simple – roti de porc aux pruneaux, lapin au citron, Bifteck haché – but the food was secondary to smoking and talking. Both were impatient to light up and push the plates aside, and when their coffee came they ladled in the sugar, to be eaten absently with a spoon.

Proust, Primo Levi, Carlo Levi . . . Claude was glad that Jim was drawn to Jewish authors and less surprised to realise they were all outsiders. 'It seemed to me we could understand each other without talking,' he said afterwards. 'Jim was a little leftist, as of course I was, too. We talked about racism, and Arabs and Jews. Existentialism – we thought alike about that, and about Karl Marx and Freud as well. Religion was bourgeois; naturally we despised those things. We liked Gide's remark, "Familles, je vous hais", as we were each most unhappy in our adolescence. We believed it was terrible to bring children into our world. And we talked a lot about girls – it was a problem for us then. So, books, families, girls – and always lots of time.' Jim made Claude read Lowry and Saul Bellow, and took him to Shakespeare and Company to buy American fiction in paperback. In return Claude pointed out the Bretagne, around the corner from the Café Wadja, where they sometimes adjourned for the afternoon and for 5f saw the latest Louis Malle or Truffaut film.

Above all, getting to know Claude brought access on an equal level to an intelligent doctor's mind, though such discussions were out of the question until Jim could overcome his reluctance to talk about himself. As it happened, the polio damage was all too obvious to Claude, but as the determination to conceal it was just as apparent, any comment was precluded. Eventually Jim took the plunge as they strolled around the Jardins de Luxembourg, and asked Claude to list the symptoms of leukaemia for a character he was creating; he would refer to the same notes when embarking upon *Troubles*. Once he had admitted his experience in the iron lung and explained the subject of his book, Claude turned out to be an ideal sounding board, with a systematic line of questioning that re-opened aspects he shied away from on his own. The most intense impression, he replied to one of Claude's gently persistent cross-examinations, had been of helplessness; back in the États-Unis he enlarged that theme.

He set out to repay him, knowing Claude had little opportunity for meeting the new girlfriend he longed for given the unsociable hours he worked. The Cité Université was a melting pot of students from every nationality, many of whom gravitated to Montparnasse in their free time, and he identified a group of Icelandic girls who liked to congregate in the Select. He fell into conversation, using Laxness, the Icelandic Nobel Prize-winner for Literature, as his pretext, and picked out a blue-eyed blonde called Anna who showed the warmth and intelligence Claude deserved. Traditionally Icelanders celebrate May Day with a picnic, and, anticipating that they would round off the day at the Select, he stationed the unsuspecting Claude beside him in the Café Cosmos, directly between the Métro and the Select. As Anna walked past he called her over to their table. 'I have a wife for you,' he announced to Claude, who would later comment drily, 'Et, voilà!'

In quick succession Jim found three girlfriends of his own, each intended for a shorter time-scale. Brash Americans in the hostel did not attract him, and he was too shy to do more than gaze at a pair of exotic students with waist-length black hair, one a Vietnamese and the other Iranian, contenting himself with having Martin Sands lust after them in his book. But he began to turn up at his meetings with Claude with a possessive Swedish student who wore her hair centrally parted and in a bun, whom he nicknamed Olive Oyl, until she was replaced without explanation by a pleasant German graduate who worked in French television, who in turn gave way to a petite and tempestuous student of mathematics named Marie Thérèse. Marie Thérèse, it became apparent, was two-timing him, and the gritty theme of adultery and betrayal began darkening *The Lung*. He would be the one to call a halt to their relationship, but not until he was satisfied with that stretch of his book.

Jim had come to loathe the impersonal États-Unis and was impatient to find a cheap room in Montparnasse, but he had paid in advance to the end of term. Putting his remaining time there to good use, he followed up the information that postgraduates in America found it easy to get grants to teach beginners' courses in French; several people assured him that it was merely a matter of applying to the French departments of a cross-section of colleges. 'If I'm ever to get back to the States this seems the most likely way to do it,' he proposed to Russell McCormmach. 'Until I become a seedy Grand Old Man of Letters, that is. I don't think I can wait that long.'

With Claude's help, he found a room on the sixth floor of 163/165 rue de Rennes, near the Gare Montparnasse, at a rent of 120f a month. A gruff concierge hovered on the alert, and there was a circular staircase instead of a lift which reduced him to a limp dishrag at the top. But though he was squeezed in under the eaves he had the table and chair he needed and a carved wooden bed, while a breath of air from the window which overlooked the inner courtyard promised ventilation for the summer ahead. The cramped space had the bonus of keeping out intruders, and when his mother and a couple of cousins visited Paris he was able to suggest a small hotel around the corner without a qualm.

Polishing *The Lung* did not take long, and once Jim had posted the typescript off to Jonathan Clowes he turned his attention to the money-making prospect of a 'sub-Chandleresque' thriller to be based on his recent study of human vice. Hoping for Robin Cook's success, he set the plot in London and wrote with film rights in mind, and since the climax had to be visually original he proposed a machine-gun duel, with rival gangs firing from skidding double-decker buses on an icy airstrip. He expected to dash it off in a matter of weeks and started briskly by naming the Mafia head Arnotti, after Gary, and toying with pseudonyms for himself. Sam Hatchet? Spike Mac-Bloodstain? It was impossible to take the project seriously. The long daily stint soon turned into an ordeal as his elegant style kept breaking through to disrupt the pace. Aware that it had to be terse, fast-moving and written for the masses, everything he despised, he put it aside with relief whenever it was time to meet Claude in the Café Wadja, where they would praise the length of Proust's sentences and the importance of the elliptical approach.

'Jim was easy to know in the beginning,' observed Claude once. 'But he had a hardness – a sarcasm. He became always a little sarcastic about me.' One problem was Jim's awareness that he had little to show for the summer's hard slog, and stepping off the teaching bandwagon could only be justified if he first completed a book to fund the year ahead. There were no plans beyond the vague mention of a meeting with Clowes and Nicol when summoned by them, and continuing silence about *The Lung* sapped his ability to concentrate. He took his frustrations out on Claude, who was sunk in gloom on his own account in the face of deferred National Service that September, and it came as a relief to both when Claude's most 'amusing' friend from medical college sent word that he was arriving in Paris for ten days.

Observing Elie Harar, Jim placed him as the most unusual specimen in his burgeoning collection of doctors. Elie was tall, tanned and lighthearted, with a hawk-like profile, slim gesticulating hands, and the knack of sitting elegantly in the most awkward café chair. He had travelled from his remote practice in Morocco to see his girlfriend Irma, but Claude smiled and Jim forgot his tribulations as Elie was drawn into trotting out case after bizarre medical case. 'Why not go back there with my friend Elie?' Claude suggested at the end of his stay, and with uncharacteristic impulsiveness Jim agreed. On the spur of the moment he booked a cheap air ticket to follow, paid off the concierge, notified Clowes, packed up everything to take with him so he could fly back direct to London, and invested in batteries for his radio, typing paper and carbons, a supply of Gauloises, tobacco in airtight tins and cigarette papers, as well as pots of marmalade and jam, and his favourite blend of tea.

Marrakesh airport shimmered under the glare of the sun as Elie drove up to meet him in a smart chauffeur-driven jeep which sported a red cross on either door, and when they gathered speed a red and white pennant fluttered in the breeze. Ait Ouvrir, the administrative centre of Elie's vast medical district, was high in the foothills of the Atlas mountains; to Jim it was P.C. Wren territory, with Beau and Digby Geste beyond every bend. In the distance inland, as they climbed above sea level, snow shone on the mountain tops beneath a cloudless blue sky, and stunted trees and solitary palms marked out the single metalled road ahead.

Ait Ouvrir had one sewer and one small souk, pot-holed tracks connected patchily whitewashed buildings, and goats rummaged in the refuse. People wore the djellabah and women were masked. They were the only two 'white men', Elie took care to advise, but power lay with the Caifa, the village chief. The large scantily furnished house that came with the post was surrounded by a scented garden, and after being shown to the spare bedroom at one end of the long narrow layout, Jim sat out there beside beds of roses and sipped his tea, made with a slice of lemon from the tree beside him, instead of the condensed milk proffered by the cook. At the gate artificial insemination for sheep was proceeding, and when he wandered down for a better look he learned that the massive ram was bred in Ireland. 'It is the same thing as with a small woman and a big man, it will work,' the owner hastily explained. Jim was charmed by it all. Lizards kept most mosquitoes in check, cases of mandarins and pineapples were delivered twice a week and fresh eggs were plentiful.

The two men settled into a tolerant routine. Jim rose first, checking his shoes for scorpions, and as soon as Elie had set off on his rounds he worked on the 'gangster book' in the airy main room, breaking off to cook an omelette or make salad for lunch. He got used to the vagaries of the gas fridge, which froze all contents into solid blocks. In the afternoons he took his customary walk, unaware of being shadowed; Elie thought it best not to tell him that the authorities insisted on a 'tail', and the villagers kept out of his way, believing that he wanted to be alone. Less philosphical than Elie about the cook's limitations, he took it on himself to make supper and shopped for vegetables in the souk on his way back. Towards dusk, before the temperature fell, he lit the fire in the room where he wrote. It was pitch black by 6pm, and the combination of unmade roads and lighting kept on midsummer schedules made it too hazardous to venture out on foot. They filled in the evenings peaceably, sitting by the big fireplace as the erratic electricity flickered and chatting over a bottle of the disappointing local wine. After their meal they read in silence, ready to turn in early. At 11pm, when a long-wave French station began broadcasting, Elie switched on his bedside radio. At the other end of the rambling building, Jim would be tuning in to the BBC World Service, intent on keeping up with Labour's election campaign. The life had many similarities with his father's in the Indian chummery days.

Spending so much time alone, dissatisfied with his output and preoccupied by the fate of *The Lung*, he became intrigued by the previous occupants of the house whose swift departure, according to the worldly Elie, had hinged on adultery: his predecessor had discovered his young wife *in flagrante* with the only other Frenchman in the district. Noticing a trail of red ants in the kitchen one day, Jim traced them to a stock of rusting babyfood tins, a troubling human dimension, and he sampled two, choosing meat extract and apple purée. The tins would re-appear in *A Girl in the Head*, and in a future anecdote their role would dramatically expand to save him and Elie from starvation, but the poignant aspect he kept to himself. It bore out everything he had witnessed: trust was better withheld.

On their regular trips to Marrakesh Jim haggled in the teeming souk, and lingered to watch the street 'doctors' cupping patients with a mediaeval technique of drawing blood from the back of the neck, sterilising their knives in alcohol only if Elie happened to pass by. In a doctor's company the horrifying deformities and diseases had straightforward explanations, and though mystery was stripped from cadaverous silhouettes, so was the sense of threat.

The chauffeur and distinctive red-cross-emblazoned jeep ensured safe passage, and sometimes he accompanied Elie on his rounds to villages within a 100-kilometre radius. In remoter areas where illegal poaching of wild sheep was the way of life, the backup of armed soldiers was also needed. Elie referred to himself mockingly as the Man from the Mountains, and revealed that despite the trappings it was a National Service posting for which he was paid a pittance retrospectively, adding that although his Arabic was fluent and he took care to build up his popularity, he was liable to be moved at whim. Burned dark by the sun in his casual turn-out, compared to Elie's crisp white coat, Jim filed away the likelihood of mundane frustration beneath the most imposing colonial façade.

Taking after his mother, he was not squeamish, and although he now hated hospitals, outdoor clinics presented fewer reminders. He watched as Elie treated stab and gunshot wounds, severe injuries, broken bones, botched abortions, a ruptured appendix or two, snake bites, scorpion stings and cases of malnutrition, and lent a hand with crowd control in the mass vaccinations. A few cases re-appear in his novels: the screams of a fleeing woman in labour, whom he was called upon in Ait Ouvrir to help overpower, echo in *The Siege of Krishnapur*. Others would become anecdotes, inventively transposed. Cumulatively their impact was intense, and he grew to prize common sense almost as highly as compassion. The practice of demanding certificates of virginity for brides offended his liberal sensitivities, until he understood Elie's approach after hearing him answer 'Yes' when called upon by a local judge in a marital dispute to rule whether it was possible for a pregnancy to last two years. 'Always say yes for the wife's sake,' Elie explained afterwards, with a wink.

The stay in Morocco, unexpectedly, was a crash course in colonial experiences. Dinner invitations, particularly from the Caifa, could never be refused, and Jim found himself the centre of attention, faced with twenty unrecognisable courses and the only one present who did not speak the language. The classic stiff upper lip, as he had always suspected, disguised amusement and boredom as effectively as fear. On one occasion a group of Berbers near the top of a mountain track crowded around to urge them to honour the family wedding feast. Jim agreed, saying that he had not yet heard Berber music. Since the road was petering out, a couple of ancient mules were led forward, and after two bone-crunching hours a village finally came in sight. They were shown up to the roof of the bride's home, honoured with the best view, and a pair of musicians were ushered below: one banged a tambourine and the other played a two-string violin. The same two monotonous notes continued without variation. 'It is just for you because you asked,' whispered Elie. 'But they are poor, so it is hard for them to afford this. We cannot leave early because that would give offence, and there is also my own position to keep up.' Food was served, tough elderly goat and a giant turnip, and dancing began; eventually, when Elie judged the moment right, they set out on the gruelling cross-country ride back to the jeep, legs dangling to within an inch of the ground.

Questioned about how his writing was going, Jim always hedged. 'It's not much good,' he would say, and change the subject. Silence over *The Lung* alarmed him, because he could not forget Jonathan Clowes's remark that the capacity to write

one good book was not unusual – and that the second novel was
'the very stiff fence' that separated the gifted writer from the
momentarily inspired amateur. By mid-October the breathtak-
ing views no longer rated a second glance, he picked his way past
drunken Arabs with distaste, and Elie, like Claude before him,
was having to revise his earlier impression. The sarcasm and
cynicism, he diagnosed, having drawn his own conclusions
about polio damage, were a long-term manifestation of shock.

Waiting for a response in Ait Ouvrir proved a greater strain
than second-guessing the fate of *A Man from Elsewhere* in
Toulon. This time Jim knew Nicol and Clowes well enough
to imagine their deliberations in tone of voice and turn of phrase,
and rejection or criticism would have a personal sting, made
more humiliating by the confessional nature of the book. His
depression was acted out in a miniature existentialist drama that
took place nightly on the terrace wall, where a hanging bulb
threw a pool of light.

> *I wonder if you've ever seen lizards eating moths? They'd
> wait there, knowing perfectly well that sooner or later their
> supper would come whizzing and bouncing and fluttering
> along . . . It was perfectly inevitable. Moths are attracted to
> light. Lizards eat moths. A rapid lunge and then sometimes
> they'd hesitate, rock-still, with odd ends of dusty wings
> protruding from their mouths . . . After a while I used to
> stop switching on the light at night. I used to sit in the dark
> thinking of the lizards getting thinner. That was rather
> depressing too. It was either one or the other; the moths or
> the lizards. That's the essence of a tragedy, I suppose, if you
> happen to like them both. Everything . . . becomes a
> responsibility once you start thinking about it. The whole
> thing became quite intolerable in the end.*

In November Clowes wrote to say that Hutchinson was hesitating, and it was necessary to meet as soon as possible to discuss
editorial changes. Jim booked a flight, borrowed 10,000 (old)
francs from Elie, and was morose on the drive to Marrakesh. Elie
knew that two chapters of the thriller had already been despatched in the hope of producing a £100 advance, and he

guessed from Jim's abstracted manner that there had been bad news about that, too. Repaying the debt promptly on arrival in London, however, Jim merely wrote to say that his days were uneventful and his nights even more so. Elie belonged to the French compartment, and that, for the moment, was closed.

'The first reactions to my thriller weren't good,' he admitted to Russell. 'The main trouble being, apparently, that I turned it into a satire on itself. This was a calculated risk. I got bored with it, you see, but thought that there was enough humour in it to make up for the decrease in horror.' Desperate for money, he spent Christmas at home in Dalkey rewriting feverishly, despite the temptation to let it 'slither down' into limbo, driven on by the need to get it out of the way so that he could turn his attention back to *The Lung*.

Clowes had told him that he had begun reading it with trepidation and felt astonished by the final page. 'Not only was it clearly superior to the first but it was also written in an entirely different manner,' the forthright agent would evaluate. 'I immediately understood why he had been dissatisfied with *Elsewhere*. He had developed a harshly lyrical style that perfectly matched the emotions and situations he was describing, and more important perhaps was what this technique was used to convey – a very deep understanding and compassion, combined with a sincerity that illuminates the entire book.' But that enthusiasm had not communicated itself to Hutchinson, despite the support of Graham Nicol. *The Lung* was best suited to the New Authors series but was disqualified by being a second book. To be accepted for the main list for publication in the autumn, Jim was warned, it would need considerable cutting and rewriting. 'There is too much of you in it,' Nicol said bluntly.

'When he first read it the publisher was ultra-enthusiastic,' Jim would make light of the following stage. 'He gave it to his readers who were infra-enthusiastic. There was some haggling about whether they were going to publish it. Finally they decided they would, largely, I suppose, because my other rotten book got good reviews. I should have been watching all this with the coldly sardonic smile of the Genius watching lesser mortals making fools of themselves, but I had a sneaking feeling that so many readers (3) couldn't be wrong. Besides, I needed the money – pitiful amount though it be. I'm still waiting for it, of course.' After extra work the typescript was accepted and publication set for 25 October.

The deeply personal content made his horror of self-promotion all the more acute, and as the date neared his apprehension grew. Clowes insisted that the most successful campaigns were author-led, and told him repeatedly that to achieve good sales he would have to drum up public interest himself. 'Can't they just advertise the book?' Jim baulked. Meetings became an uphill struggle – 'It was very difficult', Clowes said with feeling, 'to get Jim to do the smallest thing' – and friction intensified when the Autumn Books section was printed in the *Bookseller* in July. Hutchinson's section was devoted to Arther Koestler, Frank G. Slaughter and Brendan Behan, with Jim's book disposed of in eight words: 'James Farrell's *The Lung* has a hospital background.' But when asked by Hutchinson's publicity department for the names of well-disposed journalists, he responded with his non-commercial friends. Corgi bought the paperback rights in September, but there was no word of American interest and the sale of French rights fell through.

On the night before publication Jim wrote up his notebook with a heightened sense of transience. 'All day, at least from the early afternoon, an odd feeling of depression pursued me. A sunny day, though sharp with rotting leaves and bonfires, which may have had something to do with it. Partly, I suppose, I dread the exposure of my book (and myself) to the massive indifference of the newspapers where one's ego is neatly filed, if at all, alongside millions of others.' All that day he had wandered about Notting Hill and Kensington, pausing at one point to watch a happy couple playing with their small boy. 'I couldn't help thinking,' he wrote on, unable to sleep, 'you think a son is something permanent but it isn't. In a way it's even less perma-nent than a book.'

The massive indifference did not occur, and the review that pleased him most was in the *Daily Telegraph*, the paper his father took, which commented that 'Mr Farrell has achieved the rare feat of writing a book which is at once very funny and very serious'. Raising his eyebrows at the *Irish Times* rebuke for a 'gratuitous sideswipe at Dublin', and 'vague hostility' from *Punch*, he was relieved to find favourable short notices in the *Observer* and *The Times Literary Supplement*. His own preferred paper, the *Guardian*, gratifyingly picked out *The Lung* for its October Fiction of the Month, praising it for the 'very strong, very subtly articulated imagination, cussed and compassionate, and prose to match it, deft in comedy, densely textured in rueful anguish'. But happiness was cut short by the *Guardian*'s ultimate assessment that 'one sees sure signs of the developing powers of a considerable talent'. Within two months that sentence had assumed a threatening tone. 'The idea that my powers should be developing covers me with alarm and despair,' he wrote in Christmas melancholia, 'as I fancy they are diminishing.'

In the desolation that he was beginning to realise always lay in ambush behind publication, his feelings about his novel suffered the same reversal as before. 'Out of this blur looms the sinister impression that the book lacks a strong enough main thread to bind it all together,' he summed up the reviews. 'The feeling [is] that the thing has been made up as the author went along and that the various events don't have a powerful enough interrelation between each other and the theme as a whole.' Signing copies for Dublin friends he kept his doubts hidden, and they hid theirs, since general agreement was that it was difficult and halting – 'Very like Jimmy himself'. His parents, however, detected a distinct improvement in his outlook. As his mother put it, when they discussed him behind his back, he appeared at last to have written out the horror.

On his daily walks, rediscovering the coastal area between Dun Laoghaire and Sandycove where he had spent so much of his convalescence from polio eight years before, Jim, too, made comparisons. Too much separated him now from the old crowd, and the subject of Judy Mitchell remained so sensitive that they all still tiptoed around it, accentuating the gulf. He was thirty and they were much the same age, but he was a free agent and intended to remain so, while they were becoming replicas of their parents. He had expected Jack Kirwan to be married with a child and very probably Jill as well, but somehow not Hilary, too, in spite of the wedding invitation that had been sent out to Mende.

On impulse he called around to see her and his unmistakable disillusion at finding her in the kitchen, untidy and up to her elbows in flour as she made bread, was mortifying for them both. His intention to stay on at home to write dwindled, and halfway through January he decamped.

Back in London he arranged to meet Russell, who was visiting England for the first time since Oxford, and on the day took along a gift copy of his new book, unsure what the five-year gap might reveal. At first they were both self-conscious but that soon fell away. Knowing the despair which had caused Russell to tear up his own long novel, the one posted over to Toulon, Jim had dedicated *The Lung* to him, and watching as Russell came across that page, he added anxiously, 'I hope you don't mind.' He need not have worried because Russell was transparently delighted. The last therapeutic task of the book was done.

CHAPTER TWELVE

A Nebulous Desire for Escape
1965–1966

On St Patrick's Day 1965 Jim took up residence at 35 Palace Gardens Terrace, parallel with Kensington Church Street; a good address, but not exactly the leapfrog in circumstances it might appear. 'I think I'll go and live in a greenhouse in Notting Hill Gate next – for £2 a week' he had decided, seeing the dramatic potential at a glance, and it made a perfectly proportioned glass case for the threatened species inside: the writer driven to self-sacrifice, careworn but game. Being a solidly built conservatory annexe, however, it was less flimsy than he implied. The structure jutted from the rear of the building, between ground level and first floor, and was entered via the front door and main staircase, through double doors opening off the return.

His recent peripatetic existence had worn him down, culminating in temporary digs in a large house in Richmond with a group of Icelanders met in Paris. There the landlady's daily meditation – 'the thought of her sitting there on the other side of the wall becomes very discouraging' – had been compounded by her addiction to 'The Saint Strikes Back' at full volume on her television, forcing a second retreat to Gary Arnott in Ridgemount Gardens. *I'd carried the luggage of my life just as far as I possibly could. My hands were blistered, my shoulders were aching.*

Taking possession of his small oblong space on a six-month lease, Jim lit up one of the Schimmelpenninck Dutch cigars he had recently adopted, justified as an investment against English colds, and took back control. The bed was pushed against the long glass-paned wall which faced the opaque, mottled glass panels of the double doors, and the table for the typewriter placed at rightangles to it, on the left. The dingy beige curtains offended him in daytime but were a useful screen against the light, as well as the distracting rear windows of the high-terraced houses beyond the dividing wall. 'I'm living in a greenhouse,' he announced at the first opportunity, promoting poverty as a natural element, like water or air.

Not everybody was impressed. Old friends saw it as a pose – 'He *wants* to live in a greenhouse,' it was frequently said, exasperation tinged with concern – and Phillip and Jill Davies, who had married since the unhappy episode in Spain, presented him with a second-hand electric heater. 'You have to have *something*,' they explained, missing the point. The effects of the greenhouse were to be on Jim's imagination, not his health, as an indelible experience rapidly overtook the astute career move. Transmuted, the poky glass-walled box in Palace Gardens Terrace would billow into the immense conservatory of the Majestic Hotel in *Troubles*, dense with jungle-sized under-growth inspired by an assortment of small pot plants from the shops in Notting Hill. Long before that, from the start, it would influence his latest – still-indistinct – hero, Count Boris Slattery.

> [Only] a theatre curtain would have been big enough to cover the vast expanse of glass that surrounded me . . . Perhaps if things had been different I might have done something – rigged up a canopy, perhaps, and broken a few judicious windows for ventilation. [But] a succession of sunny days and cold nights . . . reduced my normally ferrous will to syrup . . . and then the weather changed abruptly . . . The bright knives of sunlight . . . were no longer there. The greenhouse was filled with greyish light. I could hardly believe my luck. A cloudy day at last . . . I had merely exchanged one torment for another . . . the endless shrieking of the wind.

Jim, too, swung from discomfort to apathy at the mercy of the weather and was compelled to wear dark glasses unless the sky was overcast, prompting disturbing flashbacks of the iron lung.

'I thought, this man doesn't *know* what living in a greenhouse is like,' he declared ten years later, trouncing the author of a book with a similar background.

'I'm living in a greenhouse,' he duly challenged Jonathan Clowes over the phone, but when Clowes investigated he declared it to be well-sheltered and quite reasonable. Russell, on his flying visit, allied himself firmly with Jim. 'It was a wonderful image of the artist exposed in a glasshouse,' he wrote. 'He had a little table for his typewriter and a teapot, not even any cooking facilities. He ate fish and chips with peas every day, always exactly the same.' Multiple vitamin tablets, swallowed surreptitiously, made up for any deficiency. 'Texture but no vitamins,' Jim explained when spotted once, indicating the peas.

Among the Oxford contemporaries with whom he kept loosely in touch was Andrew Gemill, star of the truncated rugby period at Brasenose, whose passions, even then, had encompassed both sport and the Arts. On going down, Andrew's stint with the UN in the Cameroons had been followed by an apprenticeship studying drawing with Annigoni in Florence, and his motive for taking a well-paid job as a BBC announcer had been to finance a parallel career as a portrait painter. The original tenant of the Pembridge Road basement Jim had inhabited in 1963, Andrew had moved to a large Victorian studio-flat nearby on the strength of his BBC salary, and encouraged artist friends who were still struggling by hosting impromptu soirées. 'We used to chat for hours, like characters in *La Bohème*,' a regular guest wistfully recalled. At Andrew's studio Jim gravitated again towards a committed playwright, John Spurling, whom he had first got to know there in his previous brief London incarnation. Spurling's conventional colonial background and military carriage belied his unyielding socialist convictions, and he was unabashed by Jim's status as a published writer. Both had been at Oxford with Gemill and they teased him for selling out. Casting up his eyes theatrically, Andrew would complain that they were always hanging around and drinking his coffee for free. Ganging up on him hastened their friendship, providing humorous common cause.

'Jim had an air of worldliness – of irony and cynicism – and I was desperately serious about everything,' John would subsequently own. 'He wouldn't exactly deflate me, but would often achieve that obliquely. Our relationship became, to some extent, mutual ribbing, mutual sending each other up.' They talked books robustly and scorned each other's favourites; John's condition – never met – for reading *Under the Volcano* was that Jim had to finish Anthony Powell's *A Dance to the Music of Time*. Fencing adroitly, however, Jim kept up his guard. He made no mention of his polio when lending *The Lung*, although John's father was also a victim, and John was never invited to the greenhouse, in spite of the fact that Jim soon became a frequent guest of John and his wife Hilary at their flat in Ladbroke Grove.

'Jim felt both the Spurlings had great integrity,' said a friend who knew them well. 'He saw them as a married couple who fed each other in both the emotional and literary sense.' He liked their hospitality on a shoestring, with talk of the latest books and theatre which alleviated the loneliness of the greenhouse; the Spurlings' priorities were very like his own. Hilary, who had been at Oxford a year or two behind him, fully supported John's determination to write, and was about to become Arts editor of the *Spectator*. She gave Jim her whole attention and convinced him of her genuine appreciation for his writing; he saw her as his first real ally in the potentially treacherous world on which he had set his sights. Wariness by now tended to put a distance between himself and old friends in the book world. Sally Bentlif from Oxford had married Anthony Sampson and become a literary agent with A.D. Peters. He kept away, though they lived around the corner in Holland Park, after realising that she had been sent the typescript of *A Man from Elsewhere*. The title, she would comment, instantly reminded her of how he had represented himself at Brasenose College.

Monday sessions in The Albany with fellow protégés of Graham Nicol continued much as before, and Jonathan Clowes suggested that, like Maureen Duffy, he should become a Hutchinson reader at four guineas a script. 'I find I'm already surfeited with fiction, with the dreary, self-therapeutic monsters I have to report on for the publisher,' he complained after taking up the idea, but the money was important and he saw the personal advantage in monitoring overworked trends in fiction. Turning up at Hutchinson's office one day on impulse, needing four guineas at short notice, he was handed a script which he would always claim had been propping up a rickety office table. 'I read the first page and thought "this is awful", ' he noted, 'read the second and thought "Hmmmm", read the third and couldn't put it down.' *Weekend with Claude* was by the unknown Beryl Bainbridge and, much to his annoyance, Maureen was given it to read as well, enabling them both to stake a claim to spotting Bainbridge's talent.

Jim's own experience of critical attention had made him dubious about any critical judgement not his own. Living frugally, he invested in the review pages of newspapers, and Kensington Public Library enabled him to keep up to date. 'I happen to have read Philip Thody's book [on Camus] and thought this [review] was very unjust . . . making points in order to squeeze in scraps of information picked up at cocktail parties but having no central approach.' . . . 'Reading Cesare Pavese's diary, *This Business of Living*, he committed suicide at the height of his literary fame at the age of 42. And this, of course, colours a lot of the things he has to say, particularly about his relations with women.' All that summer Nabokov possessed him, sparked by discovery of the autobiographical *Speak, Memory*. As the small garden below him bloomed, viewed as from a box at the theatre, the butterflies it attracted were Nabokov's butterflies, and on his walks the people he moved between were Nabokov's creations. One day a parcel with Canadian stamps arrived from his older brother Robert, whose choice of books matched his own. Inside, by uncanny coincidence, was a copy of *Lolita*.

'I have a craving to write something good', Jim had written to Russell McCormmach in February. 'I've been ruminating the idea of doing a love-story. To write a love-story that would be moving without being naïve, simple-minded, sentimental, sordid, unreal or any of the other thousand and one ghastly things it might be – this seems a supreme challenge.' By Easter, haunted by the refrain from 'Smoke Gets in Your Eyes', he had a hazy outline in mind. 'Briefly, the idea is now to present a man's love-affair with his wife and an idealised, poetic love-affair he is living through in his imagination concurrently,' he noted with relief. 'I think I may finally have hit on a satisfactory way to do this – a problem that has been dogging me for the last few weeks.'

The title *A Girl in the Head* would come later; initially Jim called his story *The White Bird*, which was a metaphor for death. His Nabokovian narrator, Count Boris Slattery, would share his own preoccupation with loss and mortality, and be dragged down by the fatalist undertow he fought constantly in himself. *Imagination can only change things for a little while, preserve the illusion for the briefest of whiles . . . Reality wins in the end. No doubt about that. And if it is destined to win in the end why bother to keep it at bay even for a while?* Although the story would unfold along the lines Jim had already outlined, it became an account not of love, but of the inability to love.

The seaside resort where Boris Slattery tells his story – *the cemetery of all initiative* – was a composite of Southport, Dun Laoghaire and Brittas Bay. Autobiographical touches stamp the book, beginning with the Victorian house called Boscobel, where Jim's latest hero lives. Boris Slattery arrives in the town on a whim, marries from compassion and lingers on out of apathy in his wife's family home, dreaming of the young Swedish lodger, Inez, in a plot constructed upon the chance rescue – while living in a greenhouse beside a station – of his future mother-in-law in a mistral-force gale. *The Lung* had examined Jim's most searing memories; *A Girl in the Head* was about the resultant dislocation. Childhood hopefulness was to be set against adult disillusion, revealing that the way Jim continued to see himself bore little resemblance to the opinionated guest at the Spurlings' table, favourite pink shirt open at the top button and collar neatly tucked into the rounded neck of his light wool jumper. *But there was another man standing slightly to one side with a pair of cymbals which he clashed from time to time. He was so thin that his scarlet uniform hung in great empty folds from his shoulders, and every time he came to clash his cymbals his gaunt, exhausted face decomposed into a look of utter desperation.*

Writing to Russell, Jim stressed Sergei Eisenstein's enormous care over the construction of his films, adding that he did not think it was the only approach, but it certainly appealed to him. 'I have the impression that the more consciously one creates something,' he added, 'the more satisfaction you get from it (the author, I mean).' He created an *unspeakable* brother-in-law, Maurice – *a poseur and a layabout* – from his concealed antipathy to Alan Riddell, a raffish Australian poet who roomed at the Pembridge Road house, and even occasional pot-smoking at parties had a use. *Once on his feet Boris realised that he was immensely tall . . . Warm oil was injected into the dry sockets of his limbs so that they flowed effortlessly . . .* Alan's sexual exhibitionism would prompt the dénouemont, in which Boris finds the graphic evidence that Maurice and Inez – shades of Ait Ouvrir – are lovers.

Engrossed by depicting the hedonistic Inez, Jim took out a Swedish au pair. But, arriving with her at a bottle party, his eye was caught by a girl with pale-gold hair and a sexual aura. Sandy Ellis, amused by his insistence, gave him her phone number while her boyfriend was getting their drinks. After a trip to Hutchinson's next day to earn the money to pay for it he took her to supper at the Ark, further down Palace Gardens Terrace. 'Don't look now,' he said suddenly, indicating another table, but a patronising male voice, unchanged since last heard at Oxford, could not be stopped. 'Oh, it is Jim! Do tell me, you still scribbling?' Unaware of the sneering Edward Gibbon allusion, conscious only of Jim's anger, Sandy was his champion from that moment on. He took her back to the greenhouse and drew the curtains, and she found him touchingly worried that she might be feigning her response.

As a girl, Sandy Ellis had been a Pony Club winner, and she drove her mini with the same pluck. She was an illustrator with an advertising agency, lived at the other end of Kensington High Street, and favoured miniskirts and thigh boots. In vitality and the confidence to take the initiative, she was exactly as he imagined Inez. 'Race you to that lamp post and the last one to reach it pays for the meal,' he would shout, jumping the gun in his determination not to be beaten over 100 yards, and he instigated singing contests, presenting her with his best Jeanne Moreau record as a prize. Even visiting the wheelchair-bound Stephen Wall in Oxford lost its customary sadness when Sandy whisked him up and down by car. '[We] literally flew back to London by 7pm with Jim holding on tightly and closing his eyes in sheer fright most of the time,' she wrote when thanking them.

'Luckily the speed limit is 70 or I'm sure I'd have gone at least 90!'

Jim never discussed his writing with Sandy, and Andrew Gemill, the Spurlings and The Albany were kept off limits. 'There was always a shadowy girlfriend', according to Maureen Duffy, 'but it was never made clear. One always thought he was involved with somebody, but who?' Once they unexpectedly bumped into Maureen in the street, and when he murmured, 'Oh, she likes you' afterwards, the inflection was suggestive. Sandy was under no illusions about his opinion of her mind. 'He liked nothing more than to take me to an intellectual gathering,' she said later, 'and know I was out of place.'

From being spontaneous, she began, as had others, to hesitate before she spoke. He held her hand as they walked and cuddled her if she was upset, but never said he loved her, nor did he enquire if she loved him. At her endearment 'Jimbo' he flinched, which she interpreted as not wanting to let anyone get too near. 'He wanted the appendage of a woman,' she analysed, 'but not the responsibility, and it was new for me to be treated like that. Suddenly I was being used, but he would never admit it.' The sudden swings from approval to disapproval sapped her faith in her own judgement and, dreading his ability to hurt, she set out to hide her feelings. In the beginning she had wondered why he was immune to jealousy; the bleak conclusion was that he was self-sufficient.

But one evening, over a bottle of wine, he surprised her. 'If we get married,' he remarked unforgettably, 'I would never live with you full-time. There would always be a room in London, some-where where I went to work, and it might be that I spent more time there than with you.' The impression was not of love or need, but fear: the horror of being dominated that also happened to be Boris Slattery's view. 'I don't think,' she reflected after much else had happened, 'I would have *let* myself marry him.' Jim never referred to the subject again, and took her cool reaction in his stride. 'These things happen to me all the time,' he consoled Russell over an unhappy love affair. 'I normally do my best to regard a refusal as her loss rather than mine. This doesn't, of course, prevent it from smarting for a while or, indeed, change the fact that you'd have been bored to death.'

Hilary Spurling, who was of the opinion that he divided women into sirens, who were threatening, and squaws, who were non-threatening, saw a sweetness in him as a friend that Sandy could never count upon.

He would turn away after making love; the parallel was not with Inez any more, but with Boris. Sandy went out with other men, hoping to prompt a reaction, and he retreated further, half-heartedly playing the same game with a separate objective. 'I'm vaguely pursuing an affair (if that's the right word)', he wrote a few months later, 'with two women of my own age (that's to say past the highest point of the physical curve). Both nice, both independent, neither with a grip on any feelings I may still have. They both . . . have a trace of something lost, mirror the dull bitterness of apartness (for once I can't claim to be lonely) that I feel myself.'

Halfway through *A Girl in the Head* Boris tires of living under glass. *And, you know, when I thought how agreeable it would be to move out of my greenhouse and into a place with brick walls, my word, the idea didn't seem altogether unattractive to me.* Jim was reaching the same point as his six-month lease came up for renewal when his landlady turned the tables by telling him the room was promised to a student. 'The idea being', he noted, still smarting, 'that she thought she could let it more easily before the weather got bad.' Gary Arnott came to the rescue once more but was on the point of moving to New York, and after a restless interval, with just two-thirds of his book completed, Jim came across cheap accommodation in a rambling block of Notting Hill bedsitters, misleadingly called the Stanley House Hotel. In the tall, seedy building at 22 Stanley Crescent he took a small ground-floor room at the back, complete with sink and cooking ring. It had a cracked windowpane that let in draughts, but it was made of substantial bricks and mortar. 'I'm now living in this hotel in reduced circumstances, as they say,' he logged after a week. 'Since I've been here I've been sleeping an alarming amount. Yesterday I discovered a gas leak from the stove.'

There were constant comings and goings within the building, and the phone in the hall – Park 8296 – rang out untended until callers gave up. Residents seemed to lead nocturnal lives and left their doors ajar by day, creating the impression of eyes watching every move. *The hotel was largely patronized, as far as I could see,* Boris Slattery would conclude in similar circumstances, *by portly retired cat-burglars and polite dusky gentlemen cooking curries over small blue flames* . . . In real life the landlord, an Irishman, owned a dog 'with a body the shape and colour of a sandbag'. Renamed Bonzo, after a boyhood dog at The Gwanda, it was destined to be the first of the manipulative animals that prowl single-mindedly through Jim's books.

In November, unable to stand the continual interruptions, Jim sought the peace of Dalkey, explaining only that the hotel was 'too awful'. His book was nearing 300 pages, and with a couple of 'major events' still to be achieved, it was likely to be twenty or thirty pages longer than *The Lung*. Forcing himself to re-read the completed chapters, the result was total dismay. 'The thing is badly out of focus,' he decided. 'The tone is wrong. It is unreal without creating a reality of its own.' He again became convinced that his writing powers were waning, a fear exacerbated by his previous good reviews, and was sure the book would be branded a step backwards upon publication unless he could come up with some new ideas. 'The way things are at the moment,' he enumerated glumly. 'No money, a vast amount of energy-draining and nerve-straining work to get through . . . Virtually nobody to talk to without a definite journey. I feel as if I'm colliding head-on with each new day. I even have curious fleeting heart-pains to increase my general feeling of insecurity.'

His parents did their best to keep out of the way, but the difficulties of working at home became as insuperable as in the Stanley House Hotel. The sensation, he groaned to Russell, was like 'being strangled by the invisible tendrils of electricity constantly wavering about and preparing to snatch me back into adolescence'. The characterisation of Boris reflected his mood, intensified by constant reminders of the incarceration after polio: he was sleeping in the same bed, looking at the same four walls and walking past the same houses in the same suburbs along roads that were drearily unchanged. *All the white skeletons of dead emotions . . . Do they somehow continue to exist once they are over and done with? . . . Time passing. How quickly it fled.*

'My own life is dull without relief,' he recorded. 'In bed last night as I was crawling painfully towards unconsciousness I was thinking how petty and sordid it was. However, before finally going under a slightly reassuring thought occurred to me: namely that my own life was sunshine and clear skies compared with that of some people (Tolstoy, for instance) who found themselves forced to conduct their business from the most appalling psychological infernos.' Sandy had been invited over for Christmas, and he phoned when she was about to set out to tell her not to come, explaining unconvincingly that his father was unwell. *A nebulous desire for escape poured slowly out of a dark hole in his mind . . . Forget it, he tried to tell himself, even as the idea wrapped itself around him in a flash of writhing coils . . .*

From January onwards he stuck it out at the Stanley House Hotel, moving the camping table at which he wrote to face a wall to stop him looking out of the window. While typing late one night, he would claim, he was interrupted by a man who was balancing on the small balcony and tapping on the window, mouthing that he needed to reach a callgirl on an upper floor. Jim let him in, pointed out the stairs, presumed that he was a burglar and went back to work. Insomnia was the penalty for so much nocturnal work.

Whenever Jim wrote a book he was conscious of feeling 'starved' of affection, while simultaneously recoiling from emotional claims. He would call round to see John Spurling, with whom he felt increasingly in tune, when he felt particularly lonely, and at one of Gary's parties he got to know Tom Wakefield, who lived in the basement next door and was always glad to go with him to a film. Being the deputy headmaster of a school for handicapped children, Tom officially hid his homosexuality, a sensible move at a time when the practice was illegal but one which would bring him up against Jim's uncompromising set of values. Told of Tom's dream of becoming a writer, Jim replied that unless he was open about his sexuality nothing he wrote would be any good. At his request Tom showed him around his north London school, where polio damage accounted for much of the paralysis, and lent Jim an orthopaedic handstretcher for daily exercises. Boris, simultaneously, recoiled from the sight of a similar ward. 'My book is coming along slowly', Jim wrote on 7 February 1966. 'I keep getting interrupted, but with luck I should have it finished in a couple of months.' But three days later an expensive envelope addressed to him stood out among the unopened bills and circulars on the dusty table in the hall. Its contents promptly blew his schedule apart.

While in France Jim had contemplated teaching French in America, but the idea had later been quashed by the American Embassy in Dublin. Changing tack, he had applied to thirteen all-girl colleges, including Vassar and Sarah Lawrence, to teach creative writing, but only Mount Holyoke had bothered to reply. Undiscouraged, though by now more fatalistic about his chances, he had followed up a prospect aired by Christian van Briesgan, a go-getting artist friend of Gary's, who set his sights on a Harkness Fellowship which funded two years of study in the United States. To qualify, a graduate needed to have a track record in the Arts, politics, journalism or academia, and demonstrate a potential for future influence, because the aim of the awards was to promote the American perspective. Incredulous at Christian's success on the vague premise of researching a book on modern New York painting, Jim had gone to the trouble of consulting Jonathan Clowes.

It had always been agreed between them that his talents lay in the direction of novels, and that he was not prepared to spend the time and energy to master a new skill. 'Providing you can stand the way of life,' Clowes had answered then, re-assessing him, 'it's more lucrative to write for films, where $100,000 for a commissioned screenplay is nothing. But first you'll have to learn the technique thoroughly, and then you'll have to put up with the crass producers.' The trump card he played for sensitive, idealistic writers was to mention Michael Winner, but Jim was undeterred. He had put in an official application for the autumn 1966 intake as soon as he discovered that the Yale Drama School ran a playwriting course that included film as well as theatre. Three referees were needed, and he whipped in Graham Nicol, as well as Peter Browne, the family friend who had accompanied him home after polio and was now teaching at Berkeley, California, and Dr Walter Eysselinck of the University of Sussex; Eysselinck was a graduate of Yale Drama School.

Ticking the category 'Literature and Drama', he had stressed his novel-writing, not the scriptwriting. He was open about his ambition, if not his motive. 'It would seem that for a novelist interested in the twentieth century', he had argued:

> some experience of the US would provide valuable, if not essential, insights, if only because it is often more rewarding to look at your own country through the window of another. I am deeply interested in trying to write universal, as opposed to regional, novels; the sort of books in which people trying to adjust themselves to abrupt changes in their civilisation, whether it be in Ireland or in Japan, may be able to recognise themselves . . . There is no point in concealing the fact that I should be grateful for the chance of continuing my work without the distraction of scraping a living and the numerous hardships stemming from the vow of poverty that seems to be imposed on dedicated writers and artists. Faulkner was reported to have said that nobody on a Fellowship ever wrote anything good. I should like to prove him wrong on this score.

But the aloof selection interview at Harkness House in Upper Brook Street, Mayfair, conducted by a committee that included Sir Eric Ashby, Master of Clare College, Cambridge, the Countess of Albemarle, and three Oxford men, F.W.D. Deakin, Warden of St Anthony's College, Sir Robert Shone, Fellow of Nuffield College, and the non-voting Harkness UK secretary Gorley Putt, had left him with little realistic hope.

Unable to believe his luck now at hitting 'the American jackpot' so unexpectedly, he gloated to Russell straight away. 'I should be getting $300 a month, a block of $400 for book and equipment allowance (I suppose equipment means French letters), car rental for not less than 6 months, a $300 bonus for Christmas travel and $500 for some other time of year, return ship passage, any tuition fees and one or two other fringe benefits.' But when the moment came to announce his coup in The Albany to the less fortunate he was embarrassed, and emphasised instead his dread of driving the American-sized car that came with the fellowship. 'We were all thrilled and envious,' Maureen Duffy spoke up for them later. 'It seemed like an accolade for us all.'

First, however, the book had to be finished, and it was as lonely and arduous a process as ever. 'I still believe myself incapable of writing when living in close contact with someone,' Jim analysed late at night as the weeks began whirling past, sped by the departure date lying in wait. 'At least having the sort of unstable relationship that I normally seem to have with girls . . . I'm now fully aware of this curious anarchy inside me that requires me to smash to pieces every promising relationship.' To Russell, too, he admitted a bad patch, due partly, he said, hastily covering his tracks, to lack of success with a girl he did not much like. Fortunately for Sandy she could not know that he now saw her in Proustian terms, as Odette to his Swann. *You know, life is really rather sad when you come to think of it*, Boris would muse in conclusion. *You can try everything to give it some colour. You can try everything and it still makes no difference.*

Handing in the typescript at the beginning of April, with its telling subtitle, *The Succubus*, Jim's customary depression took no account of the forthcoming fellowship; if anything, upheaval ahead made the reaction worse. His sleep pattern remained broken and he suffered nightmares in which he was isolated and unloved. In the most upsetting of them his mother was stonily indifferent. 'There's no reason', he resolved, steeling himself against despair, 'why it shouldn't be solved like everything else by exercising the mind.'

'My agent read it with rather muted enthusiasm; his eyes narrowed to inscrutable, oriental slits when I asked him for an opinion,' he told Russell, mask back in place. 'At present he is dangling it seductively in front of various publishers here. I'm still not happy with it, I'm afraid, and feel that I shall have to perform some surgery on the beginning.' The session had been bruising, in fact, with Clowes pointing out that the book would be improved by more work and extensive trimming. 'Jim *wasn't* happy to have me involved on the editorial side,' he recalled long after the dust had settled. 'He was polite but clearly very unhappy with making cuts, and he didn't trust my judgement.' Hugging reservations, Clowes sent a copy to Tom Maschler of Jonathan Cape. Maschler was interested, but stipulated ahead of a meeting with them both that cuts would definitely have to be made. Eventually a contract was agreed, with the final draft to be delivered by 31 July, and only then did Jim realise that he would be in New York when the book came out.

At Cape he found himself in company with Anthony Burgess, Kingsley Amis and John Fowles, and he came away from the offices in Bedford Square elated, greatly taken by the scholarly impact of the Georgian townhouse. Cape proposed to utilise his two initials to distinguish him from his American *bête noire*, James T. Farrell, a suggestion he liked; the gravitas of J.G. Farrell appealed to him, especially as he was dedicating this book to his brothers. Soon, however, he was complaining to Hilary Spurling about the proposed cover design, which featured a nude, see-thing that it was typical and crass – 'Because "girl" is in the title they think they need a nude, and it's such a *homely* one' – and when a line drawing of the Botticelli Venus was substituted he disliked the orange background. Resentment about editorial changes spilled over towards Cape, and he began criticising publishers so bitterly that she ticked him off for being ungrateful.

Like the tidal metaphor used so often within the book's pages, Jim's personal feelings about *A Girl in the Head* ebbed and flowed. In some moods he considered it the best thing he had done, and was prepared to ally himself with the sculptor Giacometti's comment, 'I'm not really very good, but on second thoughts I'm better than everybody else.' In others he recoiled from the proofs, and flinched at his presumption at calling himself a writer. 'At one time I used to think that after publication I would merely be "myself who had written a book",' he reflected after an encounter with another author. 'Strange how quickly one becomes armour-plated with one's profession, with thinking of oneself in a certain way, or competitively. I noticed [how] disarmed I was by the fact that I couldn't patronise him . . . In the last year or two I seem to have become quite sickeningly ambitious.'

But as soon as the burden of his book had been transferred to Cape, he was casting around for a new and 'mammoth' theme. 'To write a book on insane revolutions,' he jotted in his latest notebook. 'The Frondes, the Stolen Days etc. Insane sporting events like the Crusades might be mentioned too.' . . . 'Not necessarily original this. A science fiction story in which "liberal" principles have to be evoked for the protection of some non-earth creatures. Does one apply earth criteria, or not?' Without drawing breath he scanned newspapers and books for ideas, which led to one or two wry conclusions. 'Reading in *Elements of Biology* about the beginnings of life on earth – well, where does this leave us egocentric novelists? On the other hand, why should I care about my origins in reacting chemicals? I exist, if only temporarily, and in my imagination I can make things as I want them.' As an interim project, he joined the library of the British Museum and began to research the life of Joan of Arc's contemporary Gilles de Rais, with a view to a play.

Whenever unease at imminent disruption sharpened into foreboding, a fresh vista swung momentarily into focus. 'How thin the shell of civilisation that holds anarchy out,' he had mused after watching news pictures of the Watts racial riots on television the previous August. 'And then every little crime is a crack that lets anarchy seep through the shell.' Sitting quietly over a pint in the nearby Duke of York as the switch to America drew nearer, a fight suddenly erupted beside the bar and showered him with broken glass and flecks of blood. On the top deck of a bus a few days later he snapped out of reverie when a couple of youths at the back began to bait a middle-aged peroxide blonde.

'In these situations', he scribbled before he forgot, 'I alway get a creepy feeling that polite society can dissolve into a bloodbath at the drop of a hat. I think it's the apparent lack of motivation that worries me.' And watching Ionesco's sketch on Anger for *The Seven Deadly Sins* he marked the chain of cause and effect, from the tiny incident of a man losing his temper over finding a caterpillar in his salad to an entire city brought to a standstill. 'I imagine this is more or less the way the Watts riots started,' he deduced, a conclusion borne out by the official investigation in which the spark that resulted in thirty-four deaths and more than 1,000 injuries was identified as a routine drunk-driving arrest in the black ghetto.

Glimpses of a mammoth theme continued to tantalise him during his final weeks in London. As he sifted current events for a starting point, hairline cracks were discernible everywhere. A radio news report led with the stabbing of a policeman by an unemployed teenager – 'the appalling first few hours or days when one is getting used to the idea that everything has been utterly changed by this one insignificant action' – and his reaction to a televised interview with striking Ford workers – 'unbelievably ignorant, aggressive, and coarse' – raised disturbing questions about himself. 'Montherlant would say "That's how they are. That's what you expect me to love",' he guessed. 'Sartre would say "Why are they like that? Because that's how capitalism has created them." And yet, can it really be that the actuality doesn't offend their sensibilities?'

It was gloomy speculation, made more so by Jim's solitary way of life. After an evening in a local Indian restaurant with Sandy, at the Gate Cinema in Notting Hill with Tom Wakefield or talking books and plays with the Spurlings, he returned to his shabby bedsitter and his thoughts. 'Would I have felt like this in a comfortable flat, travelling in taxis and with a healthy bank account?' he wondered during a sleepless night, as the 24 August departure date came near. 'Even then there still must be the moment when you turn the key in the lock, switch on the lights in the dark rooms, look around at the empty furniture standing exactly where you left it . . . Really one must live an idea if one is not to be wounded by the moment that lies between opening the door and taking off your raincoat.'

In the summer of 1966 London was the centre of the world, according to *Time* magazine. In July an entire issue was devoted to the Swinging City, as the headlines called it, with maps provided to enable newcomers from America to find their way around. Carnaby Street was only a short tube ride from the Stanley House Hotel on the Central Line, but Jim was conscious of little else but being in the wrong place at the wrong time. 'In my experience,' he had once recommended when Russell was similarly blocked, 'changing locale can do a lot for changing one's inner scenery too'. He had to hope that his own advice was well-founded.

He was peremptory with Sandy when the time came to say goodbye. 'I shan't expect you to hang around waiting for me while I'm away, because *I* shan't,' he instructed as she burst into tears. 'You'll soon see someone else,' he soothed in meagre consolation. And without a backward look he walked away.

CHAPTER THIRTEEN

The Extreme Outer Edge
of Endeavour
1966–1967

T he sea – once more – as catalyst. Harkness Fellows had to cross the Atlantic by ship and embark on the understanding that no early return would be sanctioned, short of an emergency. The psychological leap of emigration was believed to create fresh attitudes of mind. Jim was resistant to manipulation and doggedly European in perspective. He evaluated the other passengers as Stolidly Dutch or Annoyingly American, the standard of food as below that of a workman's cafe in the Portobello Road, and toyed quite seriously with the notion of being back by Christmas. It was the 100 dollars of spending money pressed upon him on arrival that achieved the desired outlook. 'I shall hope to startle American Express with the enormous efficiency with which I shall try to handle their correspondence,' he resolved in the Abbey Victoria Hotel on 7th Avenue and 51st Street, where the fifty-four assorted Fellows were initially put up.

Harkness House, the fount of munificence, was a beautiful brownstone on the corner of 5th Avenue and 75th Street, entered through a Tuscan portico at the side, and Jim showed up for the introductory dinner impressed by the contrast with his only other visit to New York. By the following year he would be irreverent enough to claim to a newcomer that he had peed in the majestic fireplace, but in a tone of such self-mockery that he was in no danger of being believed. The original Harkness fortune had been made with Standard Oil, and Jim's knowledge of John D. Rockefeller's business practices clashed silently with the Ivy

League atmosphere that prevailed. Martha English, who was responsible for his welfare, congratulated him upon being the only writer to be selected, and John B. Fox, his chief liaison link, turned out to be literary-minded and reticently benign. 'The richness was the people you met,' an awed English contemporary observed. 'It was the first time I was clubbed together with dancers, artists and poets, as well as rising stars in science and business, and I felt special – privileged. These were the most prestigious awards of all.'

The elevated beginning was tailor-made for bathos, the style to which Jim naturally inclined. A two-hour train journey from Penn Station took him to New Haven in Connecticut, where the accommodation he selected for his stint at Yale was Apt 3, 173 Park Street, within walking distance of the Drama School, and the cheapest he could find. His financial bonanza of 350 dollars a month, on top of the liberal books and travel allowance, car hire, health cover and paid-up fees, had to be marshalled as scrupulously as time itself if he was to obtain the maximum tenure in which to write. 'I've found myself buying sheets and a blanket for the first time in my life,' he noted sardonically. 'I feel sure this is in some way symbolic of my decline.' Gallon jars of Californian burgundy from the local liquor store, a telephone and a fifty-dollar typewriter completed the basic preparations. The typewriter, pleasingly, was a bargain compared to English prices, and the Hermes 'Rocket' which he chose was the same model as the Hermes 'Baby' marketed in London; the psychology behind the different names amused him.

New Haven struck him as provincial and architecturally gloomy, with only two bookshops deserving of the name and drip-dry shirts and polyester suits on display in Macy's windows. His portable radio drew a blank on classical music stations, instead proffering rock and repetitive 'ads', and to see the latest films involved an eight-mile round trip to a movie supermarket in Orange. 'Saw *Khartoum* last night and liked it,' he wrote to Brian Knox Peebles, nostalgic for London. 'Also read *The Millstone*, which I thought very good indeed . . . What news of Caute? I saw that his book got a bad review in the two papers I read in England. I have the feeling it went down better over here though . . . The slightly peculiar style of this letter is

William (Bill) on his return from India in 1934, Josephine (Jo), and little Robert Farrell. On the right is Jo's seafaring grandfather, Joseph Russell, whose adventures would help to inspire *The Singapore Grip*.

Jim Farrell (left) as a sturdy baby, with his older brother Robert.

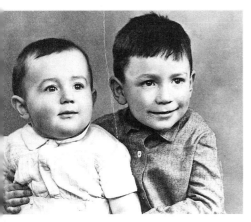

Jim and Robert on holiday from Terra Nova prep school, at their grandfather's house in Ireland, 1943.

Travelling abroad for the first time as a schoolboy, equipped with open mind, broad shoulders, and Brylcreemed hair. Jim's passport photo, March 1951.

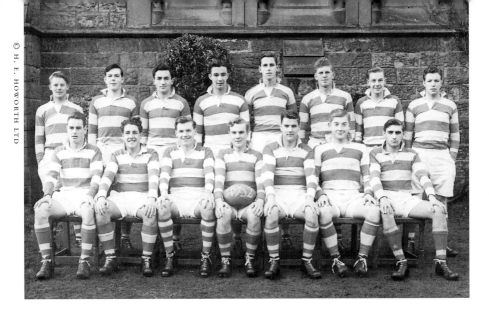

ABOVE Muscular centre-three quarter in red and white strip on the Rossall 1st xv. (Back row, third from the left.) Also on the team: Frank Taylor (third from the right, same row), Nevill Phillips (third from left, front) and Alf Tansey (third from right, front).

LEFT Working on the DEW LINE. Canadian Arctic, Winter 1955/56.

BELOW Full member of the 'Dalkey Set': Jim (circled at right) at a teenage party at the Kirwans' house in County Dublin.

The yearning, the boredom, the heartache. Jim (centre, behind the girls) and Jill Kirwan (front, right).

Sitting alone with
aching neck and back.
After polio, while
recuperating at his
parents' home, 1957.

Gaunt and purposeful
at Oxford, deflecting
pity by a *screen of
cheerful irony.*

Judy Mitchell, photographed by Jim at Trinity College, Dublin, 1958.

Bob Cumming, Rhodes scholar.

Tom Farrell winning the 800 metres at White City in 1960, two weeks before breaking the British record again for the 400 metres hurdles.

© JEREMY MOORAN

Martin Gilbert, who shared digs during Jim's final year at Brasenose

John and Hilary Spurling.

Monsieur Farrell, in Paris
at the time of writing
The Lung.

UNIVERSITÉ DE PARIS

INSTITUT BRITANNIQUE

6, Rue de la Sorbonne - PARIS

CARTE D'ÉTUDIANT Nº 305

délivrée à Mr. FARRELL James

valable jusqu'au fin Décembre

Signature de l'Étudiant,

J.G.Farrell

Date : 20/11/63

Signature de la Direction,

Validité prolongée jusqu'au fin Juin
année scolaire

Signature

The author as model. Jim's
head projects from the sand,
at Frances Humphreys' feet.

On the threshold of *Troubles*.
Jim in New York, autumn 1966.

Erwin Fleissner

Russell McCormmach and Jim
(New York, early autumn 1966)

Troubles: the breakthrough on Block Island.

a) Contemporary account in Jim's journal.

b) 'A flight of stone steps leading up to thin air'. Remains of the Ocean View Hotel

This morning I went up to look at the remains while the sun was still shining. Old bedsprings twisted with heat; puddles of molten glass; washbowls that had fallen through to the foundations; a flight of stone steps leading up to thin air; twisted pipes; lots of nails lying everywhere and a few charred beams. I think the way the glass had collected like candle-grease under the windows impressed me most. When you picked it up it was inclined to flake away into smaller pieces in your hand. I must remember to ask someone how many storeys it had. Anyway, this gave me an idea, which seems to me a good one, for the dwelling place of the family.

Sandy Ellis

Diana Saville

© BELA ZOLA, DAILY MIRROR

Sarah Bond

Patricia Moynagh

Ann Colville

Carol Drisko at her desk overlooking the Algonquin Hotel.

Bridget O'Toole, photographed by Jim beside the Serpentine in Kensington Gardens, where he often took walks after the day's writing.

Preparing a meal for Russell McCormmach (note Jim's difficulty cutting bread).

Writing *The Singapore Grip* at his desk in Egerton Gardens.
On the wall: two favourite works by Mary Newcomb.

Mike Roemer

Malcolm Dean

In 'distinguished writer' pose: Booker Prize, 1973.

© JERRY BAUER

Claire Tomalin

Francis King

Margaret Drabble

Jim in the doorway of his 'own house', Gortfahane, in West Cork. July 1979.

The small jetty at the sea, a short walk downhill from Gortfahane. The rock from where Jim fished is away to the left, out of the picture. In the distance is the far side of Bantry Bay.

© MICHAEL LEON

A conversation with Jim Farrell.

the result of reading Robinson Crusoe all night. Infantalism is setting in.' The theme of David Caute's new book, *The Left in Europe since 1789*, highlighted the isolation he himself was in; too late he would discover that Caute had been almost on his doorstep, as Visiting Professor at New York University and Columbia. Solitary, disapproving, Jim mooched about New Haven. After a while he heard with satisfaction that one Yale professor referred to it as Taganog, after Chekhov's hated birthplace on which all the remote dull towns of his plays were based. The coincidence that two old friends from Paris, separately, now lived near enough to visit by train promised temporary escape.

'Last weekend I went to Boston to see Patsy Cumming and, on the way back, Franz Beer,' he wrote to Russell McCormmach, who was living in Philadelphia. 'Well, all through the weekend I felt ill at ease somehow; rather the feeling one gets on seeing a good film for the third or fourth time – it's wonderful, but I've ceased to react.' Russell was doing a Ph.D. at the University of Pennsylvania and Bob Cumming was also out of weekend reach, having returned to North Carolina to teach in the English Department at Chapel Hill. But Gary Arnott worked on Wall Street, and Roger Donald and Erwin Fleissner were also in New York. Roger was married with two children and too senior in his publishing career for Jim to feel they had enough in common any more, and Erwin's research into tumour viruses at the Sloane Kettering Cancer Research Institute made him feel a lightweight in comparison. Roger appeared to have moved on, but Erwin downplayed himself as a rational scientist, and insisted that a writer's contribution to the quality of existence was no less valuable: both, in his view, contributed to improving public health. Revolutionary strides were being made in his branch of molecular biology with the discovery and systematic unravelling of the genetic code, and in his comfortable apartment on West 96th Street, off Central Park, Erwin enthused Jim with the remaining challenge for the results to be encoded and expressed. It was hard to recover intimacy, Jim noted, none the less. To Erwin's strong-minded wife Norma, a prolific writer, who took him sightseeing, overcame his objections to posing for photographs, and lectured him on feminism and equal rights, he portrayed himself defensively as the archetypal bachelor. 'He has developed an inner life,' Erwin reported in turn to Bob Cumming. 'A citadel – a centre.'

Jim had not been happy at Oxford, and Yale was even less his sort of place. He took against it as a WASP enclave, as unimpressed by the gothic resemblances to Oxford as he was by gaudy fraternity signs, and he recoiled from anti-semitic jokes and the unrepresentative ratio on campus of blacks and homosexuals. Roaming about in his unobtrusive way, taking his bearings from the soaring Kline Biology Tower and checking out institutions like the Beinecke Library and the Branford Buttery, he had to fight down a 'crushing sensation' of déjà vu. Yale Drama School, particularly, fell well short of his expectations, which were based upon famous alumni like Paul Newman and Elia Kazan. 'In particular the Drama School seems to have attracted every phoney and poseur on the continent,' he fumed to Knox Peebles, whom he knew would understand. 'The place is crammed to the rafters with pretentious and acneous youths with shades on. I haven't yet discovered whether there are any among them who are talented [but] for the moment I'm fearing the worst.'

The incoming Dean, Robert Brustein, was a radical New York theatre critic who had chosen to announce the revolution in store by painting the Green Room and theatre bright red, a move judged to be a communist ploy by members of Yale Dramat, the outgoing regime. Determined to replace tradition with training relevant to contemporary theatre, Brustein had moved fast, hiring a new faculty, revamping the course catalogue and revolutionising the forthcoming theatre season. Jim was arriving at the most disruptive period in the Drama School's history. Whispers swept about that Brustein had powerful friends on Martha's Vineyard, where he had a holiday home, and that he owed his job to being a member of that clique, among whom Kingman Brewster, the President of Yale, could be counted. But Jim was more interested to hear that Philip Roth was a near neighbour there, as were John Hersey, William Styron and Art Buchwald. In due course *Little Murders* by Jules Feiffer went into rehearsal, and Feiffer turned out to be a Martha's Vineyard local, too. Little remained secret among the warring factions, and his favourite story was of the disastrous introduction of Brustein's actress wife, Norma, to a bristling Yale Dramat supporter. 'Have you met Mrs Brustein yet?' 'No. Thank God I've been spared *that*.'

The staff included Stella Adler, a Stanislavsky pupil; Jan Kott, who lectured on dramatic literature; Arnold Weinstein, who taught playwriting, and the controversial Brustein himself. Peter Brook, whom Jim would much have preferred, had refused the job in protest at America's growing involvement in Vietnam. 'The Drama School looks as if it is going to be not only valueless for me, but also positively obnoxious, thanks to the garrulity of the students, who are a rare collection of imbeciles,' he scribbled angrily before the end of the first month. Brustein was dismissed as 'a nice man', not a fiery comet, no-one had any original ideas, and the entire faculty were 'straining their guts out to be dynamic and hip . . . In general, everyone around here seems to be equipped with a king-size ego that renders an exchange of ideas impossible. Well, there it is. I expect I shall gradually phase myself out of it all and take to sitting in my apartment and scratching my scalp while waiting for something to happen.'

By the end of September he had stopped going to all classes except one, justifying the boycott in Drama School phraseology by drawling that they were escalating his demoralisation. Instead he sat at home and practised on his new typewriter with a variety of short stories, each of which proved a dead end rather than the intended short cut into a mammoth theme. The lack of inspiration was doubly oppressive because, having got his Harkness award on the strength of producing something important, and now refusing to take up the tuition, he felt under increased pressure to perform. 'This is really the root of my problem,' he pondered glumly. 'I haven't yet found an idea I can absorb myself in.' As his longing to withdraw completely into 'the private world of another novel' intensified, he also began to chafe about the commercial fate of *A Girl in the Head*.

'Writing for the Camera' was the only course he continued to attend. He did so on the grounds that it salved his conscience and kept his options open, but concentration on film technique would hold unexpected literary relevance. The showing of a film was followed by a lengthy dissection of the influences upon it, and he soon made a point of arriving early for the three-hour, twice-weekly classes and taking the same side seat in the front row. In the small projection room he cut an unassertive figure, slipping down in his seat, hunched in silhouette, when the credits began to roll; his prematurely white hair and English accent drew less attention than the pointed-toed cowboy boots of Sam Shepard, who had a success Off Broadway, or the dogcollar of a Jesuit named Scully. Most of 'the oddballs' were on ABC playwriting grants or avoiding Vietnam by claiming student deferment and, though none could have guessed it, Jim felt hardbitten in juxtaposition. As the classes notched up he made two exceptions: Ken Brown was a powerful and sensitive ex-marine from Brooklyn tipped to win a Pulitzer Prize for his celebrated play *The Brig*, a harsh autobiographical production based on his experiences of military punishment in the Korean War, and John Guare brooded in the back row, sharing Jim's reservations and contributing many of his own. 'I must say, I like him,' Jim noted as he got to know Guare. 'Big, dishevelled, bespectacled, breezy in manner and with a quick wit, there is something very genuine about him.'

He also approved of the two film-makers – '*steeped* in films' – who ran the new course, Mike Roemer and Robert Young. 'Both highly intelligent and sympathique. The methodical and ruthless way they work is just the example needed for someone like me who is always ready to grow flabby and self-satisfied on a few crumbs of journalistic praise.' The small New York company of Roemer-Young Associates Inc., of 245 West 55th Street, made innovative film documentaries on a shoestring and had caught Brustein's eye by winning an Oscar for their most recent, *Nothing But a Man*. Roemer took the role of presenter, leading the class in analysis afterwards, and Young advised on camerawork, completing an unlikely double act. As a Jewish refugee in childhood, Roemer retained his German accent and expressive European gesticulation, while the athletic Young, a member of the wealthy Duarte film-processing family, was matter-of-fact and relaxed. 'My aim was to get the class to really think about each film,' Roemer said of his teaching methods. 'To draw back from being absorbed and to put a distance between experience and its intellectual construction. It could get quite personal. I wanted to put enough consciousness into the process so they would see how it was put together from the literary-critical perspective, not camera angles. I wanted them to develop what I called the film sense.' Jim needed no persuading.

That term twenty-six films were examined, ranging from *Ninotchka*, *The Gold Rush* and *Citizen Kane* to *Some Like It Hot*, *The Cranes Are Flying* and *Zéro de Conduite*. Roemer's choice was as eclectic as it was personal. Jim liked the concentration on Fellini, Visconti and Bresson, approved the inclusion of Lean and Polanski, and was more than willing to take a fresh look at the antics of Buster Keaton and Charlie Chaplin. Roemer stepped out from behind Young's more glamorous shadow, a short, slim man with authoritative mannerisms, implacable standards, and a sudden watermelon smile. 'I'm a very severe realist,' he would emphasise, 'and you must understand that *all* good films have the quality of painstaking detail.' By November Jim was prepared to admit that he attended with passion.

Young's contribution was the practical side of photography, given weight by his reputation for daring award-winning shots, including hanging out of a plane in flight, and being lowered deep underwater in a steel cage to film sharks. He provided hand-held 8-millimetre cameras and told them to make a short film each by the end of the year, and Jim was partnered with Bart Teusch, a youthful New Yorker. 'Why didn't they have something like this at Oxford?' he challenged Knox Peebles by post. 'We wander about the streets of New Haven trying to aim our movie cameras at girls' legs. All very stimulating.' In practice, he felt pretentious squinting through the viewfinder, and the definition was too grainy for such a perfectionist when projected on screen.

Jim knew that Roemer and Young had him pigeonholed as the only novelist in a class of playwrights, and that apart from Brown and Guare the playwrights noticed him as a freak, if at all, but occasionally he surprised everyone and, perhaps, himself. After the showing of Leni Riefenstahl's film of the 1936 Berlin Olympics he sprang up and attacked it so furiously for over-glorification of the human body that Roemer, who had far greater reason to hate Nazi propaganda, was taken aback; no-one present was allowed to know of the lost athleticism Jim still mourned. 'It takes confrontation with that one's deepest likes or dislikes,' Roemer tipped off Young, 'to stir him into speaking.'

. Away from class, however, things were not going well, and Jim gave vent to Russell. 'For the moment I feel that to preserve my sanity I must get myself involved in some work, which in turn partly involves staying here and getting used to living in this apartment. I'm not actually sorry to have left London but it's brought a lot of problems; the main one being life in a town where you don't know anyone you care to talk to.' On impulse he spent ten dollars on Lowry's correspondence – 'with the result that today I'm identifying madly with him' – and loneliness was sharpened when he went to see Beckett's *Endgame* performed by the touring Theatre of Living Arts, in which Hamm and Clov were played as Laurel and Hardy – billed as a vaudeville production – and mimed a masturbatory sequence which led to anti-Brustein uproar. Back in his quiet room Jim was haunted by Beckett's lines, which he knew almost by heart.

'So far the only moment when I've felt at all glad to be here', he recorded, 'came when I went to the Yale Gymnasium to register as a user of the pool and a rugged, paternal old man (no doubt a football hero of the '20's) enclosed my hand in his massive fist and told me that he'd been to England and that after Italy and France it had seemed like home.' Solace also came from the technicolor reds and oranges of the New England Fall, and from the potential of the compulsory Harkness summer tour of America, which he suddenly realised made Lowry's Mexico accessible. He began to look up maps and routes and wrote to Sandy to suggest she join him for it, puncturing any romantic misconceptions by adding that he needed her to share the driving. 'Bring some money,' he commanded.

But by December, unable to admit defeat – 'I've been getting progressively more bushed here, progressively more tantalised with dreams of returning to Europe' – he set about making more immediate changes. He applied to Martha English, in compliance with the 1 January deadline for revisions, for permission to move to New York and commute back to New Haven twice weekly, and purposefully bought a grey leatherette record book. 'Alright then,' he wrote in it on 22 December:

The idea of this diary is to help me to get control of my talent for writing. I hope that it will help in the following ways: 1) That I shall bring myself face to face with things that I normally discard through sheer mental laziness. 2) That I shall be able to remember things people say that make an impression on me as well as things I read. 3) Get in the habit of discussing problems with myself. 4) Catch some of my life before I forget it . . . However, avoid being garrulous or it will become a chore. Avoid self-pity and sentimentality. Avoid haranguing myself uselessly like this.

His first entry pinned down the previous day's discussion with Roemer, and at once one nugget stood out. 'R. repeated his theory that writers use up their experience when young, then go through a middle period of hard work before they can *learn to invent their own material*.'

After Christmas spent with Bob Cumming's family in North Carolina – 'Only when I discuss my work with someone else do I begin to see its glaring deficiences. It's inevitable that it will be deficient in some respect; the disturbing thing is that I'm inclined to forget this except when seeing it through my interlocutor's eyes' – he was notified that his Harkness liaison link, John B. Fox, was coming down to hear his case. They met over an early lunch to fit in with the 2pm start of class. Jim brought him up to date about the Drama School – 'in pretty serious trouble' . . . 'demoralised' . . . 'disjointed' . . . and argued that as no-one showed any interest in creative writing he felt unable to start another novel there, but he could not afford to live in New York unless Harkness paid for the extra train fares.

'Not having read anything Farrell has written,' Fox wrote when recommending the plan, 'I find myself at something of a loss as to how to judge him. He seems to be an extremely kindly and sympathetic and also intelligent person. He talks a great deal of sense about what he is doing . . . I think he is still trying to work out his own relationship with his craft, and it may be some time yet before he works out just what kind of writer he is and how he wishes to write . . . Given his present somewhat insecure relationship with his scriptwriting, he will fare better working by himself in New York than he will exposing himself to the constant criticism and evaluation of others, which of course is part and parcel of working in an academic atmosphere.'

Jim's next address was the Belvedere Hotel in Manhattan, situated on West 48th Street, a stone's throw from Madison Square Gardens. It had opened shortly before the Depression to cater for the great days of boxing, when it had been the choice of Joe Louis and Kid Gavaghan; in the 1930s the show-business crowd appreciated its proximity to the Paramount theatre. The front-facing room Jim took was on the twelfth floor, where – he was told – Marilyn Monroe had lived not long before, but the Belvedere's glory days were long gone and John Guare was surprised by the choice of 'a fleabag hotel'. For a nominal outlay there was a kitchenette and shower, and the characterless square room held a bed, table and telephone, plus a nocturnal army of cockroaches. 'They're built in,' he was told when he complained. The paintwork was fake wood, the corridors vinyl-floored, and the small refrigerator only worked if a block of ice was bought each day. All 450 rooms could be rented by the week or by the day, and no-one asked any questions because nobody cared. Jim christened it Heartbreak Hotel.

From his two windows when he looked right – down Lonely Street – the grey Hudson River glinted; to his left, beyond the corner of 8th Avenue, Broadway was blocked off by skyscrapers topped by the Empire State Building. Down below on the side-walk, reminding him of London, tattered pigeons strutted and pecked, and directly opposite was Public School Number 17, thankfully out of earshot at that height. He settled in and commuted back to Yale twice weekly as agreed, but a mammoth theme was as illusory as ever.

His pace had, if anything, stepped up. He was devouring Montherlant, Lampedusa, Olivia Manning and E.M. Forster, he had tried a script of the Molly Ellis affair, and he was persisting with a new story, miserably aware that it was wrong, and smoking heavily. 'It's the idea of seeing familiar things from different angles that is so valuable', he spurred himself on and, ignoring the long hair, beads and fringes, barely registering the pungent whiffs of pot, he kept his daily exercise on Manhattan's streets to an anguished minimum and spent most of the time indoors, alone. Muriel Spark's *Memento Mori* provided the first tangible clue. 'This book give[s] me an idea of what I failed to seize in *Girl* and *Lung*', he wrote. 'How the world is *different* for a cripple, how ordinary actions are made new and interesting when they are no longer taken for granted; an old lady getting out of a car and cautiously feeling for the ground with her foot. It's all in Ecclesiastes, of course. Things we don't think about now we'll think about later. The trick (for a novelist) is to think about them now. Think about all the possible angles.' In the sweeping novel that he envisaged, all the characters would approach events from different attitudes, but quite what they would see, and where and when, remained stubbornly out of reach.

Mike Roemer, who commuted from New York for classes, offered him a regular lift and refused to take a cent, saying that having company broke the monotony of the $1\frac{1}{2}$-hour drive along Route 95 at the regulation 65mph. 'I felt Jim was completely alone,' he disclosed his motive later. 'Not unhappy, but always so frail. He was as I'd been when I first went into film. I knew he was having a bad time and was very blocked in terms of his work. There was a good feeling about the fact that he was clearly getting something from our talks in the car, so I was getting something back myself. But it was his privateness that struck me most.' On the first day in the front passenger seat of the green VW stationwagon Jim was withdrawn, contemplating a suicidal state of mind for the main character of his latest story – *he, too, found himself in a situation where dying required no effort* – but very soon the journeys became the high points of his week. 'I must be more aggressive,' he echoed dutifully, but it was Roemer's ability to respond from the same frame of reference that made their conversations so valuable.

Six years in England with a benevolent middle-class foster family and a Harvard course in English Literature had not dimmed Roemer's Freudian fascination with the subconscious, nor his veneration for Chekhov, Dostoevsky and, above all else, Proust. It was Proust's portrait that he kept on his desk at home, the Scott Moncrieff translations that he treasured as his bible, and when Jim asked whom he would most like to meet among the greatest influences on his life, the answer came as no surprise. 'Marcel!' Roemer shouted as they sat trapped in a tailback. 'Followed by Van Gogh and Emily Dickinson.' When Jim confided that his favourite moment was Swann's fruitless attempt to break the news that he was dying to friends who were concerned with getting to a fashionable occasion on time, the steering wheel was thumped in recognition.

The methods Roemer employed to get a response, which he called intrepid sincerity, frequently left Jim stunned and on guard – 'Another admission that I would have found difficult to make. The English wife of his school-friend Reiner who told him that he was "insufferable" ' – but there was no attempt to turn the car into a confession box. Anything to do with sex, Roemer guessed, was taboo. 'I didn't known Jim's orientation, which wouldn't have worried me either way,' he observed. 'But I felt there was a neutral quality and I sensed a kind of fear.' He would conclude that Jim was afraid of someone else obscuring his own impressions.

The moment came when Jim dared to invite Roemer's honest assessment of *A Girl in the Head*. There was something tired about it, Roemer responded, and the fact that he projected a character that wasn't his own made the book ring false. 'I'm not sure I understand what he was trying to say and, if I understood, that I agree,' Jim noted when alone. 'I like to think that there's a music in the book that R. can't hear. The snag is: can anyone?' Alert to Jim's dilemma, Roemer redoubled his efforts to help, empathetically retreating to the neutral ground of film.

A director should avoid the obvious and enable the audience to infer things for themselves, he said as they drove down Route 95, stressing that the most terrifying thing was to get past a danger and suddenly be confronted with it again. Creative people, he asserted, waving impatient drivers past, had first to 'go out' in order to go back inside themselves productively, because mastery of detail was the key. 'The inward passage is treacherous, dynamite everywhere. You can't go into it until you know what you're doing because the thorough examination of reality beats sitting at a desk attempting to conjure up images. Call it Zola research,' he added astutely. 'There's a whole world of solid, indigestible *reality*', Jim wrote in his grey notebook, 'between fiction and the outside world. Between the life of the mind and the physical facts.'

His writing was reflecting the pressure he was under, with

plots exuding claustrophobia and lack of control. 'I wonder how long I shall be able to last out,' he speculated in his record book. 'Even after eight months the streets of Manhattan still seem intolerably dirty and hostile.' Zola research to the fore, he was conjuring up the ordeal of Andrew Robertson, a visiting English biology lecturer in New York who, while checking out apartments to rent, was to become trapped in a soundproof penthouse without electricity or water when the self-locking front door slammed shut. Jim referred to it as his modern Robinson Crusoe, but was hesitating between two endings. Should Robertson be saved from dehydration by the discovery of water in the central-heating humidifier, or be too parched by then to swallow? Simultaneously, two lesser stories were causing him greater frustration. Sebastian's suicidal despair on a train to Marseilles had to be illuminated by the sweep of Conradian adventure in the Far East that proceeded it; and the decline of an American general called Kastner, an alcoholic widower posted to London with his teenage daughter after the Second World War, was tediously in train.

Disheartened, at bay, Jim was thrown further into self-doubt by having to correct proofs for *A Girl in the Head*. 'My verdict, there's lots of good writing in it [but] simply it lacks momentum. It takes ages to begin and never picks up speed. It's like a Christmas cake, solid with fruit and nuts and sugar decoration like cast-iron – but leaden to the palate. I hope to God someone will disagree with this verdict.' And the information that the book had been turned down by Pantheon, the only American publisher to show interest, was made more humiliating by the fact that the Pantheon editor who signed the letter was André Shiffrin, Roger Donald's room-mate at Cambridge. The comment that Shiffrin liked it, intended to ease the rebuff, infuriated him. 'All I can say is that he can't have liked it too terribly much,' he scribbled, 'if instead of it he prefers to publish ephemeral bilge . . . Harsh words, but I'm convinced it's good and that Shiffrin is an imbecile.'

Brooding on the slight, Jim took his feelings out on Elsie Donald, Roger's young sister-in-law, when they met in a bar. He was morose on arrival and soon launched into sarcasm, suddenly swinging the attack towards her. She walked out when she was unable to take any more, and drew her own conclusions. 'I thought, This man is impotent. I suddenly saw something quite wrong – that essentially a sexual problem was at the base. And I think it was *not* drink talking. His soul was black.' But Jim's quarrel was entirely with himself. Snow fell outside, he ached with cold when indoors, and on the other side of the thin Belvedere wall an elderly couple waged unremitting verbal war. Shouts of 'I'll kill you!' 'No, I'll kill *you*!' punctured his concentration, a fitting accompaniment to the book he was trying to envisage.

At his most desolate, in the dead centre of winter, an idea began to take shape: he ought to write about Ireland. He had told the Harkness committee that he wanted to write about people caught up in abrupt changes in their civilisation, and Roemer's advice about the need for convincing detail singled out Irish independence as the logical setting. 'Having lived there,' he would explain when the task was completed, 'I was very interested in the situation of the Protestant Anglo-Irish, who were left rather stranded in the new nation and finding it rather difficult to adapt themselves.' But relief at the decision to focus on Irish independence gave way to dismay when he realised that his ambition had grown to weave in all shades of opinion – 'to comprehend and interpret for universal experience' – which called for a story capable of sustaining such a theme. He could not envisage how it could be done.

'What I need to do now', he resolved on 20 February, 'is to think more deeply about plots, about events, about binding books together into some sort of homogeneity.' The structural complexities were daunting, but if Roemer was correct they promised a way in. Jim read widely from that angle alone – 'Bellow and Nabokov set things up for themselves, finding a form (letters and pseudo footnotes respectively) which allows them great freedom and flexibility' – and, looking back through his Yale Drama School notes, he was struck by Brustein's arguments for breaking with tradition when staging the classics. The justification was 'freshness', which Brustein believed came only from applying resourceful – 'though respectful' – intelligence to create 'a synthesis between the past and the future, between tradition and experiment, between text and performance technique'. If an ancient play could benefit from contemporary resonances and still keep its historical distance, a new novel set in the past needed them even more. In Yale jargon the trick he now had to pull off was to be insightful without being chic.

Jim began spending every Tuesday, Wednesday and Friday in the public library on 53rd Street, where he knew no-one. 'I plough resolutely on through books about the Irish rebellion,' he noted on 11 March, 'gathering more and more information but scarcely adding to my feeble conception of how the thing should be . . . Meanwhile, I'm lonely and find it hard to work. I need people like a flower needs water. Self-confidence, too.' Detail was all very well, but he still lacked the format – 'once one has that then things can begin to fall into place, *having* a place to fall into' – and the fruitless conjecture was made no easier by endeavouring to cut down his smoking.

On St Patrick's Day, to the faint sound of Irish pipers tuning up in the street twelve floors below, he took the plunge. 'I wrote the first page of "It",' he congratulated himself afterwards. 'In the parade along 5th Avenue they carried banner portraits of Sean McDermott, Kevin Barry and, no doubt, other martyrs. I didn't stay since the wind was bitter, the pavement covered in slush and my bones frozen to the marrow. These parades make the Americans look like imbeciles. But the first page: I wrote it twice, satisfactory neither time.'

The snow settled, trapping him indoors, and the old tensions mounted. 'Mainly, no doubt, because I'm still groping around in the maze looking not even for the way out but merely for a likely direction in which to start going.' He thought about getting drunk to nudge his brain into making new connections, and wondered if his ambition had outgrown his talent. If that was the case he was finished as a writer, because if there was no way forward there was also none back. 'Certainly the thought of writing an ordinary novel has no attractions whatsoever,' he concluded. 'If it doesn't have some sort of personal impression on it it's not worth doing.'

Russell McCormmach came to stay for a couple of days, and both lamented the lack of girlfriends; in the lift a couple necked passionately, oblivious of them both. 'How to make a large novel centripetal instead of centrifugal?' Jim pondered on his departure, as unaware as the exhibitionist lovers of external factors. 'Musil does it with the character of Ulrich who, by being uncommitted to anything, acts as the touchstone to all the characters around him . . . Another is by using a very tightly organised plot that draws all the disparate elements together. Perhaps it should have both those things but . . . the centre must be substantial like the stone in a peach and it must exist before one can even begin to start thinking constructively.'

The Barnum and Ringling Circus had arrived at Madison Square Gardens, making a surreal contribution to the Belvedere Hotel. 'I now ride up and down in the lift with dwarfs, giants and clowns in full regalia,' he listed, momentarily distracted. 'One giant of almost 9 feet tall and a lady, perfectly formed and mature, who reached only up to my knee . . . Roemer is right. Reality throws up things far more powerful than our imaginations can devise . . . Damp, foggy weather. My hair falling out. Knowing nobody here I want to talk to. The heels falling off my Japanese shoes and refusing to remain stuck on in spite of a lavish investment in glue. Only minor progress in work . . . In the public library this afternoon I stood and looked at the vast shelves of novels travelling at a brisk pace into limbo and savoured my own anonymity . . . The difficulties both of living and working satisfactorily seem, at this moment, to be quite insuperable.' Sipping Benedictine, bought as a tonic, he remembered – 'the sweetness and sharpness, perhaps' – clandestine port in the dormitory at Rossall, and indistinct images of the Irish Rising faded and dissolved. A few mornings later he awoke to find his door ajar, his trousers on the floor and his wallet missing, and not even the bizarre concept of the thin man from the circus in action, his number-one suspect, could ease the financial blow.

Once again Jim turned to Gary, who gave him space at his apartment on East 14th Street, bordering on Greenwich Village. He ordered a rubber stamp with the new address – c/o Arnott – in the likelihood that he would be there for a while. No breakthrough came about. Instead, the influence appeared to be the other way around, as the 1920s perspective of rural Catholic Ireland imposed a censorious view of Gary's homosexuality, and found something to frown upon at every turn. Suddenly the only thing that stopped Jim from taking up Franz Beer's invitation to spend a few days in Rhode Island was the fact that it would indicate acceptance of Franz's second marriage.

In revised drafts of the three short stories he was working on, the characters similarly eased back towards that moral climate. Andrew Robertson's modesty increased and blended with Sebastian's ennui to indicate an observer – English, unattached – who might play the role of Musil's Ulrich. General Kastner lost rank and ribald vocabulary and as the Colonel – echoes of Lowry – was renamed Smyth-Archer for a trip to an earlier America and confrontation with battalions of cockroaches. No sooner did Jim re-shape the stories one way than he re-shaped them another. The cockroaches were abandoned, to swell in due course into cats, while Smyth-Archer's territory shrank as Jim repositioned him in Protestant, middle-class Ireland as the nephew of a country solicitor, where he attended funerals, met two girls named Faith and Charity, and put down roots by marrying a widow, Mrs Spencer. That line, too, ran into the ground. Renaming him Spencer, deaf to contemporary news stories, Jim typed on in Gary's flat, grimly refusing to give up.

'Somehow I have the feeling', he probed, 'that the answer must lie in the character of Spencer, the protagonist, perhaps his very passivity would act as a foil to the other characters?' But the voice of Spencer narrating in the first person struck a jarring note, and the hallucinatory, all-encompassing focus which Jim wanted to achieve required a more insidious approach. He returned to the shadowy English character, more passive even than Spencer and so more suitable for an outsider whose experiences could be shared. A rank was necessary to define him, less dominant than that of colonel now that his shy and thoroughly decent personality could be glimpsed; someone like that who had served in the First World War would have risen no higher than Major. A mass of fair hair, he jotted down, and a long bony face: detail by detail Major Brendan Archer, the name too apt to lose but no longer hyphenated, took on substance. Spencer, meanwhile, had his army career stripped away, becoming peppery and insecure like Kastner once more, competing for attention.

All three stories remained in play. On the same page as a sketched floor plan of Robertson's New York penthouse, Jim jotted glimpses of the Irish book. Lads from Kilnalough serving with the United Nations made an appearance, raised from real-life counterparts in the doomed Congo battalion; as peacekeeping was a euphemism for potentially lethal buffer policing, they coarsened, changed nationalities, and mutated into Black and Tans. Frustrated by being unable to find a role for the insistent identity of Edward Spencer, Jim turned his attention elsewhere, retaining Kilnalough for his place-name, and speculated how Kastner's manipulative daughter might have behaved under different circumstances in 1922.

At the end of April, still fundamentally deadlocked, he decided that a short break might produce results; after all, changing the mental scenery had worked before. Overcoming his reservations, he took up Franz Beer's invitation, because Providence was easily reached from New Haven after class by taking the Boston train in the opposite direction. Disapproval evaporated as soon as he met Franz's new wife, Marlis, but there was no repeat of the hoped-for uplift he remembered from Paris. Unable to face returning to Manhattan, he asked if there was anywhere far from people and cities where he would be able to think. Without hesitation Franz recommended the quiet Surf Hotel on Block Island, where he himself escaped to paint, and phoned across to book a room, assuring Jim that it cost little out of season.

On Friday 5 May, fatalistic and worn down by anxiety, Jim took the ferry to Block Island and checked into the hotel. One other guest, a brisk New Yorker, had been aboard, and Jim stood back to allow the man to enter his name in the ledger first. There was no hurry. As they had neared the island, the miniature jetty and backdrop of weatherbeaten clapboard houses – 'not much of anything except rocks, birds, beaches and empty shuttered houses belonging to summer residents' – had shown that he had come to the end of the line.

As the days unrolled he ate and slept well in the bracing air, reminded of Ireland by the feel of sand, sea and wind. The small hotel was run by Ulric Cyr and his wife – 'he is a fat, genial chap and she is severe with elegantly rolled white hair that makes her look like an immigrant from Versailles' – and dated from 1876.

Its Victorian seaside feel was underscored by a rocking chair on the verandah that overlooked the harbour, good plain cooking and massive portions at every meal. He was initially put at a table with an older English couple named Porter and conversation drifted back to wartime and drinking Pimms at the bar of Cairo's Shepheard's Hotel, but that was not the decade Jim was in search of, and he contrived to make his excuses and sit alone. He was reading *The Garden of the Finzi-Continis* – 'very struck by it, by the great air of sincerity Bassani manages to convey' – and the diplomatic gesture of rapt concentration was no trouble to portray.

Out of doors he ranged as far afield as the large inland ponds and sudden storms allowed, coming across boarded-up guest houses and deserted holiday homes, ghost-town images of apathy and decay on an island only three miles wide and seven miles long. His longest hike was to Sandy Point on the western tip, but the satisfaction was quenched by finding a seagull struggling in the dunes, entangled in twigs, and though he succeeded in freeing the bird he found its wing was broken, triggering flashbacks of the dead sheep at Brittas Bay. At Sandy Point the remains of three lighthouses were identifiable, each washed away in turn by the tides, and all the energy expended in the battle against the sea reduced to futile, crumbling brick. His guidebook brought no relief from poignant introspection: the discovery, as recently as ten years before, of a note in a bottle written by a local schoolboy in 1908, was headed 'A Message from the Dead'. 'Please send answer just to know where found', Percy N. Littlefield of Sandy Point had scribbled hopefully, but Littlefield had died at the age of twenty-one in 1916. That was also the Battle of the Somme, Major Brendan Archer's date.

On a cliff overlooking Old Harbour and the jetty a spectacular ruin drew Jim's eye as he sat out on the windswept verandah each evening before dinner, and he mentioned it to the Porters, with whom he remained on friendly terms. 'A place with a thousand rooms,' declaimed the husband, a poet. 'Two hundred to two hundred and fifty,' corrected his wife. The husk was identified as the remains of the once-famous Ocean View Hotel, which had burned down the previous July, and seeing his interest, the Porters were happy to elaborate. In its heyday, equipped with a sumptuous ballroom and the world's longest bar boasting 101 stools, the Ocean View had been known as the Queen of the Atlantic Coast. The loyal clientele had included President Ulysses S. Grant and the Vanderbilts; and with so many judges, company presidents and politicians in summer residence, a telegraphic link to the New York Stock Exchange had been installed. The hotel had even held a session of the US Supreme Court.

Jim's imagination was caught: Zola research came into play. In the Historical Society old photographs leapt into sepia life and stiffly posed guests gazed back, buttressed by stuffed sofas, mahogany tables and potted plants. The vanished dining room materialised as a panorama of starched tablecloths, and a marble statue of Venus in the Blue Room indicated where gentlemen were allowed to behave as they did in their clubs. Fading postcards showed the harbour bristling with smart yachts, and plumes of smoke on the horizon from approaching steamers on daily schedules from New York and Boston. Ocean View devotees had taken care to book ahead from one season to the next, whereas at the time of its demise, according to the Cyrs, most rooms were barely habitable. Jim borrowed their press cuttings for details of the fire, to be replayed against crimson DEW Line memories, and he discovered that the oil-fed boiler at the rear had exploded, igniting fuel tanks. Strong winds had whipped the flames into an inferno visible half a mile out at sea, and so intense had been the heat that water from the hosepipes of the throngs of firefighters had evaporated before reaching the flames, causing the immense clapboard building to be gutted within four hours. Sitting in the rocking chair, glad of his wool jumper that evening, he recognised the brick chimney in the rubble and could trace the angle of the long porch on the eastern side. On 11 May, before the other guests were up, he took an early breakfast and set off.

'This morning I went up to look at the remains while the sun was still shining,' he recorded with exhilaration. 'Old bedsprings twisted with heat; puddles of molten glass; washbowls that had fallen through to the foundations; a flight of stone steps leading up to thin air; twisted pipes; lots of nails lying everywhere and a few charred beams. I think the way the glass had collected like candlegrease under the windows impressed me most. When you picked it up it was inclined to flake away into smaller pieces in your hand. I must remember to ask someone how many stories it had. Anyway, this gave me an idea, which seems to me a good one, for the dwelling place of the family.'

Jim left Block Island at once, without returning for a second look. His mammoth theme had abruptly materialised, and the Ocean View was about to take on a new lease of life – one with infinite practical and symbolic possibilities – on the far side of the Atlantic as the Majestic Hotel of Kilnalough, under the eccentric ownership of Edward Spencer, the Major's prospective father-in-law. Block Island, with exquisite irony, had removed the block.

In due course the fictional Major Brendan Archer would retrace Jim's steps, burdened with the dazed comparisons of a long-staying guest. *On his last day in Kilnalough the Major paid a melancholy visit to the charred rubble which was now all that remained of the Majestic . . . there was very little to see except that great collection of wash-basins and lavatory bowls which had crashed from one burning floor to another until they reached the ground. He inspected the drips of molten glass which had collected like candle-grease beneath the windows . . . He stepped from one blackened compartment to another trying to orientate himself and saying: 'I'm standing in the residents' lounge, in the corridor, in the writing-room.'* And so it would be left to the reliable Major to pay Jim's formal respects.

CHAPTER FOURTEEN

A Traveller through Unmapped Country 1967–1968

'Dear Carol, My name is Jim Farrell and I'm an old friend of Franz Beer from his rue Joané days. When I was staying with Franz in Providence a couple of weeks ago he gave me your address and suggested I call you. I'd very much like to invite you to lunch one day. If you're not too busy maybe you could call me at 982 5585 so that we could fix it up. Virtually any day would suit me.' Carol Drisko phoned back and a lingering meal at a French restaurant in the West 40s ensued; despite the hurt in store, she never regretted the call. Divorced and five years older than Jim, Carol had an apartment on 3rd Avenue and was a senior editor with Scholastic, the educational publishers, but none of her attainments proved sufficiently insulating when rejection came.

In the beginning the scales were weighted the other way. Jim walked to her office to collect her, and hung around till she was free. Her spending power was greater, and she kept to her plans to holiday in London that June, leaving him behind. Later she guessed her imminent departure had concentrated his mind. 'I'm afraid I've given you the wrong impression of myself,' he retreated hastily. 'I'm not normally so affectionate (partly because being affectionate always seems to lead to complications and threats to my independence). But I think you took me so much by surprise – and then disappeared before I had time to take a grip of myself. Actually, even now I'm still not able to accuse myself of being an idiot with any conviction. By the time you get back, however, I should have recovered my refrigerated poise. So, baby, there it is. [That] expression is intended to sound Anthony Quinn-like so that you'll expect the worst. I'm no good for a nice girl like you.'

Carol's degree was in English Literature and Stendhal was a passion. As a teenager, her immigrant mother's descriptions of picking mushrooms in misty Polish forests had struck her as Chekhovian, and she knew the sanatorium in *The Magic Mountain* as well as she knew her way around Manhattan. She marched against Vietnam, combated racism through CORE, heckled, got up petitions, and could always be relied upon to take a stand. The evidence of Jim's polio elicited her protection, too. 'I picture you', he saluted after they had become lovers, 'in that coat of yours (which seems to be made out of eiderdown) bristling with anti-nuclear buttons, with your library of reference books and instructions to yourself.'

Christian van Briesgan's Harkness Fellowship ended with that academic year, and Jim took up the option of his rent-controlled fourth-floor apartment at 205 East 27th Street, conveniently near Carol. He re-assembled his life methodically, down to the new rubber address stamp identifying Apartment 14, and promptly shattered her peace of mind by announcing that he would be touring Mexico and the West Coast of America until mid-August with 'a cargo of boring slave-girls', soon revealed as one English girlfriend and one small ridge tent.

Sandy Ellis flew in on a charter flight on 1 July, the day before the trip was scheduled to start, bearing a bottle of whiskey and the unwelcome news that she had met two students on the plane and offered them a lift south. "Did you bring the cuttings?" he interrupted her, brushing the bottle aside. With misgivings she handed over the envelope containing early reviews of *A Girl in the Head*. He read them on the spot and steered her without comment from the airport, excluding her in the old infuriating way. 'My book got nothing but abuse from the critics,' he grumbled to Russell as soon as he got back. 'This sticks in my gullet as I'd much rather be an instant ephemeral success than have to seek election as one of the great misunderstoods. One is more likely to end up as an ephemeral misunderstood, now I come to think of it.' Telling Sandy she needed to rest, he left for Carol's flat, carrying his typewriter and a spare set of keys so that she could send on his post. 'Oh, don't be so silly,' he cut short the accusations when he returned two hours later. 'She's much older than I am – a purely literary friend.'

The Lowry pilgrimage began early next morning in a Chevrolet four-door automatic sedan collected from the Harkness garage, polished, taxed and insured. The car felt twenty feet long and as unmanoeuvrable as a whale to Jim, and the silence with which he negotiated the New Jersey Turnpike owed more to apprehension than guilt or scorn. He drove with elaborate care, and Sandy took refuge in her diary. 'Vast concrete ribbons converging with others, often six lanes wide . . . Nobody is going to slow down and let you move over, but sometimes you manage to make it [and then] another highway will merge and you find yourself completely surrounded by the same tearing traffic, in the middle lanes again and with the same battle to move over to the right and comparative safety.' Their route carried them through Chester and Wilmington, past gas stations, motels and neon signs, into the Delaware peninsula, where a violent storm broke overhead and drenching rain accompanied them down through Virginia and all the way to Chapel Hill. There Bob Cumming's hospitable family had invited them to stay, and laid on tennis parties and picnics in their honour.

At Bob's house Jim was poor company, conscious of having got himself into an invidious position. The last thing he wanted was to break off his newly apparent storyline, and the row with Sandy over Carol had been balanced by an ultimatum from Carol, delivered during the two-hour absence, to the effect that he would have to choose between them. Shunning the socialising, he tried to put matters straight. 'I haven't the slightest intention of getting married or engaged to "her", you or anybody else,' he set out the position in a letter to Carol. 'If I could get rid of her without hurting her feelings, disappointing her and reneguing on my idiotic invitation, I'd do so instantly. I find I have nothing whatsoever to say to her and vice versa. It also irritates me (and this is the main cause of my irritation) to be spending money on such a futile enterprise. I'm sick and tired of feeling no other emotion but exasperation. My former womanless state now seems like a time of bliss . . . I'm an idiot. I'm sick of the whole mess.'

Sandy flirted with Bob's friends and Jim sulked, on tenter-hooks for a reply. 'Why shouldn't you hook up with women without having them hook onto you?' Carol unexpectedly agreed, regretting her 'nagging, possessive, female' impulse. 'It is not so odd that your former womanless state now seems like bliss. Even I, sorry as I was to see you depart, felt for a time the great pleasure of peace, quiet, silence and being accountable only to myself.'

Released from one corner, at least, he took the wheel for the stage to New Orleans, via Chattanooga and Tuscaloosa. When they arrived, the city reminded him of France, putting him in better form, and the presence of the students saved money as well as tempers, since they smuggled them in and split the cost of a double motel room four ways. But at Laredo, on the Mexican border, Jim and Sandy were on their own and his mood soured. Harkness rules did not allow cars to be taken out of the country so there was no alternative to leaving the Chevrolet there and taking to the train, and to make matters worse, Sandy had stumbled into poison ivy in the dark while making camp the night before. The Lowry odyssey was not turning out as he had dreamed.

'We're on the train about to leave', Sandy noted miserably at the start of the 26-hour journey to Mexico City, the burning rash on her legs exacerbated by the crush of people, goats and chickens, and by the fumes of onions and garlic. 'It's chaotic and very hot.' Jim had stopped shaving and his beard was growing out pepper and salt, accentuating the whiteness of his hair, and he glowered back. 'I hear my book got massacred by the critics,' he scribbled to Brian Knox Peebles, shutting her out.

Adjustment to the high altitude of Mexico City was hampered by his reduced oxygen intake, and the weather, in further anticlimax, was cold and wet. Jim became so irritable in their lodging house that Sandy went to stay with family friends in Valle dei Bravo and he wandered about the city on his own, smoking and absorbed in *The Conquest of New Spain* by Bernal Diaz. On Sandy's return he grumbled about bourgeois chums, but was appreciably kinder. In cafés they drank mescal, the Consul's tipple in *Under the Volcano,* and he confided that he was reminded of North Africa by the blend of deprivation and great beauty. 'We live but a day,' he murmured aloud the haunting Aztec philosophy. Claude Simha was sent a postcard of Lowry's Popocatepetl volcano, and Dublin friends got cheerier views, signed El Farrello.

The object of the exercise was to visit Cuernavaca, renamed Quauhnahuac in Lowry's novel, and as Jim's anticipation built up so did his anxiety about the second batch of reviews that should have reached the post office in Laredo, which he had given as his first forwarding address. 'I still haven't seen the *Times* and *Observer*,' he reminded Carol in New York. 'Were they *very* bad? Or merely indifferent? I am being consumed by retrospective anguish.' Seeking distraction, he took Sandy to Acapulco – 'a cross between Cannes, Nice and Blackpool' – and after checking into a cheap hotel they headed for the crowded beach, where her blonde good looks attracted a group of bronzed and muscled-up American surfers. In his *Oxford Opinion* days Jim had sketched a glamorous James Bond vision of himself in that very spot, and he set off for the breakers defiantly. The undertow threw him over, his arm went up and back as he shouted for help, and Sandy and the beachboys raced down to drag him out. They laid him on the beach, pale grey with shock and with a dislocated right arm that was already black and blue. He spent that day and the next in bed, putting off consulting a doctor, and then, groggy from the prescribed drugs, pressed on. 'Every word is torture,' he scrawled with difficulty to Carol. 'Life no fun with arm in sling.' And he ignored the portent from the sea.

The next postcard featured the Borda Hotel in Cuernavaca, and he wrote it sitting in the garden which was all that remained of the model for Lowry's Hotel Casino de la Selva. He was in too much pain to commune in the way he had intended and it took a supreme effort of will to shut out the television aerials, souvenir shops and retired, disgruntled Californians. So tangible had Lowry's world been before setting out that he had almost expected a listing of the fictional hotel – 'Palatial, a certain air of desolate splendour pervades it' – in his borrowed copy of *Mexico on $5 a Day*. Nothing was as he expected, and even Popocatepetl, the volcano, was scaled down by reality. The feat of transformation however held an unexpected bonus: it endorsed the powers of imagination, and the quantum leap on Block Island.

Accompanied by Sandy, and invisibly by Monsieur Laruelle, 'resplendent in white flannels', and the Consul, 'a lock of fair hair falling over his eyes and one hand clasped in his short pointed beard', Jim left the bougainvillaea-hued gardens and explored the backstreets, noting that even the cobalt of the private swimming pools was the exact shade Lowry had depicted. He came across the shop sign Piggly Wiggly – 'The Consul, with his stick, was indicating through the trees the little American grocery store . . . "Peegly Weegly" ' – and surveyed the barrada, finally to linger, arm in sling, over the ruins of the tragic Emperor Maximilian's Summer Palace.

Back in Laredo there were letters from Carol but no reviews, which stretched Jim on the rack for a further month. The next forwarding address was that of his brother Robert in Canada, where a reunion, their first for eleven years, had been planned for the finish. Taciturn and in agony, he allowed the student who rejoined them for a short lift to California to do the driving, and on the straight roads between El Paso and Tucson took back the wheel, resting his injured arm on his lap. The temperature soared on the interminable desert crossing, imposing regular stops at gas stations for ice-cold tins of Coke and root beer, and he fulfilled a childhood dream by frying an egg on the bonnet of the Chevvy; the result was unanimously judged inedible. At night his pain was aggravated by the hard ground and constrictions of the sleeping bag, and he developed breathing problems which frightened him sufficiently to give up smoking. On their own again Sandy was instructed to bang him hard between his shoulders, and the nadir was a sleepless night in the car by the side of the road, after mixing bourbon with some of the Mexican sleeping pills, and a repetition of the anger unleashed on Elsie Donald. 'He put me down seriously, real emotional bruising,' she would recall. 'I felt, "I don't want to know this man." But I did nothing, and we sat in silence till it got light.'

On 1 August they camped at Lake Wohlfort, Escondido. 'Nom de dieu, those reviews were pretty awful, weren't they?' he vented his feelings upon Carol. 'I really can't believe that the book is *that* uninteresting. In fact, I still think it's the best thing I've done and it perplexes me that no-one else thinks so.' In San Francisco, five days later, they checked in to the Hotel Sequoia on the corner of the aptly named Ellis and O'Farrell streets near Haight-Ashbury – 'It was good to get into a place with walls and a roof. Pretty soon I won't be able to look another magnificant panorama in the eye' – but the wearying habit of observation was impossible to unlearn and, discovering that the Beatles were giving a concert, he took her along. 'We just wandered around,' Sandy commented later. 'Looking at everybody else.'

With his shoulder on the mend and the cough gradually improving, they headed on up the West Coast, camping off the beaten track: Redwoods Forest, Rogue River Camp, Cougar Camp. He took evident pleasure in travelling light, and when the owners of a luxury motor-camper asked if they had a knife or gun to stop predators, he flourished his potato peeler. One camper presented freshly smoked fish, another a salmon straight from the river, and he prided himself on being able to make a cooking fire from dead wood and a few well-placed bricks. Day by day his mood improved. As they approached Mount Rainier National Park along an empty road, the pale pink summit tipped with snow hovered above the early morning mist, as delicate as an ancient Japanese painting.

Jim met up with his brother Robert in Victoria, British Columbia, instructing Sandy to disguise their relationship in case his mother was informed. Robert, anticipating his priorities, left him alone to read the collected reviews. Only *The Times Literary Supplement* considered *A Girl in the Head* to be his best work and even then the reasoning was noncommittal, the ultimate verdict unfavourable. 'The consistency of tone . . . in spite of a certain flagging of energy towards the end, is an advance on the grey narrative efficiency of the first [but] its world cannot be taken seriously except as an occasion for a fascinatingly written *tour de force*. Its verbal assurance and resourcefulness show that Mr Farrell is not content to coast along merely imitating his previous work, and such a deliberate extension of range is perhaps a hopeful sign for a talent which after three novels still has not found the mode in which to fulfil its attractive promise.' When he emerged from the room his face was grim and, dedicating one copy, he wrote: 'Frankly, all one can say is: Arrrgh!'

The combination of Robert's agreeable company and the long drive back through the cowboy country of Wyoming did much to restore his equilibrium. 'Actually the reviews were so awful, with only one or two exceptions,' he was able to claim within a month, 'that I feel maybe I should be pretending that the author was James T. Farrell, "the Small Bore from the Mid-West", as Cyril Connolly once described him. Hardly anyone, even the people who liked the book, had any sympathy for Boris and his predicament. Well, apart from all his appalling defects of character, pride, dishonesty, self-centredness and so on, I couldn't help thinking that Boris was significant in some way . . . Anyway, authors have been right and critics wrong about their books before now (though not too often) . . . so I refuse to allow it to be counted out so soon.'

Sandy left for England with alacrity, convinced there could be no mutual future, and 3rd Avenue and East 27th Street became Jim's main territory; after the long break from writing he had little desire to go further afield. Mornings were devoted to writing and afternoons to research and, walking to the stop where he caught his bus to the New York Public Library, he winced at the shamrocks and sour smells of Guinness in the Irish bars he passed, and made no attempt to seek out corroboration inside. Evenings were spent mostly with Carol, who shared his new interest in cooking; using the small stove in his seedy brown-painted apartment, he produced supper on alternate evenings. Home-baked brown bread and casserole-roasted chicken with tarragon led to the mastery of Béarnaise sauce. He tried out recipes from the *New York Times*, watched TV cookery demonstrations, became a fan of Julia Child, buying her book *Mastering the Art of French Cooking*, and found encouragement in a line of argument contained in *Michael Field's Cooking School* that might almost have been tailor-made for him. 'Marcel Proust', cajoled the bow-tied American chef, 'writes rhapsodically of cold *boeuf à la mode* served upon enormous crystals of jelly, like transparent block of quartz, and goes on to describe its preparation as a task of great complexity. But literary license being what it is, cooking beef à la mode is in reality far less difficult than he implied. In fact, it is not difficult at all.' Cast-iron Le Creuset saucepans were another matter: Jim needed two hands to lift one, even when empty.

The relationship with Carol was filled with badinage, with her contempt for the English class system balanced by his for American vulgarity. 'The day America is no longer vulgar it is no longer powerful,' she retorted one day. 'Oh God,' he drawled. 'I guess it must be reaching the pinnacle of power.' When they ate out, usually at El Faro's on 14th Street or at Moonfetas on 49th Street, they split the bill, which she thought more than fair as the sole wage-earner; and though her loquaciousness exhausted him, he could tell her that he wanted to be alone without giving offence. The only jarring note was his growing importance in her life, and as they sparred she would sometimes catch him looking at her, and falter.

Absorbed as Jim was by Ireland of the Black and Tan period, he relied on Carol to keep him abreast of current events. She had subscriptions to the *New York Times*, the *Wall Street Journal*, the *Weekly Guardian*, *The Economist*, the *New Left Review*, the *New Statesman*, the *Observer* and the *Sunday Times* and stacks of newspaper crowded her apartment; in his gallery of vignettes these would bloom into paper sofas, tables and chairs. He used the lengthy New York garbagemen's strike to clear them all out, carrying them down in piles to add to the refuse in the street, and a grand piano with a broken leg was revealed, supported by a three-volume biography of Trotsky. 'Trotsky is under this piano', ran the cardboard sign he put in place. But more usually it was Carol who took decisive action, impelled by a childhood spent in the coalmining region of West Pennyslvania, where she had witnessed the company exploitation of miners at first hand. He liked to prompt her and play devil's advocate, a tactic she recognised but could rarely let pass. As she held forth about the Chicago riots of 1919 or produced statistics of the sharecropping and segregation that kept blacks in their place long after the abolition of slavery, researched for her educational book, *The Unfinished March*, he speculated about religious intolerance and tribalism at another time and another place.

The most graphic image, magnified by Carol's unflagging

opposition to it, was of the Vietnam War. She staked out the Pentagon, marched down Fifth Avenue as crowds threw red paint, stuck stamps of the US flag on her mail upside-down and took him to task for the British Empire's bad example of colonialism, which he would defend with an analysis of why imperial visions were justified. But radio and television coverage was less easy to set aside, and even in the short period since he had stopped living in New Haven 100,000 extra servicemen had been drafted. In mid-February the weekly rate of US casualties had reached an all-time high. The continuous front-line news reports and interviews that he watched on her television prompted thoughts about the manipulation of history through official despatches, as well as the coping mechanisms for transcending fear. He followed the 77-day siege of marines at Khe Sanh avidly, aware that it was a contemporary version of the psychological testing-ground he intended at some point in future to create. 'I have the feeling I should be doing more,' he began to fret to Carol, 'I should be further along.'

Among the Harkness Fellows, a journalist and two artists passed muster. Hans Dorflinger – 'a German painter of a rather teutonically playful disposition' – found him 'astonishingly visual' for a writer, and shared his keen interest in wines, while Paul Huxley impressed Jim for a more personal reason. 'Very young,' Jim singled out, 'and yet already married with children'. In the 1967 intake he particularly liked Malcolm Dean, who was exchanging the *Guardian* for Chicago. 'This is Malcolm,' he took to introducing him after a gaffe by Malcolm led to the discovery of a mutual sense of humour. 'He was educated in the University of Life.' In Malcolm's view, Jim was an intellectual in the true sense of the word, because he loved to explore every idea, wherever the avenue might lead. 'Jim was very serious,' he explained once, 'but he hated being solemn. And that was the secret.'

Malcolm was not a Harkness rival, however, unlike another newcomer, Piers Paul Read, whose latest novel, *The Junkers*, was said to be in the running for the Geoffrey Faber Memorial Prize. When Piers and his eighteen-year-old bride Emily turned up at the East 27th Street apartment to collect the keys of the Chevrolet in their turn, he ushered them in with mixed feelings,

glad to be free of responsibility for the car. On his mettle, he
served Earl Grey tea and home-made brown bread, and took
private offence at the lack of a mention of *A Girl in the Head*. An
invitation to Sunday lunch with the broadcaster Alastair Cooke,
a Harkness Fellow of many years standing, caused the same
hackles to bristle. 'It was like visiting royalty,' he complained to
Gary Arnott.

The removal of the car brought home the fact that his fellowship would run out at the beginning of the summer, when his
return passage on the *Queen Elizabeth* was pre-booked, and he
no longer smiled when Carol teased him about being broody. As
the weeks sped past and the Majestic of Kilnalough rose all too
slowly from the ashes of the Ocean View Hotel, the sole
relaxation he allowed himself centred on his book. The rhythm
of walking was more conductive to the imagination than pacing
up and down in a room, and during those periods he plotted
ahead and occasionally laughed aloud, which attracted no
second looks in a city where drunks and madmen traditionally
got a wide berth. 'Jim is very much absorbed now in his work as
a writer,' noticed Bob Cumming upon his move that winter to
New York. 'But not always confident about his aim or abilities.
We're walking on Sixth Avenue: "My novel is like that painting"
– a crude, ornate, huge drawing in many colours of chalk that
went on over several slabs of sidewalk – "with its large cast of
characters and semi-historical [scale]." ' Meanwhile, following
Bassani's trail from *The Garden of the Finzi-Continis* through to
his introduction to *The Leopard*, Jim rediscovered Lampedusa.
'He does *so well* almost exactly what I've been trying to do in the
book I'm writing at present,' he noted, losing headway. 'Clear,
very concrete images, the characters beautifully portrayed. He
never puts a foot wrong! It's uncanny, I don't know how he
manages.'

At the end of January 1968 he suggested to Carol that they
should take a ten-day break in Puerto Rico. 'I thought, "Gee, this
means something," ' she would say wryly later. 'That was like
Jim. He kept raising your hopes.' In the early hours of 16
February they took the 720 bus from East Side Terminal and
joined returning immigrants on the 3am red-eye flight, but in
their double room in the Old Town or over paella at a table for

two his remote politeness remained in place. The vast rubbish dump of La Perla, which they inspected at uneasily close quarters, came to symbolise her despair. 'He would get silent and I just couldn't ask,' she reflected. 'And sexually I couldn't pursue him if he didn't want that. Part of me said, "Well, maybe he's trying to make up his mind, as he's about to leave the States," but I always hate to kid myself. I thought I was hiding it, but there was a tension from my desire for a permanent relationship which pervaded the whole trip. I wanted him to say, "Come to England with me." And of course he didn't.' Two nights after they returned to New York he asked her round to supper, and the table usually cleared for the meal was piled high with books. He spoke of Russell McCormmach and she realised that he was matchmaking, building upon the coincidence that her ex-husband was also a physicist. 'You are the only woman I can imagine who is intelligent enough for him,' she heard with disbelief.

With only twelve weeks left in America, the book consumed Jim in a race against time. He was trying to depict the Major's love for the girl who had evolved from General Castner's daughter – now older, Irish, and Catholic – who was to shake his convictions to the core. 'It's as if while writing my imagination dilates and begins to gorge itself not only on the characters in my book,' he would admit revealingly later that year, 'but on me and my private life.' Carol had been witness to the Major's postwar numbness. In April an English newcomer, Sarah Bond, would lift him into the sphere of intensity he now sought.

Sarah entered his life with a suitably dramatic impact in the electric three weeks between Martin Luther King's assassination and the violent confrontation between police and students at Columbia. A unexpected letter arrived on 11 April saying that Robin Cook – 'a mutual friend in London' – had suggested that she get in touch. 'Dear Sarah, How's this for service?' he delivered a reply by hand. 'The reason for the speed is that I happened to acquire some fresh mackerel this morning and plan to cook them with an English friend this evening. If you happen to be free give me a ring . . . In any event, give me a ring.' Glamorous and radiating zest for life, Sarah regaled them with her adventures the previous night rescuing a naked man from a smoke-filled room in her new digs, summoning an emergency ambulance crew when he went berserk – "*twice!*" – and drinking brandy at dawn with her landlord. He appraised her with pleasure, from the long dark hair and huge eyes down to the miniskirt and good legs, as charmed by her jolly-hockey-sticks vocabulary as by her degree in French and German and an openly stated determination not to marry in her twenties.

'Actually,' he was soon to discover, 'I'm amazed at the amount of things we think the same way about, from Richard Hughes to sleeping in the same weird position, to being malicious about other people (though in the nicest possible way). Perhaps another thing we have in common is being impermeable to romance.' Sarah kept him disturbingly on edge, illuminating the Major's still-indistinct emotions. She was the one who went off a man, she challenged, not the other way around. 'I remember distinctly you saying how you are never jealous', he would remind her later, 'even when your boyfriends slept with other women, since you always knew they liked you best. You see, my memory for this sort of thing is prodigious.' But by then – as with the Major and her fictional namesake – that was a two-edged sword.

They spent most of the six weeks he had left, she later reminisced, either eating or in bed. It stood out in her memory as a wonderfully exclusive time, when they were cut off from everyone else. 'When we were together we never quarrelled, did we?' He, too, would recall, 'I don't remember ever enjoying a girl's company a much as yours.' She mended his elderly corduroy trousers with Girl Guide efficiency and introduced him to Edward Lear's nonsense recipes, learned by heart as a child. He extended his culinary repertoire, and mastered her favourite roast duck. Only many years later did she question the nature of their intimacy. 'All the things he liked about me,' she conceded then, 'were really the things he *didn't* approve. He needed someone far more cerebral, literary, left-wing, cause-oriented and uninterested in how she looked. I sported all the things he said were signs of superficiality in someone else.'

At a noisy party Gary warned him that she was pushy after she jumped on a chair and shouted to get her opinion across, but Jim was inhabiting the Major's mind, mesmerised by her nerve. The pile of pages was already two inches high, and she carried them off, chapter by chapter, to xerox in her office after hours, overcoming his protestations by telling him that he had to take advantage of such an opportunity while he could. She was allowed to read through and thought it eerie to recognise him so unmistakably in the Major, but she made no connection between the unfurling behaviour of Sarah Devlin and herself.

At the end of the month she thought she was pregnant, and briskly announced that a hot bath and lots of gin should solve the problem. The absence of any claim bound him closer still, and his role that inconclusive night was to top up the bathwater from a boiling kettle and pour liberal measures of gin. 'It really *is* lucky that the Gin and Bathing Regatta was a success', he teased afterwards, 'since the result would have been positively *tone deaf*, inclined to sleep in fantastically odd positions and given to exceedingly boring monologues on Lamartine and Verlaine. Not to mention having grey hair and bandy legs and a paralysed arm.'

Both Sarah and Carol believed they had his sole attention, and he juggled his evenings deftly, as Carol's diary reveals, '12th April: Dinner with Jim. 13th: Fish soup and soufflé – dinner with Jim. 14th: Dinner with Jim and Fred Myer. 18th: Dinner with Jim and Hans Dorflinger. 20th: Film *Charlie Bubbles* with Jim. 22nd: Jim visit. 24th: Jim and Bob to dinner at Sorrento's in Little Italy. 26th & 27th: Dinner with Jim. 30th & 1st May: Dinner at Jim's with Bob and a Bergman movie after – 2 films in 2 days. May 4th: tears and hysteria. 5th: With Jim and Bob to Moonfetas. 8th & 9th: Jim – crab soufflé. 11th: Metropolitan Museum with Jim. 12th: A Sunday – to Philadelphia to meet Russ with Jim. When we came back we made a soufflé together. 14th: Dinner with Jim. 25th: Dinner with Jim. 27th: Jim and Bob – curry. A pre-departure dinner.' In a whitewashed restaurant that she was never able to locate again, with time running out, she knew he could sense her longing and a shadow fell over the evening. 'Sex continued off and on during all those months,' she mused later. 'But there was such a brooding quality. In the privacy of the bedroom I would think, 'What does this mean to him?'

Bob Cumming, who liked them both, watched sympathetically. 'A note about relationships between men and women which I've observed,' he wrote in his own diary concurrently. 'Women are fascinated by men who reject them.' Like Carol, Sarah was taken to Bob's East Village address, and to Rittenhous Square in Philadelphia to meet Russell McCormmach. By force of habit or design, Jim was operating in an arena that was dangerously small. In the same time frame Sarah found herself sitting opposite him in Moonfetas on West 46th Street, the Greek restaurant where he took Carol on 5 May. 'It has a great reputation,' he observed blandly, glancing through the menu as if he had never seen it before.

At the end of his New York sojourn Jim emptied his savings account at Chemical Bank and thanked Martha English and John B. Fox in person, relieved by the progress on his book. It was with some satisfaction that he filled out the report in which Fellows were expected to compare their actual accomplishments with their original claims. His plan to bequeathe the good-value apartment – as well as Carol – to Russell was unsuccessful, and by the pre-departure curry dinner there were no loose ends left. His intention was to slip out of New York as invisibly as he had slipped in.

Early on 28 May Carol phoned him with a pre-arranged wake-up call and they breakfasted quietly together at her apartment before she left for work. At the door he forestalled emotion by handing over a cardboard box containing his left-over groceries. Sarah, similarly, was kept well away from the docks. He said goodbye to her privately later that day in a parting so harrowing that she cried long after he was out of sight. Rain gave way to fitful sunshine, and in the late afternoon Bob accompanied him to the 52nd Street Pier, tactfully helping to carry the minimal possessions, and at the last minute presented him with a Dostoevsky paperback – *The Friend of the Family* and *The Eternal Husband*. Clutching that lifeline, Jim went aboard.

The voyage across the Atlantic was dull and his cabin-mates bored him, from the grumpy pensioner who had been a store manager in Nicaragua – 'the climate, he said, was very debilitating' – to the two weatherbeaten Irishmen returning home, one of whom spoke exclusively of his accordian, the other of his fourteen children. At his table in the dining room two humourless girls from California lectured him about the consequences of drinking tap water in France. 'I could think of no reply,' he groaned by post to Russell, 'but eyed my plate gloomily.' The most interesting passenger was the son of an IRA veteran, renowned for killing an informer during the Troubles, who talked freely about his father. But after eliciting the details, Jim kept himself to himself, his low energy level re-asserting itself. The well-worn sea passage induced thoughts of transience and the bleak human condition. 'I'm thinking of how lots of sad little old men got sloshed crossing the Atlantic,' he reached out companionably to Carol, rather than to Sarah. 'That reminds me of Roemer's image of a twentieth-century death, an old man dying in a taxi. Well, I guess it's just me that's hypersensitive to such things.'

Polite, reclusive, his mood matching the approaching low cloudbase, Jim was struck suddenly by the irony implicit in making good his Harkness boast. He had wanted to alter course and he was aware of having done so: he was bringing back the solid framework for a fittingly mammoth theme. But the real price of the still-unfinished manuscript was a greater sense of displacement, something the proximity of England threw sharply into relief. Like Major Brendan Archer, he, too, was now haunted by the unattainable. *He could go anywhere in the world*, Jim would in due course touch up his final draft. *He no longer had any ties, either in London or elsewhere. Yet this was precisely the trouble. In all the aching void of the world where should he go? Why should he choose one place rather than another? For wherever he went, Sarah would not be.*

But Jim was not the Major, for all that; he remained a child of his time. When the *Queen Elizabeth* docked at Southampton there was Sandy in a bright flowery mini-dress waiting to meet him, as they had arranged long before. She waved and smiled without the slightest sign of rancour, and he eased back in the familiar front passenger seat of the tiny Mini. After a while he slid a hand appreciatively up her tanned bare leg.

Part Two

CHAPTER FIFTEEN

Out into the Open Sea
1969–1970

The first thing John Spurling noticed about Jim after the period in America was that he had shaped himself – that description at once sprang to mind. Being a playwright, John paid keen attention to development of character, and he was intrigued by two opposing explanations. Was it, he speculated, because Jim was shaping his books? Or were his books now shaping him? The change was emphasised by the familiarity of the Stanley House hotel room with the cracked windowpane, as unobtrusive as a well-used stage set.

Jim put up his customary smokescreen of dry humour, which indicated that a return to the conveniently vacant room was a positive choice. Privately he wrote of taking cover there because it was easy to leave, and of feeling too bereft to want a lease. On his own, the pangs of 'Sarahlessness' multiplied, and he remained sexually absorbed. 'I want a photo of you, preferably with no clothes on . . . Do wish you'd send details of your amorous exploits so that at least I could enjoy them vicariously if not actually . . . PS. I wish you were here right at this moment so that I could take off your clothes and get inside you.* – *This autograph postscript is supposed to make the letter invaluable to collectors and is definitely *not* written while drunk!' But distance took its toll: the reality was that teasing led nowhere and letters were ultimately arid. 'I'm becoming faintly more resigned to these withdrawal symptoms', he analysed, but bitterness showed through. 'As a doctor once said to me while in the iron lung, "You can get used to anything." (Thanks a lot, I replied.)'

Both Sarah and Carol, were informed by post, about Sandy,

and Sandy knew about Carol, but not about Sarah. Jim, for his part, was put out to discover that Sandy was on the point of becoming engaged, and his arrival made her hesitate, but not for long. She thought she had grown impervious to his jibes, but his scorn of her attendance at evening classes at Hammersmith Art School – 'Oh, you're very good at cotton-wool daubs' – was the final straw. News of her engagement came by letter, and his polite reply claimed it was 'a bit tough' as he had come back from America expecting more. She showed him her ring when they met unexpectedly in Knightsbridge, and made sure to invite him to her wedding.

But Sandy's impression that she had had the last word was mistaken, because the Major was about to put pen to paper in similar circumstances.

> *He wrote to her immediately. He said that* of course; *he minded (after all, one could hardly say that one didn't mind in the least), but he hoped that nevertheless she would be very happy. In fact – he wrote, warming to the task – in fact, . . . he was positively gnashing his teeth with despair . . . It served him right – he wrote, feeling a flood of compassion for this other person wandering, like himself, at large in the minefields – that she should choose someone else and leave him for ever outside in the cold and clammy darkness . . . Had he not written with too much haste and warmth? 'My God supposing she regards it as a counter-proposal, calls off the wedding and comes . . . to get me!' Fortunately . . . it gradually became clear that he would not be held to account for his rash outburst of sympathy.*

One relationship made no such demands; in fact, made no demands at all. Jim slipped back into the old relationship with the callgirl he would salute as Lucy Hughes, and with his concentration directed inwards, her principal attraction was that she had not changed. When Russell came to visit from America he, too, was introduced. 'Also there was a Corsican gangster,' Jim jotted with satisfaction, 'who had shot someone in the Victorian Sporting Club 3 or 4 years ago, so she said. Russell was very impressed with [her] and thought she was very warm-hearted and sexy, which indeed she is.' In low moods he thought it said a great deal for her kindness and simplicity of nature that she had put up with him for so long.

Carol Drisko flew in on holiday, and he arranged for her to stay in his old digs in Pembridge Road. 'You could throw all caution to the winds, buckle on your armour-plated pyjamas and bunk down with me,' he suggested half-heartedly, 'but I doubt if it will come to it,' and signed off Uncle Jungle Jim, a further backward step. The visit unfolded on his terms, and by its end Carol accepted that if she wanted to go on knowing him it would have to stay that way. The freedom of the past two years had made him extra-sensitive to emotional shackles, and when his parents passed through London, travelling between Dublin and a newly bought retirement flat in Malta, they left him grumbling in their wake. 'One very much got the impression', according to John Spurling, 'that he despised his parents and family which I didn't like and thought an unexpectedly conventional attitude.' It was also clear that Jim was still being partially subsidised by them, since he could not possibly be living on royalties alone; the crunch for John came with the curt rejoinder that it was a bonus for them to have a novelist for a son.

Jim was already worrying about his 'meagre' Harkness savings, squirrelled away to complete the book. During his absence Graham Nicol had left Hutchinson, with the result that the useful Albany network was disbanded, and resentment against Jonathan Clowes, whom he blamed for not pushing Cape harder to promote *A Girl in the Head*, prevented him seeking his agent's advice. Anxiety about money was matched by anxiety about his self-imposed deadline, which aimed for publication in the summer of 1970 to coincide with the fiftieth anniversary of Irish independence. The obvious course was to become a reader for Cape, but as manuscripts could not be taken off their premises, to qualify he would have to spend an entire afternoon there for each small fee: his determination to make writing headway seemed under threat from every side. He was consulted about the paperback cover of *A Girl in the Head* for Pan, and proposed Frances Howard, a fleeting successor to Sandy, as the model for the blonde in the bikini, and in due course he posed with her, his head leering up from the sand at her feet. There were also time-consuming demands from Harper and Row concerning publicity for the American edition. His frustration built at the slightest provocation, and inscribing a copy of *The Lung* for Norma di Marco, who owned the Pembridge Road house, he wrote: 'A cheap novel for Norma', and explained with sarcastic inflection that it was remaindered, and so genuinely cheap. Told that she liked his early books, he groaned. 'They're rubbish,' he corrected.

'I've been suffering from mild despair in the past few days', he wrote to Sarah within a week of moving back into Room 17 of the Stanley House Hotel. 'And gloomily deciding that we should abandon writing to each other: the trouble is that I decided there was *nothing to look forward to*. I wouldn't mind if there was and I could get happily down to work . . . Two or three weeks [together] really wouldn't change the basic problem, would it? In fact, it would just take us back to square one. Walking around the King's Road I've been feeling that I *am* Square One – excuse the weedy joke. Misery. The only other thing I can suggest apart from [the idea] that you should chuck in America and come and live with me indefinitely (I could give you a voucher good for one year and a day but you could apply for an extension by submitting an application in triplicate with nude passport photographs) is that you wheedle some extra vacation . . . Maybe the best thing is to meet, have a terrible row and then part again, feeling relieved. Otherwise I *genuinely* think the best thing is to drop the correspondence until one fine day you appear back in Blighty . . . because my letters are inclined to get morose and aggressive . . . a mixture of professional arrogance and personal misery . . . and we'd merely end up by having our row by post, which is highly unsatisfactory since one can't throw things . . . I think this is really what I want to do.' But that resolution, too, dissolved. 'I really can't write letters and remain detached. I started off just now planning to soothe you with honeyed words and instead of honey there is nothing but acid bubbling out of my typewriter.'

In Kilnalough the Major was fighting a parallel battle, convinced that he was liable to be *poignarded to death by the painful 'absence of Sarah' that had suddenly started to afflict him – indeed, the pangs of self-pity and Sarahlessness became appallingly acute . . . Compared with his feelings for Sarah all his desires were tepid . . . It was as if he had been skinned alive; the thought of contact with anyone was more than he could endure.* Jim read and typed and walked alone, and at mealtimes cooked for one and ate with little appetite. A haze settled, dimming impressions. 'Oh, bugger the whole business', he wrote one day.

Walking back up Kensington Church Street after breaking off to buy a loaf of health-food bread, he was accosted by an old man holding out a leaflet, and his reaction disturbed him sufficiently to take stock. '"Are you giving me this or selling it to me?" I asked him. "Selling it," he replied. I thanked him and wandered on a few yards and then he started shouting at me. "Giving you it! I'll give you something!" For some reason I lost my temper at this, went back and asked him what about it in an ugly manner. To my amazement the fellow looked terrified and said sheepishly, pointing to his glasses, "Oh, anyone could beat me, I can't see." I slunk off then, feeling bitterly ashamed of myself . . . Me with my paralysed arm threatening an old man with glasses. If it had occurred it would have been The Fight of the Century. My only consolation is that he won anyway since I could hardly have felt worse if he'd laid me out with a right hook.' That night Jim slept fitfully and got up at 4am, intent on getting down to work. 'I was really *amazed* at how absurdly I've taken to behaving recently,' he resolved, 'and decided it was high time I called out the Red Guard for a cultural revolution on myself. For someone still reasonably young, in good health, eating when I feel like it, coming and going as I please, working at something I like, I have been doing an awful lot of moaning and groaning. Time for that when I'm old and sick, dependent, hungry and the work has gone down the drain.'

Sarah had not sent on the last section of the manuscript completed in New York, which she had kept back for copying and half-seriously viewed as a hostage for his permanent return. Fresh reading of the work he did retain depressed him – 'awfully scrappy and inconsistent and inconclusive' – and he was aghast when her letter mentioned lending the missing pages to a friend. '*Please* don't show what you have to *anyone*,' he pleaded. 'You're the only person I've *ever* allowed (actually I couldn't really stop you) to see my scribblings before completion (big deal).' He bombarded her with instructions to return it; spectres of suspicion, jealousy and rejection stalked and the interlacing of plot and private life grew tighter.

When the missing pages did arrive, a sense of loss at the sundering of his and Sarah's only remaining tangible link broke through his concentration. 'My empty sails filled out with great gusts of despair,' he wrote afterwards. 'And I sailed over to Paris.' But during a stroll around Montparnasse, prompted by the fleeting notion that it might be a more productive place to work, he was confronted with a plaque – 'Dans cette Maison Bond . . .' – which channelled his thoughts straight back to Sarah Bond and the slow progress on the book. Claude Simha, his host for the few days, listened understandingly and advised him to follow Sartre's example. 'Claude gave me some amphetamine pills which have increased my productivity about 200%,' he recorded after a test run, 'but I get worn out in the evenings . . . When stoked up on these pills I feel obliged to hammer away nonstop to get the full benefit.'

Off-duty interludes, from supper with the Spurlings to film outings with Tom Wakefield, were strictly rationed. On unproductive days he sometimes sought out Heathcote Williams – whose fondness for anarchic slogans like 'Don't Vote: Vomit' raised an answering grin – or went with Norma to a small arts club with a wine licence in Kensington Park Gardens. The disorientated period came to a head at a dinner with Oliver Marriott, an Oxford contemporary who had become a financial journalist on *The Times*, and his Swedish wife, when he was put opposite the actor who had played Death in Bergman's *The Seventh Seal*. Jim gazed back appreciatively, remarking later, 'He lent a weird quality to the evening.' The autumnal damp aggravated the aches he had to live with, which he was able to disguise; fatigue, his normal condition, was too familiar a state for him to recognise when it was dipping lower.

Unexpectedly, October brought an opportunity to turn his introspective routine inside-out. His mother had entered a Texaco competition to win a weekend for two in New York, nominating her younger sons as recipients, and won first prize. 'I shall very likely be in New York on the weekend 25th–28th

October to say hello to old Broadwa-a-a-ay – tum-ti-tum –
Farewell Leicester Square!' he exulted to Sarah straight away,
adding the characteristic qualification, 'It's such a short time it's
bound to be somewhat unsatisfactory.' The irony of petrol
profits conveying him once again where he most wanted to
go was rubbed in by the accommodation specified: in an eerie re-
run of his Harkness arrival, merging past with present, the hotel
chosen was the Abbey Victoria. He warned Sarah about mutual
disillusion – 'One tends to stylise people in one's imagination,
and the reality sometimes comes as a shock' – and approached
another matter more elliptically. 'Affections, like everything else
in this vale of tears, being subject to the second law of thermo-
dynamics, have a tendency to cool off, decay and get reborn.
Well, what I'm trying to say is that I won't be too astonished if
by now (without my magnetic presence) someone else is pluck-
ing your heartstrings (to put it at its most delicate). That would
be only natural. But I would like to *know* if we're lovers now or
old friends, so that I can get acclimatised to the idea and digest it
(to mix a metaphor) rather than spend the weekend with that
awful skinned-alive feeling one gets when things come to an
end.' No reply came by return and at once he shared the Major's
insomnia. [He] *began to feel drowsy. Yet even as, hands in
pockets, he strolled peacefully away into the tall waving grass of
sleep, baleful yellow eyes were watching him, and then . . . Ah!
the thought of Sarah once more pounced and clawed his sensitive heart.*

Jim swung from being comforted by the recollection that she
had said she never allowed friends to quarrel with her – 'I only
hope I don't turn out to be the exception that proves the rule' –
to horror that she had taken offence at his comments in a string
of highly charged letters that he regretted as soon as each was
beyond recall. 'I swear to God I can't use my typewriter these
days without turning everything into a drama,' he apologised,
and stopped taking the amphetamines, ascribing most of the
blame to them.

Escorting his brother out of John F. Kennedy airport towards
the exhilarating skyscrapers of Manhattan on Friday afternoon,
Jim was still on tenterhooks. He had not worked out how to give
Richard the slip, nothing had been fixed with Sarah beyond the

vague mention of Saturday, and Sunday was entirely taken up by Carol's arrangements for lunch in Chinatown with Bob Cumming, followed by supper with Erwin and Norma Fleissner. When Carol called around to the Abbey Victoria after work he told her that regrettably he would have to devote some time to his publisher. Covertly, he made the call.

'So that *was what she looked like . . . of course, now I remember'; but to tell the truth he only half remembered her; she was half herself and half some stranger, but neither half belonged to the image he had had of her while reading her weekly letter . . .* The meeting at Sarah's apartment on West 11th Street, followed by a walk around the Village, was disastrous, demoting her instantly to the limbo separating lover from old friend. 'It was all too rushed and too awkward, and clearly we were doomed,' she said subsequently. 'We didn't have a row, we just clammed up because we knew it was over, and that was a horrible feeling. Why those endless unhappy letters? I had no money and he had none, so there was no question of any future. And I was twenty-four, in no frame of mind to languish for more than a few months over someone, which upset both him and me. I felt I'd let him down.'

But in one crucial way, she had not. As Jim did his sightseeing duty and brooded, making small-talk, his turmoil of emotion shed light on the Major's experience. He was monosyllabic on the flight back, too preoccupied to read the copy of *Rosemary's Baby* bought as a memento of Manhattan. His charter flight was scheduled to land in Dublin, where he had intended to spend a day visiting the County Waterford location he had in mind for the Majestic hotel. Too upset to contemplate research, he took the first connection through to Heathrow instead and got down to work. Sarah had told him about a new boyfriend who had already beaten her up, and the fictional Sarah's fate was to be elopement with an equally aggressive Black and Tan officer. She would abandon the Major, who would continue to worry about her in spite of knowing it to be futile. *After all, he was not a complete fool. He knew that now there was really no further hope on earth of a successful union with Sarah. Apart from everything else, he now bore her a considerable resentment which would prevent him (probably against his will) from being friendly. Doubtless one day it would fade into indifference and allow him to be friendly again; but it would only disappear* on one condition: *namely that he was no longer in love with her. Thus, his only hope of success depended on his not wanting to succeed.* On cue, Jim's letters to Sarah ceased.

'I literally haven't spoken to anyone for days (except in shops where I buy my food),' he noted absently. 'I'm beginning to feel like one of Dostoevsky's mad students [in] *Notes from Underground.*' Simultaneously a character named Stavrogin took shape as a veteran of the Ulster Regiment at Thiepval, only to be banished by the second draft. Jim re-established his routine of writing all morning and researching in the afternoon, boosted by a reader's ticket for the British Museum and access to the Colindale Newspaper Library in Hendon. 6" × 4" cards of detail proliferated, stapled on to strips hung from the back of his door where they could be read without getting up from his desk. The pace was unrelenting, although there was no longer much chance of meeting the self-imposed publication deadline, and occasionally he flagged. 'Writing is simply too neurotic-making unless one has a woman one can get some psychological support from in the background.' . . . 'I've now reached ms page 425 and somehow suspect that it's unlikely to go on much further than another hundred pp or so (of the first draft).' . . . 'My inspiration has somewhat deserted me in the last day or two; I've had one or two nagging suspicions that I no longer remember why I started writing the book or what it was all supposed to be about. Rather like someone who starts telling a long joke and then, when he gets to the end, can't remember the punchline.'

Jim moved in one world and mentally inhabited another. He went to see the nude scene in *Hair* and in Kilnalough the sheltered Major glimpsed a naked maid. Elderly people drew his eye in rush-hour crowds on the tube, and the Major surveyed the Majestic's elderly residents and thought *after all, there is not so very much difference between an old lady and a young girl, only a few years diluting the exuberance with weariness, sadness and a great sensitivity to draughts.* He disguised his shallow breathing, exacerbated by two harsh winters in America, and his latest fictional doctor picked up the thread of transience. *People are insubstantial. A doctor should know that better than anyone.*

They are with us for a while and then they disappear . . . A man must not let himself become bitter and defeated because of this state of affairs, because really there is no point to it . . . There is no rock of ages cleft for anyone and one must accept the fact that a person . . . is only a very temporary and makeshift affair. The melancholy that pervades *Troubles* was laced with surrealism and humour, but a familiar man made a cameo appearance. *And yes, it had been a bit hard getting back to one's studies – at least, he added with an agonised smile, he'd found it so at first anyway . . . And his sad, shocked eyes returned to the faces of his high-spirited companions . . . he trailed after them, a walking reminder . . .*

By 10 January 1969 Jim was on page 561 – 'a month to go' – and he allowed himself a day off on the eve of his thirty-fifth birthday. 'For the past few months,' he summarised, 'I've been possessed by this vast and dreary novel. A classic case of monomania, retarded development and God knows what else.' The awkward fact, he concluded, was that he didn't work hard enough or quickly enough, and the work still to be encompassed loomed like an unscalable mountain. But on 26 January a surprise signal was fired off to Carol – 'Finished first draft of book and am despondent. More and more I fear that after all the roaring and bellowing I'm about to give birth to a mouse.' Almost at once he started into the second draft.

'I'm being steam-rollered by my re-writing', he noted in April, 'though I'm enjoying it too. On the whole I think I'm making it better than I hoped I could make it . . . But whether it all blends as I want it to blend, I know not . . . Ages since I read the papers (other than those of 1919) but I suppose the world can manage without me.' . . . 'My energies are all being channelled into my enormous chef d'oeuvre. I reached page 400 of the retype yesterday; another 400 odd still to go. I feel I'm on a ghastly treadmill.' . . . 'The things I like best in the book because I feel that they're the best written are the usual small change of farcical seductions etc., entirely without historical interest. So it's certain that I'll keep them in preference to the cautiously written surgings of the Irish people.'

The daily newspapers straddled the fifty-year divide as soon as British troops were sent into Northern Ireland, and Jim often

took the tube home from North London or Bloomsbury surrounded by commuters reading *Evening Standard* accounts of
disturbances that mirrored events he had just been unearthing;
superstitiously he wondered if he had somehow evoked the
current troubles. Personal experience was invaluable: on one
occasion he was stopped by police outside Victoria Station as the
IRA bombing campaign intensified – the surname Farrell was
not a help – and the banality of the exchange served to illuminate
the exact composition of historical milestones. 'The real experience', as he would point out, 'is not composed of treaties being
signed or pincer movements. It's smoke in your eyes or a blister
on your foot.' *Every now and then, however, he would become
aware with a feeling of shock that, for all its lack of pattern, the
situation was different, and always a little worse.*

The double fetters of his room and his book increasingly
chafed, and he longed to be free of captivity in 'this small, seedy
cage'. One evening Norma di Marco heard a knock on her door
and found him standing on the step holding out a bottle of wine
and a carton of cigarettes. 'I haven't spoken to anyone for four
days,' he said, handing them over. 'This is just for being there.'
At the end of July the Spurlings were the recipients of a very
different communication. A note written on a scrap of a Marks
and Spencer paper-bag and pushed through their letter-box
abruptly informed them that he was swapping Stanley Crescent
for Pont Street Mews, and later that day the sum of his possessions fitted into three plastic bags at his feet as he waited for a lift
across the gulf that divided Notting Hill from Knightsbridge. In
the late afternoon he bolted back to buy a jar of coffee in
Queensway; like a rabbit into a burrow, according to his
chauffeur and new flatmate, Diana Saville.

They had met at a party given by the editor of a small poetry
magazine, and a shortlived attraction had ended without reproach on either side, enabling him to take up the unexpected
offer of a spare room in the flat she had just taken with a friend.
Both girls, ten years his junior, felt that he needed looking after
and were prepared to set a purely nominal rent. Jim moved into
the best room, overlooking the cobbled mews, willingly donated
because he would be writing there all day while they were out at
work. Free of the unsettling pull towards Sarah Bond, he dyed

the carpet, painted the walls and bought a Habitat work table and anglepoise lamp. Once installed, he took great pleasure in his famous 'corner store'; a fresh Harrods Edinburgh loaf from the Food Hall, within 200 yards of the mews entrance, superseded the health-shop bread. The general agreement was that he could pay his way by keeping an eye on things, and he signed household notes 'J. Mellors, gamekeeper'. It quickly became apparent to both girls, however, that life ran more smoothly if his routine came first. Diana's cat dutifully curled up on an orange cushion placed upon his new table beside the typewriter: aware that the real attraction was the warmth beneath his lamp, he appreciated its company during the lonely hours of rewriting. In deference to Tiffany, the cat was renamed Mappin, after Mappin and Webb. Webb's turn would come, fictionally, in *The Singapore Grip*.

Jim continued to avoid Jonathan Clowes, and the information that the agency was severing ties with its New York partners bought an excuse to move. 'Really,' he commented, 'I feel one might be spared this sort of thing. Agents acting like ballerinas,' and he turned to his editor at Pan, who recommended Deborah Rogers as a newcomer with good American connections. Spurred by the recollection that Piers Paul Read had said she acted for him, Jim called round to her office at 29 Goodge Street that same day. The phone call about *Troubles* that Clowes was expecting finally came through, but instead of the guarded male voice he remembered so well, he recognised Deborah. 'I've been approached by Jim Farrell. Do you mind?'

Jim approved of Deborah's youth, as well as her warmth and optimism, the necessary qualities that in his view Clowes lacked. She had set up her agency while he was away, based upon English representation for the list of the American agent Lynn Nesbitt, with whom she had become friendly during her New York apprenticeship with Curtis Brown, Jim liked the transatlantic combination, as well as the enthusiasm with which she spoke of finding the best individual strategy for each writer she chose to take on. 'She wears one of those fashionable chain belts and has dark glasses on top of her head,' he described her delightedly, 'like Rommel the Desert Fox.' The comic potential of an office sited in a red-light district with 'Miss Deborah

Rogers Ltd' by the top bell was the crowning touch. One of her stories featured a man in a macintosh who had been ushered in by her baffled assistant with the briefing, 'A rather strange man. He says he's a friend of Keith.'

Deborah praised Jim's three published books, and he took round the *Troubles* typescript expectantly, but silence ensued. Eventually he learned that she was in Malta visiting Anthony Burgess, another client. Since Oxford he had loosely kept in touch with Janet Dawson who, in her role as film critic for *Sight and Sound*, boasted of Hollywood links. He lent a copy to her, and again was disappointed. 'Having at last sampled 60pp,' he recounted to Carol Drisko, 'she rang me invoking the names of Henry James, Scott Fitzgerald and Ford Madox Ford. At the 200pp mark I snatched it back from her. She was no longer invoking the literary heavyweights and seemed a tiny bit apathetic. She observed that she thought it was "a mistake" to kill Angela off so soon – "the most interesting character". You can imagine the state of alarm this threw me into.'

Could it really be no good? There was too much time to worry in the unexpected lull. 'In spite of everything I find this hard to believe. I've never felt as confident about a book as about this one and if it should be judged mediocre then it means that my judgement has seized up.' Cape's enthusiasm was tempered by advice to cut it by 30 per cent, and before beginning a third draft in Deborah's absence he despatched a letter to Tom Maschler demanding a substantial increase in the advance, threatening to find another publisher if they did not pay up. 'To hell with the fellow anyway,' he noted angrily. 'He hardly misses an opportunity for heaping me with oily praises but does nothing for my books. It would be a relief to find someone, an editor, with whom I had a better relationship. But I guess all publishers' editors speak with forked tongues.' He revised and returned it by September, doubting whether he had cut enough, and considered *Troubles* aptly named.

Things had slowed to a point, he observed to Carol, where only God and a trained observer could tell they were moving at all. 'Deborah promised action but then her office was burgled, next the ceiling of her office fell in; the latest I heard was that she was in a car crash and hospitalised with a suspected fracture of the spine. All this time the ms of *Troubles* lies in her office like a sinister gem, stolen from a mysterious Oriental figurine, and radiating a sort of weird miasma (if a weird miasma can be radiated). I expect to hear next that one of her cleaning-ladies, who has pinched the ms in the hope of a nice dirty read in bed with her hot-water bottles, has been found strangled . . . Could it be, these disasters aside, that I was over-optimistic about her?'

A cut-price charter to New York that autumn promised movement, at least, and he scraped together fifty dollars to get him through the fortnight. 'To Whom It May Concern', attested Carol, as sponsor. 'I have undertaken to support Mr J.G. Farrell during his projected trip to the United States' – and Gary Arnott offered his flat on East 14th Street. After an interminable flight the flat turned out to be already occupied by a male Japanese lover who spoke no English, the national topic of Nixon bored him and, emerging with Carol from Moonfetas in heavy rain, he clashed with a macabre woman with piercing eyes over the only yellow cab to pull across. 'May you turn into a frog,' she hissed, grabbing the handle of the door first, and his bad mood was exorcised. He hopped away down 49th Street in the torrent, crouching and leaping until out of sight, and Carol was forced to run to catch up.

'Incidentally, I've read *Cold Comfort Farm* and everything is clear to me!' he had taken care to set the tone for Sarah, with whom he had resumed sporadic correspondence. 'You are *exactly* like Flora Poste. If I'd read the book I'd have recognised you instantly on the day we first met – when you'd just been frightfully sensible with naked men dashing in and out of flames, drugged up to the eyebrows. However, I was alarmed to recognise myself in the writer, Mr Mybug, who loves striding over the moors and saying how phallic everything is . . . "We're friends, aren't we?" he (Mybug) asked. "Certainly," said Flora pleasantly. "We might dine together in Town some time?" "That would be delightful," agreed Flora, thinking how nasty and boring it would be. "There's a quality in you," said Mr Mybug, staring at her and waving his fingers. "I should like to write a novel about you . . ." "Do, if it passes the time for you," said Flora; "and now I really must go." ' On his return to London Jim faced a grilling about the glamorous photo of her on show in his room, and responded mildly, saying she had turned him down 'like a bedspread'. To Sarah he now signed off, in Mybug key. 'Although, apart from the one evening when you told me about your lover, I felt that we weren't communicating at all, I was very glad to have seen you and managed to remain on friendly terms. A triumph of British sensibleness, in my view.' But his earlier change of heart about dedicating the book to her was not rescinded.

No progress had been made on the Cape contract for *Troubles*, there was no paperback interest, and it was being turned down by New York publishers. When Malcolm Dean, who had returned from Chicago to the *Guardian*, suggested to Jim that he should write career leaflets at £50 a time, he was desperate enough to have a go. He soon grumbled that he spent as much time polishing ads as a book, and the 'hacking job' was set aside. Determined to raise his morale, Malcolm introduced him to an American journalist who had just written a book about Bobby Kennedy. 'I was making some of my usual disparaging remarks about my namesake James T. when this Bill Shannon, who is otherwise a nice though rather prissy fellow, announced that he was a very good friend of his. My mind boggled irretrievably.'

Reviewing promised a more congenial income, and Hilary Spurling, in her capacity as Arts Editor on the *Spectator*, was surprised by his request for a regular film column, and even more surprised by its didactic tone. All her diplomacy was needed to deflect him to the literary pages where, she earnestly assured him, he belonged. Jim welcomed the prospect of occasional £20 cheques, but was wary about becoming identified with the *Spectators*'s right-wing politics. 'Who cares about Scotland?' he asked, distancing himself by means of a review of *Memoirs of Modern Scotland* edited by the influential Karl Miller. 'Almost nobody, to judge from the melancholy tone of [these] essays . . . What they add up to in the end is a glum picking of fleas out of the Scottish fur . . . A light drizzle is falling on the reader [and] presently the drizzle increases to a steady downpour.' It seemed petty to be airing his opinions on other people's work that he had not even read properly, he wrote to Russell McCormmach. 'It seems to me that one must suffer an instant drop in one's already precarious self-respect – From Novelist to Man of

Letters, like a Victorian boy's story by G.A. Henty I once read called *From Powder Monkey to Admiral* (this book would have been more interesting if it had been the other way round).'

The idealistically driven *New Society*, which was centre-left without being party-political and determinedly non-metropolitan, raised no such hackles, and he reviewed for it occasionally without quibbling. As a bonus, he was becoming friendly with its editor, Paul Barker, who had been introduced to him by Gary Arnott as an Oxford near-contemporary; Barker, too, had read French at BNC under Shackleton, whom he saw in a kindlier light. Labour-supporting election-night parties at Paul and Sally Barker's house in Kentish Town became a tradition.

One evening in November Diana, who worked in publishing, inveigled him to the Chelsea launch of *The Beatles' Illustrated Lyrics*, ostensibly to glimpse David Hockney but in practice to make a match between him and her friend from Oxford, Bridget O'Toole. Jim loathed the scrum, depressed by such graphic evidence of publishing priorities, and politely squired Bridget, who found the celebrity cult equally alien, back to the flat. To break the ice on the way she mentioned that she was doing a literary Ph.D. at Warwick University, at which his pace slowed. 'Have you read anything of mine?' he queried, and she admitted she had not. In silence they reached Pont Street Mews and she unrolled her sleeping bag in Diana's room.

'When you want to see me, summon me to your side, m'dear,' he left the first move to her, addressing his letter to her digs in Leamington Spa. 'Rub the magic bottle (preferably gin) and I will appear, or even better, come to London again . . . PS. Life is very, very short. (Cliché of the week.)' Bridget's research brought her regularly to the British Museum, and by their next meeting she had read *A Girl in the Head* and detected the Nabokov dimension. Jim was impressed by her critical judgement and her equally keen sense of the ridiculous; and while deploring her academic world – 'What could be more barren than dessicated analysis?' – he appointed himself her mentor.

At twenty-five, Bridget was unselfish, intelligent and perceptive, with an aura of vulnerability that allayed his usual suspicions. All the same he made a point of reminding her that he was still in love with Sarah. Her family background in England, as the daughter of a

Liverpool Irish father, the son of a 'mixed' marriage, and an English mother who had instilled the importance of individual choice, knitted up the conflicting patterns that still preoccupied him. Even more importantly, that background had bred a subtlety of humour he had not been aware of missing until they met. *Troubles* was not yet at the proof stage, and within a few weeks he took the significant step of including her among the guests, along with Sarah, Carol, Bob and Russell, at the climactic Majestic Ball. In a reversal of his usual practice he wooed her unhurriedly and on paper, the medium where both were more at ease.

'I was just thinking the other day how nice it must be to be sealed up in such good skin as yours . . . but what has been happening to the person inside? What of the steaming passions of Leamington Spa? . . . I now see that a grey fog hangs in the Pump Room. Faces are expressionless, people seldom speak, and never above a whisper. From time to time, however, one of these figures looming out of the fog will exchange a searing glance with another, a brief glint of passion or hatred, before their faces are rendered once more as impenetrable as masks. Sort of thing.' . . . 'I wonder what you'll think of *Troubles*, the book I'm now going through, the last of many editings (I hope) before it goes into the works . . . I wish you were here now instead of in two weeks' time to advise me whether to keep or drop a couple of chapters. My own critical faculties have totally atrophied.' He posted off *A High Wind in Jamaica* and she sent *The Good Soldier* and there was soon so much to discuss, unlike their first stiff encounter, that as they crossed a side road in Chelsea one day an oncoming car had to swerve to avoid them. Politically, they were in tune and cast their votes for Labour together.

Jim talked lightheartedly about getting Bridget trained, by which he meant undemanding and unpossessive, as well as scrupulously tidy. He liked her, he once said revealingly, because he could forget she was around. The ten-year age gap created a seniority that he made no attempt to lessen, and the advantage only swung the other way in the presence of Malcolm Dean, who became her ally. '*Poor* boy!' they turned the tables once. 'All those public school hang ups, while we grammar school products have been educated in the university of life.' Bridget was allowed to smoke in his room, and he made no protest when he was typing if she wound the scarf she was knitting for him around his neck for size. 'You'd *better* come at the weekend, or who knows?' he teased her back. 'Your mustard may be flavouring the victuals of one of my other numerous women. From where I sit I can see them herded resentfully on the cobbles below, waiting for a glimpse.'

He had worked out that £200 was due in December from paperback royalties of *A Girl in the Head*, and grudgingly co-operated with Deborah's advice to compromise with Cape on the strength of a small increase for *Troubles*, simmering down to the point where his young editor, Catherine Peters, found him shy and helpful. When the royalty cheque arrived, however, it was made out for £20, accompanied by a statement to show that £180 had been deducted to repay the previous unearned advance. Too proud to ask Tom Maschler for the money he was relying on, he rushed across town to Catherine, unable to hide his distress. 'I got hold of Tom and asked if he could advance anything,' she later revealed. 'He was adamant that he would not, and I found myself in the curious position of defending my author against my own firm. Naturally Jim was very unhappy afterwards about Cape; already *Troubles* was in trouble.' Back in Pont Street Mews, with Christmas less than three weeks away, Jim let his feelings rip to Carol. 'I haven't a bean . . . So you see I must do some work, get something else finished. You can imagine the state of desperation I'm in.' Simultaneously the absentee landlord of the flat sent a notice to quit, and without a lease they were in no position to stall for long.

In the weeks left before they had to get out, Jim decided that he would be better off living by himself again, although he had begun to enjoy giving small dinner parties, and the sparks from mixing the girls' friends with his own. 'Although life is more pleasant living with other people,' he acknowledged, 'I find that I spend too much time in idle conversation and not in "creative" day-dreaming. It's sad that one has to be lonely in order to get up the steam to write fiction but this seems to be the case – as far as I'm concerned, anyway.' Attributing that to the archetypal writer's lot was preferable to harking back to invalid status; by now the low level of energy from his diminished oxygen intake was the normal state of affairs.

Harrods Food Hall had, insidiously, become his daily focal point. Reluctant to move away, he patrolled the neighbourhood for estate agents' signs, undeterred by the area's prohibitive expense. At 16 Egerton Gardens – 'a redbrick Victorian canyon' – he eventually found what he sought in Apartment 2, the rear ground-floor flat, which consisted of an unfurnished bedsitting room, a bathroom and a kitchen the size of a ship's galley. The set rent was a mere £3.50 a week, there was a not unreasonable asking price for the five years left of the 21-year lease, and he knew that under the Landlord Tenant Act sitting tenants in rent-controlled properties had security of tenure. He made a lightning trip to his parents in Malta, told Gary Arnott afterwards that he was given £750 as his stake in a distant Farrell will, and the lease was signed in May, with Bridget as his witness. Separate copies of the *Troubles* typescript were lodged with Diana, Norma di Marco and his former Brasenose room-mate, Brian Pearce, in case of fire. He ordered his customary rubber address stamp and, finally prepared to put down roots, opened an account with Barclays in the King's Road.

'It formerly belonged to an ageing faggot with a seigneurial taste in fake grandeur,' he noted caustically. 'Old-fashioned, plastic-dripping electric candles on all four walls and hanging from the ceiling enough Regency stripes to satisfy a colony of zebras and some luscious red and white brocade curtains that wouldn't have looked out of place in the Field of the Cloth of Gold (Hollywood version).' The curtains were replaced with cream ticking, the red carpet toned down to mulberry, and the kitchen walls papered with aluminium foil, while the long wall of his main room was given the Proustian treatment, accomplished with Habitat cork tiles. As the weather warmed up, pots of herbs appeared on the steps that led down from the bay window, and in boxes on the strip of grass he raised seedlings of marjoram, rosemary and bergamot; the tubs intended for honeysuckle and roses were filled with earth he claimed to have smuggled out of Hyde Park in a suitcase. Seeing a way to save money and simultaneously take more exercise, he bought a second-hand collapsible bike with a low central folding hinge instead of the usual high straight bar, which made it much easier for him to mount and dismount by easing pressure on his damaged arm and shoulder muscles. 'Isn't it great', he hailed a passing friend, 'to get out and about and know you're not in debt to anybody?' Overhead lived the celebrated concert pianist Alfred Brendel, who appreciated tranquillity as much as he did, judging by occasional irritated knocking on the ceiling.

Before moving to Egerton Gardens, Jim had checked over the typescript that Cape had prepared for the printer – 'in the nick of time to save some gleaming pearls of style from the too-severely toilet-trained copy editor's dreary insistence on the rules of grammar and syntax'. But as soon as the proofs of *Troubles* were delivered on 1 June the familiar tension about losing time clamped down. 'I trust that I've finished with the Home Beautiful for a few more years,' he noted with dismay. 'It'll certainly take me that long to recover. In all this time I've abandoned both writing and reading [and] my financial plight is desperate.' Publication was set for October, but his doubts returned as he set about yet another reading.

'To say that excitement is running high in the book world about its forthcoming appearance would be an exaggeration,' he wrote to Russell McCormmach, disguising his misgivings. 'Indeed, excitement appears to be running low here, and even lower in the US where, after months of study and a course of electric shock treatment, the editor in chief of Harper and Row reached the conclusion that he didn't know whether he wanted it or not. He's waiting now until he sees a proof copy, hoping no doubt that this will inspire him to a decision. If not then it will be a question of calling in the seers to consult the tripes in the H & R boardroom. He was heard to murmur however, that he thought "not enough happened" in the book (although within its pages the entire British Empire crumbles).'

Bridget, meanwhile, had made up her mind to take a teaching job abroad as soon as she qualified in the summer, and with the book now out of his hands – 'What a life. Either one is agonised or bored stiff' – the impact of her imminent departure struck home. He found that he did not want to let her go, and for the first time since the early months of his love affair with Judy Mitchell, fourteen years before, he cast caution to the winds. At Easter he took her to Paris to stay with Claude Simha and Anna, who had moved to a general practice in the north-eastern suburb of Noisy le Grand. Tense and, uncharacteristically, needing to confide, he told Claude when the two men were alone that he had seriously proposed to her and was even prepared, if need be, to have children. Claude was astounded: he knew how non-committal Jim was in his relationships with women, and afterwards he was thoughtful; the word 'sacrifice' had been used, and Bridget described as 'undecided'.

In the countdown to the publication of *Troubles*, Jim's emotions remained in well-camouflaged turmoil. Bridget attended interviews in London for posts as far afield as Bermuda, Hong Kong and Singapore. Each new prospect affected Jim, too. His only attempt to influence her, however, was over a summons to the New University of Ulster. 'I might live with you in the West Indies,' he responded then, nonchalant mask barely slipping, 'but not in Northern Ireland.' They understood one another completely: for each of them the riposte held warning.

In the week of the General Election Jim had two pieces in the *Spectator* and four more in the pipeline, and his alarm at the large Tory swing was as nothing compared to the immediate financial loss when the editor Nigel Lawson was sacked upon the loss of his Eton and Slough seat, and Hilary Spurling resigned in protest. She had been planning to send *Troubles* to Elizabeth Bowen for a prominent review. Piling on the pressure, Harper and Row in New York backed away from publication, bringing to four the number of US publishers who had turned it down. 'As this book is easily my best,' he commented grimly, 'I can only conclude that publishing companies are staffed by idiots.'

In Cape's Fiftieth Anniversary list of autumn titles in 1970, Jim was placed fourth, given the same prominence as Patrick White and supported by a full-page advertisement in the *Bookseller*. But vying for the limited review space were Irwin Shaw, Agatha Christie, Len Deighton, Ngaio Marsh, Günter Grass, Nicholas Monsarrat and Gore Vidal. 'I feel the tide is running against me,' Jim wrote to a friend a month beforehand, tongue-in-cheek as usual in letters. 'This suspicion became a certainty when I learned that my book is coming out on the same day as new novels by C.P. Snow and Hemingway. (Yes, Ernest is getting at me from Beyond The Tomb).' It was not a good time to learn that Bridget had decided to take up the lectureship in English and American Literature at the New University of Ulster in Coleraine but he waved her off without implying blame. 'When the book business has settled down,' he concealed his hurt, 'I shall probably come over and pay you a visit to make sure you are behaving yourself.'

Thin-skinned and despondent, he braced himself for further blows, and as the publication date approached he described his mood as one of grey dissatisfaction. 'When I look in the mirror,' he confided in his notebook, 'I notice that I'm growing old and still haven't done anything good. I remind myself of the main character in Chekhov's masterly *A Dull Story*.' His best work had to be completed within five years, he let slip to Diana Savile, and, seeing her puzzlement, his thin expressive face hardened. Tolstoy had finished *War and Peace* by the age of thirty-eight, well before that, he explained with an emphasis that chilled her. 'I'm the most ambitious man you'll ever know,' he added softly, getting up to go.

Troubles was published on 8 October, and the *Observer* and *The Times* reviewed it in glowing terms; the *New Statesman* took a different tack, and savaged it. 'In general,' Jim countered, 'I think I prefer outright (or do I mean downright) praise or abuse to vague suggestions that "this novel isn't too unreadable if you tackle it with a bottle of whiskey and a box of Black Magic at your elbow." ' But the damage was done. Appreciation by one of his heroes, William Trevor, who singled out the 'feeling of the particular reflecting the universal, a feeling so successfully pervading page after page of this clever book' for making it 'a *tour de force* of considerable quality', and a separate *Guardian* interview by the kindly Malcolm Dean, could not remove the *New Statesman* sting. In December Elizabeth Bowen's judgement finally surfaced in the small-circulation *Europa*, and caught the exact dimension he had set out to achieve. At her comment that he had captured yesterday 'reflected in today's consciousness', the sun, as he ruefully put it, at last began to shine; she, alone, had noticed his attempt to write 'about *now* as well as *then*'. Angus Wilson chose *Troubles* as his Christmas recommendation, and at the end of January the tardiness of *The Times Literary Supplement*, the only major paper to ignore him until then, was made up for by a review there which praised the book as 'subtly modulated, richly textured, sad, funny and altogether memorable'.

On a warm afternoon three months later Hilary Spurling phoned to tip him off that he was about to be awarded the Faber prize. She had just been with Olivia Manning and Francis King, two of the judges, and neither had been able to stop talking about the traditionally acrimonious lunch, which for once had been fun because everyone had put foward the same name. 'Whose was it?' she had probed. 'Someone called J.G. Farrell.' Jim's elation was the keener for knowing that his predecessor was Piers Paul Read.

Overnight, and without any further call on his own resources, he was a literary star. The transition was so abrupt it was unreal. A cheque for £250 was presented to him on 6 May, followed by a ceremonial meal at the Étoile. 'I ate so much I almost doubled the value,' he mocked his moment of triumph in the aftermath. 'I also had my hand shaken by Lady Faber in front of a spotty photographer. A picture of the event subsequently appeared in *The Bookseller*, myself smiling oilily like an Arab rug-seller.'

At a stroke, in the world where he most wanted to succeed, his reputation was now made. Malcolm Dean's advice to seize the opportunity for further publicity, however, was brushed aside, and in the next *Author's and Writer's Who's Who* he made no addition to his entry, beyond mischievously adding the hobbies of Mexican politics and gastronomy. At the small informal dinner parties that had resumed, he continued to do all the cooking and washing-up on his own; old friends and new were made welcome around the hastily cleared Habitat table that still had to double as his desk. Progression from past to present was incorporated into letters in matter-of-fact commentary; *que sera, sera*.

'I had lunch the other day at the Café Royal with Sonia Orwell and Jean Rhys, who is a friend of hers. She is incredibly old and frail and her voice is rather weak, but I liked her very much. She told me that she had fallen over six weeks earlier and broken three ribs, after drinking a bottle of white wine. I hope to be doing the same in my eighties. She's a bit helpless and Sonia had to cut up her food. In the incredibly lush turn of the century plush decor . . . she seemed like a fly in amber. It was also poignant to hear someone talking about Djuna Barnes and the Joyces as acquaintances in such a setting ("Nora Joyce was very sweet.")' . . . 'Saul Bellow [wore] a jacket with two buttons on the back, like a frockcoat.' . . . 'One evening last week saw me bowling along the King's Road crammed into a car brimming with literary talent: viz Anthony Powell, Edna O'Brien and a nice American girl called Alison Lurie, on the way to supper at Alvaros.' . . . 'Powell is very entertaining in a malicous, gossipy Old Etonian sort of way. He also had lots of harsh words about Malcolm Muggeridge, a former bosom friend, whom he declared to be completely mad, adding "Mind you, hardly anyone over forty is altogether sane." . . . He looks like a suburban bank manager down on his luck (if suburban bank managers are ever down on their luck), greasy tie, lumpy suit.' Ironically it would come to be said, behind Jim's back, that he himself was like a character out of *A Dance to the Music of Time*.

A solitary character, however, and now likely to remain so. On Bridget's first birthday away the previous November he had crossed the Irish Sea to spend it with her, and they walked for miles along the beach at Portrush. He tucked a toy monkey she had been given inside his coat, and peeped it out at everyone they passed. She was happy, sure that they were closer than before, but his good humour hid the distancing fact that he was repelled by the religious bigotry of the province, and did not share in her belief that Labour shop-floor solidarity might unite the Catholic and Protestant working classes. He listened in his teasing way, and christened her Red Biddy. 'I'm having a few misgivings about your firebrand political activities,' he admonished from London, 'but I suppose you know what you're doing.'

Mild and responsible, emanating bafflement and concern, he began referring to her as Bríd Ná Thuille, and at Christmas went out to Heathrow to meet her as a surprise. She came into view laughing with a man he did not know, and, catching sight of him, she waved and introduced a fellow lecturer. Jim's icy acknowledgement gave away his sense of exclusion. By the time he introduced her to one of his new allies, the Irish poet Derek Mahon, the balance had shifted back. 'I remember her being tremendously excited to be there with him,' Derek noticed. 'As for his feelings, there was no telling.' Their impatience with each other's circle mounted. Bridget found little in common with his exclusively literary friends like Olivia Manning and Sonia Orwell, and Jim's scathing opinions about Northern Ireland hardened. Alone together, they remained harmonious but, although she took every opportunity to come to London, such interludes were dwindling.

The years go by and [he] undoubtedly felt, as many of us feel, that one uses up so many options, so much energy, simply in trying to find out what life is all about. And as for being able to do anything about it, well . . . Coming back into his room after seeing Bridget off, re-absorbed by insistent characters beguiling him from a more distant century, Jim shut the door into the hall and prepared to start work. But before immersing himself he got out the diary he had kept in America, which he had recently unearthed. 'I now think of the time at the Belvedere as the lowest point of the last few years,' he made a final entry, 'although I had a regular supply of cash coming in and no worries except complete inability to get a book started. I was evidently very lonely: it's hard to remember what loneliness actually *feels* like if you've stopped being it. My life has taken on a much more settled apearance since then; partly because of an increase in self-confidence, I suppose. Bríd has meant taking a more stable view of things too.'

Meanwhile, a Cunard liner was getting up speed at the start of a long sea passage to Australia, and among the passengers aboard was Judy Mitchell, to whom he had also, long before, proposed. She was travelling abroad on her own for the first time since the Spanish holiday they had taken together, only a few months before her near-fatal car crash. With apprehension she set out to explore the vast ship and, coming across the library, she stepped inside. Prominent among the new purchases on the table, she saw the name *J.G. Farrell*, highlighted in large white letters against dark blue.

Judy borrowed *Troubles* and took it to her cabin where, unable since her head injuries to concentrate for a paragraph – let alone a page – she kept it on the locker beside her bed. It was her talisman as the ship crossed the Equator and sailed far south, and when it was time to disembark at the end of the voyage she handed it in with regret. The librarian thanked her, and re-marked on its untouched state. Had she not liked it? she was asked. Judy looked back from the doorway, and smiled. 'I used to know the author,' she replied.

CHAPTER SIXTEEN

A Foot Wedged in the Door of Eternity
1971

F our years after confiding that his ambition was to match the achievement of Camus in *La Peste*, Jim's chosen setting was taking shape, wafer-thin brick by brick. *Bricks are undoubtedly an essential ingredient of civilization; one gets nowhere at all without them.* But his original besieged town had dwindled to a British enclave under siege in the Indian Mutiny of 1857; a smaller community, but a much broader theme. Since Yale he had had a name for the unresolved idea, and he continued to refer to it privately as 'his' Robinson Crusoe.

India, like Ireland, evoked a possessive glint, because rapt attention in childhood to his father's colourful stories had merged Bill's experiences with his own. As the research for *Troubles* had stretched out he had made notes on the Amritsar massacre, the mutiny of the Connaught Rangers and Gandhi's repeated calls to drive out the British. Each was a historical turning point, but none ultimately caught his imagination. And then, while idly glancing through a tome on Victorian social history in a public library, he had come across a love letter addressed to 'Tony', and instantly the mid-nineteenth century sharpened into focus. The subject selected itself. 'Naturally I read it greedily,' he recorded. 'Actually it was only half-written – the unnamed girl was begging forgiveness for some unspecified unfaithfulness which had merely been "experimental" but that ever since "the first time on the camp bed" (!!!) she had really known that he was the only one.'

Jim returned to the period whenever he could, and a leaden day in the British Museum was lit by the discovery of a personal diary kept during the Indian Mutiny's most sensational confrontation, the five-month siege of Lucknow, by a survivor, Maria Germon. 'What really interested me,' he would acknowledge, 'was that it talked not about heroics and strategy but about how people were actually living, how they washed their clothes, what a nuisance the flies were, and so on.' Authentic detail could now give strength to a suitably dramatic pivot, and the historical timing of the mutiny provided scope for a new and ambitious subplot. Contemporary newspaper reports of massacres of wives and children across Northern India had shattered the widespread belief held by the Victorian home public in the happiness of grateful native servants. By assigning notions that were equally misguided to characters with whose thought processes modern readers would still identify, current 'certainties' could be questioned.

Putting aside less appealing alternatives (one based upon de Gaulle's period in England – 'a gossipy popularised history explaining why he hates the Anglo-Saxons so much' – and the other probing the exploitation by Father Fischer – 'a diabolical priest' – of Emperor Maximilian in Mexico), Jim set about assembling the background. He was unsurprised to learn that the spark for the mutiny had been bureaucratic pennypinching combined with scorn for other cultures, as a result of which the cartridges for the army's new Lee-Enfield rifles were greased by a mix of cow's fat and lard to save money, a source of defilement for Hindu and Moslem sepoys alike; complacency and rigid narrow-mindedness heralded an empire in decay.

Victorian England was within walking distance of the Egerton Gardens flat. In the Science Museum Jim examined surgical and medical procedures of the period, and compassion rounded out respect. He prowled the Victoria & Albert Museum, hunting down individual items from the British Museum catalogue of the Great Exhibition of 1851, and studied costumes, making sketches. Afternoon walks took in the cemetery in the Old Brompton Road, winding between the headstones and vaults collecting inscriptions that captured *the spirit of the times*. On his desk the stack of specialised research cards accumulated: social etiquette, political events, religious controversies, scientific inventions, administration, artillery and siegecraft, military tactics . . . *What an advantage that knowledge can be stored in books! The knowledge lies there like hermetically sealed provisions waiting for the day when you may need a meal . . . this was a culture so flexible that whatever he needed was there in a book at his elbow. An ordinary [man could] turn himself into a great military engineer, a bishop, an explorer, a General overnight, if the fancy took him.*

Well before the publication of *Troubles* Jim had made a false start on the India book with too little preparation, which had proved the wisdom of Roemer's emphasis on research. 'I'm still trying to get into my Robinson Crusoe with only moderate results,' he backed away with exasperation. 'I've started it a number of times but am still not satisfied that it's off the ground. The irritating thing is that I'm sure Defoe just reeled his version off without a thought, the son of a bitch.' In 1970, however, he was much better briefed, and the distant voice of one of his father's favourite authors, John Masters, set a benchmark: 'It was the Collector on the phone . . . the head man of the Bhowani civil district . . . It's an old custom to call the D.C. the Collector.' Jim's figure of authority, too, was evolving as a fair-minded Collector, unlike E.M. Forster's Turton in *A Passage to India*, and conflicting loyalties were to be acted out against the similar backdrop of a Residency, a cutchery and a Maharajah's palace. One of Masters's fictional towns was Kishanpur; Jim, intrigued by Ramakrishna, renamed Lucknow Krishnapur. There, however, all resemblance ended.

In *Difficulties*, the irresistible early working title, Jim was prepared to rework history to suit his need. Rumours of atrocities had swept from regiment to regiment in 1857 as the sepoys mutinied, and at Lucknow the decision had been taken to bring all Europeans into a single defensible area, the British Residency. Once corralled there, however, they were surrounded and pinned down in compound buildings that were soon pounded into a maze of shattered walls and no-go areas by sniper fire and cannon shot. The 1857 Lucknow siege began later in the year than Jim's fictional siege of Krishnapur and lasted longer, and he dispensed with the unsuccessful attempt at relief which led to the surviving soldiers becoming trapped inside with the already starving garrison for a further fifty-three days. His Collector,

Mr Hopkins, would be imbued with the decisiveness of Sir Henry Lawrence, who in real life instigated the stand, but on the second day Lawrence had been mortally wounded, while Hopkins survives to disillusioned old age. In the matter of casualties, too, Jim saw no reason to stay with official statistics. Three thousand or so had been cooped up at the start of the Lucknow siege and 979 were ultimately rescued, a figure which included the less-famished soldiers from the doomed rescue attempt. To make control of plot and characters easier, Jim's numbers were far fewer and his losses less stark.

When writing *Troubles* Jim had viewed events through the experiences of one hero; this time he inhabited two. The outlook of the Collector had to contend with that of an idealistic newcomer to India, George Fleury, who was initially named the Griffin, utilising the contemporary disdainful slang. Increasing the challenge, each main character was intended to embody a separate personality trait, since the intention was to pit them against one another and allow debate to dictate the pace. On Bridget's trips to London she was banished while he worked, and if she heard him laughing and tiptoed in she found him smiling over the exchanges as he typed.

Walking back from the Victorian-tiled Harrods Food Hall with his morning loaf, Jim daily re-entered a more claustrophobic hall, that of the Residency under fire, *crowded with ladies and children who sat huddled on trunks and boxes . . . Now every room, every corridor, every staircase was occluded with the garrison's acquisitions . . .* The impact of Boscobel's wartime evacuees blended with the newspaper thickets of Carol Drisko's Manhattan apartment; the rationed biscuit tin kept for Southport air raids multiplied, and old press photographs of Dublin street barricades of 1920 were given a surrealistic change of scene. For the first time Jim was conscious of moving fairly smoothly from one book to another.

That was especially fortunate because his anger with Cape redoubled as soon as sales of *Troubles* tailed off at the low figure of 2,000. He saw his editor, Catherine Peters, as his only champion within the company, and was rewarded by the unexpected loan of family letters from Edward and Charles Metcalf MacGregor, distant uncles on her mother's side whose regiment was serving in India when the mutiny trapped them in Lucknow, where Edward died of cholera at the age of seventeen. 'As you may have guessed,' he told her gratefully when Fleury and the heroic young officer, Harry Dunstable, a foil for Fleury's intellectual values, were fully fledged, 'the character of the two young men – or perhaps it was just their healthy youthfulness – was suggested to me by the letters you let me see.'

In the spring of 1970 progress was aided by the award of an Arts Council grant of £750. It was immediately earmarked for a trip to India and put in a deposit account until the first draft was completed, because Jim correctly guessed that the shock of exposure would play havoc with his imagination. In the meantime he monitored India keenly at second-hand, sitting through the latest Satyajit Ray film at the Paris Pullman twice, and meals in the Standard, his favourite Indian restaurant in Westbourne Grove, were spent studying accents and mannerisms. In December Norma di Marco accompanied him there and he waited by the door as she got her coat and wished the staff a happy Christmas, adding, 'But you probably don't keep Christmas, do you?' White with anger at such apparent lack of sensitivity, he intervened and marched her out.

As happened with every book, the euphoria of research without warning drained away. A pivotal Indian character was to be the Maharajah of Krishnapur's weak son, Hari, who remained tantalisingly indistinct. And not only was Jim writing from twin perspectives this time, he was also writing on two levels, with the aim of bringing off the ambitious double, for commercial purposes, of an adventure story and literary work combined. The complexity of the task had been further increased by the discovery on a street book-barrow of several nineteenth-century volumes of the *British Medical Journal*, which revealed the rival theories within the profession about the cause of cholera epidemics. He instigated medical debate, siding with his enlightened doctor, McNab, as a beacon of order in disorder, of control in fundamental lack of control. Another accidental discovery, that of fervent mid-Victorian ecclesiastical battles, launched a parallel investigation, and he became fascinated by the Lucknow diaries of the Reverend Polehampton, a poignant victim. Into the religious pot went Darwinism and the agnostic backwash from scientific advance.

On the other side of the Atlantic Bob Cumming made a telepathic entry in his diary. 'A man – like Jim – who suffered a good deal at the hands of fate and of people, and who dared to let himself come in conflict with them, comes to see that the only truths are those of his imagination. So he goes his own way.' Bob had condemned Jim at Oxford for being too fatalistic; now he saw him as a model of self-determination. It was a comfortable view that, ironically, Jim himself no longer shared. 'I'm distressed by my inability to hit the right style and tone with the thing I'm doing now,' he was castigating himself at the time. 'Although I've written some forty pages, to me they are difficult to distinguish from forty corpses stretched beside my typewriter. Life is not in them. I waste hours massaging their hearts and holding mirrors over their mouths. From time to time I become convinced that the mirror has clouded faintly. But the next time I look the thing is as dead as ever.' . . . 'I tried writing again yesterday but only managed to reveal to myself once more the present barrenness of the land.' Each character under siege in Krishnapur had to find it a severe test of their belief. Jim placed a statue of 'The Spirit of Science conquering Ignorance and Prejudice', a marble bas-relief from the Great Exhibition catalogue, on show in the Collector's study. By the outcome, would Ignorance and Prejudice wrench back the upper hand?

He restricted writing to the mornings, when he was at his most productive; the comparison he preferred was to a clockwork mouse, which raced off when wound up and slowed as the spring ran down. The descent into deep concentration depended upon routine, and the bed had to be made without a wrinkle and every crumb wiped off the table before the blank A4 sheet could be lifted off the previous day's completed work and wound into the typewriter. Michael Leonard, a neighbouring artist who was the son of an Indian Army officer, was occasionally invited to share the afternoon walks. 'He wanted to know everything about my childhood,' Michael noticed. 'The way I treated servants at home in Barreilly, my school, and moving to Mussoorie in the hills during the hot months.' Another useful introduction was to Shiv Chirimar, whose contribution was the alternative Indian view. Born to a prosperous Calcutta family, Shiv had been educated in England and was studying at the London Film School.

From Malta, Jim's father supplied authentic detail. '*Ghusl* means bath, *ghuslkhana* bathroom. The traditional method of having one's ghusl was to take the water out of a reservoir about a yard square with a tin dipper and pour it over oneself. Another important part of furniture in the ghuslkhana was the thunder-box. *Chota* means little. A *peg* I always took to be a measure for the use of native bar-tenders. A *chota peg* was the usual call if one wanted an average whisky and soda . . . Another useful imperative in Hindustani was *lao* – bring, e.g. on arrival home from the office or golf course the usual cry was "Boy, chota peg lao!" ' Jim's main purpose in consulting Bill, notwithstanding John Spurling's view of their relationship, was to distract him in retirement with happy memories of youth; as a private joke for his father's benefit the Krishnapur opium agent, Mr Rayne, was made as vulgar as he was venal.

The portrayal of the Collector was conjured as much from his father's tolerance and common sense as from the author of *Personal Adventures of a Magistrate During the Indian Mutiny*, his newly found influence, Mark Thornhill. *What use is it if we bring the advantages of our civilization to India without also displaying a superior morality? I believe that we are all part of a society which by its communal efforts of faith and reason is gradually raising itself to a higher state.* It is significant that the ultimate fate of the Collector, too, was to be that of stoical isolation, but the verdict on imperial administration was un-sentimental. 'Being half Irish and half English,' as Jim once pointed out, 'I'm able to look to the same thing from both sides – from that of the colonist and the colonised.'

The baking plains were becoming peopled by recognisable individuals in disguise; some pen-portraits were fond, others decidedly not. Dr McNab's chief model was Robin Stott, a Brompton Hospital registrar whom Jim had got to know and admire for holding to the Marxist view that the genesis of illness lay in social structures. Martin Gilbert coloured the agreeable Fleury, and his French tutor at Brasenose, Professor Shackleton, was ridiculed in the guise of the local magistrate. The rollcall included the elegant Miriam May from Oxford, now married to the critic John Gross and met again at literary gatherings in London, recast as Fleury's widowed sister, Miriam – a character he assured Tom Wakefield mischievously was inspired by him – and Bridget, whose political activism was also affectionately reproved. *What can be more distressing than to hear a member of the fair sex exclaiming: 'In the first place, this . . . and in the second place, that . . .' while she chops the air with her fingers . . .? No, a woman's special skill is to listen quietly to what a fellow has to say.* 'Lucy Hughes' was well to the fore as *a sensual little angel*; and in Fleury's true love, Louise, a doctor's daughter, he made amends to Judy Mitchell – blonde and chaste, *the beauty of the cold season.* Fleury would begin his courtship with the gift of a dog, in tribute to Tiffany the cat, and he would win and cherish Louise – a second debt repaid – but on the last page a future extra-marital liaison on his part would be mentioned casually, as if inevitable. Jim had no illusions, either, about himself.

Again he lived in one world and surveyed quite another. Invited to a dinner party, he would cycle up punctually with a bottle of good wine in the handlebar basket and be gone by 10.30pm. Sitting at the table, apparently relaxed, he would check his watch and monitor the amount he drank: by 9.30 next morning he had to be burying the dead, supervising medical treatment, spiking cannons and orchestrating arguments. He usually worked seven days a week, and even at the christening of a godchild he was unable to switch off. *The infant . . . began to cry . . . screwing up its tiny face and fists with the effort it was making. The Collector's mind wandered again . . . Soon . . . he himself would become superfluous . . . 'Dost thou . . . in the name of this child, renounce the devil and all his works . . .?' 'I renounce them all,' said the Collector, not very firmly, it was thought.* Jim took pains over choosing appropriate presents for his godchildren – Nina Knox Peebles received an antique cross and little James Pearce an early edition of *Robinson Crusoe* – but his low opinion of Christianity was reinforced by his research.

As soon as the rough first draft neared completion, Jim's exposure to India could no longer be postponed. He had hoped to start before Christmas in order to be there during the cool weather – 'and miss the British cool weather' – but was delayed by the amount of preparation to be done. With regret he abandoned the idea of joining one of the many advertised overland expeditions, and instead settled for the cheapest return air fare to Bombay he could find. Allowing time for doing some writing while he was out there, he expected to be away for five months. Warnings about his physical limitations were listened to courteously, and ignored.

Jim flew to India, via Paris, Rome and Cairo, on United Arab Airlines in January 1971. He was glad to be getting out of Edward Heath's England, and he brought with him more agreeable company in the shape of Conrad, Mrs Gaskell, Dickens and Paul Scott. A returning Vietnam war correspondent dozed in the seat beside him, leaving him free to skim through *India on $5 a Day*. It painted rather a contrary picture to his father's farewell letter, which counselled that when choosing a bearer it always paid to select the one who looked most likely to impress his comrades.

He landed in the early hours of his thirty-sixth birthday, and as he wandered about Bombay in the heat, lightheaded with tiredness, the smoky, rubbishy smell conjured up Mexico and Puerto Rico. The splashes of scarlet on the pavements made him recoil, and the discovery that they were gouts of betel-stained saliva, not blood, was of little consolation: the graphic TB wards of the Wingfield Morris hospital were unforgettable. 'It is very easy to be a sahib in India, it seems,' he was berating himself within a short space of time. 'Servants are automatically deferential even to the most bizarre whims . . . Moreover, I wish my eye were better able to see the *differences* between them. I see things without understanding them.'

Jim kept his usual work notebook for impressions and wrote up a detailed diary of his odyssey, but was relying on writing letters for the sense of communication he needed. 'I'm having very mixed feelings about India and found the rapid transplanting from Kensington to Bombay a considerable shock,' he informed Russell McCormmach soon after he arrived. 'Being treated as three parts American tourist to two parts white sahib has a debilitating effect on you in the long run.' 'I don't think this would be a place for you, Brid . . . with your sensibility,' he remarked in a letter that same day to Northern Ireland. 'Even heartless old me finds it hard to get used to; in the course of a few moments I saw an Anglo-Saxon hippy in dreadful condition, arms and legs covered in scabs, wearing a dhoti and stoned beyond hope of recall, staggering along in a filthy street, then all sorts of maimed beggars with naked babies playing beside them in the dust. What hope have they of living any sort of a life?' Without a typewriter, so much writing increased the customary ache in his weakened hand and arm, and his breathing problems were compounded by unavoidable noxious traffic fumes. He was philosophical about the added burden of discomfort. Unlike London, where he was convinced he stood out as an invalid, it was almost liberating to be one of so many. It also made him feel less guilty.

Driven out of the Tea Lounge of the Taj Mahal hotel by the smug tenor of overheard conversations, he came across a stone bench beside the great arched monument, the Imperial Gateway to India, and sank down on it with relief, tired of the non-stop appraisal he could not set aside. All of a sudden, most unusually, he was enclosed entirely by the present. 'There were a lot of people, rich and poor, some utterly in rags sitting there enjoying the cool evening sunlight or strolling about', he felt compelled to record afterwards. 'The girls look wonderfully feminine in saris, one has no idea from seeing the occasional frost-bitten begum in Knightsbridge how lovely they can look. What was good was the harmony and tranquillity of everything.' Completing the moment, a bespectacled man in a dhoti sat down beside him and opened a well-thumbed book, revealed as Bertrand Russell's *Power*.

Jim's plan was to start with the traditional tourist route to Jaipur and Agra, and adjust to the country by means of a first-class train ticket, but any hope of conserving energy was wiped out by the cut and thrust of political argument over Mrs Gandhi into which he was promptly drawn in the carriage. 'I must have eaten about 1/2 lb of dust and I don't know what the dhobi made of the shirt I gave him to wash,' he wrote to his father on arrival in the Jai Mahal Palace, a hotel in a time warp which brought alive his parents' era. The sensation was heightened by the *Times of India*, which carried advertisements for films in Delhi that he had watched years before with his brother Robert in Dublin; and in the bazaar a fortune-teller dogged his steps, intent on telling him his mother's name for ten rupees. 'Tipsy cake was the dessert last night. I'm expecting Brown Windsor soup to appear sooner or later,' he wrote to his parents. 'There is a splendid garden in which I am writing this letter as green parrots with red beaks fly about.' But as he bent over the airmail letter resting on a book upon his knee a turbaned gardener theatrically handed him a rose, a touch of stage-management that broke the spell. 'An encampment of untouchables live in a dusty grove just outside the gates,' he made a separate note, 'to remind you that things are bad here, beneath the charm.'

Hard-headed enough to haggle, he explored Jaipur by cycle rickshaw, gasping in the scrum of diesel-spewing rickshaws, overloaded scooters, bulky 1950s cars, meandering cows, fast-striding camels and the occasional swaying bulk of an elephant. Offered a less-stressful tour in her chauffeur-driven Ambassador car by Roshan Lala, a young sari-clad businesswoman staying in his hotel, he accepted, undeterred by her explanation that he seemed a sad and lonely person. As Parsees, she added, her family felt friendship for the British, and she was not to know that the Parsee custom of putting their dead out to be picked clean by vultures fascinated him so much that he had already been to see the Towers of Silence, and stared up at the bodies placed on racks in the trees. They strolled together around the Maharajah of Jaipur's cremation ground in the sun, and behind the energetic small-talk he mused on the certainty that she would 'end up as a meal' there too. The keynote of his Indian experience, the transience of human life, was set.

Shaking off the fortune-teller – 'I told him I didn't want to know the future' – he booked a third-class ticket to Agra and was rewarded with a punishing twelve-hour ordeal. Lauries Hotel turned out to be a single-storied Empire relic with a long sweep of whitewashed colonnade. Indoors, foxed watercolours of Highland scenes adorned the walls, and a Coronation photograph of the Queen and Prince Philip was displayed beside a framed letter of thanks from the British High Commissioner in Delhi for accommodating the Royal Party in 1961. He felt uneasy in the 'little island of satisfaction' when he learned that the hotel had continued to bar Indians for many years after partition, but in its heyday Lauries' staff had numbered 300. Now they could be counted on two hands.

In Agra Jim visited the Taj Mahal and the ghost-town of Fatehpur Sikri – 'The world is a bridge,' he copied down Emperor Akbar's choice of Koranic inscription, 'pass over it but do not build a house upon it' – but he had not come all that way to sightsee. The Red Fort was another Mughal empire attraction, but for Jim it was the scene of Mark Thornhill's most harrowing experiences in the 1857 Mutiny. Blanking out loud voices and the clicking of cameras, he roamed about the rooms, familiar with the layout after so many hours spent poring over Thornhill's account in the British Museum. At Agra station, as he left in the cold early hours, the floor was covered with shrouded forms, and as the sun rose they sat up, coughing. An old man of seventy, a former canteen worker with the British Army, spoke to him nostalgically of the good times he had had when the British were there.

Peering through the dusty ochre-tinged windows of the train was like watching from a hide. 'A small boy in a cap covered from head to foot in black grease like a sweep out of Dickens. Open drains full of bluish black water and sludge. On date palms long green tresses where the dates grow hang from the lower branches and move gently in the wind. Sikhs, fat and white-bearded and fierce, look very imposing as they get older – Old Testamentish.'

In New Delhi, his first mailing address, Jim was informed that the post to England had been suspended due to a strike, and he left the American Express office in Conaught Circus empty-handed, with the depressing news that letters out were similarly affected. It meant that no post would catch up with the remaining forwarding addresses on schedule, sealing him off in the sub-continent. 'I wish I'd brought you along,' he wrote to Bridget nonetheless, 'as I think I would be enjoying it more and possibly noticing more things. I find that unless I actually acknowledge my thoughts by voicing them or writing them down they tend to melt into a vague blur.' Delhi was seedy and provincial, further Empire enlightenment, and two parallel threads wove through his daily notes: one was bright, assembling detail, and the other sombre, documenting transience. 'A cloud of servants, tiny and old and rather stooped. They must select them for their physical qualities. The British give funny names to the natives. One called Falstaff.' . . . 'Incense sticks smouldering in jars in the old Muslim tombs – very often these look like miniature flat-topped houses. Around them are more conventional graves, some a cut-out head and shoulders, the mound in the dusty earth remains, giving the impression of the body beneath.'

He missed Bridget acutely and it was her response that he sought most often. 'As for old Delhi railway station late at night waiting for the Mussoorie express,' he wrote chattily, 'it reminded me of pictures of bedlam jail. People slumped everywhere on the crowded platforms, great racket going on, lights so dim one could hardly see well enough to read. When the train finally drew into the platform a howling mob descended on it while it was still moving, wriggling through windows to bag seats. Meanwhile Smoothy Sahib surveyed this leaning on his cane with a faint smile playing on his lips. Then, signing to the two dusky Malabars to pick up his steamer trunk and follow him, he picked his way through the malodorous natives to his first-class accommodation.'

The destination was Dehra Dun, where Jim had an introduction to John Spurling's uncle, Sir Edmund Gibson, and roving about aimlessly on arrival, he bought six tiny cakes which turned out to be inedible. 'Perhaps it's just as well,' he addressed another letter to Bridget. 'Already I think I hear whispers in the bazaar that the Fat Smoothy Sahib will soon be having to buy new *churidars* (trousers to you) to enclose his ample proportions.' But he woke next morning immersed in sadness and loss, and handing his breakfast tray to the Hindu bearer, was wounded further by the instinctive reluctance to take it, due to caste taboos on physical contact.

An advance letter from Sir Edmund Gibson – 'Dear Farrell' – proposing lunch at the Dehra Dun Club had reminded him of his father's insistence on the wisdom of adopting a correct turnout. As a result, new black shoes bought in Delhi complemented his badly creased blue suit. But his shyness evaporated when he saw that his elderly host was equally uncomfortable and afterwards, moved by compassion, he wrote an account to John. ' "Heaven

knows what they're giving you", he muttered, peering suspi-
ciously at a dish (delicious curried eggs) and "I have no idea
what this is supposed to be," (salad) and "I don't know what
those glasses are for, not champagne anyway," (fruit salad and
cream) . . . We chatted for a while on the verandah and he
seemed pleased when I remarked on how peaceful it was, though
he added "sometimes too peaceful".'

The compromises of those who outstayed their time stood out
as the exact reverse of his father's frustrations. In the Kwality
café earlier he had recorded an exchange between a wistful
elderly man – 'dressed the way Englishmen no longer dress' –
and a kindly Indian who enquired how he was enjoying his
retirement. 'He nodded his assent, but he didn't look as if he
was.' Studying the flushed face and stubble-white moustache of
85-year-old Sir Edmund over lunch, he assessed that the details
that together made for parody were composed of individual
loyalties, each one of paramount significance. John's uncle, who
became breathless on the slightest gradient, still counted on
buying clothes from England and fretted about the replacement
of his hat. He was not wearing his good suit to impress, it
became plain, but to give it an airing and outwit the moths. Jim
took the older man's arm as they walked and talked after lunch
and mused about isolation, his empathy the sharper for recalling
Sir Edmund's distinguished career in the Indian Civil Service,
and John's description of him as 'quite a ladies' man' in youth.

'He has a rather peeling house surrounded by thick woods and
land which he farms, and his rooms are *exactly* how one would
imagine they should be: the rooms of a colonial bachelor who
read Greats . . . (Pliny in the bookshelf and volumes of P.G.
Wodehouse). Picture of the Queen . . . and King George V.' But
the books had to be locked behind glass to preserve them from
white ants, and when writing up his diary Jim enumerated
further deprivations. 'There was something rather sad about
his bed neatly turned down in that very bachelor-like room –
everything rough and masculine, dark leather or wood, slightly
grimy . . . He seemed gloomy about the prospects of getting
back to England. As I was getting into the car to depart I noticed
his fingernails were bitten down. He told me to give his love to
John and Hilary and added, "I do love them very much." He

said he didn't suppose he would ever see them again.' Two and a half years later a signed copy of *The Siege of Krishnapur* would reach Sir Edmund's remote farm at Ramgarh and be received with unflagging Empire spirit. 'I shall', the shakily written letter of thanks ended, 'get someone to read it to me.'

Back on cigarettes, smoking the cheap biris of tendu leaves, Jim accelerated his pace, going up to Hardwar for a first glimpse of the Ganges, and next day sharing a taxi to Mussoorie, even higher in the Himalayas. He explored the town on foot in the 'extraordinary' chill, noted the ruined skating rink and evocative Housi-Housi sign outside the Co-op Club and made the recommended steep ascent to Gun Hill, where mist hid the panoramic view. Glancing down to the town, far below, he identified a British cemetery among the houses that were now spread out like a map, and hurried on down for a closer look, aware the taxi was about to leave. 'Some of the lead letters of the inscriptions – thin leaves made to fit into grooves in the marble – have been prized off,' he noted. 'Death of Major Bromley's son 1875 accidentally shot aged 13. Bengal infantry, Bengal civil service. Edward Hardinge of Monkstown aged 32, Royal Engineers. Not lost but gone before. 1871.' As he sat back in the taxi, limp from the altitude and exhaustion, there was no indication that the seeds of a future book on India had been sown, nor did it become apparent when he wrote up his diary on the train during the next leg to Lucknow. 'Many young people, girls in their twenties, no doubt young wives in sickly condition, sent up from the plains who didn't make it. Even if I had had more time I'm not sure that I would have stayed much longer. Gravestones don't tell you nearly enough about people – only enough to depress you.'

First impressions of the sprawling commercial city of Lucknow were disconcerting, but the Carlton Hotel on the outskirts had once been a Raj staging post, and in its oriental architecture and formal gardens he found something of the dimension he expected. The hall contained a magnificent stuffed Gonda tiger and a snarling leopard, and, felicitously, the library held a copy of Elizabeth Bowen's *The Last September*, which drew on the same Irish period as *Troubles*. The Residency, where almost all the action of his book took place, was open to the public and within half a mile. On his walks about the area, postponing confrontation with reality, small boys chorused, 'Good morning, Sahib!' as he passed. Finally he braced himself to visit, and took breakfast early on the dew-covered lawns. His gentle bearer, Peter Julius, brought out a marsala omelette, freshly buttered toast and raspberry jam and his tea was poured with unobtrusive care, the cup and saucer placed by the open notebook on the table which faced a huge banyan tree by the compound wall. 'Vultures hunch like witches and quarrel in a tall tree. Very heavy birds. The banyan has thick oval leaves varying in size between a hand and a foot. The roots hanging down act as supports, the thickness of a tree themselves. The result is a mass of pillars. Very graceful.' He snapped shut the notebook; it was time to go.

'Let me say', he would stress during a pre-publication interview, 'that it was not the least like what I had imagined.' The once-imposing Residency was heralded by evil-smelling drains, and a ticket-seller lolled beside the shell-pocked, instantly recognisable Clock Tower Gate. The winding incline of the drive led past overgrown memorials and ruins towards the incongruous peace and order of a public park, where citrus-yellow butterflies warmed their wings on shattered, cobwebbed walls and fluttered over ranks of cannons towards neat displays of blood-red flowers.

A stone tablet with Canning's tribute as Viceroy – 'There does not stand recorded in the annals of war an achievement more truly heroic than the Defence of the Residency at Lucknow' – still stood beside the steps down to two small cellar rooms where the women and children had taken refuge, and there the foetid horror of death from cholera, dysentery or childbirth in the crowded space was startlingly brought to mind by the undamaged, handsome chimneypieces. In the mouldering Model Room, surrounded by crumbling wreaths with faded ribbons and the dusty cairns of cannon balls, a plastercast small-scale groundplan of the original buildings awaited inspection under glass, complete with defiant Union Jack. Groups of Indian schoolboys standing around it were being instructed in their opposite perspective, a reminder of Ireland's contradictory myths. 'Susanna Palmer: killed in this room by a cannon ball on 1 July 1857 in her 19th year', commemorated a plaque a few feet away. It was known that at the end of the siege 2,000 bodies had been buried in the compound churchyard; the modest dimensions struck Jim as suitable for 200, at most. Anger blazed out from the taut inscriptions on the graves, and he endeavoured without success to find Edward MacGregor's name.

Three days later Jim went back for a second visit and climbed the ninety-one steps to the flagtower, his breathlessness a help in comprehending the cost of keeping the Union Jack flying while faint from hunger and thirst and prey to injury and disease. Widening his research, he took a different route back to the Carlton Hotel, and came upon the body of a black water buffalo covered by seething crows. As he paused, appalled, one bird hopped forward and pecked inside a nostril, at which the animal's head twitched, and it sat up.

There was no respite from the draining concentration on two levels, and even leaning over the Carlton's verandah to watch a bagpipe band tuning up for a wedding reception – 'dark red uniforms, dark blue trousers, the contrast they made against the green of the grass . . . was very striking' – he could not escape his book. *Over there, beneath that group of now shattered Eucalyptus trees, had stood the band of one of the infantry regiments. Once [the Collector] had looked out from the upper verandah of the Residency as the bandsmen were assembling; it was evening, and somehow the deep scarlet of their uniforms against the dark green of the grass had stained his mind with a serious joy.* The effort of adapting to hotel after hotel was becoming an ordeal, made worse by the inevitable stomach problems he had been warned against. 'All day,' the final Lucknow assessment ran, 'I've been feeling defeated by India.'

In the Hindu city of Benares on the sacred River Ganges death held court. Jim chose a tourist boat for economy and joined a group of young backpackers, his notebook at the ready; record-taking distanced reaction and justified the avid curiosity he felt. 'The burning ghat: a woman in white, unmarried or wife died before her husband, whose feet are sticking out of a pile of logs. The chief mourner who has his head shaved bustles around. The house of the chief official who superintends the ghat stands over the river; twin tigers about to pounce, Kali in between. Wood piled up everywhere.' The brightly painted tigers, it was explained, were there to remind passers-by that death might spring at any moment, and though Jim gagged on the oily smoke he held his gaze, despite the acrid stinging in his eyes. That lunchtime he ate with undiminished appetite, and afterwards went back alone to sit within a few yards of the nearest pyre. The trail that had begun in the iron lung in Oxford led to Mannikarnika Ghat.

> 'The outside bits tended to burn least quickly, the feet and the head; a couple of feet stuck out for some time, toes rather splayed, nails paler than the dark skin (the feet of a not young man I should say) while the middle portion of the body burned, the shin-bones showed very white, the skin having burned off quickly and there being little flesh to carbonize; presently the attendant turned one of the legs over – it was when it went right over against the natural articulation of the joint that the body really stopped being a person for me and became an object . . . From time to time . . . I heard a dull report from one of the half-consumed bodies. Also the white ribs showed plainly for a moment, as the cloth and skin burnt way. When the bodies were consumed down to small pieces the attendant picked the charred lump . . . up with two sticks and manoeuvred it into the river; it went in with a hiss of steam.'

Cows wandered about, mangy dogs snatched at corpses, sparrows played on dampened shrouds and boats full of cheerful people chugged by, one containing a wedding party.

'All this, which sounded distinctly gruesome to me yesterday when someone described it to me, now doesn't seem at all so,' he reflected. 'I think this is because a dead body being burned is so completely a body; which is consumed so quickly . . . that one sees people, bodies and so on, in a completely different light.' The lesson from Benares, unexpectedly, was the peaceful one of acceptance. *A lamp was burning . . . and in the glass of the bookcases he saw his own image . . . the face of a man like other men, who in a few years would be lost to history, whose personality would be no more individual than the shadowy reflection in the glass.*

Ram Nagar Fort, the palace of the Maharajah of Benares, loomed over the opposite bank of the Ganges, further down-river. Jim booked a second package trip and blended in, his white hair adding an eccentric touch to the hippy camouflage he had taken to wearing in the hope of deterring scroungers. In the fort he hung back, and as soon as he was on his own began the inventory he had come to make. 'The griffin might find the rajah's son sitting on a chair constructed of antlers. His indented cushion on the floor showed where he had been sitting a moment earlier. The griffin admires apalling Victorian objets d'art . . . Into anteroom 20 feet high. Not rectangular . . . Palanquin – 6 poles . . . Duelling pistols . . . Rifles . . . Swords . . . An elephant wearing a tasselled crown . . . Shutters on window . . . Check chandeliers.' Piece by piece, the Krishnapur palace of 1857 materialised, with its magpie collection of Empire trophies.

'My rajah', Jim envisaged before leaving Benares, 'might be sitting in the middle of all this gloomily eating a boiled egg and reading Blackwood's Magazine.' As with the Residency in Lucknow, he returned for a second look, and scrutinised the public rooms and armoury with a more proprietorial air. *Near a fireplace of marble inlaid with garnets, lapis lazuli and agate, the Maharajah's son sat on a chair constructed entirely of antlers, eating a boiled egg and reading* Blackwood's Magazine. *Beside the chair a large cushion on the floor still bore the impression of where he had been sitting a moment earlier . . .*

Jim reached Calcutta weakened by a severe bout of dysentery, and the city recalled Malcolm Lowry's description of Mexico City: 'the most christ-awful place in the world in which to be in any form of distress, a sort of Moloch that feasts on suffering souls'. He compared the squalid bustees near Howrah station to Dante's underworld, aware that the cumulative effect of weeks of outstretched hands and horrifying deformities was contributing to his debilitated state, and made for the Salvation Army's Red Shield Guesthouse in Sudder Street – 'the Red Shithouse' – rather than the Great Eastern Hotel, where both Kipling and his own parents had stayed. Stifling heat exacerbated his collapse and put paid to his intention to stay on in the city to write, and as soon as he was on his feet again he applied for a visa for Nepal. 'I don't know whether this was the place to stay in the 1920s,' he teased his father when he was up to letter-writing once more, 'but it certainly is now: very clean and cheap and a good breakfast for Rs 8 per night . . . I'm kicking myself for not making a note of your old address in Calcutta. I would have liked to go and see if the house was still there.'

On impulse he rang Shiv Chirimar's family in Alipore and discovered that he was home; it was the first familiar voice he had heard for eight weeks. Refusing the invitation to stay, he made an arrangement to meet, and surprised Shiv when they did so by displaying the same quietly purposeful air as in London. They walked over the Howrah Bridge to the Eden Botanical Gardens – *Their way led past the Great Banyan and Fleury was filled with awe at the sight* – and returned by ferry. Tea and ice-cream in Flory's awakened childhood memories of Southport's Matti and Tissot's tea-room, and they rounded off a day of contrasts in the élite billiard-tabled realms of the Saturday Club, where Shiv's tennis-playing older brother was a member. Jim's disgust at hearing that Indians had first been admitted only four years earlier subsided in a haze of bhang, the herbal cannabis said to induce high concentration and relaxed talkativeness which he had been hoping to try. The effect, like so much else in India, turned out to be the other way around. 'We were lectured by an Indian lady . . . half an hour of non-stop boasting about her husband's job . . . My mind was working so slowly I could think of no way of putting her down, though I should have liked to.'

With time to put in until his Nepal visa came through, Jim strolled around the atmospheric Park Street cemetery – *Fleury . . . was fond of graveyards; he enjoyed brooding in them and letting his heart respond to the abbreviated biographies* – and found a credible explanation for Fleury's presence in India which did not conflict with the work already put into the book. The idea was influenced by Mrs Gaskell's *Cranford* – 'the griffin might be transfixed by the appalling notion that he too will never again see his dear mother alive' – and in the finished version, twisted about, it would be to pay his respects to his mother's Park Street grave. *All the same, once he had spent an hour or two pondering . . . he decided to call it a day . . .*

Giddy after exertion in the stifling heat, Jim kept on the go. St

Paul's Cathedral was selected for Louise Dunstaple's experience as a bridesmaid which would seal her destiny – *Fleury could see that Louise had been moved* . . . *He found this vulnerability strangely disarming* – and the Victoria Memorial's mixed bag of memorabilia was sifted through for extra detail. 'Sepoys wore, according to the water-colour of Atkinson,' he logged, 'white caps and trousers and red tunics with white frogging.' A short distance away across the Maidan stood Fort William arsenal, where the fateful greased cartridges had been manufactured. His final impression of Calcutta, appropriately, was of being under siege. The flight to Nepal left on the spring festival day of Holi, and from dawn onwards his hostel was invested by crowds of jostling youths. Relief eventually came in the form of a shabby airline bus, and he was conveyed in stops and starts through mobs of shouting Holi-dyed faces and gesturing arms.

Nepal was cool, but Jim's energy had run down; the clockwork mouse could only go so far. Mrs Gaskell was dismissed as over-sentimental, Conrad as fatuous, and Dickens's highmindedness had become an irritation. Defying apathy, he hired a bicycle in Kathmandu, but although the scenery enchanted him and the rigours of India were on the far side of the Himalayan barricades, life's transience continued to intrude. At the stupa at Swayambunath he was shown the burning platform and, stopping at a low bridge to rest while cycling back from the Sleeping Vishnu at Budhanilkantha, he realised that a Buddhist cremation was in progress on the river bank directly below. On the outskirts of Kathmandu he overtook a dozen men carrying a dead cow slung from poles – 'how flies buzzed about the cow's eyes and upside down its udder sagged inwards' – and, cycling past the burning place again, his eye was caught by 'a couple of perfectly serviceable looking feet crossed in a rather casual manner . . . though the rest had been consumed'.

There was sardonic amusement to be taken from wondering what his London friends would say if they could see him. His hair was long and his hippy outfit now sported an authentic string of beads; he had a hacking cough, shadows under his eyes and he had lost weight that he could ill afford. More alarmingly, the book had become insubstantial, and on some days he barely thought of it at all. In Kathmandu he gave up hope of making any writing headway while abroad. All that remained to be experienced was the blistering heat on the plains, and that would be accomplished automatically on the arduous train journey south to redeem the return half of his charter ticket in Bombay. Halving the time he had intended to spend away, he rattled out of Nepal in an ancient Mercedes bus – 'half-broiled by the heat of the engine, half-ecstatified by the panoramas' – with dwindling morale and the mental snapshot of a portrait of the young Queen Victoria, due to be transposed from Kathmandu's National Museum to the fictional cutchery at Krishnapur.

In his exhausted state he took the overnight train to Patna, crossing the river on a steamer, and waited six hours on the platform, existing on oranges, for the connection to Benares. Raging thirst accompanied each lengthy stretch in third-class carriages that lay ahead. 'A trunk was shoved under my feet, a woman with a naked infant sat on it; another child half sat on my lap. No room to move in any direction and I'd already been sitting there for twelve hours,' he summed up a typical ordeal. 'I did my best to read *Hard Times* by the very dim light [while] the young man opposite me hawked and spat endlessly out of the window.' In his sapped condition most people contrived to annoy him. At one stop he lost his temper when a hotel proprietor 'rudely' questioned him; and in a Railway Retiring Room – 'grimly adequate' – he was tricked out of his proper turn in the shower. During a lull between trains further south, he ached to escape a bore – 'dreadfully loquacious' – who praised the British without drawing breath; three months before he would have hung on every word. In a densely crowded compartment a young engineer harangued him about Louis Malle and accused him, by association, of showing India in a bad light. 'He annoyed me enough for me not to bother about hurting his feelings.'

There was a last detour for the erotic sculptures at Khajuraho – *Fleury found . . . such an intricate mass of limbs that he was quite unable to fathom what it was all about (though it was clearly very lewd indeed)* – and there the effort of keeping his diary became too much. The journey had surpassed his grimmest expectations and shown that mutual access to the English language was misleading; if he came back, he resolved, he would learn Hindi first. But in the cave temple at Ajanta, at his lowest ebb, he was shown around in the company of a young Indian whose curious response to the guide's patter was to say 'Correct!' instead of 'I see', and at a stroke the missing piece of the jigsaw fell into place. The Maharajah of Krishnapur's son, Hari, emerged into full view, no longer in danger of being overshadowed by his possessions from Ram Nagar Fort.

On reaching Bombay Jim sought out the Salvation Army Hostel – '10/- a day for three meals plus afternoon tea *included*' – and the city that had seemed so shocking now felt civilised in the extreme. He booked a night flight to London for 7 April, in time to be home by Easter, donated his hippy garb to the guesthouse, shaved with elaborate care and in the evening sun headed for the stone bench beside the Gateway to India, where he had found tranquillity before. Now the vastness and immutability beyond pressed back against him.

'I know that the general feeling of unavailingness increased and the depressing aspects of life there intensified', he reflected after he had taken time to readjust and recover. 'I do know that I utterly failed to make any contact with the sort of India Bob Cumming knew; this was a failure of character really. I can no longer meld myself with another culture; I have an advanced case of spiritual hardening of the arteries and didn't even try.' But the recurrent stomach cramps that plagued him on return were diagnosed as psychological, a delayed response to poverty and suffering, and as his health gradually picked up, so did his anger. When it came, the explosion – rather muffled, in John Spurling's opinion – would take Jim and all his friends by surprise.

A couple of years afterwards, following the publication of *The Siege of Krishnapur*, he was introduced to the author of the popular Inspector Ghote detective books, Harry Keating, who quizzed him on whether he had gone to India to research. Jim said he had, and added in all honesty that he wished he hadn't. 'I had a firmer idea of what India was about', he explained in his careful way, '*before* I went.'

CHAPTER SEVENTEEN

In the Right Place at the Right Time
1973–1974

T *he Collector had become calm again . . . How pleasant it is to sit . . . and watch the waves rolling in. You can see them beginning so far out . . . you can see them slowly grow as they come nearer and nearer to the shore, rise and then thresh themselves against the beach. Some of them vanish inexplicably. Others turn themselves into giants.* Unpredictability now became the order of Jim's day.

His bulky collection of books had been stored in a family-owned woodmill near his mother's childhood home after the sale of Balholm in 1967, and on his return from India their retrieval became the excuse for a reunion with Bridget. Meeting up with her under circumstances in which armed police wore flak-jackets, law courts had to be protected by coils of barbed wire and the military presence was conspicuously being strengthened, however, he sensed at once that she had changed. He reminded himself that Ireland always depressed him and took the wheel of her Mini without comment, heading south across the border to Portlaoise. She was silent and he drove jerkily, trapped in a vicious circle which neither could break.

'I know he was sensitive to mood,' she would acknowledge from her new standpoint. 'But he never could say "What's wrong?" and he didn't like talking about feelings, even when things were going well. So we didn't communicate. I can remember turning my back on him in the hotel room and reading Germaine Greer and thinking "This is not being nice to Jim", but being unable to help it, though I knew it was a childhood defence. The more that happens, the more apart you grow.'

Ironically, the postal strike, which had confirmed to Jim how much she meant to him, had revealed to Bridget how separate they had become. 'I rationalised', she reflected later, 'by saying Jim was cold, because I was being emotionally – though not physically – unfaithful. He thought that we could pick things up as they had been, but I'd got too sucked into an alternative way of life.' Jim appeared unruffled, apparent confirmation that her instinct was correct, but he was letting fatalism take over. 'We zoomed down south to pick up my books,' he telescoped the experience for Carol Drisko's consumption. 'Ulster was full of fresh-faced young troops with guns.' *There's nothing one can actually do with love once it has passed a certain stage. It's not an ointment one can rub on one's soul or a hallucinatory drug with which one can effect a semi-permanent transfiguration of one's life. One has to go on living in the ordinary way.*

Jim burned off his feelings elsewhere, siding with the miners as their strike escalated, and joining the Public Lending Rights Campaign spearheaded by Maureen Duffy, which re-acquainted him with his trenchant Oxford contemporary David Caute. 'We felt the greatest intimacy,' Caute recalled, 'and as we agreed that all publishers were crooks or incompetents Jim's toughness was extremely congenial to me.' Veering away from the gentlemanly Society of Authors, Jim embraced the more militant Writer's Guild. His friends noticed that he was becoming argumentative about politics, and at supper parties he was liable to criticise public schools and the monarchy, as well as the Tory Party, and if he came upon anyone being rude to a waiter or bus-conductor he called out, 'He's only doing his job!' As a *Private Eye* fan, he referred to Heath in public as The Grocer, and he spoke out more elegantly through the Collector, who allows himself to feel *a cautious contempt for the greedy merchants of England*. But though letters to Bridget ceased in the immediate aftermath of the journey to Portlaoise, he shared too much with her to lose contact. Whenever she stayed in his flat on her occasional visits to London, though, she slept on the floor.

Carol kept up her moral support from New York, and he had grown to depend on her tenacity. She still turned up at anti-war demos and could be moved to tears by the sight of crippled Vietnam 'vets' throwing away their medals. 'Yesterday an

American girl from Radio Liberty arrived to interview me about Dostoievsky for a centenary programme they are beaming at Russia from Munich,' he wrote to her shortly after the break-up with Bridget. 'She said she didn't know who sponsored Liberty but wouldn't be surprised if it was the CIA. She revealed that among other British writers being interviewed were such notorious commie-bashers as Kingsley Amis and John Braine. I managed to say, among remarks about Fyodor, that I thought Dostoevsky would have appreciated the Kent State girl who handed a flower to the National Guardsman the day before she was shot.'

That summer Carol came to London on a brief stopover from Istanbul, and he did not object when she offered to make her own way back to Heathrow. Travelling out, the coach neared Egerton Gardens and in the distance she saw him standing on his back steps, looking in her direction and waving. 'I waved and called out', she wrote as soon as she reached Manhattan, 'but of course you couldn't hear me.' 'Yes, I did attempt to wave goodbye when I heard the bus passing,' he replied, 'but I couldn't spot you.' The tableau that summed up their relationship so wryly would be her final sight of Jim.

'I feel I've bitten off more than I can chew this time, but have long since passed the point of no return.' . . . 'Too much research left me and the book in a near-hopeless muddle. I'm trying to sort it out but am tempted to strip it of all ideas and just leave the action.' . . . 'I'm working hectically, but with deep dissatisfaction at what I'm producing.' . . . 'You've no idea how morally exhausted writing a novel makes you feel.' . . . I'm making progress of the painful kind – but so much remains to be done and I'm pretty sick of it. Soldiering on, though.' Progress was hindered by publication of the Knopf edition of *Troubles* in September and the hostile tone of American critics, with a *Saturday Review* piece exhorting readers to skip the book and read Yeats's poem *Easter 1916* instead. 'How simple-minded can one get?' he jeered back. 'Answer: very simple-minded indeed.' But Mike Roemer sent congratulations, which encouraged him, and *Book World* likened him to a daring mixture of Evelyn Waugh, Henry Green and P.G. Wodehouse.

Difficulties, as Jim still thought of it, was not yet divided into chapters and, like *Troubles*, fully justified its name. 'I'm still hoping to get it finished by the early summer,' he estimated the following February, 'so I can start something new', and from then on he worked 'day and night', cursing his debilitated energy. With unfortunate timing a contact made in India looked him up and decamped with a loan.

In July 1972 Jim typed the dedication – 'For my father who as a young man once found himself defending the Raj, armed only with a mashie niblick and a bottle of soda water', subsequently truncated to 'For W.F.F.' – and in a final burst of effort cycled over to Deborah Rogers's office with the manuscript in the wicker handlebar basket. 'I've now finished my India book, which is actually less about India than about the 19th century,' he wrote wearily to Russell McCormmach. 'Although reaction among publishers has been favourable (publishers use a hyperbolic language in which "excited" means "apathetic" and "very excited" means "faintly interested" etc.) I entertain private misgivings about its superficiality.'

Being a Faber Prize-winner made his name a more marketable commodity this time, and at a price-guide of £5,000 Hamish Hamilton expressed immediate interest, acting on the advice of its chief editor, Gillon Aitken. Jim remained adamant about not going back to Tom Maschler at Cape, despite Catherine Peters's attempt to mend the breach by inviting him to dinner to meet a more emollient member of senior staff; on the understanding that Hamish Hamilton had first refusal, Weidenfeld and Nicolson and Hodder and Stoughton were also allowed copies. By now Jim had got to know Hodder's senior editor, James Hale, and since the editorial director, Robin Denniston, was away on business Hale went directly to the chairman to speed up a deal. When this was refused, Jim concluded, wrongly, that Denniston must have been to blame. He hung on every movement in the water and endeavoured to be as philosophical as the Collector, but without a great deal of success.

In August there was a startling 'bite'. 'What an extraordinary relationship it is between a reader and a novel,' Tony Godwin, deputy chairman of Weidenfeld and Nicolson, wrote without preamble. 'Quite unlike those towards other types of books, and varying as much as relationships and attitudes to other people.

Some novels arouse no more interest than someone occasionally met and enjoyed at a party, while others, from the very start, plunge one into intimacy . . . All this is just a long-winded and clumsy way to say that I was swept away by your novel. I have just returned from a week in Majorca where I've been staying with some friends who've taken a little house in a hill village. Deborah lent me a manuscript and I read it there, on holiday, under the blaze of August sun and lying on the hot ground, an appropriate setting, wouldn't you agree?'

The letter was addressed to him directly, instead of being routed through Deborah as agent, and, praising the 'exactitude and concreteness' of observed detail, Tony Godwin went on to enumerate, scene by scene, his favourite moments. 'I can't remember', he concluded, 'when I last read a novel as affectionately expressive of the sheer human humorousness and incongruity of life . . . But in the end I think what most compelled my admiration was the development of the narrative itself and the masterly control of pace and tempo from that leisurely opening . . . I must stop or my letter will become a catalogue. But I hope I have written enough to show you my enjoyment, admiration and affection for your novel. It is a wonderful advance on *Troubles*, the handling of the complexities and its theme among them . . . The creation of an utterly convincing society of another age in another place, all this is masterful . . . I congratulate you.' Jim's immediate response was to pick up the phone and ask for Godwin's extension.

Tony Godwin was widely considered to be a phenomenon in publishing, in that he was able to combine the mutually exclusive roles of career executive and nurturing editor. Weidenfeld had headhunted him from Penguin in 1970, but the senior job on the board had not altered his priorities: if a stand had to be taken he was still trusted by writers to take their side. One of his maxims was that the book, not the balance sheet, was the important thing; another held that a really good novel had first to go molten in an author's brain. Deborah already knew him well, as they were neighbours, and attributed her grasp of the business almost entirely to him. 'Tony regularly woke at 4am, made a cup of Assam tea, and read manuscripts and edited,' she once said. 'At 6.45am he'd phone me to say, "Come on. Get up! It's time for your walk." So we'd walk over Primrose Hill and along the canal. "What are you reading?" "What do you like?" "Why is it so good?" "Should it be published?" I never got away with an easy opinion because he'd immediately say, "Why? You must justify that." ' Her consternation was the greater, as a result, when she discovered that Tony had gone behind her back just as the commitment to Hamish Hamilton was about to be formalised.

'I got a hysterical letter from Tony pushed underneath my door. It was handwritten and several pages long, defending his move. It went on to say why he wanted to publish Jim's book and how aggrieved he was that I hadn't sent it to him first. And I was aggrieved because I thought it was characteristic of how Jim worked and I was now put in a very awkward position.' In the event Hamish Hamilton proved understanding, and the contract was signed with Weidenfeld and Nicolson. Deborah shifted the blame from Tony to Jim, and realised that he was extremely hard to represent. Proving how close they had become without her knowledge, Tony was already referred to by the nickname 'Dogwin'.

Within a month Jim received a second dynamic missive, ending: 'P.S. What about *Ordeal at Krishnapur* as a title?' The package contained his manuscript, marked up with all suggestions, eleven typed pages listing 136 proposed changes, two pages of structural re-organisation to arrange the book into four parts and thirty-two chapters, two further pages of character notes, and one and a half more itemising major cuts or reductions. It was important, chivied Dogwin, to get the book moving, and by November 20,000 words were expected to be cut. 'Is your reader likely to follow your aside? I don't.' 'Cut, overdoing it.' 'One is confused by the sequence here.' 'Seems to me superfluous.' . . . 'Timing a little askew here.' . . . 'Final sentence seems a non-sequitur. It needs a bridge.' Jim read it all through, one craftsman to another, and double-checked before making his own annotations. 'No, keep it.' 'Keep this, too.' 'It is a *bit* long but shouldn't be cut much.' 'Dogwin is quite wrong about this here. I think it works.' After one clash Tony rang Jonathan Clowes to ask for advice on how to handle Jim. The reply was diplomatic.

Bridget owed Jim thirty pounds and had written to say that

she could at last afford to repay it. 'Maybe,' he proposed, 'you could do a job for me instead . . .' Her next London visit was spent with the typescript, Tony's reams of advice and her own editing notes, and no quibbles were forthcoming. She was both surprised and relieved, having expected him to be possessive.

It greatly helped that Jim and Tony had similarly exacting standards, on top of a mutual appreciation of walking, cooking and French wines, but there was also a less apparent bond. Tony was a chronic asthmatic who had come near death, and he relied on cortisone to survive. His fear of a fatal attack was as unmistakable to Jim as the rasping wheeze, and he understood both the perfectionism and the mercurial switches of mood. Imp-like, with a shock of grey curls and his customary worn jeans, Tony became a regular guest at Jim's sociable dinners, unfazed by accusations of being a typical publishing parasite. 'I enjoyed myself enormously,' he shot back after a bruising session. 'I liked your friends. I only hope I didn't strike *too* jarring a note.' And Jim was invited back to the untidy, black-curtained eyrie in Primrose Hill where Tony had moved on his divorce from the writer and photographer Fay Godwin. 'Dear Jim. Can you come to dinner on Saturday May 12th? I have Frank Kermode coming and I would like you to meet.'

As an established author Jim was treated with respect at the Weidenfeld and Nicolson offices in Clapham. Rosemary Legge took over the editing in mid-production, by which time his choice of title had been agreed. She found him sure of his work but kind, and he presented her with a basket for her bicycle. Yet although they had occasional meals together, she was always conscious of a barrier. 'I used to think he must be slightly bisexual,' she observed, 'because he was a little effete. Mainly, though, he came across as lonely.' Soon afterwards, Tony was appointed company chairman, but that made no difference to his attentiveness. 'Many thanks for the blurb wonderfully trans-formed,' he characteristically took the trouble to write on a flight to New York. Jim also got on well with the influential Christo-pher Falkus, but when congratulated by Robin Denniston, who had just joined the company from Hodder, and whom Jim held personally responsible for that company's decision to turn down *The Siege of Krishnapur*, he responded glacially. Well-meant politeness on Denniston's part, ironically, came across as conclusive evidence of the insincerity of all publishers, and when, shortly afterwards, Jim was put on the regular guest-list for Sir George Weidenfeld's famed parties, he attended warily, distrust rekindled.

Arriving at Weidenfeld's Chelsea Embankment home, putting on a plain tie for the occasion, he would announce his name on the intercom to the penthouse suite on the first floor. There a footman would relieve him of his elderly macintosh and indicate the right-hand corridor lined with Klimt drawings, which opened on to a panorama of sofas, soft carpets, lamps and bookcases presided over, most suitably as he privately thought, by one of Bacon's Screaming Popes. The Weidenfeld salon was founded on the prerequisites of influence and success, the exact antithesis of his own idea of entertaining, and eyeing the throng as he took a glass of white wine, he would make for someone he already knew. The sensation, novices agreed, was of being a guppy in shark-infested waters. 'I'm making pathetic attempts to change my habits by wearing different clothes, doing things I wouldn't normally do, and so forth,' he reported with some embarrassment to Russell.

As publication at the end of August neared, the pressure to perform increased. Tony was as keen an advocate of publicity as Jonathan Clowes, and Jim was instructed that in the current market it was hard to sell books unless the author helped with promotion. 'It's all word of mouth,' Tony emphasised when the title appeared in the *Bookseller*'s listings on 11 August. 'And nobody's going to talk about your book unless you talk about it first.' Reluctantly, Jim agreed to be interviewed again by his old friend Malcolm Dean, and although the questions were submitted in advance, the process was as uncomfortable as before. Satisfaction at his third billing in the Weidenfeld autumn fiction list was eroded by being included in advance columns for the trade as John Farrell, and once again he had to compete with Piers Paul Read. Julian Symons bracketed their new novels together in his *Sunday Times* review, and in the *Observer* Piers was not only given the top spot with two-thirds of the space, but the only photograph.

Jim dwelt on the criticism that he had trivialised his theme by being too funny. By far the majority of reviews, however, with the usual exception of the *New Statesman*, were laudatory. His 'wry and capricious talents' were praised, as was his ability to 'construct a work of art on two levels' and 'distil emanations of time and place to an extraordinary extrasensory degree'. Compassion, recommended the *Daily Telegraph*, informed his work, 'though it, like much else in this multi-faceted book, must be pieced together from the black shards of his humour'. Jim took refuge in banter. 'For Lavinia,' he inscribed a copy for a new friend, the young agent Lavinia Trevor, 'and I still don't think she's read this book.' A few months earlier, after a shared evening of unintended black humour in Egerton Gardens as their host blithely described the smell of the burning ghats in Benares while carving his favourite charred lamb, Tony Godwin had made her pay 50p to read the proofs.

Some waves vanish inexplicably; others turn themselves into giants. *The Siege of Krishnapur* was among the forty-two books submitted for the 1973 Booker Prize of £5,000, and Tony had been sufficiently confident about its chances ahead of time to ensure publication within the fifteen-week qualification period. Jim did not share his optimism and pointed out that Karl Miller of the *Listener*, which had savaged *Troubles*, chaired the judging panel, and owned up to his own scathing treatment of Miller's book on Scotland. The two other judges were Mary McCarthy, about whose opinion he could only speculate at such a distance from America, and Edna O'Brien, who alone gave him cause for hope. She, too, was published by Weidenfeld, under Tony's wing, and when he had met her at Alvaros in the afterglow of the Faber Prize she had told him how much she admired *Troubles*.

'With the horses in their stalls, the breeders and trainers and owners settled in the stands, and the stewards buzzing around in the background, the going seems good for the season's most expensive classic,' trumpeted the *Bookseller* in September. 'The organisers can be assured that the gentlemen of the press will be present by the dozen to record the finish. For many authors . . . the metaphor is perhaps inappropriate, since the idea of literary league tables has traditionally been regarded with a certain amount of distaste [but] the field itself is full of interest.'

Of the forty-two runners, shortest odds were laid on David

Storey and William Trevor, but Jim was heavily tipped, along with Iris Murdoch and his own discovery, Beryl Bainbridge. Also in the frame were Barry Unsworth, David Garnett, John Banville, Ronald Harwood and Isobel Colegate, and outsiders included Bamber Gascoigne, Dennis Potter and Michael Frayn. When the shortlist was announced it consisted of four names only: his was one, alongside Iris Murdoch, Elizabeth Mavor and Beryl Bainbridge. At once the phone began to ring and the post increased. 'I don't want to gush,' wrote the journalist Janet Watts, a chum since his first summer in Egerton Gardens, 'but it was so very good to hear your Booker nomination falling out of my Saturday afternoon radio. Jim, many congratulations. I do hope you get it and are at least half as pleased about it as your friends.'

The Siege of Krishnapur, according to one source, 'might just turn out to have the kind of success with the intelligent common reader that the founders of the Prize have always hoped for.' But from two quarters the competition was stiff. Beryl Bainbridge's *The Dressmaker*, set in wartime Liverpool, was believed to be favoured by Karl Miller, and Iris Murdoch was expected to win for the sake of achievement, if not for *The Black Prince*; the reticent Miller was on record as saying the book was 'one of the best things she has done'. Jim sought a calm outlook by sticking to his routine, and coming out of Harrods Food Hall, toting his housewifely string bag, he bumped into Edna O'Brien, who was also laden. Unlike his bag, he sighed to Derek Mahon, hers was going clink, clink, clink.

In 1973 publishers were told the name of the winner in confidence a month in advance to enable extra copies to be printed, and as soon as the call came through to Tony, Jim's ordeal was over. 'Dear Stephen and Yvonne,' he wrote to the Walls before the result was officially announced. 'You don't feel like selling me one of your many properties, do you? I'm thinking of starting a NEW LIFE outside London (!!!) and I think I see where I can lay my hands on some cash.' Lunching with Piers Paul Read in The Ark, near his old greenhouse room, he could not resist a gloat when asked if he was nervous. 'No,' he drawled. 'I know I've got it.' Brian Knox Peebles rang to suggest 'a few drinks' if he won, but assumed that Jim had been passed over when told that the result was already known. He was indignantly put straight. 'Don't tell anyone,' Jim whispered to Bob's philanthropic cousin Alan Cumming while on a visit to the East End youth mission where Cumming now worked. 'I've definitely got the Booker Prize. It's pretty good.'

'I doubt', Karl Miller told the press at the time, 'whether there is much to be said for reporting the falterings and last-minute semi-fallings out. Such things generally happen, and they happened here.' Jim gave the credit to Edna O'Brien, but the outcome was less straightforward. 'At the meeting in the city Mary McCarthy, too, voted for his book,' Edna subsequently divulged, 'and Karl Miller thought it was all settled. Soon after he rang me up and said Mary had changed her mind and it was now up to him to vote a decision between her choice, Iris Murdoch, and mine. Karl said he would ring whoever he disagreed with, and as I didn't hear back I assumed he voted for the *Siege*. I admired Karl greatly for the way he handled it.' The relegation of Iris Murdoch took most spectators by surprise, and gossip centred less on who had voted for Jim than on the decision to pass her over. Allowing that *The Siege of Krishnapur* was 'a more than respectable choice', one critic spoke for all with his summing-up. 'I think Mr Farrell will understand as well as anyone that what's mildly sensational about this year's prize concerns not who has won it, but who, once more, has not.'

The midweek ceremony was held on 28 November in the Café Royal in Regent Street. As his partner, Jim invited Deborah's blonde younger sister, Sue, from the Christopher Mann literary agency. He had met her through Tony Godwin the year before and invited her to one of his dinners in the flat, but she had not returned his interest. He asked her to accompany him in the guise of reliable good scout, and she agreed to pick him up beforehand in her beat-up white Mini. Punctually he opened the Egerton Gardens hall door looking thoroughly conventional. Unfortunately for Sue, who was sensitive and much shyer than she appeared, she had no way of knowing about a phone call he had made to Tom Wakefield earlier that day. 'I'm going to be very angry.' 'What about?' 'Oh, things . . .'

The gilded *fin de siècle* Grill Room had played host in its time to Beardsley, Wilde, Beerbohm, Whistler and Sickert. In honour of Jim it was crammed with nine white-clothed round tables, each with nine places laid, and the winner's table was pushed up against one wall, which left little room for manoeuvre. Tony Godwin, beside himself with pleasure, and Deborah, elated at having her first Booker winner, were among the group, but it soon became clear that the two Rogers sisters had been counted as one, leaving one place short. Jim paced around the table, more put out than Sue. 'My instinct', she said later, 'was to say "Do you want me to go away? I'll go home.' He told me to shut up and not be ridiculous. He was very disparaging about Booker making such a mix-up and said they had to sort it out. There was a hasty summons and much jostling while another chair was brought, and for me it was all most embarrassing.' Suavely, George Weidenfeld held court at a table nearby, and it was noticed that Iris Murdoch had elected not to attended.

The presentation was to be made by Lord Butler, the former deputy Prime Minister and Foreign Secretary. The painful experience of the previous year, when John Berger had won with G and used the occasion to donate half his money to the Black Panthers and lash out at Booker in front of reporters for 'sweating blacks' in the West Indies, was in all minds, and the organiser, Martyn Goff, was acutely conscious that Booker might withdraw from the sponsorship, which was shortly coming up for renewal. A few hours earlier Goff had taken a call from Booker's managing director, John Murphy. 'We're not anticipating any trouble with Farrell, after last year, are we?' 'No,' he affirmed. 'I was talking to Weidenfeld's only this morning, and they assured me that we wouldn't.' Goff had also taken the precaution of assessing Jim covertly at the most recent Weidenfeld party, judging him to be eminently mild and pleasant. 'We all went into that dinner', he said ruefully afterwards, 'expecting him to purr and say very sweet things.' At the table by the wall wine was poured and dinner served; the lack of imagination in the menu did not escape Jim's comment. His speech of thanks was fifth in running order, preceded by a formal welcome, Rab Butler's speech, the announcement of the winner's name by Karl Miller, and the handing-over of the cheque. Sensing his nervousness, nobody probed.

As was imediately apparent when the moment for the presentation at last came, Lord Butler was manifestly drunk and Martyn Goff became more discomfited by the minute. 'Butler started his speech with two jokes and both were antisemitic. A Scotsman, an Irishman and a Jewboy – that sort of thing, and not even relevant to the book world. Terry Kilmartin, books editor of the *Observer*, got up and walked out at the end of the second, and everyone looked round to see if George Weidenfeld would do the same, as he had far more reason. But he just looked down. We pretended that nobody noticed anything and gave no indication it was happening.' The custom of inviting an outsider to give the presentation would be changed as a result, but a winner's speech could never be deleted from proceedings and, remembering Berger's diatribe, Goff held his breath. A portable microphone was set up, and with hands twisted together, as taught in hospital, shoulders tensed and diffidence in every line, Jim began. 'You may think, after last year, that you had got someone who was going to say Booker were most wonderful, but I, *too*, disapprove . . .' The soft voice, curiously paced by the need for extra breaths, became etched into Martyn Goff's memory.

'I know the moment capitalism shows its more acceptable face is not the time to punch it on the nose, but I have to confess that I am no more enamoured of capitalism than my predecessor. Yes, I thought that would silence you.' Jim had a go at privilege, public schools and the Royal Family, before turning to overpaid company chairmen and executives, and finally rounding on Booker's exploitation of low-paid workers. He did not mind being poor himself, he stressed, and rather than compromise he willingly made sacrifices. The greenhouse at £1 a week was flourished, as was the drudgery of reading manuscripts for a living, which neatly brought him to his part in Beryl Bainbridge's career. The £5,000, he affirmed, would be used to document his next novel and that was to be a full-scale study of commercial exploitation, set around the fall of Singapore in 1941. He regretted that 'like the sea monsters in Racine's *Phaedre* which made the waves recoil in horror, every year the Booker Brothers see their prize washed up a monster more horrid than the last'. And he was back in his seat before general reaction set in.

At least John Berger had given back half the money, muttered some listeners; Jim had tried to cash in on his predecessor's notoriety and kept the lot. For the second time that evening Sir George Weidenfeld looked down at his hands. The Booker representatives sat stoically as Michael Wilby, a director, hastily wound up proceedings. 'With the pain from his hand, bitten while feeding,' commented the *Bookseller*, 'it was not surprising that he sounded as if he were performing sad memorial rites, and said that with the Booker Prize now in its fifth year, the company would decide in January 1975 whether or no to carry it on after the seven-year period. It will, to put it moderately, be a pity if this generous fiction prize is doomed to end but, faced with a press sometimes uncooperative, publishers sometimes unhelpful and authors sometimes unmannerly, few could blame Booker if they decided to abandon this sour scene and stick to sugar.'

Unmannerly? That the epithet should be flung by the book establishment at Jim, the politest of authors, revealed the perilous mast to which he had nailed his colours. Without Booker funding, publicity for the industry would be back to 1969 levels, with authors now tarnished as undeserving egotists in the minds of the public and potential commercial sponsors. Jim was alert to those issues, too, as they affected sales, and his own aim was that capitalist one, a record profit. But writing history had evolved into a crusade. Childhood indignation on behalf of the less fortunate had been salved by giving pocket money; glimpses from the adult perspective, most hauntingly in India, called out for a written indictment. The Booker reproof was a clarion call to proclaim the socialist thrust of his next book, and the £5,000 would fund his offensive; it was like capturing the enemy's campaign chest.

Jim left the Café Royal exhilarated, unaware of the irony that the freehold belonged to the National Union of Mineworkers' pension fund, and was whisked by Sue to a big party in Pelham Place, where his behaviour continued to astonish her. 'He was terribly elated and high, really revved up,' according to Piers Paul Read, who was also present. Exalted and triumphant, he was deposited back in Egerton Gardens as Tony Godwin was drinking the first cup of tea of his pre-dawn ritual and scribbling a congratulatory postcard. 'My hero! Marvellous speech. Salutations! I can see you've got a second career to fall back on – politician rabble rouser.' But old friends were not impressed.

Malcolm Dean reproached him – 'Corny as well as phony' – and John Spurling mentioned treading in larger footprints. Brian Knox Peebles, now a member of the book trade, grew tired of having to defend him to irate booksellers, and concluded sadly that he no longer really knew him.

Jim's reactions were a mixture of bravura and deflation. Photographed for the *Sunday Times* in December with the winners of six other literary prizes, including Eugène Ionesco, he dismissed the line-up as a rogues' gallery. Yet he was also doing his utmost to persuade a friend at W.H. Smith to devote a window of the Holborn branch to *The Siege of Krishnapur*, and complaining lightly to Bridget that only the *Daily Telegraph* and the *Daily Worker* had reported his speech. He still felt, he confided to his former editor Catherine Peters, that if anything of his survived it would be *Troubles*. 'Though, being more readable, no doubt the S of K was the better book to win the Prize with. Believe me, I'm ready to be spoiled by success, but am not too sure how to go about it.' In Malta for Christmas, where he was witness to his parents' pride, he spared a thought for his cousin Tom Farrell, for whom running shoes and adulation had since given way to a clerical dog collar and relative obscurity. Who was the winner now?

Perhaps, if one takes the long view, this . . . might be seen as a solstice in Fleury's life . . .' Meeting Jim unexpectedly after the long gap since Pamplona, Andrew Sinclair was impressed. 'He seemed much more assured and at peace with himself,' he observed, 'and it occurred to me that most of us had outlived our childish complaints.' The win was popular in literary circles; his celebrity gained him no new enemies and a wider circle of friends. Invitations filled the evenings, but he kept his head. 'Someone told me that Auberon Waugh had made a disparaging assessment of the book somewhere,' he noted after a barrage of compliments from Olivia Manning and Alison Lurie. 'I shall be interested to see what he has to say, as, though inclined to be erratic, he often hits the nail on the head.'

The Weidenfeld print run was doubled and foreign rights began to sell, with his work receiving particular attention in Denmark. He was wooed by Penguin – 'Peter Calvocoressi is a very nice fellow' – and Booker announced that they would, after all, continue sponsorship. He was invited to lunch at the company headquarters in Queen Victoria Street and equipped himself with the glamorous foil of Sarah Bond, who happened to be back from New York on her annual visit to her family. In a backhanded compliment he assured her that she was the only friend he had who could deal with a corporate lunch. But listening to him boast afterwards about his 'eye-glazing' performance, polished instantaneously into one more witty story to be told against himself, Sarah detected a growing trait she did not like. 'He was disparaging of himself moving in grand circles and yet engineering it,' she said, and she flew back to America with a revised mental picture and no idea that it was the last occasion they would meet.

Derek Mahon, in his part-time role as *Vogue* features editor, suggested a full-scale profile; like Malcolm, Derek would come to compare the process with that of getting blood out of a stone. Jim said little in the interview and hid behind whimsy, as when he praised Booker for producing Tia Maria. 'An acquired taste, perhaps, but delicious poured over vanilla ice-cream and served with a sprinkling of Ovaltine for the texture. I call it Sepoy's Surprise.' Derek let him check the copy, to which a couple of minor amendments were made, but over the accompanying photograph he was not prepared to compromise, and Lord Snowdon was commissioned: at the very least Derek expected the photographer and the subject to take to each other, having Ireland and polio in common. But things did not work out quite like that.

'We had a photo session in Jim's flat, white umbrellas and the lot, but the light wasn't good enough. So Snowdon said, "Let's go out and find light somewhere." All of a sudden Jim noticed two cats and we all stopped to admire them, and Snowdon said, "That's it!" Then we went to the Bunch of Grapes in the Brompton Road and everybody pretended not to recognise Snowdon, who was wearing his dark glasses, but they kept giving surreptitious glances. When he and his young assistant went off I asked Jim what he thought. "Not very intelligent, is he?" he said. It was his way of saying he was not impressed at being photographed by royalty.'

On film the disapproval is preserved, and in proletarian

jumper, jacket and dark trousers Jim leans against the window of a derelict shop, a stray cat on either side; tailor-made, in due course, for the back cover of his polemical new book. A few months later, when Derek wrote the poem *A Disused Shed in County Wexford*, inspired less by *Troubles* than by a passage in *The Lung*, he asked permission to dedicate it to Jim in print and, greatly touched, Jim assented. His own preferred method was to spring the surprise when presenting a hardback copy, and he had never before been on the receiving end.

Abandoning the idea of a move away from London, he considered briefly the advantages of returning to Ireland under the Artists' Tax Exemption scheme – 'Future history books', he observed to a Dublin journalist, 'will cast a most favourable light on this action' – but decided he was not yet ready for rural living, either there or anywhere else. 'In the end,' he faced facts, 'I couldn't quite picture myself sitting in the country in solitary splendour for more than a few weeks a year . . . having lived so long in a small room I would hardly know what to do with anything bigger.' For once he was where he wanted to be, and on his own terms.

'Sir George gave a lunch party for Olivia Manning the other day to which I was invited. Olivia has just signed up with Weidenfeld, ditching Heinemann whom she found disappointing. Olivia and I were agog because Antonia Fraser and Harold Pinter, who have just "run off" together (figuratively) were also there. They behaved with perfect decorum, however, under our four beady eyes.' He became friendly with Francis King, another of the Faber Prize judges, whose family had long connections with India, as well as with his childhood magician Richard Hughes. In Olivia Manning's hospitable St John's Wood flat he was introduced to Margaret Drabble and, with the quizzical smile she would come to recognise as a danger signal, murmured that he had once written her a fan letter. When they got to know each other, her discreet Quaker philanthropy recalled the Russell outlook of his grandfather, and he approved so much of the voluntary tuition she gave at an adult-education course in Lambeth that he stood in for her at short notice when she was taken ill. Their friendship flourished, although she was plain-spoken where he was elliptical, serious where he liked whimsy, and combative in situations in which he tactically changed ground.

Diana Saville, who had married since the Pont Street Mews days and settled in the country, took him to task for allowing himself to become affected by the attitudinising of the literary world. 'But then,' she relented, 'you can't keep a coterie going without subscribing to its rules.' Jim, however, was unlikely to take anyone too seriously. Told that Christopher Sinclair-Stevenson, the popular editor at Hamish Hamilton, was an admirer, he shrugged. 'I think the world of him,' he noted drily. 'Is he a very tall thin fellow with brushed-flat hair?' Ruth Prawer Jhabvala was introduced after her Booker win with *Heat and Dust*, and he was polite but withheld approval. 'A disaster,' said an observer, who had expected them to click. His respect for Manning's *The Balkan Trilogy* was undiminished but he saw great comedy in her behaviour, and his patience with the unpredictable Sonia Orwell was not that of a courtier but a sympathiser, as conflict with George Orwell's accountants over royalties threatened to engulf her. Recounting insights from the marking of A-level English Literature papers, Margaret Drabble castigated one southern school where the results had been uniformly bad. 'Oh,' he said, smiling that smile, 'that was *my* old school.' V.S. Naipaul and Rosamond Lehmann were accorded no star status when invited to the Habitat table; when Gabriel García Márquez came, he was expected to perch on the bed.

The plots of all Jim's novels put his characters under test, and he applied the same slide-rule across the board; there was no excuse for lost potential. Sally Sampson realised that he considered she had opted out when he was staying at their weekend cottage in Suffolk. She left the kitchen briefly, exhausted from juggling cooking and housework with the demands of small children and the deadlines of a publisher's reader, to sit beside him in the garden, where he was quietly reading. 'You have quite an easy life, Sally,' he remarked, with a hint of censure. But his reserve was not entirely concerned with her; he felt troubled all weekend, he noted privately, 'perhaps because of the massive tides'.

Andrew Gemill's disqualification stemmed from settling for family life, suburban commuting and a City job. 'I don't think',

Jim pronounced from the passenger seat as John Spurling accelerated away after a joint invitation to Sunday lunch, 'I shall ever see Andrew again.' He was not averse to dividing his own guests into A, B and C teams, using Terra Nova terminology, and 'lowering the mental temperature' meant instant relegation, signalled by an elaborately mimed yawn. 'You had', said one offender, 'to work hard to ignore that.' At some parties he stood on the fringe in judgement and surveyed the Second Eleven, at others he radiated a benevolent magnetism. 'Jim did what a lot of novelists do,' said a fellow writer, aware of scrutiny. 'He helped people to define themselves. He said things that made you feel a particular person, and his analysis held up a mirror that did not distort.'

Jim allotted some of the Booker money to buying wine by the case, attending Berry Brothers auctions in St James's and patrolling local wine merchants and off-licences in the company of the artist Hans Dorflinger, whose expertise he had discovered in New York when they were both Harkness Fellows. They looked mainly for good, mid-priced French clarets and burgundies – Chambolle Musigny, Château Grillet – and Château Yquem, his favourite sweet sauterne. They tasted before buying, and cases were stacked in his bathroom, leaving narrow passages to the basin, the lavatory and the bath. He stepped up his entertaining, keeping glasses filled and pulling corks with a liberality he could not condone for himself, but otherwise lived frugally. No attempt was made to swap his bike for a second-hand car, and he waited throughout the winter for the new mac he needed until the Aquascutum January Sale. His choices, it occurred to Derek Mahon, might have been drawn directly from Cyril Connolly's advice in *Enemies of Promise*. He had not married, he avoided journalism, he did everything in moderation and he imposed a daily discipline on his life; the only pleasures allowed were the ephemeral ones of food and wine.

With the curtains drawn and friends around the table, however, he had family security without ties. If talk about the collapse of the Western world dragged down the prevailing mood, he raised his glass – 'Well, this is the last bottle of this vintage and let us drink to the end of civilisation'. When called a cripple by a guest with an unhappy private life who was promptly labelled an emotional cripple by the others, Jim pointedly opened a bottle. 'I'm not having my friends called emotional cripples, even by my other friends,' he soothed, pushing it across. 'Speaking of cripples, however, I don't know if I'm strong enough to pour you all another glass of wine . . .' Under his hospitality people did things they did not normally do. *He was like the ring-master of a circus . . . Crack! The whip of [his] personality would sail out across the ring . . . Crack!* A well-endowed novelist unbuttoned her dress and thrust forward one naked breast, challenging, 'Not bad, is it?' during an argument about physical decay, and the young agent Felicity Bryan sang the madrigal 'The Silver Swan' in harmony with her husband by candlelight. Margaret Drabble's novel *The Gates of Ivory*, in which the hero Stephen Cox is based on Jim, would preserve those discursive evenings, in which conversation might flit towards the disarray of the Labour Party, council-house sales and the failure of *Marxism Today*. 'Was it partly a sense of failure that drove people into aggression? Does a sense of inferiority breed violence? Discuss.'

Jim sat back when his catering chores were done, and Derek watched Jim watching them and guessed that everyone was a bit afraid of the satire taking place in his head. 'I thought, "I bet he told the story damn well," and shrank a bit,' one victim of a barbed anecdote admitted after being tipped off by a third party. 'I thought a little less of Jim after that, which shows how much I thought of him until then. But of course I'd laughed at his stories myself.' He excoriated journalists as leeches of the writing profession but invited many, perhaps with an ulterior motive. 'I always thought', said Malcolm Dean, 'part of that may have been that he could sit there and seep in the information.' The fictional portrait in *The Gates of Ivory* did not omit the flickering ghost of his 'sardonic, cold, gentle little smile. It had always been a latter-day smile'.

Around the time of publication of *The Siege of Krishnapur* Jim had jokingly offered the film rights to the fledgling video company of Richard Rawlinson, a business-like new friend, for £15, but his ambitions for a film breakthrough were serious. The highlight of 1972 had been meeting Robert Bresson – 'one of my all-time heroes' – and his reaction on getting to know the young BBC director Stephen Frears was to float the idea of a film of *Troubles* with Alan Bennett as scriptwriter. The Booker win raised his hopes, and at last in the spring of 1974 an approach was made by Jules Buck of Keep Films in Belgravia, proposing Peter O'Toole, who co-owned the company, for the lead of *Siege* and John Osborne for the screenplay.

'It now seems pretty certain that I'll sell a film option for a year, renewable for another,' Jim kept his parents up to date. 'We're at present having the contract conned by a specialist with the impressive name of Irving Teitelbaum, a solicitor who knows enough about film contracts to see that we aren't taken to the cleaners.' In June, however, fortuitously coinciding with a visit from his older brother, Robert, a far better deal was mooted. Answering the phone, he was stunned to hear Fred Zinnemann, another of his all-time heroes for *High Noon* and *From Here to Eternity*, suggesting a meeting at his Little Venice home. A copy of *The Siege of Krishnapur* had been sent to him, explained Zinnemann matter-of-factly, and it met his two-fold criteria of an extremely visual plot and a gripping story.

Jim was greeted by a small methodical man without pretension, whose courteous European accent was overlaid with authentic Hollywood slang and who with humour and equanimity took his reluctance to write the script himself in good part. 'Jim was humble and overcome by the whole thing, which made me feel very protective,' Zinnemann recalled. 'He seemed the type of person who could be taken advantage of easily and I guess I'm a Jewish grandmother at heart! People of great talent I like to help, because a lot of them don't know how to protect themselves and if they come into the wrong hands they can get crushed. Writers are especially vulnerable. If they're not careful, their talent gets commercialised too soon and they become hacks. Awe of film is dangerous and I had a feeling it was all new to him.'

Mesmerised by being in the presence of the legendary Oscar-winner, Jim was not too dismayed when told that Zinnemann had come to the conclusion that he did not know enough about the Raj and the English mentality to proceed with making a film. He could not do justice to it, Zinnemann explained, because the crucial thing was to get the rhythm right, and he was disqualified from that by background and experience. However, David Lean – 'a good friend' – was the ideal man, and knowing that Lean wished to make a picture in India, he had sent him a copy. 'And, well,' Zinneman paused for effect, 'he likes the book.' Jim rushed home and hailed a taxi to Deborah Rogers's office, bringing Robert to share the triumph. 'The T-shirts alone will make a quarter of a million,' he exulted. 'Do you realise none of Lean's films grossed less than two and a half millon?'

'There have been some promising developments on the film option front,' he composed himself for the tip-off to Malta. 'In brief, we're preparing to gazump Jules Buck . . . in favour of a similar arrangement with David Lean, who is reported to have read the *Siege* throughout the night in a lather of excitment. However, the point is that if [he] did make a film of it, it would . . . put me beyond financial want for the rest of my days. I expect to sign a preliminary option agreement with him next week. All this is in strictest confidence of course . . . I'm beginning to realise that I'm going to have to give some thought to the problems of success (relative) and danger of having one's private writing life steam-rollered by lucrative sidelines. However, all that may never happen.'

But promising incentive for a film came from frozen rupees, the industry's term for the large sums which many studios had tied up in India which could only be utilised by filming there. At a meeting with Judy Scott-Fox, the William Morris agent who had originally sent the novel to Zinnemann, David Lean made no secret of his enthusiasm. 'We had lunch,' she reported, 'and David kept saying how much he loved it. He said it would make the most *wonderful* film.' To Jim's elation Lean followed through and took out a year's option for £2,000. 'Since I last saw you,' he brandished his coup to Russell McCormmach, 'I've sold the film rights to the most gaudy film-maker in the business and if he actually makes the film I may simply retire and build a shack next to yours in Washington State or Oregon.'

The agent's percentage on a potential David Lean blockbuster drew Jim's attention once more to that role. 'What sort of advance are you getting?' he now grilled most writers, however established, sooner or later. 'That's very bad – your agent should demand more.' Encountering his first agent Jonathan Clowes again, at a book launch, he acknowledged him with a cool 'Hello' and moved on. Not only could he do the job better, he was coming to the conclusion, but he could save a great deal of money into the bargain, as much as the price of a car on a £20,000 contract, said to be the likely advance a Booker winner could expect. Next time, he began to tell friends, he was going to do the deal himself, and, re-examining his contract, he found a clause that he considered should not have been there. Agents, he pointed out in literary company, were compromised by being too close to publishers, since they would never risk total confrontation on behalf of one author because they were simultaneously negotiating for several. His brother Robert reminded him that P.G. Wodehouse had said that getting an agent had been the most sensible thing he had done, and pointed out that, even if it was possible, it would cost too much in time and energy. There was no indication that Jim had heard. Old galley proofs, guests at his suppers noticed, were now being put out as loo paper.

'Some time after the Booker,' in Deborah's recollection, 'his attitude changed. It was not necessarily the Booker itself, but with recognition steel entered his soul. He could have made a good barrister, and my way was not an accurate reflection of how he would have handled it himself. He enjoyed the whole negotiation and especially loved the money side, about which he was meticulous. At the end of the day, I was having the discussions he wanted to have himself.' She was much closer to Jim than Jonathan Clowes had been, and when the blow was dealt she remembered Tony Godwin's ominous comment on their dawn walks that she would never grow up as an agent until she was prepared for the writer she most cared for to leave her. Even so, when authors left it was usually approaching the end of a book, not at the beginning of the next, which gave the rejection added sting. Seeing the hurt Jim had inflicted, her sister Sue made little attempt to be understanding when he continued to call around.

'He was one of those people', Deborah analysed later on, 'whose confidence was really arrogance, yet at the same time he was hesitant – very ambitious, but concealed. He presented himself with that self-effacing modesty, but while listening to

you he noticed everything, and that unassuming quality completely belied the real thing. Only people with a very powerful
ego manage to be quite shy and underneath as tough as an old
boot.' To be a successful novelist, the chill thought occurred to
her as she packed up his papers, it was probably necessary to be
like that. Hilary Spurling looked on his actions with indulgence.
He had become, she informed him, a grand cocotte.

Jim equipped himself with an accountant and a solicitor and
became his own agent, fortified by the year of Law at Brasenose.
He decided to write his next book free of contract or advance,
and to invite publishers to auction for it at the end. 'Jim was
remarkable for making the breakthrough,' David Caute gave
him full credit. 'His decision was to master the field, unlike the
95 per cent of authors who want the money but feel they can't
brazen it out, and to have someone as distinguished as a Booker
winner wandering around without an agent by his own choice,
that's a phenomenon. We saw it as a great source of encouragement to all authors to become self-reliant.'

But there was a downside, which quickly became apparent.
Roger Donald's young sister-in-law Elsie, who had exchanged
New York for London, introduced him in a pub one evening to
the editorial director of a major publishing house, with whom he
stayed up late, drinking and talking. He was persuaded to show
his work in progress, which had then to be retrieved with
difficulty when it was circulated without permission to someone
else within the business. 'I thought it was me he was interested
in,' he complained to Elsie, 'but it was just my book,' and the
aggrieved tone reminded her of a beautiful woman who wants to
be loved for her mind. No prop was secure, as he should,
perhaps, have learned. Halfway through 1974 Tony Godwin
left Weidenfeld and Nicolson to take up a senior post with
Harcourt Brace Jovanovich in New York, which meant that the
September launch of the American edition of *The Siege of
Krishnapur* would be well-supervised, but had far graver
long-term implications.

Jim prepared to go over to do his bit for publicity, but on 9
August, twenty-six months after Watergate, Nixon resigned,
and he guessed that the attention of the reading public would be
elsewhere. With additional bad timing, Nixon's official pardon

by the newly installed President Ford coincided exactly with the launch. Jim reached New York on 6 September and stayed with Tony in his mid-Manhattan apartment, but the experience was to be wretched. Selling himself was becoming no easier, and Tony was a changed man; not only was he unsuited to the American publishing market, but he was possessive and deeply lonely, prone to self-doubt and in constant dread that the atmosphere might lethally aggravate his asthma. On Fifth Avenue Jim bumped into Anthony and Sally Sampson and impulsively asked them up to the flat, but Tony was so unwelcoming that they did not linger. 'There was a long, favourable but very muddled review in the highly influential *New York Times* which Tony said he thought would be a good selling review,' Jim monitored unenthusiastically. 'He also said they expected a rave in *Newsweek* . . . but Tony often gets things muddled and is quite capable of having confused *Newsweek* with *Time*, which it resembles.' And when the *New Yorker* did get around to printing a review in November, it was the harshest the book had received.

Without an agent, and with Tony faltering and Bridget absorbed elsewhere, there was no buffer any more. The cork-lined bedsitting room had taken on the appearance of the library of an eighteenth-century recluse, with a metal reading stand beside the frequently solitary table-setting. And at the Old Rossallian dinner in the Army and Navy Club – 'densely packed with elderly generals and clerics [which] justified my worst fears' – Jim felt more set apart than ever. Penguin launched the paperback edition of *The Siege of Krishnapur* and Philippa Harrison, who had known him at Cape, was taken aback to glimpse him standing alone outside, shielding his eyes and gazing in at his own party.

Nothing further was heard from David Lean about the film option, and Judy Scott-Fox moved to California. 'At first people purred up in Rolls-Royces to talk about film rights,' Jim quipped when asked, 'then they came on bikes and then with bus tickets.' In July 1975 he made a note that Lean's option was up that week, 'but nothing has been heard of him so it seems he doesn't plan to renew it. He's said to be travelling in the south seas, which makes it difficult to get a straight answer.' Eventually Fred

Zinnemann passed on the disappointing confirmation that Lean no longer wanted to do it. 'I can't face the idea of those dead bodies all over the place,' Lean was unofficially reported to have said.

Such was the reward for complacency, he reflected, not without a certain stern satisfaction at the justice of this retribution. Cycling through London one afternoon, he stopped at a red traffic light in Piccadilly and sat back in the saddle, short of breath as always and gazing into the middle distance. A man materialised abruptly at his side, and he flinched, expecting to be mugged. 'Oh, it's J.G. Farrell,' the stranger exclaimed, recognising him from the full-page Snowdon photograph. 'Well done!' And his precarious balance was toppled by a powerful clap on the back, leaving him dizzy, trembling and retching.

CHAPTER EIGHTEEN

At Large in the Minefields
1975–1978

Jim had taken to wearing a suit of bleached Indian cotton in summer which accentuated his greenish-blue eyes and his tan; in winter he sported a melodramatic dark hat with rakish brim and high crown. Women noticed him, as he was well aware. 'Physically he was delicate-looking,' wrote one, 'with prematurely silver hair swept back from a fine brow with surprisingly thick, dark eyebrows. He had an Irish face of the neat, elfin kind with a large nose and a sensitively humorous mouth. His voice was educated, English and tinny, with a tendency to trail away on the ends of words which he had emphasized.' 'He was absolutely correct,' approved another, 'and slightly unusual. Very immaculate, but not boringly British.' If he was asked to put a label on himself, he usually chose cosmopolitan, an apt description. 'He seemed un-English in his manner, openness and generosity,' a normally waspish male American novelist pointed out. 'He was much warmer, more friendly and there was less sense of class.'

In the close-knit book world Jim now became, as it was put, *un homme fatal*. Sex, he admitted, gave him a wonderful feeling of mental clarity. 'One knew he saw women but he never brought them along,' noticed Alison Lurie. 'They tended to be younger and not up to the dinner parties.' 'He rather liked nymphets,' said Sonia Orwell's younger colleague, Ian Angus. Women sometimes said that going to bed with him, Jim confided to Margaret Drabble in a tone of self-mockery, was like going to bed with a good book. 'And they do tend to complain', he added, highly amused by the un-exciting comparison, 'that they are not the only woman in my life.

So I say, "Why should they be?" Each girlfriend believed she was the only one, until made aware when she was in love with him of the quality and quantity of equal candidates. But anyone with a slim volume behind them, he was heard to ridicule, could attract women. 'I believe', one casualty concluded, 'that the makeup of these men is such that, whatever happens to their career and fame, it can't possibly work out. You almost can't blame them for having a terribly unhappy effect on you.'

The compartments Jim employed were not visible until too late. The young graduate Brigid Allen had met him early in 1973 but after the Booker Prize saw him much less often, a sequence made no less painful by her ability to be as analytical as he. 'On one hand,' she said later, 'he was easy, natural, willing to start a relationship, even if it was to fail. That would be a relationship of talking about good books, art, food and, in his cautious way, involving sex. On the other hand, there was a strong negative-ness; he was from the carping generation, inclined to quarrel with things. And on another level he enjoyed being famous. He could be bitchy about well-known writers, but he would like the idea of being on the same level himself, and knowing someone as an insider made him more generous towards them. He enjoyed feeling he could do things, and he was exhilarated by success.'

Rose Knox Peebles was in a position to matchmake for him, but she made no attempt to do so. 'I couldn't see anyone resisting him,' she explained, 'and I wouldn't have liked to have seen them unhappy. The only woman who could have coped would have been someone genuinely content with being a housekeeper, because he had to have a separate existence.' Jim's own image for disillusion had been on record for seven years and offered little hope that he might one day change. *I was like a man who sees a breeze playing over a field of corn and is so inspired by its beauty that he buys it. Well, I bought the field but I couldn't buy the breeze. The breeze dropped.*

His choice of flat was a statement in itself, and a woman was unwise to ignore the space for a single occupant, or the self-sufficient blend of male and female capability. A night with Jim was stage-managed for voluntary early exit, from the unaccom-modating bed to the monosyllabic toast and Bovril breakfast which made plain the expectation of being left alone to work.

One girlfriend, realising she was about to drive past his flat, was rash enough to suggest to friends that she would surprise him. He came to the door, kissed her cheek and went back in. 'He just dismissed her,' said a witness. 'I was so stunned, I said, "Oh God."'

'He operated from his dinner parties,' observed Paul Huxley, who had known him since their Harkness Fellowships. 'He would invite an interesting mix of people – couples mostly, and among them would be his potential girlfriend. Nothing as crude as the first date alone; instead "Come to dinner with some of my friends". At the table there might be an artist, a writer, a broadcaster, and a critic, and gradually, as one assessed who everyone was, you'd realise which was the girl. Invariably she was in publishing or an art gallery and just his type – intelligent, nothing terribly glamorous, decent, never tall. It was a gentle and, we thought, very dignified approach designed to let them see him among his friends and decide for themselves whether they would like to see him again.'

Jim was attracted to lively, witty women who seized the initiative, but he was more compatible with the vulnerable, which put him in a dilemma. *I loved her above all because she was so shy and lonely . . . She reminded me of an anxious, lost dog on a crowded street at rush hour, dashing back and forth looking for its master vanished somewhere in the flood of hurrying strangers. And not only had she given up hope, she had put up defences against it. And when I came along . . . how pitifully lost she was then . . . She had barricaded herself into her loneliness and bolted the door. She had pushed tables and chairs and bookcases against it.* As soon as that door was open, however, it threatened to close behind him, too, and he would seek escape. The pattern began to repeat itself, at accelerated pace.

'There is a tide in the love affairs of men,' he had made a note within a year of going down from Oxford. 'So much depends on the chance of the first acquaintance which can transcend all that comes after it, though what comes after is most humdrum and would never have given rise to the affair in the first place.' The small-breasted Cranach nudes in the Courtauld Institute remained his ideal, and he admitted that if a woman did the slightest thing to shatter the image he had of her, she was no longer of interest. As 'Lucy', his callgirl, put it, 'Jim always wanted the unattainable, but he would soon have bolted if she'd come after him.' The conundrum was the same after the Booker Prize as it had been a decade earlier when he had first posed the problem in print. *How on earth could he disengage himself immediately without hurting her and without appearing utterly heartless and calculating? Especially if he was heartless and calculating . . . It had been exclusively his own idea. All the responsibility was his . . . he had won something he did not want.*

'He could draw those women like moths to a flame,' his American school-friend Roger Donald observed after their paths began to cross again in the 1970s. 'And then he would reject them. But they had not pursued him until they'd had definite signs from him that they were welcome. I guess he angrily saw himself from the woman's point of view and the better known he became, the more that festered. He'd say, "I'm a combination of the perfect writer and" – always such bitter emphasis here – "a *cripple*".' Listening to a friend's complaint about being sexually involved with two domineering women, however, Jim observed wistfully, 'I haven't enough for one, let alone two.' In such rare confessional moments he was beginning to talk, with some incredulity, of being able to manage without a sex life at all. 'I'm nearly forty,' he sighed after making love to one of the girls whom Paul Huxley could now spot. 'It's high time I gave this thing up.' She blamed herself for being too sexually inexperienced and too much in love.

Celebrity made disengagement more troublesome. Jim had told Bridget O'Toole that he was still in love with Sarah Bond, but now word filtered back that he was claiming to be in love with her. With dismay Bridget recognised the device. A master of nuance, he would provoke unease with intimate tales of 'Lucy' and prostitution, and a clinging girlfriend might be told that someone they both knew was chasing him, or be expected to offer sympathy when he reported a disappointing assignation with one of her friends. After taking one girl to France on a cycling trip he made sure that her rival heard about the difficulty of zipping two sleeping bags into one. If need be, his tactics were more brutal. On a mellow summer evening beneath the trees of Diana Saville's lush orchard the discussion centred on French nationalisation of the Renault car industry, and his companion dared to chip in. 'Of course, politics are a matter of emotion,' allowed Diana. 'But there was more to this than that. Instead of defending her when she was subjected to an unpleasant attack by an aggressive male leftwinger, Jim joined in. She was conservative politically, as I am, but it was all directed at her and not at me. She was unfairly humiliated.' From a distance Brigid Allen likened his behaviour to the tides of the sea, continually retreating and advancing. She removed herself, first to New York and then to India, out of self-preservation.

In January 1974 Jim stood near Claire Tomalin at a Weidenfeld party, fixed in the guise of his latest hero. *The Collector admired pretty women . . . 'She has a mind of her own,' he decided. 'Why can't all women be widows?'* Claire's late husband, the journalist Nicholas Tomalin, had been killed when covering the war in Cambodia the previous year, and in *The Siege of Krishnapur* vivacious young widows were accounted fair game. He asked Tony Godwin to act as go-between, and a drink at the Fitzroy Tavern on Shrove Tuesday led to a Woody Allen film. Unknown to them both, Tom Wakefield saw them together and thought, 'Oh, that's it!,' and Francis King, separately, jumped to the same wrong conclusion.

Claire found him attractive and he was certainly attracted to her, but when confronted with her stronger personality, he acted less like the Collector than the hesitant, shy Major. Her widowhood brought out his protectiveness and he was happiest when they were alone, but as soon as she finished her biography of *Mary Wollstonecraft* she joined the *New Statesman*, and her book was published that September to acclaim. She grew more confident and he grew less, the reverse of his usual experience. 'He was being extremely sweet,' she said of the embarrassing finale to one of his small dinners, at which she had been the last to leave. 'And, as a woman sometimes does, I phoned him up when I got home. He quite obviously took fright, and it was panic stations. I concluded that he preferred fantasy and flirtation to any serious involvement.' After a few months he made his peace by coming to a crowded party in her house and sat beside her at the dinner table, serving out the fish. Among those he passed a plate to was Martin Amis, fifteen years his junior, who was then, as he knew, romantically linked with Clare. Afterwards he reached out to her with a late-night phone call of his own which proved her point. 'Everything would be alright between us,' he rhapsodised, 'if you were a milkmaid and I were a shepherd.' In due course she cried on his shoulder about an unhappy love affair, and he reprimanded her for allowing herself to become dependent on anyone.

'I always fall in love with impossible women,' he teased Margaret Drabble, giving the impression that she was too well-balanced to qualify, but she was not upset. She considered that his attitude to women in his books was curious, even hostile, and had heard rumours about his treacherous behaviour. Depending, as she did, on his astringent sympathy to put professional reverses in perspective, she preferred to be in the safe squaw category – as were the wives of his friends – and so able to count on unstinting warmth and support. She was not aware that girls liable to be impressed by big names in the book world were led to believe that she was in pursuit of him. Jim was ringmaster in this arena, as well as at the dinner table, and intent on keeping the space about him clear.

Like Lowry's Consul, who simultaneously prays to be reconciled with his wife and prays to be alone, Jim was ambivalent, and his growing reputation as a womaniser disguised the actual problem. 'All you need', he let slip to a publisher who was complaining about widespread falling standards in submitted novels, 'is enough *time* to write well.' Past the age when most of his friends had married, several more often than once, his yearning for companionship and sensual fulfilment was coming into increasing conflict with the urgent need to be alone. 'I can't work', he fumed, slamming out after one minor scene, 'if I have *any* kind of emotional upset.' The dilemma was that the women who most attracted him, those who were cerebral, sensitive, tinged with self-doubt and many years his junior, became dependent precisely because they lacked the self-sufficiency and independence that he could have lived with, yet fled from. ' "The women I like I cannot love," ' cries his well-observed alter ego in *The Gates of Ivory*, ' "the women I love I cannot like, the life I seek I could not endure. I seek . . . simplicity." '

The undemanding alternative of a cat or dog would have been both shackle and distraction and, aware of his own affectionate nature, he restricted himself to keeping a watchful eye on the welfare of a hunchback local feline stray which he named Pussimodo, bringing gifts of sardines for Diana Saville's cats, and composing a rueful fairytale for adults, as revealingly autobiographical as it was intentionally political. The plot centred on the unexpected sexual behaviour of Rameses, the big tomcat belonging to Hans Dorflinger and Monika Beisner, when Hans's mother came to stay from Germany and unpacked her fluffily-covered leather luggage. He called it *The Cat Who Fell in Love with a Suitcase*.

Being compassionate, Jim got himself into situations from which he had to extricate himself, and he then went about that clumsily, retreating and temporarily advancing; in the process he inflicted greater pain than a more ruthless man. He longed for emotional intimacy, but with women it came at an unacceptable price because, unlike male friends, they then expected permanent access to the centre of his life; to share his flat, not just his bed. He had to be constantly on his guard, and mistrust occasionally slipped out. 'It's funny how men so often are more amusing,' he remarked in front of Alison Lurie and Margaret Drabble. 'I think I'm quite funny sometimes,' Alison rapped back.

Jim was managing to lead the life of a Victorian bachelor, an anomaly in late twentieth-century London. When Paul Theroux was invited to a midweek lunch he cycled up from Wandsworth on his F.W. Evans bike, convinced that his host must be a dilettante. 'To my mind lunch meant the total ruin of the day and I was really surprised that he was prepared to slack off. All that effort directed at other people – if he was a serious writer, what were we doing having *lunch*?' He could not place Jim, and Ireland brought them no closer: as a Catholic, Theroux had grown up among the Boston Irish and in London he was used to watching nationalists in his local pub shout obscenities if Prince Charles appeared on television. He expected an immediate rapport between an American and an Irishman, and Jim's brand of Irishness was suspect. He was equally perplexed by the mixing of host and hostess roles, and speculated freely about Jim's sexuality as he peddled back to resume his costly family responsibilities, convinced that his was the toughest literary life. Ironically Jim criticised Theroux for the identical flaw. 'He spends so much time on television chat shows', he complained, 'that he isn't a real writer.'

Cycling forays across northern France, lasting from a long weekend to a month, were occasional escapes. With a small ridge tent and minimal equipment Jim averaged twenty-five miles a day, allowing time for picnics, sitting at cafés, and resting to admire a view. One pilgrimage was to the Grand Hotel in Cabourg, the setting for Proust's Balbec, and he struck camp in a field outside the town before cycling in. The evening bettered his expectations as the name of the manager, who displayed a lofty approach to cyclists, was Monsieur Parodi. 'When I woke up this morning my tent was covered in dew and spiders' webs', he wrote on a postcard to the Spurlings, whose son, Nat, was his latest godchild, the recipient of a specially commissioned set of child-sized bowls and mugs by the talented potter, Anne Stokes. 'P.S.,' he added for John and Hilary's benefit, 'Much more buckets and spades here than suntan oil and heaving breasts.' Passing an impoverished, dungaree-clad elderly eccentric in a London street, who was solitary, serene of face and unkempt of hair, he turned to the girl in her twenties at his side and predicted that he would look like that, too, when he was old.

But a transition had already taken place, as was evident when a letter appeared in *The Times* – from 'Mr J.G. Farrell' – about the building of the new British Library. 'I am no less certain than Professor Thomas', the authorative voice reproved, 'that the administration simply do not realise *what will be lost*. Committees, it is well known, tend to ignore matters, such as atmosphere, which they cannot quantify. And yet where a reading room is concerned that is the very heart of the matter.' Only a few years beforehand Gary Arnott had offered to put Jim up for the London Library and to pay his subscription, and had been rebuffed on the grounds that it was too much of an inner sanctum.

From within that sanctum, however, getting a new book off the ground was no less difficult. If anything, it was harder. 'I'm badly blocked with the Singapore book at the moment,' he bemoaned within nine months of committing himself to the agenda in his Booker speech. 'I keep writing and rewriting the first few pages, which get duller and duller. It's a bit like one of those dice games where you have to throw a double six before you can even start. But the more I cudgel my brains, the fewer ideas I get.' Tracing the hidden crosscurrents of financial and psychological motivation would complete the Empire circle, but the subject was dense and external pressures had increased. Everyone's expectations, including his own, were raised, and the annual Booker Prize build-up regularly re-awoke attention. To keep faith with the stand he had so publicly taken, it was necessary to recreate fictionally the fall of Singapore, and there was a certain grim irony in the knowledge that when he had first seen its potential, in 1972, the large scale had acted as a deterrent.

Jim's ambition was greater than he had intimated in the Café Royal. His dream was of emulating Tolstoy, and this book was to be *a jolting passage over the switched points of history*, his personal *War and Peace*. But the jump from eccentric hotel to violent siege had been minimal compared to that necessary for bridging the Residency compound and the geographical complexities of Malaya and Singapore. Instead of a single drawn-out confrontation, he had to take on the military campaigns of both the Allies and the Japanese, and he felt 'handcuffed' to too powerful a theme. The climax was intended to be the last day of the British Empire in that part of the world, but where should he begin?

'I did think of not dealing with the war side of it at all,' he later admitted. 'My first idea, my very first idea, was to have merely the civilian side of things and have my characters arguing about the problem of commerce and so on and then at the very end have a servant appear and say, "Excuse me, but there's a Japanese gentleman at the door." However, I reluctantly abandoned that. Obviously you can't completely ignore the military side of things.' He was historically boxed in, and that constrained imagination. Everything had to take place on the right date, in the right sequence, even under the right weather conditions. From the point of view of plot a delayed advance down the peninsula and an earlier Japanese air strike would have been preferable, and he had to take account of the dynastic contortions of the real-life mercantile houses of the rubber industry. The Singapore Grip of the title was not simply the erotic speciality of local brothels, recounted to him in the buzz of Sonia Orwell's drawing room, but capitalism and its crushing coils.

Matthew Webb was Jim's new hero, an idealist in flight from the family firm of Blackett and Webb, of which his estranged father had been senior partner. The rubber company was based in Singapore under the capable management of Walter Blackett, and on his father's death Matthew was to be summoned to inherit his share of the company, arriving in time to witness both the complacency of the final months and the Japanese attack. Into that short period a huge theme had somehow to be inserted, and Jim reverted to drawing his curtains in daytime and switching on the overhead light. Christmas that year was spent in Paris on his own, walking up and down the icy embankments obsessed by his book. *He found himself . . . brooding on what makes up a moment of history; if you took a knife and chopped cleanly through . . . what would it look like in cross-section? Would it be like chopping through a leg of lamb where you see the ends of the muscles, nerves, sinews and bone of one piece matching a similar arrangement on the other?*

He extended his working day, allotting the lion's share to research. In the British Museum, the Liddell Hart Centre for Military Archives at King's College, and the Public Record Office, bent lower these days, chin cupped by left hand to ease his aching neck, he made notes on to separate cards from fifty-one books. These ranged from P.T. Bauer's *Report on a Visit to the Rubber Growing Smallholdings of Malaya* to M. Tsuji's *Singapore, The Japanese Version*, and included autobiographies as contrary as *The War in Malaya* by Lieutenant-General A.E. Percival, and *Men and Rubber*, co-written by Harvey S. Firestone. 'I'd already been interested in some govt. papers I'd come across in the PRO about a serious strike in the Firestone factory in Singapore at the beginning of the war,' he noted as late as March 1975. 'Now I'm reading about Harvey's attempts to get alternative sources of supply by starting his own rubber estates in Liberia. So far I have not discovered whether or not he was successful as I've just reached the Depression and they don't need much rubber anyway.'

News items about the current 1970s recession served as an intriguing counterpoint. 'I'm afraid I am now responsible for the impending collapse of the Western economy,' he encouraged himself sardonically. 'By turning my attention to the last great slump I've conjured up another.' To his boyhood hero, Richard Hughes, who nowadays regularly came to supper and extended warm hospitality in Wales, he remarked on how little had been written militarily about the fall of Singapore. 'If it had been a victory,' Hughes observed tartly, 'the bookshops would have been crammed.'

Jim was faced with a massive organisational effort if he was to assimilate so much documentary material, and sleep disturbance was already cropping up. Gary Arnott gave a crash course on how money markets worked; Bridget weeded out the simpler tracts of Marx, Lenin and Engel; Robin Stott argued their relative points, as well as those of Trotsky and Stalin, and gave an explanation of Jung and Taoism. Malcolm Dean, now a *Guardian* leader writer, lent economics textbooks, and Jim's older brother, Robert, scoured the University of Victoria Library. His younger brother, Richard, now married and a father, produced investment research on Asian Trading houses. At Rossall Jim had been bored by maths; now he was determined to follow the trail of cause and effect. *'Strong nations . . . will always take advantage of the weak if they can do so with impunity. This is a law of nature . . .' 'But surely government has a duty to act in the moral as well as the material interests of its people?' . . . 'Let's not be naïve, my boy . . . Strong nations survive. Weak nations go to the wall, that has always been the way of the world and always will be.'*

In the early stages Jim had an experience that affected him deeply. During his parents' summer visit from Malta he took them to the Proms, and in the Albert Hall the effect of the tinnitus was cruelly underlined. Bill's wish was to hear the range of orchestral instruments, however indistinctly, and they tried first one place in the auditorium, then another, and finally a third, at which Bill shook his head and gave up, sitting back. The loss glimpsed there would take Murphy's Law to its pessimistic limit as Ehrendorf's Second Law, which holds that *in human affairs things tend inevitably to go wrong. Things are slightly worse at any given moment than at any preceding moment.* Captain James Ehrendorf, a philosophical young officer in the American military attaché's office in Singapore – *quite simply a gentleman . . . first met at Oxford . . . a Rhodes scholar* – was Jim's coded signal to Erwin, Bob and Russell.

In the human situation he envisaged, Walter Blackett's ambitious daughter, Joan, would toy first with Ehrendorf and then with Matthew, shrewdly aware, unlike her lazy brother Monty, of the long-term needs of Blackett and Webb. Diligently doing his best for everyone as the Japanese threat intensified would be Major Brendan Archer, *a tall, rather anxious-looking man in his fifties*, now turned civilian and a confirmed bachelor. But this was to be Matthew Webb's book, not the Major's, so he was evoked dispassionately, and from a distance. *The Major was a discreet and sensible fellow, although sadly lacking in ambition . . . [He] was just the sort of conscientious individual with time on his hands who can usually be relied upon to volunteer for . . . charity balls, picnics in aid of orphans, Buy-a-Bomber-For-Britain Funds and so forth.*

As always, the book was studded with private allusions. Malcolm Dean, representing the *Straits Times*, was reduced to a junior reporter. *'What's your name, son?' 'Malcolm, sir.' 'Well, you're a bright lad, Malcolm,' said Walter with magnanimity. 'Work hard and you'll get on in life.'* And François Dupigny, a cynical Frenchman whose presence is ascribed to having left Saigon hurriedly with General Catroux, was Jim's wink at Claude Simha. The school tie borrowed to distract a tennis opponent *by its disagreeably clashing colours* was his own, and the Russells of Portarlington were honoured by the ship *Felix Roussel*, on which refugees escape the Japanese in the nick of time. One cameo was of Captain Brown, based on Bill's elderly seafaring friend Dick Roberts; Major Akado was named after Jim's favourite Japanese restaurateur; Berry Bros wine cellars got a plaudit, and Sir Edmund Gibson's Indian bedroom was about to be reassigned to the late Mr Webb. Even the Maharajah of Benares's ancient Rolls would be called upon to transport Chamberlain to Locarno. There were old scores to be settled, too. *Walter . . . pictured Mr Webb standing on the lawn of Brasenose College holding up fistfuls of white hair to the icy wind that howled through the quad, while dismal dons, looking up from their books, surveyed this representative of suffering humanity with distaste from leaded casements.*

The mental effort was considerable, and once again Jim found himself in two contrasting dimensions. Borrowing Lowry's pariah dog device from *Under the Volcano*, this time to embody self-interest and wickedly christened 'The Human Condition', he kept up with the partisan Dog versus Cat row in the correspondence columns of *The Times* and had supper with its instigator, Bernard Levin. He went to see the West End musical *Happy as a Sandbag* – 'It was crammed with useful odds and ends of 1940s detail' – and ordered the record so that he could use 'snippets' of the songs. After staring in silence at a Knightsbridge window display of expensive and unnecessary items, he sighed and commented to a girlfriend, 'It makes you wonder what capitalism is all about.'

The atmospheric warble of Vera Lynn on the record-player accompanied his typing. As soon as he noticed with a start that the long-playing record had ended, he would break off to turn it over. Matthew Webb was falling in love with the sensuous Lara, who was to be renamed Vera partly in acknowledgment of the musical debt, and her sexual initiation of the inhibited Matthew would be his final testimony to 'Lucy'. Over his desk, where he could double-check the streets as he moved his characters about, hung a large-scale map of Singapore.

The conversational tone of his narrator's account of bizarre and humorous predicaments could not disguise the book's pervasive mood of despair. Matthew, the Major and Dupigny were destined for the horrors of a Japanese prisoner-of-war camp, and Walter Blackett, commercial zeal incarnate, was doomed to lose everything he most prized. Life was to take on the aspect of nightmarish unreality, as had Jim's life after polio, and his rising tension kept pace with the Japanese advance. He had consistently supported Labour since being old enough to vote, but at dinner parties now he was dogmatic, as liable to drag an argument out too far as to turn it into forensic cross-examination: a smug ex-deb was reduced to tears for saying she took pride in her Englishness and rarely travelling abroad.

Jim's suspicions about the ethics of business expansion were colouring Walter Blackett's attitude, and in the process uncovering aspects of his father that he had not considered before. His parents' retirement to Malta was about to come to a premature end because of the changing political atmosphere and Bill's declining health, which shone further light on the dominant part in his parents' joint lives that illness had always played. He had grown closer to his mother during the consultations for *Troubles*, and he began to have more sympathy for her resourcefulness, given the lack of freedom of choice. Yet again her life was to be disrupted, and the proposed move to England to be near medical care, as well as their first grandchild, meant extra responsibility for himself. Seeing one useful contribution he could make, he spent a weekend in the Walls's Oxfordshire cottage, which was again on the market, to test it out on his parents' behalf. The cottage was warm, and easy to run; his recommendation was taken up. They began living all year round in Oxfordshire as his writing momentum gathered pace and he sensed with alarm that they would expect to see him more often.

The Booker cheque was drawing interest in a savings account, but it became obvious that it would be impossible to complete the first draft without utilising it, despite Francis King's naughty suggestion that he should follow Conrad's example over *Nostromo* and write the entire book at home. Reluctantly Jim set a date for the New Year of 1975 and, playing his cards close to his chest, consulted Paul Theroux, who had taught at the University of Singapore. So guarded was the exchange that Theroux despised him even more, convinced that he was tackling the trip as superficially as a travel writer. Jim was tired beforehand, and the last-minute arrangements were exhausting. In December he was recognised in the street by a pinstriped Old Rossallian, the brother of his old study room-mate, Nevill Phillips, and an account of his dejected appearance was passed on. Nevill phoned out of the blue, plainly taking pity on him across the seventeen-year divide, and invited him to spend Christmas Day *en famille* in commuter-land Kent. The answer was dusty in the extreme.

Touching down at Changi airport on 2 January, superimpos-
ing Matthew Webb's wartime arrival in an Avro-Anson, Jim was
shocked into alertness. The jail area was transformed and
Raffles Hotel diminished by skyscrapers – 'more like Los An-
geles'. After one symbolic night there he switched to a cheap
Chinese-run hotel, the South Asia at 12 Belcoolen Street. His $3-
a-night room had a shower, bathroom and fan – 'which I find I
prefer to air conditioning' – and he was within walking distance
of Tanglin, home territory of the Blacketts, Matthew and the
Major, as well as Collyer Quay, setting for the head office of
Blackett and Webb.

Jim took Matthew's bearings between cloudbursts, armed
with a red notebook and the map unpinned from Egerton
Gardens, which promptly tore at the dampened seams. 'In
Market Street Chettian money lenders doze over their accounts
in dim interiors [and] this reminded M of somnolent alligators.'
'Near the [arcade] entrance is a growth of bamboo fenced off in
which Matthew vaulting the iron fence might take refuge.'
'Matthew standing in the doorway of a metalwork merchant
glimpses his own worried face upside down in a steaming
concave silver wok.' 'A heavily built short-haired British matron
in the Cold Storage causes me to think that in many ways there is
still a lot here that would have been familiar 35 years ago.
Matthew might glimpse [her] being conveyed gasping by half a
dozen diminutive Chinese during an air-raid.' Scenting immu-
table Far Eastern whiffs of drains and river, he blocked out the
high-rise skyline and paused to gaze or to sample pavement
cooking. The city teemed with Chinese girls in miniskirts, and
many smiled at the stooped pale man with white hair and
youthful face, shirt collar open above narrow hock-bottle
shoulders, and sleeves rolled only as far as the gaunt elbows.

'I'm glad I didn't leave my trip any later as many familiar
buildings have a boarded-up look about them . . . Of John
Little's department store in Raffles Place all that remains is a
sad façade . . . No sign at all of Whiteways and Robinson, the
most famous store of all, burned down some while ago. I went to
have a look at the Great World amusement park for which I had
a walk-on part; it's still there but no longer functions as it used to
(British tommies whooping it up with the various races) and is

also due for "renewal" by the look of things.' A diary, as in India, harvested the retrospective view, and he wrote frequently in French to Claude Simha, whose droll gourmet standards infused Dupigny. *At [Matthew's] side . . . Dupigny was eyeing his plate dubiously, prodding the meat here and there with his fork . . . 'Today, no, we are out of luck. But sometimes, when Walter invites his fellow merchants of Singapore the cook makes un petit effort.'*

Jim retreated to the Blackett world, going to watch bowling in the nets at the Cricket Club – 'I was seized by a powerful sensation of "privilege" surviving from earlier days' – and a rugby match on the padang. '*Not*', he drew a veil over proceedings, 'the ideal temperature for rugby.' He took up Malcolm Dean's introduction to a friend in the New Zealand High Commission and was plunged into the spotlight, as *The Siege of Krishnapur* had been lent around in advance and the High Commissioner, whose previous posting had been to New Delhi, turned out to be a long-standing fan. An invitation to a cocktail party for Sir Edmund Hillary, who was in transit to Nepal – 'He looks like a massive, wrinkled sheep' – was less appreciated than the useful list of Chinese and British survivors of the Japanese invasion, and the leisurely briefings to round it out over ice-cold drinks in the timewarp of the Cricket Club. *How he loved the tropical Victorian architecture . . . with its vast rooms, high ceilings and ornamented balconies! Behind his chair a segment of the green padang could be seen . . . No doubt cricket would continue despite the bombing; important matches could not be expected to wait until the Japanese had been dealt with.*

But Jim was not tempted to linger in the reassuring cocoon, and the reaction of a young British stockbroker to the name of his hotel gave him one reason, among many, for moving swiftly on. 'He was overcome with astonishment and amusement', he noted, exasperated, 'and kept telling everybody he met in his club as if it was the most amazing thing he had ever heard. *Plus ça change.*' It was an authentic 1940s encounter which, in subtle revenge, Matthew Webb would share.

A letter reached him from his parents with the news that Dick Delaney, his soulmate on the DEW Line, would be in Singapore for a couple of days. 'I shall get him to photograph a certain house I have my eye on not far from his hotel,' he resolved, 'which looks remarkably like one I have already described from imagination in the early pages of my book.' The most likely candidate for the Blacketts' dynastic ambitions is at 3 Chatsworth Avenue in Tanglin, appropriately near the gradient – *more psychological than real* – of Orchard Road. *The ranks of fat white pillars that supported its upper balconies [gave] a classical, almost judicial appearance and yet, at the same time, an air of ease, comfort, even sensuality.* He spent his fortieth birthday combing the city for detail, and keeping up with international developments through the *Straits Times.*

Two days later he set off up the Malayan peninsula to Bangkok by train – 'the carriages', he jotted in his notebook, 'still have FMS Railway and a symbol of a tiger engraved on the glass of their doors' – and the mild Ehrendorf went with him as companion-in-chief. *The insignia of the Federated Malay States Railway, palm-trees and a lion, had been engraved on the window beside [him]; he gazed at it, thinking of the vanished comfort and security of earlier days in Malaya, and found it beautiful . . . A man ran back along the train blowing a whistle and shouting 'Air Raid!' . . . Another train travelling in the opposite direction had stopped beside their own . . . Ehrendorf, still drugged with sleep, glimpsed a little cluster of illuminated brigadiers poring over a map . . .* At the station exit in Kuala Lumpur Jim was brought up short by a faded colonial building opposite named the Majestic Hotel and, astounded by the coincidence, he booked in. Similarities with Kilnalough were not hard to find. 'Only a handful of guests seemed to be camping there in its vast collection of rooms, and elderly Chinese servants doddered about forgetting what you had ordered and coming back to ask you what it was.'

A day-long journey through jungle and kampongs – *Ehrendorf had the impression of travelling through an interminable dark green corridor* – led to Penang, which took on Proustian overtones at the unexpected sight of a promenade. By *half closing your eyes and very vigorously using your imagination, you might, for a moment or two, think yourself in a tropical Balbec on your way to meet some dark-skinned little Albertine.* The less built-up city was nearer the Singapore of his imagination, and he stayed on for a week to assemble detail, studying a Chinese funeral, comparing the techniques of beggars and street performers and tracking down the exact Malayan currency for 1941. 'A railway station is spelled "steshen". At the PO this morning I noticed the delightful "teligeram", the plural is formed not by adding "s" but a 2, thus teligeram 2 . . . The word for "closed" was "Tutup", which I feel sure must be a corruption of "shut up".'

By the time he reached Bangkok the bulk of factual research was completed. The congested traffic and air pollution – 'both atrocious' – were in sharp contrast to the complex, beautiful and self-contained life on the river. At a disadvantage with his chest problems, he visited the floating market, examined the teeming klongs, was whisked up the Chao Phraya river by long-tailed boat, and across country to sightsee by minibus. By now he was part of a fractious foursome which consisted of a young French physicist with an irritating habit of muttering, 'Incroyable, mais vrai,' a glum German dentist, and L, an American girl. Arranging an assignation with her at the Majestic Hotel in Kuala Lumpur, he put her on the plane south with relief. 'L had gradually revealed a tendency to use her appeal for men to help her along life's road,' he noted with detachment. 'She spent such a long time making-up in the ladies room (her flight had been called twice) that we parted on not so cordial terms . . . This extra regard for her appearance was so that she should make the strongest possible impression on any men she met on the plane.' L's relevance to the unscrupulous Joan Blackett, however, could not be ignored, and he was confident of keeping his head when they re-met. 'While in Bangkok . . . she made a declaration about having decided she wanted a permanent man and had come to the conclusion that I might suit her specifications. I was discouraging and the matter was dropped.'

The Vietnam War was more tangible in Bangkok than in Singapore, where he had read all about the North Vietnamese Army's ominous capture of Phuac Long Province, and the sight of bristle-headed GIs on leave drove home the idea that Saigon might resemble Singapore under advancing Japanese threat. On impulse he costed out the flight across to the Vietnamese capital and booked a seat, reminded that Lacy Wright, a likeable

American diplomat of his own age whom he had met through Malcolm Dean when Lacy was attached to the American Embassy in London, was now posted there. Impatient and with time to kill, he went to see the Reclining Buddha at Wat Po.

'I was standing by a tree,' he scribbled at the airport, 'when two, three butterflies . . . kite-shaped with tails, and with pink and yellow on their wings, came fluttering all around me as if they had taken a liking to the colour of my shirt and wanted to settle on me. They fluttered very beautifully, with a much slower beat of the wings than usual; a magical experience. I spent several minutes gazing at them with delight.' But not even rapture could be lived entirely in the moment, and Matthew would be granted the abandonment that Jim could not allow himself. *One, two, three butterflies, astonishingly beautiful and of a kind he had never seen before with pink and yellow on their wings and long, trailing tails like kites came fluttering around him, as if they had taken a liking to his freshly ironed linen suit . . . He watched them, filled with wonder, noting how the beat of their wings . . . made them rise and fall as if in slow motion, and swoop and glide almost like birds.*

Jim flew into Saigon's Tan Son Nhut airport on 9 February, the eve of the annual Tet celebrations, sitting beside a dignitary whom he took to be the British Ambassador; reserve and courtesy prevailed, leaving the matter unresolved. 'Novelist not journalist?' probed the immigration clerk, and with a grin he gave the reassurance sought. A rickety taxi took him into town, in close proximity with the driver's inquisitive family, and dropped him off at the Continental Palace Hotel, once the choice of André Maurois and Graham Greene. His room on the second floor was high-ceilinged and shaded by shutters, and looked out on to a three-sided square of leafy tamarind trees and the heavily fortified theatre which housed the National Assembly of South Vietnam. Erhendorf, for the moment, was banished, and at his elbow once more was Dupigny. *[He] remembered Saigon mornings, waking in a vast airy room, treading the waxed tiles of the Continental's long corridors which had a special, indefinable smell of France about them, on the way to a quiet inner courtyard to a breakfast of coffee and croissants . . .*

In Saigon the American presence was strong, despite much-publicised cuts of $300 million in US military aid. From Singapore Jim had pictured the city as about to fall, but the lax airport security and quantity of American military aircraft on the tarmac spoke otherwise, and on the spot he felt secure. Substituting British insignia and 1940s transport, rephrasing conversations into clipped tones and dated jargon as he waited for the menu, he ordered supper, downed with local 33 beer, on the open hotel terrace he recognised from *The Quiet American*; the war correspondents referred to it as 'the Continental Shelf'. Black-haired girls in ao-dais solicited with transatlantic slang and mutilated beggars in battledress shuffled up, while a child amputee with a stump severed at the shoulder tackled another boy in one-armed kung-fu. 'Being raised three or so feet off the street level,' he noted laconically, 'one feels as if one is watching a show from a balcony.' Saigon reminded him of Casablanca, and at the river end of Rue Tu Do – Greene's Rue Catinat to Jim – was a second, even larger, Majestic Hotel. The streets were thronged with scooters, bicycles and US military trucks, and on all sides gaudy decorations celebrated the public holiday of Tet. The name of the coming year, recalling Tiffany, Mappin, Rameses and Pussimodo, was the Year of the Cat.

Lacy Wright welcomed his call, and Jim extended his stay by four days, a decision clinched by warnings in the *Saigon Post* that the long-awaited Red Offensive might coincide with the anniversary of the 1968 Tet attack, which he had watched in televised close-up in New York. Closer inspection showed that the South Vietnamese Army was on full alert, public buildings were guarded by troops and civil service holidays had been cut, but newspaper reports of the latest local shellings and sabotage were carried beside advertisments for films, with prominence given to the opening of four new luxury cinemas. Twice Jim bought a 500-piastre ticket, justifying attendance as siege mentality research, and the newsreel footage of President Thieu distributing Tet gifts to SVA soldiers confirmed his opinion that the communist threat was being exaggerated to persuade Congress to relent. Tucking into *salade niçoise* and *boeuf à la corse*, he concentrated upon a gross American sitting at the bar who was fondling a Vietnamese girl. 'He must have been about 50, bald, and with a very thick chest and stomach and thin bent legs hooked on to a foot-rail. He looked very like a frog.'

Jim's French was useful, but Lacy spoke fluent Vietnamese. 'In a lot of ways, Lacy reminds me of Claude,' he recorded his train of thought, 'particularly in his air of good-natured resignation . . . plus a conservative *muflerie*.' Lacy brought along his assistant, Thé-Anh Cao, who offered to show Jim around, and the embryo character of Dupigny filled out and developed a sexual taste for little girls, a tilt at Claude's medical speciality of paediatrics. 'A Monsieur who hangs about outside the Lycée Marie-Curie at noon to watch the young girls coming out,' he jotted. 'Thé-Anh says the élèves christened him Monsieur Marie Curie.' With Lacy and Thé-Anh as his guides he was taken behind the scenes, one day to a restaurant entered through an unmarked door which was run by a retired French mercenary, another to lunch in the American Embassy that was so familiar from televised scenes of the earlier mayhem, and was now encased in an outer wall of rocket-shield. As Jim left, after shaking hands with the deputy ambassador and a leisurely tour, there was no premonition that he would be seeing the embassy in frenzied news clips once again, within ten short weeks.

The Cercle Sportif was an old colonial club with an Olympic-sized pool, much in demand by the contemporary élite, and there Jim was introduced to Général André Tran van Don, the Vice-Premier Ministre. As a student in Paris on the outbreak of the Second World War, the urbane Eurasian had volunteered for the French army and won the Croix de Guerre, only to be captured by the Nazis and made a prisoner of war. In Vietnam he had led the successful coup in 1963 against President Diem. 'He was wearing bathing trunks (when we met; not when he led the coup). A very jovial fellow, given to chasing women. TA approached him to ask for New Year money: he immediately fished a red envelope out of his briefcase: it later proved to contain 500 piastres. In return the custom requires the recipient to wish the donor something. TA wished the *général* to become *Premier Ministre*. He then exchanged a cheerful word with me, complimented me on my *guide charmant* and moved on.'

But a taller French-trained soldier of the same vintage, tipped

as a regular patron of the tennis courts, failed to show. Jim ached
to study Général Doung Van Minh, known to Lacy and the
other Americans as Big Minh. Born in the upper Mekong Delta,
Big Minh had achieved early public acclaim under Diem's
presidency by leading a successful military campaign against
a terrorist sect, but his popularity had been viewed by the
government as a potential threat, leading to prompt sidelining
from troop command. A key player in the coup, he was said to
be the officer responsible for Diem's assassination, but after
taking control as head of the Military Revolutionary Council he
had been deposed by a counter-coup, and exiled for five years.
He was understood to be waiting in the wings, keeping physically fit for the challenge, until the time was ripe for a third force,
neither Communist-led nor associated with President Thieu. Jim
considered that if anyone was taking a jolting passage over the
switched points of history, it was certainly Big Minh.

On the last night in Saigon, at a small party on the patio of
the *Time* bureau chief, Peter Ross Range, who was a friend of
Lacy, Big Minh came within his sights, and through borrowed
binoculars, in magnification, he watched the *général*'s hospitality, while simultaneously appreciating the *Balkan Trilogy*
flavour of the evening. Range's guests included the deputy
Papal Nuncio, 'a cheerful Portuguese we addressed as Mon-
seigneur, very hot in his ecclesiastical shirt and jacket until we
persuaded him to strip off and dine in shirtsleeves like the rest
of us'; a thick-set young Tory from the British Embassy, 'upper-
class, right-wing and quite pleased with himself'; a slinky
Vietnamese siren, and the Reuters correspondent David Laulicht with his well-read French wife, Martine. Delicious food
was handed around by an elderly Vietnamese with a sensitive
face who seemed oddly familiar and, just before leaving Saigon,
Jim realised why. 'I saw him again this morning. He's one of
the waiters at the hotel.'

In Kuala Lumpur, stopping off on the flight to Singapore, Jim
met L at the Majestic and rented a white Hertz Volkswagen to
reach the most recommended source on the New Zealand High
Commission list: a retired planter named Perkins. But Perkins
was away – 'the only stroke of ill-luck so far' – and to get full
value from the rental charge they drove on together to the east

coast, where he risked a repeat of the Mexican experience by taking a swim in the white-tipped breakers, and won. The elements, however, were about to snatch back the initiative.

In Singapore Jim took a late-afternoon cruise from Clifford Pier on a Port of Singapore Authority boat, and was standing on deck lost in admiration of the view – 'the duck-egg blues and greens of the water' – when sparks and debris rained down on the rail and the emergency siren began to blast. The boat lost way, the lights and loudspeaker failed and passengers began fighting for the lifebelts. 'I didn't join,' he mused afterwards, 'either through an elaborate anti-herd snobbism, or from a just appreciation of the lack of danger, most likely a mixture of both.' In the tropical twilight he watched as the boat was manoeuvred back to the pier, a tug lashed to one side and a fire-boat to the other. 'I was an hour and a half late getting back to where L was waiting at the Lovers Bar. It caused me to reflect a bit, though, that in a similar situation . . . I might be at greater risk than more modest and realistic people.' Retelling the tale, he invariably said he would have gone down with the boat if it had come to that. 'But why not escape?' 'Because I could never swim so far, and it was obvious there weren't enough lifebelts to go round.'

But did fatalism stem from lassitude, or lassitude from fatalism? Ducking the conundrum, Jim scrapped the planned journey on to Indonesia, although he had intended to see Java, where his father had worked as a young man. He cut short his Far Eastern stay, repeating the pattern of the Indian reconnaissance despite the fact that the Singapore tome threatened to be twice as long, and booked an early flight home for 27 February. And once again, as with the discovery of Hari's personality in the Ajanta caves, the wan period of relinquishment brought the structural breakthrough that he still sought. Re-absorbed by Matthew Webb as he threaded his way between sailors from the visiting US aircraft carrier *Enterprise* who were behaving like men on shoreleave in 1940 – 'shouting, swearing, drinking and vomiting in Bugis Street' – he suddenly glimpsed the solution to loose ends in the plot.

'Before [Matthew] finds the Chinese to hide [Vera] they have a terrible row that seems to split them permanently.' 'She might claim that her mother surrendered to her father, an ancient Chinese smallholder, for a few dollars to send to her parents starving in Harbin.' 'She is a Eurasian, of course; that would be the reason the Blackett girls won't have anything to do with her.' '~~Russian~~ Chinese father, ~~Chinese~~ Russian mother or vice versa, rather. Claims her mother was a white Russian princess. She did something in Shanghai which displeased the Japanese.' 'Matthew, having failed with Joan, finds an old Chinese to hide her. In Changi he hears of hooded informers and mass killings of Chinese and assumes the worst but in 1943 while on a working party on the aerodrome a Chinese presses a tiny parcel on him containing two cooked mice and a lump of sugar; and he reflects that perhaps, after all, at whatever terrible cost, she would survive and so would he.'

Making safe his Boots Ringplan notebook, with only forty-nine of the eighty pages filled, Jim spent the 36-hour stopover in Moscow with Brigid Allen, as arranged in advance to tie in with her route back from India. They explored the city on foot, but she was to be edited out of the anecdote about landing in the middle of a Moscow winter wearing light tropical clothes. 'You can do anything,' he used it to emphasise his point, 'if it's mind over matter.'

Within a couple of weeks of Jim's return to London it became clear from the emergency news flashes from Vietnam that while he had been strolling around Saigon, Communist troops had been pouring down the Ho Chi Minh Trail. In mid-March a three-division assault through the Central Highlands turned into a rout, and within ten days half a million people were in flight, while in a second prong, in a blitzkrieg down along the coast, Hué fell on 26 March, and Da Nang within four days. In his quiet room in Egerton Gardens Jim kept track as Saigon was encircled and André Tran van Don promoted, not to Prime Minister, but to Minister of Defence. The timing was eerie, given the development of his book. *Such was the swiftness with which the Japanese followed up their attacks throughout the campaign that [General Percival] knew he could not count on more than a week's grace before they launched their attack on Singapore Island itself. There was so much to be done, so little time in which to do it.*

President Thieu resigned on 12 April, with Phnom Penh abandoned the same day and the American Ambassador, whom Jim instantly recognised, pictured running for a chopper with the US flag. Saigon was invested, its situation hopeless, and by 28 April sixteen Red divisions were ranged around the city, within five miles of the Continental Palace Hotel. Tan Son Nhut airport, where he had taken reassurance from the low level of security, was overrun, and Big Minh was installed as President, the third within eight days. 'Citizens, brothers, patriots!' exhorted Minh in his clouded hour of triumph. 'In these difficult hours I can only beg of you one thing: be courageous, do not abandon the country, do not run away.' But within two days US helicopters were landing on the Embassy roof that Jim could recall so well, and lifting off fully laden, rotor blades tilted towards the 7th Army Fleet offshore. Outside the compound those who were being abandoned fought and struggled to get in.

Again the crowd pressed forward, pinning Matthew's arms to his sides and squeezing the air out of his lungs. He at last managed to free an arm and reach out towards Vera . . . but as he did so he saw the back of her reddish-black hair vanish beneath the thrusting mob. In a rage he shoved his way through the crowd to where he had seen her go down, shouting at people to stand back from her. But nobody seemed to hear. As he groped for her on the ground his hand closed over a piece of wood and he picked it up, flailing about with it until he had driven everyone back from where she lay . . . To the north the thud of guns continued. The Japanese assault on the island was only a few minutes away.

It would transpire that Lacy stayed to the end to help evacuate politically compromised high-risk Vietnamese, and in one press account he was described as visibly distressed at having to leave so many without connections behind. In the last hours he risked his own escape to bring in a group of three cut off in the US Information Service compound, half a mile away. Big Minh was captured by the Communists and his imprisonment illuminated the fate of Matthew, Ehrendorf and Dupigny; when *The Singa-*

pore Grip was published Minh would still be indefinitely confined. *In the weeks, then months, then years that followed . . . Matthew found that his world had suddenly shrunk. Accustomed to speculate grandly about the state and fate of nations he now found that his thoughts were limited to the smallest of matters – a glass of water, a pencil, a handful of rice. Hope had deserted him completely. It came as a surprise to him to realise how much he had depended on it before.*

Over 400,000 civil servants, doctors, lawyers, teachers, journalists and academics were to be consigned to 're-education' concentration camps under the Hanoi regime, but the provisional Minister of Defence resurfaced smartly in America. Indeed, something of the opportunistic Joan Blackett had gleamed that day at the Cercle Sportif. Jim, like all newspaper readers, saw the classic photograph that encapsulated the final moments of the fall of Saigon: anguished figures queueing on a rooftop stairway and an American CH-46 helicopter lifting off, as the man at the front of the queue clawed upwards and a passenger, safely on board, reached down a muscular arm. The panic-stricken escapee would be identified as the Vietnamese head of the secret police, and the man snugly aboard as that consummate survivor, Général André Tran van Don. *At long last they began to near the dock gates and could even make out the funnels of the* Felix Roussel *silhouetted against the pink glow of the night. Suddenly a rickshaw loomed out of the darkness . . . Matthew, astonished, just had time to glimpse Joan sitting in it amidst a pile of luggage while Ehrendorf, stripped to the waist and streaming with sweat, galloped on as best he could between the shafts.*

In London, life reverted to normal pace: a plodding round of writing, rewriting and research. In May 1975 Ehrendorf's Second Law came into effect for Jim in the form of a personal taste of the capitalist squeeze: the five-year lease on his flat expired and his monthly rent cheques began to be returned. Suspecting the mechanisms of eviction, although the law was on his side, he lodged each cheque with his solicitor, and kept to the contractual terms. He was in a grip of his own making, he realised with unease, as he needed at least two years more to complete and sell his typescript. The same month he was invited to appear on

Robert Robinson's book programme. When he watched it with his brother Richard and sister-in-law Lindy, who had a colour television in their London flat, he was aghast at how round-shouldered he looked. Defensively, he began referring to himself as the Hunchback of Hyde Park.

'I have no news at all as I've been working away and refusing all invitations in an effort to get my book under control. This has been hard to do in the sunny weather, with the added inconvenience that they've been tearing up the road in Egerton Gardens and much of the day is taken up with drillings and hammerings.' . . . 'I've been working hard, having found that most of what I'd written was unsatisfactory and a new return to page one was indicated. Writing a novel has a lot in common with snakes and ladders, as I've probably said before.' In the evenings he read Turgenev, and visitors found him polite but remote. 'You could always see a little bit of agitation,' said Alan Cumming, who dropped in occasionally if a light showed.

'I don't feel I accomplished anything,' Jim wrote of 1975, 'except hopelessly to complicate my Singapore novel with everything but what it really needs: viz. some believable characters and a sensible plot. Old age comes on apace . . . My novel lies on top of me, something like a large boulder on top of a beetle, and I wonder whether I'll ever manage to roll it off and start living again.' A friend driving beside Hyde Park spotted him running near the Serpentine, white hair streaming in the wind, and he strode unseeingly past another late at night, swathed in coat and scarf, clearly in a different world. As the strain mounted Jim pushed up his daily exercise, diagnosing distance fatigue and loss of 'grip' on detail as the main danger from sustaining a state of imaginative overdrive. He was beginning to hate the constricting 'robotic sensation' of being a writing machine. 'How *boring* it is,' he frequently lamented. Asked by the Society of Authors to join the selection committee for their travel bursary, he saw no decent way out of accepting. 'I'd prefer to be awarded it,' he noted absently, 'than dish it out.'

Twenty years after polio, a deterioration in his health was becoming evident to observers, as well as to Jim. He was used to the reduced vital capacity and diminished oxygen intake, but the damage done to his diaphragm and intercostal muscles was taking a greater toll. He slept propped high with pillows to ease his breathing, and Yvonne Wall's professional scrutiny took note of the early signs of untreatable scoliosis, which indicated that his spine would gradually curve as a result of weakened muscle support. As he became round-shouldered and concave-chested extra pressure would be put on his lungs, which would cause his heart to enlarge. She kept her counsel, since nothing could be done. Jim did his best to ignore the increase in colds and chest infections and attributed symptoms to the usual depression associated with finishing a book, but he bought himself a new writing chair with a high back for neck support, explaining it away as an irresistible bargain from Maples winter sale. In spite of his breathing difficulties, he had begun smoking a pipe and favoured a blend of Escudo tobacco and Balkan Sobranie.

Ehrendorf's Second Law held true. Jim still took reassurance from knowing that Tony Godwin was, at most, a letter or a phone call away, and he was encouraged to hear that Tony had adjusted sufficiently to be making plans for a New York imprint of his own. But in the spring of 1976 came the news that he had died of an asthma attack, and that his body had remained undiscovered for two days. Fittingly, Tony had taken some promising typescripts home to read, and when found he was still holding one in his hand. Jim put his grief into *The Singapore Grip*, as Tony would have appreciated, and ascribed to Walter Blackett *a real pang of sorrow, that painful sense of absence, of being deserted almost, when someone whose life has been closely intertwined with your own suddenly disappears.*

When informed that his apparently indestructable housemaster at Rossall, Harry McNair, was dead, he replied with a trace of the Major's disorientation at the end of the First World War. 'Altogether this has been a poor year. My New York editor, an Englishman not much older than myself to whom I was much attached . . . was followed by the novelist Richard Hughes, whom I greatly liked and respected. Hughes and his wife, both apparently in splendid form, had had supper with me a bare couple of months earlier . . . It comes as a particular shock when people so alert and so animated disappear.' *And slowly a peculiar feeling stole over Matthew, almost like a premonition of disaster. All the different matters, both in his own personal life*

and outside it, which had preoccupied him in the past few weeks
and even years . . . all these things now seemed to cling together,
to belong to each other and to have a direction and an impetus
towards destruction which it was impossible to resist. He read
Jung's *Memories, Dreams, Reflections* and dreamed on two
consecutive nights of separation and loss.

In the first dream he was with a group of people near the coast
and a cross-country run was proposed to a pub where there was
a photographer. 'When the parties rejoined . . . I was moved to
see my father [who looked] tired and old; as I went to him he
explained that he was helping Uncle Will [who] was much older
and more spent than himself. I interpreted this as meaning that
differences of age and birth-date have no meaning; that we are
all contemporaries and must help and be part of each other . . . It
occurred to me [that] the photographer referred to a wish to
leave some trace or record of ourselves, though perhaps it was
suggested by a sense of shame at wanting to be a well-known
writer – vanity in other words.' The second dream needed no
analysis, since it confronted him directly with his father's decline. 'I dreamed I was in a cinema with my parents, watching
Kubrick's *A Clockwork Orange* . . . Then my father and I were
travelling down towards the exit in a lift; at first all was normal,
but then the direction of the gravity-pull seemed to change, with
the result that the floor . . . I was standing on became the
bottom, that on which my father was standing the side. I had
to support him on my shoulder, which was not difficult [but] he
was perplexed and kept asking which direction we were going
in.'

Tony's death, and the manner of it, affected Jim profoundly.
'Oh dear, does one get wiser [about pain in others] as one get's
older? *Yes, one does*,' he answered his own question savagely.
The Mahons were asked to supper and found only one other
guest, a middle-aged neighbour who had just been widowed.
'We had no idea of grief of that dimension till then,' recounted
Derek's wife Doreen, 'and the poor man sat there weeping while
Jim stirred pots tactfully in the kitchen. Instead of avoiding him,
as most people would have done, Jim knew he needed to talk and
provided a young couple to bring back happier times. "You
remind me of my wife," the man told me when he left.' The death

from lung cancer of Elizabeth Bowen in 1973, when Jim was still buoyed by her perceptive review of *Troubles*, had pointed up mortality, and when Sonia Orwell, ill and broken by anxiety, left London for an isolated bedsitter in Paris, he kept up support by post. 'Old people are terribly defenceless,' he noted angrily on her departure.

The Siege of Krishnapur had been criticised for portraying the sepoys as cannon-fodder; now compassion fleshed out his miniature portraits, shaped by the silence from Communist-held Vietnam. On impulse in Saigon, viscerally moved by their unity in misfortune, Jim had given an elderly couple helping each other along, arm in arm, a couple of hundred piastres – 'i.e. about 30 cents, big deal', he had punished himself at the time. What was their fate under the harsh Vietcong regime? *The starlight glints on the silver wings of the Japanese bombers . . . In one cubicle, not much bigger than a large wardrobe, an elderly Chinese wharf-coolie lies awake . . . It was here beside him that his wife died and sometimes, in the early hours, she returns to be with him for a little while . . . Later, when official estimates are made . . . there will be no mention of this old man for the simple reason that he, in common with so many others, has left no trace of ever having existed either in this part of the world or in any other.* Throughout 1976 the writing and rewriting was interminable, and he found a good use for his parents' garden in Oxfordshire. 'There's three days' work going up in smoke,' he commented acidly one day as they stood together watching the flames. His pipe-smoking increased in tempo with the writing,

In September 1976 Jim joined Bridget O'Toole, who was on holiday at her parents' home in Cornwall, bringing with him a finished manuscript of 950 pages. She read it and approved, assuring him that few cuts were needed. Now all that remained to be done was the publishing deal. Diana Saville showed him the printed contracts favoured by her company, Gary Arnott warned against negativity, and Jim unblushingly consulted Deborah Rogers, asking for – and getting – her advice. Instead of circulating his manuscript, he sent out copies of the first two books of the trilogy, accompanied by a letter announcing the imminent completion of the third, and invited tenders for autumn 1978 publication.

The Bodley Head responded first, proposing a meeting without commitment on either side but, tipping his hat to childhood recollections of *Uncle Billy Possum*, he was immune to sentiment. 'I shall want to decide things mainly . . . on objective criteria,' he responded with a hint of steel, 'rather than on personal contact.' After a brief and inexpensive holiday in Venice he returned to the fray in mid-June, and set the week ending 3 July as his closing date. Cautiously he renewed contact with Weidenfeld because John Curtis, whom he liked, had been appointed editor of Tony's old province, the General List. 'I'm aware of the difficulties of producing a book of these nineteenth-century dimensions . . . Other things being roughly equal, however, I'd prefer in the interests of continuity to be published by you again . . . What interests me most are: a) the number of copies in the first printing. b) the projected price, on the assumption that you would (i) have no share in any paperback sale. (ii) that you would have the same share as with *Krishnapur*. c) and, of course, the advance in either case . . . If you *are* interested I should prefer to conduct negotiations by post rather than viva voce.' The Bodley Head were informed of identical terms. 'If you are still interested,' Jim signed off, 'I shall leave in a copy to your office before the end of the week.'

The brisk tone gave no indication of his real feelings, which were of despair and dread. His father's health was giving serious cause for concern, so much so that he had been admitted to hospital in Oxford. 'I still feel shattered,' he wrote as negotiations limped along, 'not just by the prospect of his death but by the way [it] is likely to happen [which is] the slow and progressive collapse of everything as his nervous system packs up . . . Thank Heaven I finished my book before his illness became apparent. I've lost all ability to concentrate on anything for more than a minute or two at a time.' Wandering out of Harrods Food Hall, consumed by anxiety, he cannoned into Olivia Manning, who promptly shielded a plastic bag. 'It's William Gerhardie's ashes,' she chided. Taking her arm, he accompanied her to Queen Mary's rose garden in Regent's Park, where Gerhardie, whose work had influenced his own, had stipulated his ashes should be scattered in his will. Just before leaving, Jim would subsequently maintain, he felt a hand on his ankle as a ghostly presence sought to detain him, and simultaneously he tripped and fell. On 22 July The Bodley Head bid came in. It was couched in flattering terms, expressing unanimous admiration for his writing, but the print run and advance were low, and the paperback terms – left open – had been discussed with Penguin behind his back. Fifty pages, at least, would need to be cut for the 'ideal' selling price, and doubt was expressed about libel. By return, Jim declined. 'For the record, and quite incidentally, I'm shocked that you should have shown [it] to Penguin without mentioning it to me. This seems to me a decidedly slippery way to proceed.' Relations with The Bodley Head were therefore at an end, which left only Weidenfeld, for the moment. 'It's us against them,' he warned an aspiring writer.

John Curtis was spending a family holiday in Sorrento, where his hotel did not allow guests to make international calls. To communicate with the office he had to queue for an open coin box off the main street, and the negotiations were carried out against an Italian crescendo from eleven other booths. Straining to hear Jim's soft voice, John was forced to shout out points that were better put delicately, but agreement was struck over a £9,000 advance and a print run of 30,000; Jim's insistence on that point was based on the reasoning that unless a publisher needed to recoup the major investment of a large print run, little money would be put into marketing. Later the Literary Guild would buy _The Singapore Grip_, with a separate print run of 75,000, and when Fontana bought the paperback rights, outbidding Penguin, he reckoned his gamble had paid off. 'It already seems very distant and hardly by me at all,' he wrote of his book in February 1978. And on the strength of the book-club interest, he negotiated a contract with Weidenfeld and Nicolson for his next book that would give him £20,000 in advance.

In the run-up to publication the Saturday Review section of _The Times_ carried a full-page extract. He gave cautious interviews to BBC Radio 4 and the broadsheet newspapers, and sales quickly reached 8,000. But at a Weidenfeld booksigning at Heffers in Cambridge, which he shared with Edna O'Brien, Antonia Fraser and Marina Warner, he was nowhere to be seen, and Marina eventually discovered him out of sight behind the wooden counter, quietly sitting on the floor. 'There's no point, no point,' he told her. On the whole, he confided to his retired Rossall French master, G.M. Arthursen, he was stoical about everything except his writing. 'I think it has something to do with the constant dislocation between my intentions and what I actually manage to get down on paper.'

The Singapore Grip was published on 7 September 1978 and critics gave it their full attention. 'Pretty mediocre', Jim summed up. The huge canvas he had chosen was considered to have been beyond him, and his former lightness of touch was mourned. Praise was almost invariably conditional, although the *Daily Telegraph* was unstinting, elsewhere Olivia Manning put him on the same pedestal as Patrick White and Saul Bellow, and in the *New Statesman*, giving rise to one of his few snatches of unalloyed delight, the prize-winning young author Timothy Mo appeared to read his mind. 'The novel may be Farrell's private attempt at *War and Peace*,' saluted Mo. 'It is both a hilarious picture of the humanly ludicrous and an acute histor- ical analysis . . . Earnest, bespectacled Matthew, ridiculously in love, tormented by the antagonism between the brutal self- interest he sees all around him and the altruism he believes is possible . . . could be Pierre Bezukhov, and Singapore in flames evokes an earlier conflagration in another city. Tolstoy's philo- sophy of history was explicit and cordoned off in a special chapter; Farrell's is implicit, informing the book's structure, themes and development.' Joy at being accorded the feat that had been his driving force all along was swiftly disguised by wry comments on the fact that the *New Statesman* was the only one – until then – that had consistently derided him.

Jim was delighted by Mo's public eulogy, and simultaneously confirmed in his distrust of literary criticism in general. 'It's too early to call the book a success,' he corrected his old friend from Oxford, Martin Gilbert, who sent warm congratulations. 'Many of the reviews have been distinctly grudging, to put it mildly. But then books seem to me, like children, to have their own destinies: all one can do is to give them a good start in life. (Corn-pone philosophy no extra charge.)'

CHAPTER NINETEEN

A Tiny Bit World-Weary
1978–1979

After *The Singapore Grip* Jim was asked if he intended to write a sequel, as the omens in the principal love story were propitious and hinted at eventual reunion. 'Oh, I don't think so,' he said flatly. 'The relationship between Matthew and Vera would never last.' The same cynicism infused his annual re-unions with Roger Donald, who stopped over in London on his way back from the Frankfurt Book Fair in his capacity as editor-in-chief at Little, Brown in New York. A ritual had evolved of meeting for dinner, with Roger picking up the tab on his expense account and Jim choosing the restaurant. At the last moment in 1977 Jim phoned to ask if he could bring a date, and, reluctant but curious, Roger agreed. On arrival, Jim brusquely introduced his companion, Judith Wright, and the evening's acrimonious atmosphere was set. It was to be a repetition of the treatment of Judy Mitchell in the Irish cottage twenty years before, and similarly spun Roger through a variety of emotions.

'I was slightly jealous when I saw this wonderful girl,' he recounted, 'because I had always been more successful in that way. But every time she said anything Jim turned on her – if she agreed, that was wrong, and if she disagreed, she didn't know what she was saying. Before the dessert came she said to me, "Do you mind if I go home?" It was hell. As soon as she went I said what I thought. "Jesus Christ, Farrell, I wanted to talk to you and you insist on bringing a woman. She turned out to be very sweet and you were *abysmal*." He was apologetic. "Oh God, I can't stand these damn women. They're all after me. We'll repair the evening. Let's go back to my place." ' The rest of the night

was spent drinking and bickering, with Jim proposing that
Roger should publish *The Singapore Grip* in America and Roger
accusing him of taking the easy way out by simply moving
Krishnapur further east. He flew back to New York convinced
that Jim had never come to terms with his changed physical
appearance, despite his literary success. 'Why in God's name had
he brought that girl? To show his power? That had been my first
thought. This incredible display of bad manners, then this
reparation of *our* relationship afterwards. I had stopped being
angry because he'd wrecked the evening, and I just felt sad.'

At the announcement that a spirited young American to
whom he was attracted was about to get married, Jim joined
in the general congratulations and later took her to her taxi,
unable to hide an air of being abandoned. Ambiguity continued
to pull him in separate directions. 'It must be wonderful to be
married and have someone to talk over problems with,' he said
with heartfelt emphasis to Stephen Wall. To Brian and Rose
Knox Peebles, who had known him very nearly as long as
Stephen, he maintained his guard until the night he found Rose
alone when he rushed back to collect his macintosh. 'We were
about to talk,' she noted, 'and he was on the verge of a
confidence and then Brian came in and he stopped. I hadn't
felt as close to him for years.'

He mentioned Bridget O'Toole's name so often and so fondly
that many old friends were sure he loved her, and though six years
had gone by since she had left to build her own career they had
recently grown closer. He signed his letters 'lots of love'; wary, but
an improvement on the curt 'Love Jim' of the period when they
were lovers. 'She fitted him more than anyone else I knew,'
observed Malcom Dean regretfully, who was about to marry
again and wished Jim could find the same compatibility. But Jim,
for the moment anyway, saw it in different terms. 'I thought we'd
got [into] a more brother/sister relationship than the stormy time
of yesteryear, or perhaps it's old age and creeping Darby and
Joanism.' Suspicion of women had not been lessened by success;
rather, it had been reinforced. In *The Singapore Grip*, in every
case, it is the woman – even Vera, whom Matthew loves – who
with ulterior motive makes the first move.

Across a crowded room Jim gave no indication of trouble

ahead; on the contrary, he appeared confident and fancy-free. 'He was looking at a painting, wearing his dark grey dramatic hat,' a girl who worked at a West End art gallery described her first impression, gathered as she ran downstairs to greet arrivals. 'And then he turned suddenly and smiled up at me. The impact was electric.' At a Weidenfeld lunch, to which he invited her, he was enclosed immediately in a circle of admiring women. He could be amusing and charming, or his asperity set a challenge. Either way, ambivalence wove a spider's web invisible until too late.

Judith Wright, whose sensitive nature initially brought out his protectiveness, was exposed to both types of behaviour. Impatience, stoked by irritation at her wealthy background, was the aspect most often shown in public. One evening he turned up with her at a small dinner party and proceeded to ignore her. Patricia Moynagh, an outspoken artist who was sitting opposite, decided to put him in his place. 'Didn't it get the Faber Prize?' she said without interest when *The Siege of Krishnapur* was mentioned. 'Something like that,' he drawled. Patricia talked across him for the rest of the evening, except for a brief exchange about opera. 'I *hate* opera,' he said, and turned away, leaving with Judith shortly afterwards. 'I hope you don't mind,' whispered her host when Patricia left to get her coat a couple of hours later, 'but he asked for your phone number and I gave it to him.' Jim took her to the Étoile, and his opening line was of demarcation. 'I just saw Judith,' he informed her, 'and said I was going to take you out to dinner.'

Patricia was socially deft and generous, with a Roedean accent and a surface imperiousness that he lacked. His request that she sew a button on his coat was met with laughter – 'I thought you were liberated, Jim' – but the balance was in his favour all along. That Christmas she accompanied him to Paris and he quoted Arthur Waley's Chinese love poems to her, which Matthew Webb also found *extraordinarily moving*, and on Christmas Day she gave him a green jersey. He wore it whenever he was pleased with her, drawing attention to its presence, but as they walked hand in hand in the Luxembourg Gardens he remarked casually, 'If I married anyone, it would be Bridget.'

Patricia's assertiveness was gradually whittled away, although

Jim still wore the green jersey occasionally, encouraged her to paint a mural in his bathroom, squired her about London and accompanied her to Italy twice on holiday, often speculating about living with her there. 'That's not how Judith would behave,' he was liable to snap and, like Sandy before her, she learned to be on her guard. 'I felt that I was only exclusive to him in that he hadn't time to see anyone else,' she described the sensation. 'I didn't believe he was having an affair with anyone, but he might well have been.' Aware that she found the opening of her exhibitions as great an ordeal as he found book promotion, he helped her to prepare a forthcoming one in Oxford as tenderly as she could have wished, and the last-minute notification that he would not be beside her on the dreaded first night, but instead cycling with Judith in Normandy, came as a shock.

The end of the affair was dragged out by a bewildering six-month pause, and she eventually found herself included again, recast in the role of treasured friend, in the dinner parties she knew so well. With mixed feelings she observed a pretty guest present him with an identical box of Thornton's truffles to the one she had bought on her first invitation, two years before. In *The Singapore Grip*, however, Jim played fair. On the wall of the home of Joan Blackett's younger sister, Kate, in the final pages, hangs *a charming painting by Patricia Moynagh of a curled up cat*, and the mysterious man nearby, presumed to be Kate's husband, wears *a green sweater . . . (we can see part of its sleeve) and that is all there will be of him until he decides to put down the newspaper.*

Ann Colville was Canadian, the daughter of the painter Alex Colville, and Jim met her through Hans and Monika, whose ground-floor Chelsea flat she rented. Soon he began turning up at the Fischer Fine Art gallery, off St James, where she was the administrator, and where Hans and Michael Leonard exhibited. 'If he could be difficult, I could be too,' she described their labyrinthine relationship. 'When he wanted me, I was looking elsewhere, and when I turned around, he wasn't there. If I did get close to him, he'd get nervous, so he'd blow hot and cold. If only we'd been *in sync*! We went out together, on and off, but it was not exclusive.' She was closest to Jim during 1977 and 1978 – 'I remember eating at a Chinese restaurant *crying* with laughter' – which implies that Patricia's instincts were correct.

'You felt he noticed what you wore,' said Susannah Clapp, who got to know him in 1978. 'I dressed up a lot then – black lacy stockings, black silky things – and I sensed that wasn't irrelevant.' She was a reader and editor with Jonathan Cape, wrote a radio column for the *Sunday Times* and tutored Americans in creative writing, a resourceful combination he admired. 'You're not someone who would be up to your arms in flour,' he told her approvingly, unable to forget the image of Hilary Kirwan in Dublin so many years before. Frequently a couple of weeks went by when they did not see each other, but there were moments when she felt she was constantly getting a taxi to Egerton Gardens – 'It was always that way around as he was such a good cook' – or setting off with him for parties. At a Weidenfeld evening Olivia Manning hobbled up with the aid of her walking stick and looked them both over. 'Oh well,' she said meaningfully to Jim, 'I'm sure you're much better now you've got a nice girlfriend.' But the assumption was wide of the mark. A single kiss outside the Brompton Oratory while waiting for a taxi had confirmed for Susannah that she did not find him sexually attractive, something she knew he instantly picked up. She thought of him as one of the most solitary people she knew, despite his attention to friendship and the number of times he entertained. 'Even his voice', she said once, 'was veined with melancholy.'

Janet Watts, who wrote for the *Guardian*, had known him now, without involvement, for ten years. 'What he would have loved', she believed, 'was a marriage that had already evolved through the agonies to the stage of sitting on each side of the fire without having to talk, both contentedly reading. But it was impossible for any woman to see it through to the peaceful reaches beyond. She would have had to be mature beyond her years, both strong and independent.' One by one, each girlfriend found herself exiled to friendship, and of necessity accepted the arrangement. 'Jim was an innately confident person who pretended to be a fall guy,' complained one casualty. 'The baby bird who had fallen out of the nest was, to me, the tough rugby player underneath.' But Jim believed the same to be true of women in reverse – *Her delicate appearance notwithstanding, Joan's tender womanhood was clad in a tough hide* – and was reacting out of self-defence. Asked for advice by a friend whose girlfriend had become pregnant when he was on the point of leaving her for someone else, he did not hesitate. 'Jim's argument was that I was morally obliged to marry her, that was when I hit the moral granite bottom of him. It was very clear that he honoured marriage and was terrified of it. I suddenly felt he could never get married himself; he saw it as far too serious, and he was also too idealistic.'

The granite layer blocked off his own choices, too. Sporadic love-making with 'his' callgirl had continued until her marriage, for which she had asked him to be best man. He had helped to choose her wedding outfit and asked the couple back to Egerton Gardens afterwards for a drink. A row ensued over the behaviour of another guest, with whom the bridegroom sided. Left alone together, Jim had treated her to a good dinner out and accompanied her to the pre-paid honeymoon suite. 'I felt it was a terrible waste, as it was so expensive,' she recounted. 'I asked Jim in, saying my husband would stay away that night. But though he was dying to, in the end he didn't. I was now married. So it was out of the question.'

On his return from Singapore Jim had found a letter waiting from the American director of *The Purple Plain*, Robert Parrish, enquiring about the film rights to *The Siege of Krishnapur*, and as Parrish and his wife, Kathie, lived around the corner at 23 Egerton Terrace the three rapidly became good friends. Bob's interest in the book had dropped by the time Lean's rights lapsed, but Jim was understanding, and *The Singapore Grip* was dedicated to them jointly. Big and expansive, a generation ahead and exuding humour and vitality, Bob Parrish, to him, was Hollywood personified in its most agreeable shape. As a child Bob had appeared in Charlie Chaplin's *City Lights*, and John Ford had been best man at his wartime wedding to Kathie. He had won an Oscar, directed Robert Mitchum, Rita Hayworth, Jack Lemmon, Orson Welles, James Mason and Peter Sellers, and worked, coincidentally, with David Lean. In 1960 Sam Spiegel had lured him to Europe for *Dangerous Silence* and, liking the ambience, he had stayed on, buying a Swiss chalet in Klosters and taking out a long lease on the London house. As Jim's relationships with women became more tortuous, his friendship with Bob burgeoned to fill the gap. His language became more ribald and Bob aired his philosophical side, but whereas Bob threw his life wide open, Jim kept most compartments bolted shut.

The gregarious Parrishes had been to Pamplona with Ernest Hemingway; their favourite companions were Katharine Hepburn, James Jones and Irwin Shaw. '[Irwin] made a great fuss of me over the S of K,' Jim, too, was soon recording, 'which pleased me as I used to be a fervent admirer of his in Gwanda and Balholm days . . . He's a very nice rather bibulous-looking fellow, more like a lorry-driver in appearance than a man of letters.' Art Buchwald was an old friend of the Parrishes, as was Eric Ambler, and their guestroom was a home from home for Hollywood stars: Kirk Douglas was shorter than Jim imagined, Deborah Kerr more talkative and Gregory Peck less smooth. 'Jim was easy,' Kathie complimented. 'he would just fit in like a glove.' On the night he sat up late with Bob and Lindsay Anderson, whose film *If* had reminded him of Rossall, she could hear them laughing downstairs until she fell asleep. In one bound he had leapt beyond the exclusively literary world.

When Harcourt Brace Jovanovich in New York published Bob's autobiography, *Growing Up in Hollywood*, Jim had made a point of introducing him to Tony Godwin, who was appointed editor. Over the American edition of *The Singapore Grip* Bob returned the favour and, not entirely seriously, proposed his own agent, the legendary Irving 'Swifty' Lazar. Swifty, whose nickname stemmed from making five major deals for Humphrey Bogart in one day, was notorious for working only with winners and Jim scoffed at the idea. Unknown to him, though, his name was already known; as was – more importantly – a cash incentive for taking him on.

After a disastrous theatre preview in Boston earlier that year, David Merrick and Roger Donald, in bad form as backers, had retreated to a restaurant accompanied by Swifty Lazar. Bristling over the unspoken charge of bad judgement, Merrick had turned to Roger and demanded to know which book he most regretted not having taken up. '*The Siege of Krishnapur*,' replied Roger absently as he glanced through the wine list, adding that it was about India so bound to be unfilmable. 'You're wrong,' hissed

Merrick, still combative. 'Every studio has millions of rupees tied up in India.' A pair of eyes bored into Roger and for the first time Swifty spoke. 'Who did you say it was by?' When Roger came to hear that Swifty had become Jim's American agent he put two and two together, and was appalled. 'I reckon he chose Swifty out of perversity. He hated agents so much! Swifty was a *dumb* choice. Why take the worst? The guy never read more than a menu in his life.'

Bob set up the meeting at his house, and Jim signed on. He longed for a film deal, had nothing to lose, and above all relished the paradox in having a celebrity agent in Beverly Hills. 'Swifty's going to make me the Big Dollar,' he liked to toss into a conversational lull, and he delighted in weaving surreal stories about a Mafia-type gangster which ended with the punchline 'and he's my agent!'. In the flesh, the tiny seventy-year-old with the heavy glasses was polite and mild, talking respectfully of the 'lit'rary field' and 'our book', and saying 'us' and 'we', rather than 'you' or 'I', which persuasively gave the impression of a team. Jim was enchanted by the performance, and at one of Swifty's London forays he was asked to lunch at the Ritz at 2pm, a curious hour. 'Anyway, there was I in good time,' he recounted with satisfaction, 'and eventually Swifty came along and pumped my hand. 'I suppose you're hungry,' he said, 'and *do* want lunch? Okay.' We went into the dining room and the waiter said 'Did you leave something behind, Sir?' So I put him through a second three-course meal.'

Meanwhile Jim was forming a working relationship with another of Bob's friends, the French film director Bertrand Tavernier. Bert, as he now called him, had expressed interest in filming *Troubles*, and they were discovering a congenial approach to the script when Bob diverted them to the more immediate project of Robert Louis Stevenson's tale *Beach at Falesa*, to which he had bought the rights with his good friends Robert Mitchum and Richard Widmark in mind. Bob suggested a three-way collaboration – himself as director, Tavernier as producer and Jim as screenwriter; with Mitchum on board Gaumont agreed the backing, and funding was obtained to pay Jim the going rate of £200 a week. He was at a loose end and, for once, unthreatened by being between books; soon they were liaising every other day and sending the finished work to Paris for Tavernier's amendments.

'I am at the moment writing a screenplay for a film set in the South Pacific,' Jim sprang the surprise on Claude. 'It is an Anglo-French joint-production (French backing) and I am working in collaboration with a French director by the name of Bertrand Tavernier . . . who is quite successful over there I am told, although exactly why, I wonder a little . . . What is more likely, however, is that the film will in fact never be made, but I will still be paid so I don't care. Anyway, that is what happens to nineteen screenplays out of twenty.' Stevenson's story, written in Papua, New Guinea, and renamed by them *The Blackbirder* after a floating brothel, was about the doomed marriage of an island newcomer and a native woman, and packed with drunkenness and disaster. 'We laughed,' said Bob, 'and even the bad things were fun. He'd say, "This is not what they told me at Yale." "Who was your professor there?" I'd shout. "He's not directing the picture. I am!" Occasionally he'd say, "I think you are wrong about that." But not all Jim's friends were happy about the direction his writing career was taking. Margaret Drabble, in particular, made no secret of the fact that she considered it a mistake, and changed the subject whenever he brought it up.

In the summer of 1978 it became obvious that Gaumont were having second thoughts; Jim talked, without any real hope, of involving Stanley Kubrick. Eventually Bob was offered a picture in Europe and left to do it, sure that he would be making a movie with Jim another day. Tavernier had proceeded no further with *Troubles*, but Bo Widerberg, the Swedish director of *Elvira Madigan*, began scouting independently for Irish locations, and to Jim's surprise the talented young English composer Stephen Oliver sketched out his ambitions for the book. 'It is a novel which has excited and moved me greatly,' Oliver put the proposal formally on paper, 'and I very much wish to turn it into an opera . . .' Jim wrote back politely, explaining that he was tone deaf and 'therefore rather lack qualifications', but said he had no objections. 'A noble and quixotic enterprise to be sure,' he commented privately, used by now to grand schemes falling through.

A good deal of the enjoyment of working on *The Blackbirder* had stemmed from collaboration, the first since the post-Oxford sessions with Russell McCormmach, as well as from the sharing of responsibility. After eighteen years of intensive solitary writing Jim felt entitled to be – temporarily – off the leash. 'Smashing party the other evening. I saw Alison [Lurie] last night and we were marvelling over how good vegetarian food could be. On the way home I sat in a deserted tube carriage and read a copy of the *Daily Mail* that I found there; it said that two of my friends were splitting up from their respective lovers. London Transport provides quite a decent service when you think about it.' Margaret – Maggie – Drabble introduced him to Bertorelli's cheerful Italian restaurant in Notting Hill Gate, and at the Spurlings' he met Elizabeth David, his cookery idol, who approved his choice of wines; indirectly he learned afterwards that *The Siege of Krishnapur* was one of her favourite books.

But discontent with inaction was building up, and it began to show in little ways. Alison switched on his electric fire without asking one chilly evening, and he marched across and switched it off. 'Mind if I sit by it?' she rallied. The landlord's unabated determination to get him out was wearing him down, and the mischievous rumour that his writing was the cover for a spy, inspired by the timing of his trip to Saigon, amused him less with repetition; instead, it raised the awkward question of his next move. He could start a new book, he could remodel his external circumstances, or he could abandon the solitary lifestyle. In a conversation with Norma di Marco, a rare occurrence these days, he appeared to rule out one of the options when he told her that he did not think he would need the coffee cups she had always promised him as a wedding present, after all.

The prospect of an extra panel in the Imperial triptych, which he had mentioned in a *Guardian* interview to mark the launch of *The Singapore Grip*, had been floated without any certainty of subject. By now issues thrown up by the Angola situation had been examined and discarded, Marina Warner's husband William Shawcross had thrown light on Cambodia, and for a while the commercial tactics behind the long-running Banana War, in which Jamaica eventually broke the American monopoly, held promise. All were false trails. Jim considered the run-up to the independence of Mauritius in the sixties, and developments in the New Hebrides where self-determination approached, while on all sides he was urged to write a contemporary novel about South Africa. Nonie Niesewand, wife of a *Guardian* journalist, was asked to supper, but the ramifications of the ANC proved as uninspiring as those of the Khmer Rouge. There were negative aspects to 'selling futures' in his own work, as he had forewarned John Curtis lightly.

He looked again at an account of the capture of a British coaster by Chinese pirates in 1925. 'It struck me immediately that it would make a good narrative novel that would be quite fun to write,' he noted, 'part of the satisfaction would be that I could incorporate one or two of Uncle Dick's salty anecdotes.' But a personal meeting with his father's staunchly Conservative – 'rabid, indeed' – old friend Dick Roberts dissuaded him of the idea, and as he continued to cast around transience was brought again to his attention by the unexpectedness of the old man's death. 'He got up one morning at 6am, as old salts presumably will, and started writing a letter to my father full of enthusiasm for the sea-story, but adding . . . "Jim has a great gift and could do it splendidly, provided he keeps his left-wing ideas out of it." [He] then switched on the immersion heater, leaving the letter unfinished, made himself a cup of tea and went back to bed. When his sister went in at 9 to tell him his breakfast was ready she found that he had died in his sleep . . . For some reason his death reminded me a bit of Virginia Woolf's essay on Captain Marryat. Sailors may be better at shoving off than us land-lubbers.' It also brought home the urgent need to get cracking, as Dick Roberts would have put it.

The theme of spiritual colonisation fitted into sequence, and there was the catalyst of a medical hero, ready-made. Early in the summer of 1971 Hilary Spurling had bumped into Jim on the steps of the British Museum: he, after a morning at home, was on his way in to do some reading for *The Siege of Krishnapur* and she, after researching her biography of Ivy Compton-Burnett, was hurrying out. Full of excitement, she told him she had just discovered that Ivy's father had isolated the tubercular bacillus, but both were short of time and the encounter was brief. The casebook of Dr McNab, however, expanded and snapped shut. Shortly after Dick Roberts's death, although Jim had been resisting the idea of a second Indian novel for fear of being typecast, he mapped out the form his next book would take. 'This time set in a hill-station in the 1870s, featuring Dr McNab as anchor-man. Hilary, to whom I described it years ago in a fit of enthusiasm, reminds me of it every time I see her.'

During his research for the Residency padre Jim had come across the religious controversies that had threatened to tear apart the Victorian church, and the grouping of India, religion and medicine together made a potent combination. As a bonus, all three were minutely documented, and he had ventured towards the theme as long before as *The Lung* in the depiction of Martin Sands's insane fellow patient, Exmoore. *I was in the pulpit one day . . . going beautifully . . . there I was, thundering away and telling them that they should all love God and then . . . well, then I stopped bang in the middle of some gorgeous bit of rhetoric . . . It's just that I realised that I wanted them to love* me *not God. I didn't give a damn about God.*

As anchorman, McNab first needed a prompt to deflect his mind into a new channel, and – consumed by TB – a church minister evolved. Inheritor of Exmoore's bony, fanatical face and the tendency towards ritual and obsession, in every other way he was Exmoore's inversion, being unworldly and spiritual. A youthful interpreter of the age was also necessary, and Jim recalled his mother's stories of travelling out to India as a bride. Eighteen-year-old Emily appeared, as McNab's visiting niece. *No, not plain exactly. She's a good, healthy girl, perhaps a little on the plump side from shipboard lethargy . . . tired and longing for a bath but excited nevertheless to arrive in this strange town.* From the standpoint of his early forties he saw beyond the strong-willed parent to the well-meaning extrovert girl Jo had been – *This brave and independent way of thinking was one . . . of which her father would have approved. She could almost hear him say 'Stout girl!' . . . 'I have a little brother the same age as you at home . . .'* And for the first time since *The Lung* he confronted his own loss: he gave Emily a withered arm and the personality to make light of it.

There was a tinge of fatalism about the setting of the story. 'In Mussoorie in 1884 a lady auctioned kisses at Rs. 5 each at a Family Bazaar,' he had copied out in 1971 without use for such a detail, and now Dr McNab, married in middle-age to Fleury's sister, Miriam, and with an established general practice in Krishnapur, would head by train with his wife and the newly arrived Emily for the cool hill station of Simla, to spend the summer months writing a treatise based on his thirty years in India – *an attempt to distil some order from the chaos of a life's work in medicine* – and launching his niece into society. McNab's intention was to pin down the moral dimension which he sensed lay behind illness – *an instinct that all things were one, that everything was connected, that [it] was merely one of many fruits of an underground plant in the community as a whole* – but in his carriage, fatefully, would be the consumptive pastor of St Saviour's in Simla, on the way back from a Delhi reprimand over his fondness for High Church ceremonial.

Jim was encouraged by the expectation that his personal magic mountain would not be too difficult to recreate. He had already examined the Indian hill station of Mussoorie, from where he had glimpsed the poignant cemetery, and he had sufficient material in his files to cut out much of the customary hard work; despite the recent diversion with *The Blackbirder*, he was aware that the effort of completing *The Singapore Grip* had taken much more out of him than usual. But he intended, nevertheless, to confront committed Christians with non-believers, the idealistic with ambitious clerics who were intent on carving out a career, and to test the rational medical view against the power of faith. Instead of being a plain tale from the hills, his Simla was to be a forcing-ground where a variety of controversies would play themselves out, and every main religion would come under McNab's scrutiny in the search for the mystic element beyond the scope of practical medicine.

Through his new hero Jim was ready to put his own conclusions on record, and spurning orthodoxy and the Bible – *These happenings at a distant point of history in a land which he had never visited had always seemed to him so remote as to deny him any correspondence with his own experience* – he reached for the indelible image of his father in the Albert Hall. *He considered himself to be in the position of a man at a concert who is tone deaf. All around him people sit rapt as they listen to sounds which to him are meaningless.* He began to hint publicly that his next novel would be historical – 'But it may not be *very historical*' – and felt more comfortable back in harness. 'I feel uneasy if I don't write, or do something towards writing, every day, seven days a week,' he told one interviewer. 'If I have a cold I'm miserable. Yet even having a cold is a way of making sense out of life if you write fiction.'

As 1978 advanced Jim took London Transport's Piccadilly Line rush-hour tube from South Kensington to Holborn in the morning and exchanged it in his imagination for the single-gauge Simla railway of 100 years before, by which McNab would make his entrance. In the British Museum he assembled the streetscape and architecture of 1871 Simla with a town-planner's care, and from E.J. Buck's memoir took the shadowy outline of Mr J.W. Lowrie, hotel proprietor and founder of the Tonga Mountain Car Company, and gave him a new lease of life as master of ceremonies. *A plump, bright-eyed fellow with curling moustaches who liked to pretend that he knew everything about everything in the hills and in the plains, or, as he put it, 'between Heaven and earth'*. The instrumental cleric with his fits of coughing and blood-spotted handkerchief was named Kingston, after the railhead for Block Island, but the genesis for Jim's manipulative Bishop of Simla was considerably nearer to hand.

'We duly assembled yesterday afternoon at Dulwich College Chapel for the christening of your granddaughter, Miss Clare Farrell, by your nephew, the Rev. Tommy Farrell . . .' Jim wrote to his father on 29 January 1979. Tom Farrell still kept fit and preached the need for young people to take a strong hand, and at the christening he pointed out that successful athletes competed to win, so that was how everyone ought to see their Christian lives. 'You must aim to be the very best,' he instructed, as he always did, 'to grit your teeth, go all out and give what it costs.' The Bishop of Simla gazed back at Jim – *a handsome, powerfully built man . . . greatly liked and respected throughout his diocese for his jovial manner . . . He was energetic, yes, sometimes people were astonished by that energy of his . . .* And Jim's subliminal retaliation for Tom's Olympic glory was to hitch muscular Christianity to avid ambition, and spike the Bishop's portrait with the aggressive need to dominate. *The Bishop had taken McNab's hand in a firm grasp and not content with that had also taken hold of the Doctor's forearm and was squeezing it.* As Tom said to his wife when *The Hill Station* was published in 1981, 'Gosh!'

'I feel that life is much too comfortable here and that I've stopped experiencing things – in a rut, in short. The years go by in a flash. Also I'm growing dissatisfied (more so, I should say) with the way I write and feel that needs waking up, too. No doubt you will simply see this as a refusal to accept the onset of middle age, as I half do myself.' Jim's burst of confidence in 1978 to the retired master who had been his rugby coach in Rossall days, Norman Ilett, was identical to the restlessness expressed in *The Singapore Grip*, published the same year. *And so, there the Major had been . . . fixed in his habits, apparently suspended in his celibacy like a chicken in aspic. But one day, abruptly, he was no longer satisfied; he had decided to give it all up, this comfortable life, to travel and see the world before he was finally too old. A man only has one life!*

In 1978 a phone call came through to Hilary Pratt, née Kirwan, in an instantly familiar voice. 'This is me. I'm at Dun Laoghaire, just off the boat, and I've booked into the Elphin Hotel in Marine Road.' The small Elphin had always been a private joke and Hilary wasted no time asking questions, but rustled up her brother Jack and as many members of the old Dalkey set as could be managed at such short notice. 'In the course of the drunken and enjoyable evening I spent with them,' Jim noted afterwards, startled, 'in a moment of intuition she suddenly said, "You just couldn't bear to come back until now, could you?" '

It was true: on every count the time was right. He was the emigrant made good, it was very nearly twenty years since the Greystones car-crash so he could no longer be a source of unhappiness for Judy, who was living elsewhere with a husband and young family, and the country, too, was coming into its own. Despite the Northern troubles there was less focus on the ex-colonial power over the water and much more on forward-looking Irish and European concerns, which made for an invigorating climate of growth. 'It was very nice to see you and the rest of the gang the other evening,' he signalled hopefully to Jack from London and there was a positive response by return. Jimmy was now a rather distinguished figure, Jack passed on the word. As if on cue, *Troubles* was broadcast as a BBC 'Book at Bedtime'.

On the second scouting trip Hilary collected him from the boat and took him on a sightseeing tour of his old haunts. He grimaced at the Top Hat Ballroom – 'No creep, no dancing cheek to cheek' – and the parapets of Castlepark, raised his eyebrows at the Astoria cinema in Glasthule and insisted on going to the Forty Foot, where in another life he had regularly marshalled noisy boys. Balholm was only partially rebuilt and The Gwanda, renamed Melmore, was disconcertingly unchanged. But Valentine Kirwan and his wife, the giants of his youth, were waiting in diminished old age at Dalkey Lodge, and there the passage of time could no longer be ignored. On the wall of the abandoned loft, as fresh as the day he had scribbled it, was the prophetic J.G. Farrell, among pencilled sightings of 'Farrell was here'; there, too, was his sketch of a pig, perpetually facing downhill.

Jim was compassionate, but he was never sentimental. 'He used to have a go at us for the orthodoxy of family life in Dublin, as if we were totally unadventurous and didn't know anything,' commented Jack later. 'In the whole of our health we hadn't done as much as he had! There is no question that his favourite theme was the rut he found us in.' But both sides of that argument had their own definition of success, and they lived prosperous, busy lives in houses into which his own flat would fit many times over. 'Too bad about the All blacks,' he communed with Jack at the start of the next rugby season. 'I really thought Ireland would get away with a draw,' and he made plans to attend the Triple Crown match against England at Lansdowne Road. In London he talked animatedly of Ireland, saying in one unguarded moment that the Irish were much nicer than the English, and to Malcolm Dean he reported the quirk of fate that the journalist Bill Shannon, whom in the early seventies they had blackballed for sticking up for James T. Farrell at a dinner party, was elevated to US Ambassador and installed in the Phoenix Park.

The tax exemption inducement of a move to Ireland had been

urged for some time by his accountant, on the grounds that when his health deteriorated he would be unable to sustain his income. It made more sense for him than for most writers to avoid giving away well over half any money due, and with Swifty's involvement that might amount to as much as £100,000. 'Jim felt a great anger that it was the first time he was likely to earn a large amount and it could be taken by the taxman,' Hans Dorflinger sympathised. 'He saw it in a strong social context and unfair, in that businesses could be taxed retrospectively. He'd lived on virtually nothing and after all that effort he was expected simply to hand it back, so he naturally loathed the idea of being fleeced.' The strict residency conditions were the only drawback in the light of his father's worsening health, but none of his family stood in his way.

There was another, less obvious, argument. 'Jim blocked off everything that stood in the way of his writing,' his old Oxford room-mate Brian Pearce detected. 'At each stage of his life something came along that threatened to divert it, and he would disengage. He was totally dedicated, he couldn't compromise, and he simply had too many friendships in London. His flat was on a beaten track, and because he liked his friends he couldn't think how else to avoid being immersed.' A move to Ireland solved the immediate problems, but it need not be permanent; Jim reviewed the tempting Paris option and opened enquiries through his brother Robert about living part of the year in Canada. The trip to poke around Paris estate agents coincided with a Cézanne exhibition at the Grand Palais, where he ran into Paul Huxley and introduced him to the Café Wadja. It was as rough and ready as ever, but the cost of a small apartment was astronomical. Martin Gilbert happened to be in Paris too, and they had a meal together in a Vietnamese restaurant. Jim's expat sensitivities remained acute; it seemed entirely appropriate that all the staff were refugees.

He scanned the property pages of the *Irish Times* and investigated a Connemara cottage owned by the County Librarian for Limerick, which on inspection turned out to be too large. He had no intention of living in Dublin and liked the idea of the more isolated western coast, since with a car he could have the best of both worlds. Bob and Kathie Parrish were also keen to get out of England ahead of the election, and they agreed to join househunting forces. 'I've more or less decided,' he notified Jack that autumn, 'that I would like to be on or near Dunmanus Bay in Co. Cork.' West Cork was remote, but the city had an airport to enable him to get back quickly if Bill's health deteriorated, a deciding factor; he was signing letters to his father 'Jimmy' again and writing often, memories stirred. 'I woke up last night thinking of how you and Oddie and I used to play cricket with a tennis ball up against a garage door in Boscobel. I don't know why. Odd and I must have been very small.'

A ruined farmhouse raised his hopes but was beyond his means, and a further sortie was called for. The Parrishes flew in and found him waiting as chauffeur with a hire car, undaunted by a heavy cold. Three likely prospects disappointed, but over lunch at Wolf Mankowitz's house in Ahakista Jim was re-charged by Mankowitz's encouragement, and driving off again they passed a small handpainted sign which read 'Irish Cottage for Sale – Ask Within'. Kathie got back into the car shaking her head, saying, 'Too old, too much work, too uncomfortable,' and Jim sat silently, gazing at its outline and the view. As they neared Cork airport, miles away, he spoke. 'Do you mind if we go back and look at that last cottage again?'

This time the owner opened it up, and Bob quipped that the stone fireplace was like a Ford movie set from *The Quiet Man*. There was no electricity, water came from a disused well, and the cottage had been empty for twenty years, but Jim bought it there and then for the asking price of £22,000 Irish punts, the equivalent of his Weidenfeld haul. The house haunted him, he told the vendor, Jerry O'Mahony, and he had been unable to get it out of his mind. 'It was quite unlike him,' said Bob, shaken. 'He was absolutely sure and excited, full of plans. "I'm going to put my bedroom here, the bathroom there . . ." ' With the cottage came two roods and twelve perches of land, about half an acre altogether. Tongue-in-cheek, they were inflated to 'my estates'.

The two-storey cottage was more than 250 years old, and at the time of the French fleet's swoop into Bantry Bay in 1796 was said to have been lived in by the man pressed into service as interpreter, a 'spoiled' priest fluent in French. It overlooked the setting for a farcical voyage in *The House of Fahy*, a story he knew from *The Irish RM*, and was within half a mile of the sea, tucked against a hill and buttressed from the rest of the world: the sensation was as snug as taking cover in bad weather against a high sturdy hedge. Jim approved of the original state that so offended Kathie, and praised the fact that no-one had interfered with the internal layout or outbuildings.

'I just got back from a rapid and exhausting trip to Cork and Dublin in the course of which I hope I bought a house – an old farmhouse on the very end of the peninsula between Dunmanus and Bantry Bays, on the side of a hill locally known as Letter Mountain,' he wrote excitedly to Bridget on 5 November. 'Ach, vot is this? We haf heard of ze vine lakes and ze butter mountain, now we are haffing a letter mountain? It's a splendid place, but very exposed, so if you need a wuthering you must come and stay. You must come and stay anyway as I'm hoping to buy a sailing dinghy and want you to give me lessons. Provided the sale goes through without a hitch I'm going to make a determined effort to settle down there . . . London already seems far away.' That day he despatched the £5,500 deposit to Jack Kirwan, who in his solicitor's capacity had volunteered to act for him, and applied to the Irish Land Commission for the necessary permission under Section 45. 'He has very strong Irish connections,' argued Jack successfully. 'His mother is Irish and he resided in Ireland for most of his childhood from 1945 up to 1960.' Shortly afterwards the Artists' Tax Exemption came through. The contract was signed before Christmas, witnessed by Bob, and the balance agreed for 16 February 1979, a close-run thing considering that 'a large slice of cash' would not come through from the publishers until 9 February; press conjecture about exchange controls if the Irish pound cut loose from sterling added to the tension. 'Now for the good news,' he thanked Jack. 'The Irish Customs say I can bring in two cases of my Château Kirwan duty free!'

Bowing out from London was accomplished with equal despatch, and his friends divided into those who supported his decision, and by far the majority, who did not. It was pointed out that he was sociable by nature so the switch to isolation was a mistake, that he would take himself and his problems with him, and that he was mad to go to the back of beyond. The London Library notified him of the availability of a sought-after Index catalogue, but people who knew him were sceptical about how he would exist so far from libraries and museums, and the upsurge in Northern Ireland violence was emphasised by headlines about threatened car bombs in London and newspaper photographs of naked men in blankets in the worsening H Block dirty protest. Margaret Drabble would subsequently put the unspoken case in *The Gates of Ivory*. ' "There's plenty of human nature here at home," Liz had offered . . . with a gesture that embraced . . . dreadlocks and strollers and buskers and cruisers and crooks and drifters; the enshrined Campden Hill dignitaries to the west, the Bayswater backwaters to the east . . . And Stephen had taken all this in, and had shrugged his thin shoulders, and had said a little wistfully, "There is nothing to keep me here." '

Jim's Achilles heel was the matter of principle, and it caused him uncomfortable moments. Why, he was asked, if he was such a staunch socialist, was he leaving the country as soon as he had enough money to qualify for the higher tax net? He had no answer, except the necessity, in military and literary terms, of a temporary retreat and redeployment of forces.

Facing into the unknown, externally and internally, he toyed with living dangerously on all fronts, and resurrected a list of marriage prospects, of which four names were ticked. Bridget's was at the top, and, in no apparent order of preference, Patricia, Ann and Judith were also flagged. At the end of January 1979 another name was added, and a small tick beside it. Unlike the others, in a significant break with his own principles, Carole Tucker happened to be married and, hearing that she was separating from her husband, he took her out to a restaurant. On the next date he cooked her a Stilton quiche at home. 'After dinner,' she revealed, many years after a reconciliation with her husband, 'I looked at his hands and saw how delicate they were. He got up and on the way to the kitchen to make coffee said, "I want to kiss you. Think about it." ' Carole fell deeply in love with him and he spent the weeks between one life and another in illusory limbo with her, unsure sometimes whether he even wanted to continue writing. Iris Murdoch had been awarded the latest Booker Prize for *The Sea, The Sea*, and Paul Theroux the Whitbread for *Picture Palace*. He longed to escape.

In the winter of discontent, as it was being christened by the media, strike followed strike in bitter weather, and Jim recoiled from the intransigence that was closing cemeteries and hospitals. He was alienated by the rise of Militant in the mortally weakened Labour government, and his anger fuelled McNab's fictional compassion. As for Margaret Thatcher's Tory values, he had a single word: barbaric. He had always been supersensitive to the spirit of the times, and felt he had nothing in common with what he called the 'soccer and money cultural ambience'. Hurt more than he cared to admit by the continuing lack of recognition from Brasenose and the Bodleian, where his old tutor Dr Shackleton had been librarian since 1966, his angry mood was sealed by the chance discovery that Weidenfeld had reneged on the agreed print run, halving it without informing him. Whenever he went into his kitchen his eye was caught by spots of mould that were symbolically spreading across the silverfoil-covered wall.

At Christmas, however, *The Singapore Grip* made a belated comeback. Hilary Spurling chose it as her book of the year – 'May you be rewarded in heaven if not sooner,' he thanked her – but she was by no means the only one, and the *Bookseller* singled him out in their annual analysis of the recommendations, in which he came third, behind Graham Greene and Iris Murdoch. 'I have no means of verifying this,' wrote the acerbic Critic's Crowner columnist, 'but I suspect that Mr Farrell's is the novel that reviewers are kicking themselves about most after the event.' It would, Jim noted sarcastically, do something to restore his reputation in the book business, 'though of course they are in any case much more interested in selling books than in good reviews, and in that respect I have been doing alright.' A bookshop encounter neatly encapsulated his frustrations. 'I spent a little time', he noted ruefully, 'observing a middle-aged gent of saturnine appearance who was deeply engrossed in my book. I felt like going up to him and saying, "Right now, you've had enough of a sample. Do you want it or not?" '

The move was set for 20 March, and in the Harrods January sale he haggled for a buttoned leather Chesterfield, stipulating that it would have to be stored until then. His parents donated a Victorian oak chest and bible box, and at an antique shop in Peckham Rye he bought a lectern, wardrobe and chair, and paid £400 for an oak refectory table. 'They must all think we're a married couple,' he murmured unfairly to Patricia Moynagh, who was accompanying him that day. The list of potential candidates for marriage was stored in a concertina file, along with the few private papers he chose to keep, and his trail was intended to go cold, so he emptied drawers ruthlessly and asked his family to do the same.

Bridget sent a tin whistle – 'I had a cautious blow, whereupon all the cats in the garden have come darting up and are standing on their black back legs trying to look in the window' – and he made two trips to the Boat Show, keenly tempted to buy a fibreglass dinghy called *The Scaffie* and undeterred by that month's explosion of the tanker *Betelgeuse* at the Gulf Oil terminal at Whiddy Island, within sight of his new cottage, with the loss of fifty-one lives. On 19 February he travelled to ice-locked Dublin to buy a car, and chose a silver Toyota Starlet in the Glasthule garage that his parents had always used. On his return he asked Patricia to design change-of-address cards – 'J.G. Farrell, Saltwater House, Letter, Kilcrohane, Near Bantry, County Cork, Ireland' – and to be sure to stipulate 'no telephone' to save friends a pointless search. In his Simla manuscript, which was getting fluctuating attention, Emily's childhood home was given the same name.

Jim eased out of London, having mentally already left. 'Everyone drank a lot, and I remember we all had a conversation about air brushing – lewd, fun, giggly,' Susannah Clapp would describe a farewell party at her flat. 'It was terrifically good fun and he wasn't in any way depressed.' Jim made the most of ethnic restaurants while he still could, and when writing out his next address for Elsie Donald and Lavinia Trevor in Kalamares he added the comment 'Piss off!' beneath; oddly juvenile, they thought. Malcolm Dean threw a party for him, where he said goodbye to Brigid Allen, who was present with her husband and baby son. And at a dinner given by Alison Lurie he slipped away from Claire Tomalin enigmatically, without telling her of his plans. 'I like living alone,' he said indignantly whenever told that he would be lonely. 'It's a new beginning for me.' Gary Arnott's send-off had a Last Supper air about it, with a feast of salmon followed by goose, followed by Rocquefort cheese. Most friends, whether old or new, were asked to a final dinner in the flat.

At the largest gathering Suzanne Lowry was present. She was an observant young journalist with an Ulster background, who thought he rather resembled Cardinal Hume. 'Jim was beaming, sitting at the end of the table, being very witty and funny, and everyone was giving him little presents – mine was a very old brass candlestick. He was benign, capping remarks and issuing invitations all over the place. People were worried about him going off on his own, but everyone was going along with his mood when someone piously said, "Ireland is such a healing place." I was so irritated that I snapped out, "How can you say that? It's a perfectly dreadful place. Beautiful, maybe, but also a place of death, despair and betrayal. I wouldn't go there at all." I said it out of bad temper, not runic warning, but I fervently believed it as I said it.' Jim smoothed over the incident by passing around photographs of the house, taken with his faithful Canadian camera.

At the last moment he had second thoughts about giving up the flat, knowing that legally he could hold on to it as long as a suitcase remained, but was advised that his Irish tax position would be at risk. In confidence he consulted Bob and took the ultimate capitalist step of opening a Swiss bank account at the Crédit Suisse in Klosters, where the Parrishes had their second home. As March ticked by he distributed farewell presents from his wine collection, ringing doorbells without warning, handing over a bottle, chatting for a moment, and cycling on.

As always, he felt 'weighed down spiritually' by the prospect of moving, and a wave of bombs across Northern Ireland, backed up by a statement from the Provisional IRA that they were not a spent force, did not help. But there was no turning back. The furniture van was booked, the landlord's solicitors informed, and he arranged to spend the three days which the van would take to reach West Cork in the company of Claude and Anna in France whose small daughter was his godchild. Anxiety about leaving his father quickened with a visit from Bill's ageing sister May – 'I explained your writing difficulties, Dad' – and sitting up late with Francis King, long after his usual hour of departure, he was monosyllabic. 'Hurry up and get your book done,' chivied Francis, attributing his black mood to the depression all writers encounter. 'Oh, I don't think it will ever get finished,' he replied, and there was such bleakness in his voice that Francis had trouble sleeping that night, convinced all of a sudden that Jim was heading towards suicide.

He locked the door, posted off the keys, and took his suitcase to the Parrishes' guest bedroom for a night until the early flight to Paris. Supper was spent alone with Carole Tucker, and he chose a local bistro which was cheap and cheerful. Afterwards he let her into Bob and Kathie's house, and she left just before they got up. 'We'll see each other again soon,' he promised.

CHAPTER TWENTY

A Place to Breathe
1979

The move to Ireland marked the start of a new ten-year cycle. Ten years of solid apprenticeship had been followed by ten years of accomplishment, and the anniversary of the delivery of the first draft of *Troubles* to Cape was practically ten years to the day. In Paris Jim felt optimistic enough to pick Avenue Junot in Montmartre for a future apartment, cheered by a meeting with Elie Harar, not seen since Marrakesh, and he talked to Bertrand Tavernier, had a drink at the Closerie des Lilas with Pierre Jean Remy who wanted to discuss a filmscript, and interviewed his French translator: a positive beginning.

'All goes well so far,' he jotted on a postcard before leaving the Gare du Nord on 29 March. 'My friends here are in good form . . . I'm off now to Dublin.' That day the Callaghan government fell by a single vote and a General Election was called for 3 May, and within twenty-four hours the man tipped to be the next Northern Ireland Secretary if the Conservatives got in, Margaret Thatcher's ally Airey Neave, was killed by a bomb attached to his car as he drove out of the House of Commons underground car park.

Jim, meanwhile, had found sanctuary. 'Three miles past Kilcrohane on the road from Durrus,' he described his exact location. 'Turn right at green shop, over brow of hill, right at a T junction, then fork left at cattle pen and first house on right. (You can tell it by the weeds.)' Damage to his possessions in transit amounted to no more than a couple of broken plates and a lamp – 'In other words, nothing at all' – and his grey fedora, somewhat incongruously, now hung on a peg in the hall of his 'own house'; occasionally he underlined those words. The electricity was unconnected, so he made do with candles; there was no post because of an entrenched strike, petrol pumps were closing because of an international oil crisis, and there was a two-year waiting list, at best, for a phone. The brackish taste of the water in his taps imposed the extra expense of boring a new well, and six weeks later he was waiting – 'philosophically' – for the well-borer to turn up.

'Actually I think the absence of post for the first three months', he evaluated later, 'was a big help in getting me settled in psychologically. I got a funny feeling when the outside world began to make itself felt again.' Painfully learned passivity came into its own. The farmer whose cattle broke in and trampled his garden found him mildness itself – 'It was my own fault for not having better defences' – and he did not allow the fact that the final cheque in payment for the house was marooned in a postal sorting office to come between himself and the sensation of full ownership. 'Oh, just wait till summer,' he memorised the assurance of a local farmer's son. 'It's like the Garden of Eden.'

The air on the coast was noticeably better than in London, and the immediate benefit was evident in extra energy and an optimistic frame of mind. He slept better, woke refreshed and ate with increased appetite, transformed from the tragic figure Francis King had glimpsed. *The sun had risen by now. It was going to be a lovely day. [He] took a deep contented breath . . . The smell of grass and wood lingered delightfully under the mild sky . . . it was hard to believe that there was any malice in Ireland.*

Jim was on good terms with the owner of the local petrol pump – 'When I appeared in her shop she did a double-take that would have done credit to Laurel and Hardy in their prime' – and eked out his tankful for visits to the town of Bantry, seventeen miles away. There he joined the public library – 'It isn't too bad' – and opened an account at the Bank of Ireland in Wolfe Tone Square, charmed by its resemblance to the premises of Sarah Devlin's father, the unctuous bank manager in *Troubles*, and by the crosscurrents of history, which had arranged for the first Governor-General of Ireland, Tim Healy, to be born in the building two years before the Indian Mutiny. Nearer home he relied on the local shop of John O'Mahony, appreciatively described as an enlightened man.

In the White House Bar on a Saturday night only Jim's accent set him apart; he was, it was said with approval, totally inoffensive. All writers were distrusted, after many local people, years before, had been recognisably lampooned, and Jerry O'Mahony, the vendor of the cottage, who as handyman and builder was in charge of renovations, warned him not to do the same. 'A brick,' Jim complimented. 'Not to mention a concrete block.' Their friendship ripened as he helped to plumb in radiators off a Waterford Stanley oil stove, and week by week the book was postponed. He was often asked to Sunday lunch by Jerry's wife, Mary, who was expecting their third child, and returned the hospitality, surprising them with oriental recipes, China tea and Colombian coffee.

Jim's fatalism was sorely tested. He had never bothered with a chartered surveyor over the sale, and the roof beneath the weathered Bangor blue slates, which once had been thatched, was found to need a large sum spent on it before the next winter. The ground-floor room furthest from the sea that was earmarked for his study was given a new fireplace, but smoke billowed from a crack in the external wall and rats got in and made a nest. 'Minor disasters', he chalked up, 'include the fact that the tractor that came to rotovate the garden which was full of brambles broke the sewage pipe to the septic tank; when I got another guy to rotovate a strip of land above the house [he] succeeded in cutting the pipe which carries the water supply . . . No doubt it happens to everyone who is mad enough to become a householder.' The new pipe, when delivered, was found to be too short, and walking into his study to arrange his books he discovered a dead rat by the grate. The property was known locally as Gortfahane, not Saltwater House, and bowing to the inevitable he ordered a wooden sign. 'You see further evidence of the Gaelic twilight', he taunted Bridget over the border, 'mounting around my ears.' He had intended to convert the stone outbuildings into guest accommodation, and regretfully that had to be postponed. He decided to do without curtains, for the present.

The clearing of the garden opened the way to heavy physical

work – 'I've been digging like a fiend' – which he had not attempted since the DEW Line. He cleared overgrown escallonias, planted sixty apple and pear trees as a windbreak, sowed night-scented stock, and made space for lettuces, onions, sweet corn, chicory, endives, celeriac, watercress, courgettes and green peppers. Jerry and Michael Daly, two farmer brothers who were his nearest neighbours, donated cabbage seedlings – 'I'm undoubtedly in the forefront when it comes to cabbage-owning novelists' – and to keep off the birds and a marauding hare he deployed nets and the miniature conservatories of glass domes. A swallow nested in the garage, so he propped the door ajar, and starlings raucously hatched in a hollow of the outside wall behind his bed. 'Not sure what date or day of week it is', he made a note. 'Today the sun is shining, the sea is sparkling, and all seems right with Kilcrohane, if not the world.'

Jerry O'Mahony, who was almost a generation younger, felt illogically paternal. 'He wanted to replace his childhood,' he would comment. 'I'm sure he was reliving it. He often talked about his mother during the war, and how they'd kept bees; when there was extra buzzing, he told me, his mother would say, "Your bees are boiling." He intended to have chickens as well, because they'd had them, and the first tree he bought was a Siberian crab apple. He said there was one when he was a boy and he and his brother found them too bitter to eat and used to throw them at one another.'

Vigorous gardening did away with the need for walks, but the sea at the far end of the narrow lane drew Jim like a magnet, and during spring storms he watched waves being pounded into the narrow rocky cove with such force that they towered forty feet in the air. He picked sea urchins from the rocks for Jane Grigson's recipe, listened sympathetically to accounts of damage to scallop beds arising from the *Betelgeuse* catastrophe, and the disastrous impact of large trawlers on local mackerel fishing, and was grateful for Jerry's occasional gifts of fresh crayfish or a lobster.

Without a postal service or a phone Jim relied on the radio, and timed his supper to coincide with 'Kaleidoscope' or 'The World Tonight'. From far away he heard that Hilary Spurling and Paul Theroux were to be among the next Booker Prize judges, and that Timothy Mo, who had bracketed *The Singa-*

pore Grip with *War and Peace*, had won the Faber Prize for *The Monkey King*; a neat correlation. BBC Radios 3 and 4 were augmented by French stations, and he listened to the Radio Eireann news. 'Paisley really is quite bizarre. You wouldn't get away with him in a novel,' he noted. 'I liked the exchange when he was being drummed out of the Euro Parliament with a Fianna Fail deputy nearby. Paisley: "You're a Papish lout!" FF dep: "And you're a bigot!"' But Dr Ian Paisley's language and behaviour were supremely relevant to Victorian Simla, and the leader of the Democratic Unionist Party was to have not one reincarnation in *The Hill Station* but two: the zealot Dr Bateman – *It is always possible to rouse [a] rabble with a cry of 'No Popery'* – and B'sun Smith, a lay preacher who orates on *Romish rituals, dangerous all round*. The struggle between Paisley and Martyn Smith, Grand Master of the Orange Order, over leadership of the Protestant community had Jim's full attention, and he relished their apt description as Ulster's leading political clergymen.

Whenever Jim was successful in 'squeezing enough petrol out of the nipples' of female custodians of filling stations, Hilary Pratt was liable to find the silver Toyota parked without warning in her drive when she got home from work, and whatever the provocation from old Dublin friends he was affable and diffident, quite changed from his old self. He would be gone again before the household woke, and on his way back sometimes called to see his uncle Harry Russell in Portarlington, confiding once that he had never been so happy. So rare an experience was it that he could not keep it to himself. 'I'm terribly happy here,' he told Hilary atypically. 'Happier than I've been in years.'

Ann Colville arrived from London for Easter and as swiftly went, taking back a raft of letters to post. He enjoyed her sensuous presence but emphasised their fourteen-year age difference, and made no effort to detain her. Although he talked of buying an apartment with her in Paris and perhaps living together in Europe, she detected that isolation was already changing him, and realised that although she now wanted to make a commitment, he did not. 'I felt very sad when I said goodbye,' she said of their parting. 'I felt there wasn't a way forward – in a sense he was clamming up. I couldn't see where the relationship was going to go.'

With most of the interior jobs nearing completion there was the mental space to return to the book. After Ann's departure he achieved two days of 'heavy work' at his typewriter in the study, but the 'really heavy work' needed more attention than he could yet spare. His planned starting date of 8 May had, with dismay, to be shelved. 'I remember that you were dubious when I explained that I was hoping to move in and start work on my book almost immediately,' he wrote in one letter, put aside for the next visiting-postman's duty. 'Only a complete innocent could have thought, as I did, that I'd unpack my suitcase and settle down without more ado.' It was a 'very bad idea', he underscored the words to Bridget, to be moving around while writing the first draft of a novel because it 'permits you not to face up to it'. The note of anxiety was unmistakable, and to Jerry's surprise he was becoming as tense as a student swotting for a big exam. But the deadline Jim had to meet was the end of the summer, when his mother was due to stay, because she would be taking back the typescript. Once arranged, the date was irreversible, as a nurse had to be booked long in advance to care for Bill. Also, the sum of £5,000 was due on delivery, an incentive made more significant by every bill. 'I'm spending like a drunken sailor,' he had fretted to Ann.

Sometime earlier Margaret Drabble's friend David Simpson, whose thoughtfulness he liked, had tentatively suggested coming to stay during a fraught week between jobs. David had been running the English branch of Amnesty and was about to head up ASH, the anti-smoking pressure group, a choice that had been the subject of a critical article by Bernard Levin in *The Times*. Sympathetic to his dilemma, Jim instructed him to come along. The mid-May visit held off his own confrontation, putting them in a similar frame of mind and, shutting himself away to work for only one day out of six, he good-humouredly took advantage of the imposed leisure and decided they would both learn how to fish. His line flew up and the hook caught in the back of his jersey, jerking it up behind his head as he reeled in, and helpless with laughter he dared David to do better. Each morning they set up their rods on the small slipway at the bottom of the lane, without success. 'Later the lad from the farm across the valley told us that we would be as likely to catch fish in the kitchen sink as in the spot where we were fishing,' Jim noted, sporting instincts roused. 'He recommended another place where we mean to try if the weather improves.'

A high wind put paid to further practice and they took a long walk to the tip of Sheep's Head Peninsula, which culminated in sheer cliffs on either side and dramatic waves raising fountains of spray. 'Great stuff!' Jim shouted into the gale. David's affinity was with medical subjects, and as they made slow headway they discussed the nineteenth-century divisions of the causes of cholera and TB. The mood became confessional, and Jim overcame his reticence sufficiently to say that he could never have become a writer without his parents' support, and that only one woman was really important to him, so much so that he really thought he might marry her – Bridget O'Toole. The name was a complete surprise to David, who was privy only to the London compartment. Heads down into the wind, they were suddenly brought up short by a rock ahead that seemed so menacing they were stunned into silence. But Sheep's Head Peninsula already held hidden meaning for Jim, recalling the sacrificial omen of the dead sheep by the sea so many years before. *How could I have forgotten? . . . You took a dead stick polished like ivory and wrote beneath it in the sand: Quis tollis peccata mundi . . . The sheep stared back . . . Life is a dream. He's waterlogged now. His eyes were glassy, his hair was seaweed when they dragged him out.* David described the jolt as 'psychic' to Susannah Clapp immediately on his return.

Letters went with David, written a day apart, for four out of the five ticked names on Jim's typed marriage list; each missive reached out in one sentence, drew back the next. To Ann he was warm and evasive, and Bridget knew him well enough to read between the lines when he asked her to let him know when she wanted to come 'so that I don't have a whole lot of people descending on me. (Actually I think I'm probably sufficiently remote to discourage all but the most determined).' But though to Carole Tucker, the newest candidate, he put up few defences – 'I'll insist on reimbursing you for your ticket . . . Alternatively, come to India with me for a month or more this winter, or possibly Mauritius if I don't have to go. Anyhow, we must meet somehow' – each letter signed off with the same noncommittal phrase, 'Love to you, Jim'. All options were open, and on the long drive to drop David off at Cork airport, slowed by the imposition of a 55mph speed limit to conserve fuel as the petrol crisis lengthened, he proposed a week's walk together in the Himalayan fooothills around Simla in the late autumn. The car they parked behind contained a graceful silhouette of long delicate neck and hair pinned up in a chignon, and he turned to David. 'That', he murmured in a conspiritorial last comment, 'is an *extremely* attractive girl.'

McNab was temporarily allotted a Christian name – *Are you worried that Simla is such a dissolute place then, David?* – but Jim was still unable to get to grips with the book because Bob and Kathie Parrish came in early June, bearing 'mail, oceans of booze, frozen chickens etc'. And they, too, returned with letters for the women in his life. 'I won't really feel happy leaving here or even having a visit,' he staked out his territory to Ann, 'until I've got at least a first draft of my book out of the way. [It's] better not to make any pretence about it and it goes for everyone.' Meanwhile, on a quick trip to Dublin he turned to Hilary and took her hand. 'Will *you* come to India with me?'

Rough notes on the backs of used Weidenfeld envelopes, unpacked three months before, outlined the writing that remained to be done, and with no traffic to break the silence except the occasional tractor rattling by, he at last succeeded in getting down to work, sorting it first into chapter summaries. *A feeling of great peace unexpectedly settled on [his] soul. Sounds came to him from far away on the still, clear air . . . And he thought: 'How wonderful it is to be young!' And he was quite annoyed for a moment to remember that he was old . . . on the other hand, he thought of poor Emily, the yearning, the boredom, the heartache . . . 'No, No. Things are better as they are.'* The self-sufficiency of his London life had been ideal preparation for solitary life in Ireland and breaking off at lunchtime, as before, he knocked up a soufflé omelette, or perhaps mushrooms à la grecque with garlic, tarragon and butter. The same cookbooks were to hand, the same herbs grew in the same pots, and being far from the shops in a petrol crisis presented no problem: he baked his own bread and kept flour in reserve, and his vegetables were outside for the picking under a 'green tide' of weeds. He could, he claimed, 'eat salad niçoise till the cows come home', and on his doorstep, as a bonus, was a potential fishmonger's slab.

The first time Jim succeeded in catching a fish, he kept it triumphantly for show. 'He was absolutely *amazed*', noticed Jerry indulgently, 'at how easy it was.' Proper equipment was immediately justifiable as an investment, and in Durrus, locally, he bought a light six-foot fibreglass rod and tackle, black rubber boots with corrugated soles, a strong penknife, and a selection of the recommended bait of feathers for pollock and spinners mackerel. In his kitchen, fortuitiously, he already had a deepfreeze. As a reward for completing his daily writing st now allowed himself an hour or so of fishing, changin jeans, jumper and anorak and, mindful of his neck, pulling woollen balaclava if it was cold.

Since David's departure his skill had improved with practice and he picked his way across the uneven shards of rock to the left of the slipway and made for the rock where Jerry caught lobster, stepping out across a cleft to balance on its slippery surface, well-used to the backward slope. He had taught himself to stand upright there with the rod fully extended, and not to be dis-tracted by the deep waters several feet below, by looking out for a bewhiskered seal that often wallowed thirty yards out 'with the air of someone who thinks he might know a better way of doing it'. In the distance ahead was the Whiddy Island oil refinery and, on a good day, the far side of the bay. Mackerel were scarce – 'they've probably been vacuumed up by some bloody trawler' – but pollock were plentiful, and he threw back any catch too small to eat.

'I feel ill-used', he wrote, 'on a day when I don't manage to drag my supper from the waves. It works out more expensive than buying fish at Harrods because I keep losing bits and pieces of tackle but it's fresher and it's fun.' He preferred to fish on the rising tide, and compensated for his weak shoulder by anchoring the end of the rod under his right arm and casting 'flat' with his left, flicking it round in a circular, swinging movement. A pollock and a couple of homegrown courgettes made 'the perfect instant supper', and in July he hauled in one weighing a hefty

$3\frac{1}{4}$ lbs. Fishing was the first sport he had been able to enjoy since rugby, and he worked diligently at improving his technique. 'Naturally I've been spending my days fishing instead of writing,' he owned up to Bob Parrish in a letter. 'Stop Press: More major fish have been caught in the meantime.'

The ancient name of the rock from which he fished was pronounced 'Conorgrahogue', and was referred to by Jerry and the Dalys simply as 'the block'. It reminded Jim that Irish had once been widely spoken in the district, and led to absorbing conjecture about subjugation by language – verbal colonisation. 'Oh, don't worry about me,' he dismissed Jerry's warnings about losing his balance. 'The water's warm, and if I fall in, I can swim.' Hilary made a detour while on business and brought her daughter Amanda, who was the same age he had been at the first meeting with the charismatic Kirwans, and before supper he took them both down to stand upon the block, chivying them to overcome their hesitation. As a concept, the rock continued to work in his imagination. 'Obviously one of the difficult things about getting older,' he wrote in one letter, 'is the constant readjustment one has to make of the mental image one has of oneself so that it continues to correspond with reality. Sometimes I find myself that I leap for a rock which has been mentally sanctioned but find it not so easy to get there.'

The end of the postal strike on 24 June put paid to the simplicity of his days. 'I'm now paying the penalty', he sighed, 'for those blissful weeks without mail or phone (still no phone, of course) by having to deal with all sorts of dull business matters which normally don't come so concentrated.' The haul of personal letters had a less peremptory tone, but one telegram from 'a certain small person in Beverly Hills' demanded an urgent call to Claridge's in London, and with the local petrol pump running low he made the supreme sacrifice and drove to the public callbox in Bantry with a heavy bag of 5p coins. Writing to Bob, he figuratively threw up his hands. 'He said "Can you call me back. I'm in a meeting." I said that was quite impossible. So he improvised a few vaguely encouraging remarks about my book. Then he said, "How did you know I was here?" "You sent me a telegram," I grated. "Oh, did I?" he replied. "Well, do keep in touch from time to time." ' American reviews of *The Singapore Grip* boded well but, dismayed by Swifty's response, he fired off a letter to Knopf enquiring about sales. He was relieved to hear the book was earning out its advance.

In the backlog of post came more good news. American rights had netted $41,250 and other promising sums were accumulating, and Penguin were talking about taking all three Empire books as a trilogy. Deborah Rogers notified him that the BBC had approached her about filming *The Siege of Krishnapur* in four instalments – 'This has happened so often before that I can hardly raise an eyebrow, let alone count on it for hot dinners' – and another BBC producer – '*not* re Krishnapur' – was on holiday in Schull nearby and sought a meeting. His mother's visit was put back until early October, pleasingly extending the deadline a little, and he arranged to meet John Curtis in Paris later that month to hear his verdict on the new book and collect the cheque. The damp-squib result of delayed victory over the Public Lending Rights Act was a request for £2 from the Authors' Lending and Copyright Society to collect library borrowings on his behalf. 'It strikes me as a bad sign', he noted caustically, 'that they start off in life by tapping me for a few quid.'

Contrary to London expectations, he had no desire to be anywhere else. 'Anyone who hasn't spent July in Kilcrohane doesn't understand the phrase "douceur de vivre" (fuck Talleyrand, what did he know?)', he wrote in one reply. 'I've been trying to write but there are so many competing interests – the prime one at the moment is fishing off the rocks . . . Then a colony of bees has come to live above my back door and I'm thinking of turning them into *my* feudal retainers.' The bees had got in through a cavity and worked so noisily near the now-empty starlings' nest that in bed he could hear them through the wall, but although Jerry extracted them and shut the swarm overnight in a box, next day they were back. Jim took the view that he was merely one inhabitant among many, and was glad to hear that their presence meant good luck, with the reverse if he interfered. 'I'm keen to have bees around,' he wrote to his parents, 'as there aren't that many insects about to pollinate my fruit trees; also there's lots of heather not far away and you remember that lovely 'eather 'oney we had in Southport. I'm trying to think of ways of getting them into a hive.' Among the garden weeds he identified Elizabeth David's favourite sorrel, and from his own 'particularly fine' specimens by the back door he made elderflower wine. It was hard to believe that he had once pictured himself in West Cork with nothing to do.

'I simply don't have time for proper horticulture with the book to write and sixty odd trees to keep watered.' 'A spell of bad weather is the only hope for getting my book out on time.' 'I'm making rapid progress with my novel but I'm still behind schedule. People keep barging in on me the way they never did in London.' From Northern Ireland news of the Unionist marching season accompanied his bursts of progress – *The mob felt somewhat cheated [but] they had caused a Romish service to be abandoned and that was not half bad* – and Southern preoccupation with the Pope's imminent visit turned the daily newspaper into a useful primer on Catholic ritual. The deadline was less than four months away when a review clipping was sent to him from *Time* magazine which likened him to a windy raconteur at the bar of Raffles Hotel. 'How dare they!' he commented, drawing two lines beneath the words.

Halfway through July Jim changed his mind about the bees. He told Jerry that he wanted to present them to him, and refused to be intimidated by superstition. 'Take them away,' he insisted. 'What the hell!' On 18 July, with hindsight, there was a third ominous incident. 'This afternoon I was walking back along the cliffs feeling annoyed with myself because I'd lost part of my fishing tackle (having got it snagged inaccessibly in the depths),' he noted without a twinge of premonition, 'when I was joined by an old farmer with a walking stick who laughed me out of it and for good measure told me about some of the terrible storms he had witnessed, pointing out on the rocks how far the water had come up and adding a few fishing tips: a much more valuable catch than the unfortunate fish I'd been planning for my supper.' The sea remained calm, giving weight to the local saying that between 15 June and 15 August the waters were safe, and he gloried in living almost for free on the produce of his garden and the sea. In the evenings he rarely managed to read more than a few pages of *Middlemarch* before dozing off.

The book now had a possible title: in the margin at the top of Chapter 16 he added 'The Doctor of Confusion'. 'I'm currently having a blitz on my novel,' he notified Bridget on 22 July, but within two days he was knocked off course once more by the unexpected visit of his garrulous American editor and her boyfriend, who had nowhere to stay. 'Well, I'm pressing on,' he turned up the pace when they had gone. 'But I have serious misgivings about its quality.'

Necessary future planning meant further distraction from the book on which so much depended. He had encouraged Bridget to take a year's sabbatical to write, during which she would be staying with him, and the upheaval over roof repairs was pencilled in for November; on condition that the wind settled into the north-east for long enough. 'Otherwise I'll have to wait for Spring, dodging flying slates,' he teased Bridget by post. 'It's very like the Majestic here. I even have what looks like a root growing up through the kitchen floor. (Jerry says it isn't: he says it's the legs of a table in what used to be the dairy, which were set in concrete and which he had to saw off in order to get the table out.)' Patricia Moynagh was also due in the autumn to tie in with her annual attendance at the Wexford Opera Festival, and the shared prospect of a Paris flat with Ann Colville was unresolved. 'What is annoying,' he hinted to Ann, 'is that I have almost enough to buy a small apartment in Paris but not quite yet . . . There are one or two small signs "no bigger than a man's hand" indeed, that I may be in a position to give the money-tree another shake quite soon – but nothing one could count on.' One future option was suddenly no longer relevant when an emotionally charged but resolute letter from Carole brought the news that she had decided to rebuild her marriage.

'I shall no doubt be wistful about not spending the better parts of this winter with you,' she wrote to cushion the blow, 'travelling, falling in love, eating, always being amused and sometimes amusing. What is a girl to do?' Jim wrote back to reassure her that it was probably for the best. 'One of the few virtues that I sometimes suspect myself of (if that's what it is) is a reluctance to interfere in other people's marriages, and if you had come in June the weather was so good and the scenery so spectacular I'd have thrown a golden net over you.' But he went on to comment that it would have been 'nice' if she and Bridget had stayed with him at the same time, a remark that convinced her of the rightness of her decision. 'I was someone who'd had a long investment in someone,' she said subsequently, 'and I knew Bridget had invested so much of her life in Jim's. I was married and I understood prior commitments, but I was used to men who did, too. If we had all three stayed together I would have been horrified – if I was sleeping with him it would be very hurtful to Bridget, and if he was sleeping with her it would have been hurtful to me. So why would he have wanted that? It could only have been power.'

On 28 July, accelerating the need to finish the book on time, he learned that the Customs and Excise demand for £2,332.67, which he had paid by cheque before setting out, was still outstanding – 'I *thought* I came away with a bit more money than I expected,' he sighed to Bob Parrish. 'This means I shall have to tap my Swiss resources' – but concentration in his study was helped by a downturn in the weather. From the start of August it rained every day – *a steady, interminable downpour that seemed to hang from the sky like a curtain of glass beads* – and he was relieved to be freed of the chore of watering the extra windbreak of young Leylandii he had just planted. In the short intervals from writing he decided on the purchase of a greenhouse and the enlargement of the main window with its view of the bay. Unable to garden in the evenings, he attended then to the backlog of letters to friends, although delivery to England was still delayed. Whenever the skies cleared and light permitted he grabbed his rod and went down to fish.

On 4 August, a Saturday evening, he was elated to catch four pollock before snagging his line on a rock and losing his last hook. 'Two of them were over 2 lbs, the other two were a pound each, which is a good size for me,' he recorded, greatly chuffed. 'I think I may have to take to filleting the bigger fish before putting them in the freezer if it begins to get full up. They'd also be easier to handle when using them later.' He cooked one that night, put two in the freezer and presented the fourth, cleanly gutted, to his new neighbours further down the lane, a Dutch couple 'so deeply boring they make Jack Hedley sound like Aldous Huxley'. The next day, confined to barracks, he replied to more letters, including one from David Simpson. 'An added hazard,' he wryly brought him up to date, 'besides slipping on the rocks and braining myself and getting snatched off them by a wave, when going fishing, is that [the Dutch couple] are likely to invite me in for a drink.'

Work on the book was going well, meanwhile, and he estimated that he would be able to finish the draft on time. He was glad of the respite to advance a scene spanning three chapters, in which a boycotted High Church service in St Saviour's was planned to end in chaos. That evening he switched on Radio 4 and heard Nicholas Monsarrat's death announced on the 6pm news. 'Pity his last book', he commiserated, 'wasn't better received.' He grilled a pollock, which left one in reserve, and listened to Bertrand Tavernier being interviewed on 'Kaleidoscope' about his new film *Deathwatch* and discussing the growing pressure on movie directors to become voyeurs; if Bert was to be believed, it was one of the central problems of the age. 'Yawn . . . yawn . . .' he communed with Bob before going to bed. 'Such mortal strivings seem far away out here on the Sea of Tranquillity where even a telegram from Lazar comes as the merest stirring in the trees or the faintest sighing in the chimney sort of thing.'

There was sufficient petrol in the car for a round trip into Bantry for the personal authorisation his bank needed to withdraw a third of his Swiss account to settle the VAT bill, so cutting his writing short on Thursday he drove in to attend to it. His account was more than £500 in credit and he was assured the Swiss transfer would come through within a month and, catching the 5pm post, he drove home in the rain.

A wet Friday was broken up by a lunch with Wolf Mankowitz – 'he's working on some dull-sounding TV series' – and in the late afternoon Jerry called to see if he needed anything in the shops, and to ask him for Sunday lunch. Jim made him the customary cup of Colombian coffee and accepted, and handed him a card to post which accounted for his upbeat mood; at last he felt able to tell Rosemary Legge at Weidenfeld that he would be delivering the novel on time. As Jerry was leaving he called out after him that he needed fishing hooks, explaining he was completely out of them. After Alastair Cooke's 'Letter from America' later on – the

mellifluous voice always a reminder of the prickly Harkness lunch
– he found the fishing hooks had been dropped back.

Jim went straight to the typewriter after breakfast on Saturday, relishing the uninterrupted hours ahead. In Derry the
Apprentice Boys' Parade that day exactly matched the unfolding
bigotry in Simla, and by felicitous coincidence the culmination of
his riot was taking shape on the tenth anniversary of the critical
Bogside confrontation. In St Saviour's the bedlam he envisaged
was almost concluded. The mob was dispersing, the congrega-
tion aghast, and a squealing pig, pushed in to disrupt the service,
was being removed. McNab had come to the rescue of Kingston,
advising him to lie down, and Emily, disturbed by the influence
of a more predatory woman, had the undivided attention for
once of the flirtatious young officer she admired. Time slipped
into a different gear, as it always did when he was writing, and
he did not hear the wind getting up.

Aproaching 4pm he reached his target. '*But I'm sure it's all a
misunderstanding. An awful lot of dreadful gup flies about the
bazaar, you know. It's the servants in India, Emily, they spread
all sorts of fanciful tales.*' Smoothing out potential trouble, as at
one of his dinner parties, he rolled the sheet out of the typewriter
to add to the A4 pile and from habit put a blank page, for next
day's start, on top. There was no rain for the moment, though it
was forecast for later in the day, and he counted it a release to
take on the elements after being trapped indoors for so long.

Leaving the single pollock in the freezer, confident of coming
back with his supper, he got ready: old denim jeans, penknife in
pocket, blue and white striped shirt, grey jumper and rubber
boots. Chilled after sitting so long, aware it was much colder
down on the rocks, he hastily did up his anorak and pulled on
the balaclava, tucking the woollen edge securely inside. He set
up his rod out of the wind, put the rest of the new hooks into his
fishing bag and set off, leaving his wallet and loose change on the
table and without bothering to lock the door.

Outside it was one of those odd days with a dry fog –
somewhere between a fog and a mist – and when the poor
visibility eased, down by the slipway, there was a promising
wash on the sea.

Epilogue

On the far side of Bantry Bay, near Castletownbere, a farmer named Ted Lowney was walking his land on 13 September when he noticed a black wellington boot protruding from waterweeds near the pier. Upon investigation the Gardai were called, and identity made from a laundry tag bearing the name of Farrell sewn to the inside neck of the sodden black balaclava. In Castletownbere Hospital dental records removed the last shred of hope for his family, and at the autopsy death was attributed to asphyxia by drowning. With fictional symmetry, the period spent in the water exactly matched Jim's immersion in the iron lung.

The small funeral at St James's Church of Ireland in Durrus was attended by family members with the exception of his father, who was too ill to travel, and by friends from his youth, as well as a good turnout of local people. The coffin was carried by his brother Richard, Jerry O'Mahony, Peter Burgess and the Daly brothers. 'It was desperately sad,' recounted Hilary, who travelled down with Jack Kirwan and her sister Jill. 'Afterwards I just remember thinking incredulously, Jimmy's *buried*. But there were two howlers which would have appealed to him hugely. As with any remote little Protestant church in Ireland, there was a record player instead of an organ and choir, and our music relied entirely on a '78 record of hymns. Halfway through one, the record stuck, something I knew, as we were standing there, that he would have absolutely loved. And when the coffin was being carried out at the end of the service I saw the name inscribed on the plate and it was James O'Farrell.' The site of the grave was within a few yards of the Bantry road, level with the spot where he used to brake for the bend. It overlooked the narrow stretch of water at the tip of Dunmanus Bay, and the inscription would be as modest and as guarded – *so eloquent, so succinct!* – as that on his books. 'James Gordon Farrell. Novelist. 1935–1979.'

The funeral in Durrus delineated the Irish compartment, with only Bob and Kathie Parrish, who were already familiar with the area, making the journey from London. On 19 October the English compartment was celebrated at a memorial service at St Bride's in Fleet Street, organised by his brother Richard and conducted by his cousin Tom Farrell, with an address by Bob Parrish, attended by his family and his London friends. St Bride's is a church with lateral pews facing towards each other across a central aisle, and the impression many took away was of rank upon rank of stylish women, of whom a large proportion was in tears. 'The memorial service was full of the best-looking women in publishing,' mused James Hale. 'One looked around and thought a little.'

The ex-callgirl immortalised as Lucy was present, on her own. Afterwards she ran up to hug Malcolm Dean and Gary Arnott before disappearing. Most of Jim's girlfriends sat together; he had, they agreed beforehand, left them to support one another. Patricia sat with the poet Derek Mahon, directly opposite Beryl Bainbridge, and Olivia Manning arrived late, wearing purple and leaning heavily on a stick. 'Looking sad and pinched,' as Hilary Spurling told Sonia Orwell, 'and perhaps just a tiny bit pleased at having survived him.' 'Perhaps these things shouldn't happen at all,' commented Sonia from Paris. 'In general they're lugubrious affairs and leave one gloomier than one was before and desperately in need of a drink despite it being the wrong time of day . . . And of course Olivia Manning was wild with joy at outliving anyone!' Margaret Drabble was one of those who could not weep, though she yearned to do so. "Nobody thinks Stephen would have wanted a church service," ' says the heroine of *The Gates of Ivory*, ' "but what else is there? You can't hold a service in Sainsbury's or Bertorelli's, can you?" '

Jim's sudden death inevitably gave rise to speculation, and conspiracy theories abounded, based upon a struggle on the rock and fatal knowledge; some suggested spying and MI5, others the Provisional IRA. But gradually the belief gained ground that suicide had to be the explanation, fuelled by the quantity of letters arriving posthumously to recipients unaware of the long Irish postal strike. 'J.G. killed himself,' guessed Andrew Sinclair tersely, remembering Pamplona, as he took a phone call about Jim's death. 'Scarred girl he was with till he left. Night. Horror about his body. His lung. Depressive.' When Carol Drisko told her lover he jumped to the same conclusion, and nothing she said could persuade him that he was wrong. Like everyone who knew Jim intimately, however, she remained adamant that he would never have committed suicide.

Mike Roemer, characteristically, questioned the role of the subconscious. 'One is endangered at times of change or stress,' he propounded. 'Concentration is so inward that you are more prone to accident, and there's a "don't care" fatalism underlying that. So often there is an intersection between the psychological and the physical. I personally believe that something coincided that didn't have to do so. I don't mean that Jim wanted to die, but he was *vulnerable*.' It is a telling argument against suicide that Jim left no will, which hugely increased the burden for his family: as danger intensifies in *The Siege of Krishnapur* the prospect of dying intestate, for that very reason, becomes the Collector's great anxiety. In his most autobiographical novel, *The Lung*, Martin Sands blames himself, too late, for the same omission.

The Coroner's verdict, brought in by a Bantry jury on 2 November 1979, was of accidental drowning. The sole witness testified that she saw him fall into the water and not move: if he had thrown himself in deliberately it would have been impossible to suppress every involuntary reflex. 'People who saw him fall', his mother informed his physiotherapist, 'thought that he . . . crumpled first. A doctor friend tells us that it is a frequent happening when people have had severe chest trouble.' Independently Claude Simha and Robin Stott, both doctors, concluded that hypothermia was responsible. The normal biochemical reactions to sustain life operate within a very narrow range, and a sudden fall of a few degrees in the core body temperature can result in coma and death. Such a shock causes cardiac arrest, which renders immediate unconsciousness and immobility. After a few minutes without blood reaching the brain death occurs, and the instinctive breathing-in of as little as two lungfuls of water in the interval can kill sooner.

But why, even so, had Jim ignored the weather danger signs, and how did he happen to fall in? In the early stages of that unexpected storm nothing out of the ordinary showed, except a higher water surface where it lapped against the rocks. 'Even when it seems calm to the untrained eye,' Jerry O'Mahony was able to explain, 'a storm can be on its way. When a storm is still 600 miles out at sea you get movement in the water with no cap on it; a well, we call it, and that comes two days before the storm, with the wind behind it.' As a newcomer, Jim had never experienced those conditions; nor would he have known that a storm with a spring tide is a more dangerous combination than a storm with a normal tide.

Concentrating on the tugging line, he would not have seen the subtle changing pattern in the number of breakers rising, and the progressive build-up from one big wave out of every twenty, to one out of every ten; the rotation was infinitesimal in comparison to the forty-foot crescendo he had witnessed. But the gulley behind the block, which under normal conditions was out of reach of the sea, now came within range of the highest crest. It seems most likely that as he stood on the small sloping surface, braced against the gusting wind with the end of the rod tucked under his right arm and playing out the line with his left hand, the wave seen by Mrs Foley's eldest child swelled up and washed into the gulley, sweeping down the line of the cleft to catch him hard behind the knees, and once in the water his three-quarter boots filled and pulled him down.

A writer may hope, it is said, for half a century of working life. Had Jim lived to write more, David Holloway assessed in the *Daily Telegraph*, 'he might well have been regarded as the greatest historical novelist of his generation.' The Collins paperback edition of *The Singapore Grip* came out in the spring of 1980, and within six months sold 45,000 copies. Underlining the brevity of his writing career – transformed from anonymous disciple within the space of fifteen years – Olivia Manning's last novel, *The Sum of Things*, appeared with the inscription 'For Jim Farrell, taken by the sea'.

And if Jim's death was unreasonable, so were the forms of

consolation, as Margaret Drabble, who did not believe in an afterlife, came to understand. Several months after his death she woke weeping in the night from a dream she thought must stem from a Weidenfeld party. 'It was an oddly frightening party, full of people I did not know, and many of them were sinister, changed half into animals, as in Circe's den. I was in a state of panic, looking around as one does, even when guests are not changed into animals, for someone I knew to speak to, when I saw Jim. He was wearing his white suit; he was always very elegant. I walked towards him, overcome with relief, reaching out my hand, and just as he was about to take it I remembered that he was dead, and he began to fade and recede from my sight. He was untouchable. But he was smiling quizzically, and was so much himself, so vividly himself, unlike all the other people there: he shook his head slightly, and continued to smile, as I began to cry, and he said, very distinctly, 'It's all right, you know, it's quite all right.'

In 1990 the novelist Timothy Mo, who in 1978 had been one of the few reviewers to acclaim *The Singapore Grip* – unknowingly awarding the accolade that had meant most to Jim, as he did so, by the comparison with Tolstoy – crossed from England to West Cork. In company with a fellow diver he changed in the empty house of the Dutch couple, and in heavy rain retraced Jim's last path. 'Underwater it became deep very quickly from shore and the scenery a few yards out was striking,' he was to write. 'Rock fingers formed a series of gulleys or narrow valleys, the walls of which were about 20 feet high. You could dive in one and not see the others in the one next to you. Returning to shore entailed swimming up walls to near the surface, then descending again, and then reclimbing. This is provocative of decompression sickness but one hardly cared: the visibility for a rainy day [pouring!] and stirred-up bottom was amazing: about 60 feet of crystalline viz, which is paradise for a UK diver. Quite a few tame wrasse and crabs going out to a sand bottom beyond the gulleys at 20 metres depth.'

So Jim, like Eliot's Prufrock but with no human voice to wake him, did for a while linger in the chambers of the sea. Timothy Mo had never succeeded in meeting him during the period when they both lived in London, and as he swam down he gave thanks that his tribute had appeared in time for Jim to read. Above the surface the rain pelted down, and below everything was bright.

The World of J.G. Farrell

It was, after all, only the lack of perspective that made it seem he
  would be swept away.

A huge house (*Troubles*) at the water's edge
whistling and groaning in the wind from the sea,
blind windows, flying slates, whole days of reverie,
'the cemetery of all initiative and endeavour',
outbuildings, tea-gold streams, a heathery road,
a yellow vintage 'motor' in the garage,
crows bickering high up in a foggy wood,
vegetable encroachments, intestinal shapes,
the click and ripple of exhausted pipes,
a creeper twining around a naked light
while a young man, inspected by binoculars,
harangues a restive crowd from a watery rock;
hill stations deserted (*Siege*), impenetrable foliage,
long bars empty (*Grip*) in tropical heat,
their pools afloat with matchboxes and driftwood,
fly-blown verandahs, ceiling fans at rest,
carnivorous plants entangling gates and fences,
the coercive empire an empire of the senses,
of rustling organism and whispering rain-forest,
a dripping silence after torrential rain,
the fluttering butterfly that starts the hurricane.
Whisper, immortal Muse, of the insanity of the great,
the futility of control, the proximity of the pit,
of babies in the dust, smoking rubbish, a circling kite.
The girls from Goa, in silk and satin and boa,

have boarded the last ship out of the opium war
while Gurkha riflemen parade at the aerodrome
to a skirl of bagpipes and the 'Skye Boat Song'
leaving to the Chinese, if they so desire,
the investment banks and polo fields of Hong Kong,
the Coke and Marlboro ads; they're going home.
Everyone's going home now, those with homes to go to;
the bugles blow and the Union Jack comes down
in the West Indies and the Antarctic soon,
Bermuda, Antigua, South Georgia and Pitcairn
and even, who knows, Gibraltar and Ulster too.
The big-game trophies and lion skins have gone
from the cold interiors of northern Europe
while the consular derelict with his jungle juice
and perpendicular terror of the abyss
can take the cure and start to live in hope.
Better a quiet life, the moon in a bucket of water
with nobody there to hear though the stars do
and a bedside book like the teachings of Chuang Tzu –
type of the unselfconscious thinker who,
never a slave to objective reality, knew
the identity of contraries, traced us from the germ
and saw our vital unity with the rest of nature;
disdained, of course, utilitarian system;
like Echo, answered only when called upon
in bamboo cage or palace of white jade.
We have lost our equilibrium, he said;
gaze at the world but leave the world alone.
Do nothing; do nothing and everything will be done.

Derek Mahon, *The Yellow Book*, 1997

Notes and References

Quotations are taken from the following editions of the works of J.G. Farrell:

A Man from Elsewhere (1ˢᵗ edition, New Authors Ltd), Hutchinson 1963.
The Lung (1ˢᵗ edition), Hutchinson 1965.
A Girl in the Head (1ˢᵗ edition), Jonathan Cape 1967.
Troubles (1ˢᵗ edition), Jonathan Cape 1970.
The Siege of Krishnapur, Phoenix paperbacks 1993.
The Singapore Grip, Phoenix paperbacks 1992.
The Hill Station (second impression), Flamingo paperbacks 1989.

Prologue

Contemporary (15 and 16 August 1979) newspapers: Guardian, Daily Telegraph, Irish Times, Irish Independent, Irish Press, Cork Examiner, Southern Star, Reuters report, International Herald Tribune and obituary columns of Observer and Sunday Times. *Interviews*: John Curtis, Malcolm Dean, Elsie Donald, Margaret Drabble, Josephine Farrell, Richard Farrell, Philip Haas, Francis King, Jack Kirwan, Garda Lupton, Jerry O'Mahony, David Simpson, Hilary Spurling, John Spurling, Carole Tucker. *Letters*: Edna O'Brien, Dr Colm Quigley, Calvin Trillon. *Archives/private papers*: Rockefeller Archives Center (Harkness); Jack Kirwan (notes); David Simpson (notes); English P.E.N. (commemorative JGF tape). *Publications*: Bookseller (18.8.79); 'Legacy of a Great Friendship' by Margaret Drabble in *People*, ed. Susan Hill (Chatto & Windus/ Hogarth Press). *Contemporary letter*: Hilary Spurling–Sonia Orwell 20.8.79.

page
1   The Major was floating: *Troubles*, p. 371.

1 At the Centre of a Vast Empire

Interviews: Sheilah Baird, Beryl Dawson, Josephine Farrell, Robert Farrell, Richard Farrell, Revd Tom Farrell, Revd J.R.I. Wikeley. *Archives/private papers*: Farrell family; Liverpool Record Office.

page
19   The train puffed steadily: *The Hill Station*, p. 18.

2 The Vanished Comfort and Security of Earlier Days

Interviews: Sheilah Baird, Beryl Dawson, John Eadie, Josephine Farrell, Richard Farrell, Robert Farrell, Revd Tom Farrell, Revd J.R.I. Wikeley. *Letters*: R.R.V. Kaufmann, Jenifer Leech, H.E. Moore, Buckley Wickham. *Contemporary newspapers*: *Southport Guardian* 14.10.44. *Archives/private papers*: Farrell family; West Derby Church Parish Records; Terra Nova School. *JGF interview*: 'Grip of Empire' by Malcolm Dean (*Guardian* 13.9.78). *JGF dialogue from correspondence*: with his parents (undated 44, 15.10.44, 29.10.44 and undated 45); with Sarah Bond (31.1.71).

page
23   a giant plant . . . insignificant petals: *A Girl in the Head*, p. 90.
23   What had happened: Ibid., pp. 87–8.
27   In human affairs: *The Singapore Grip*, p. 306.
27   stared about them: *The Siege of Krishnapur*, p. 92.
28   full of freshness and hope: *A Man from Elsewhere*, p. 25.
29   nobody is superior: *The Siege of Krishnapur*, p. 139.

3 Run Very Fast, Very Fast Indeed

Interviews: Brigid Allen, Pat Booth, Ralph Burrows, Roger Donald, Josephine Farrell, Richard Farrell, Robert Farrell, Revd Tom Farrell, Tom Gover, Norman Ilett, Geoffrey Lee, Prof. J.K.B. Nicholas, Nevill Phillips, Dr A. Tansey. *Letters*: Ralph Burrows, Glenys Ilett. *Contemporary letters*: G.M. Arthursen–John Spurling (27.8.79, 30.12.79 and 9.7.81); Revd C.E. Young to the Principal of Brasenose College, Oxford (1.12.53). *Archives/private papers*: JGF papers (Trinity College, Dublin); Farrell family; Brasenose College; Rossall School. *Publications*: *A Very Desolate Position* by Peter Bennett, Rossall Archives 1977; *The Rossallian* (1951–53); 'J.G. Farrell' by Brigid Allen (*London Magazine* 1992); 'Jim Farrell – A Memoir' by John Spurling (*The Times Saturday Review* 11.4.81); 'A Personal Memoir' by Malcolm Dean (*The Hill Station* 1981). *JGF dialogue from correspondence*: with Carol Drisko (undated).

page
36   An old man: *Troubles*, p. 100.
37   asphyxiating, ammoniac stench: Ibid., p. 146.
37   If that had been all: *The Lung*, p. 67.
38   large and jovial figure: *Troubles*, p. 344.
39   His father was sitting: *A Man from Elsewhere*, pp. 41–2.
41   Moreover, he was surrounded: *The Singapore Grip*, p. 287.
42   Edward had grasped: *Troubles*, pp. 46–7.
42   eminently normal: *The Lung*, pp. 154–5.
43   the smoky savagery: Ibid., p. 96.
43   that dreadful lurching: *Troubles*, p. 362.
45   'No thanks, quite alright': *The Rossallian, c.* 1951, 'Memoirs of a
       Fragile Three-quarter' by J.G. Farrell.
45   'When my housemaster': *The Rossallian, c.* 1951, 'Excuses' by
       Seamus.
46   There was something very depressing: *The Lung*, p. 42.
48   to stand reluctantly: Ibid., p. 53.
48   Good articles usually start off: *The Rossallian, c.* 1952, 'Relations'
       by J.G.F.
49   On the whole . . . next four hours: *The Rossallian, c.* 1953, 'Life at a
       French School', by James Farrell.
50   I . . . just wanted to get out: *The Lung*, p. 101.

4 The Yearning, the Boredom, the Heartache

Interviews: Pat Booth, Pamela Bradley, Jill Cox, Roger Donald, Josephine
   Farrell, Richard Farrell, Robert Farrell, Patricia Johnson, Jack
   Kirwan, Bridget O'Toole, Alison Palmer-Carter, Roy Parker, Hilary Pratt. *Letters*: Geoffrey Drought, Robert Farrell. *Contemporary letters*: (Solicitors James W. Lane, St Stephen's Green, Dublin 2
   (16.2.54); Donald Pringle (27.7.55). *Archives/private papers*: Farrell family; Castlepark School; Cunard (RMS *Saxonia*). *Publications*: 'Not a Crumb, Not a Wrinkle' by Bridget O'Toole (*Irish
   Studies* Autumn 1995); *Bookmark* – '*Writers on their Reading*', ed.
   Frederic Raphael (Quartet Books/Jonathan Cape 1975). *JGF interviews*: 'The Quandary of £5,000 Prizewinner' by David Brazil
   (1973); 'Epitaph for the Empire' by George Brock (*Observer*
   magazine 24.9.78). *JGF dialogue from correspondence*: with Russell McCormmach (19.11.65).
page
54   I arrived punctually: *The Rossallian*, 1952, 'Further Memoirs of a
       Fragile Three-quarter', by J.G.F.
55   From his window: *A Girl in the Head*, pp. 38–9.
56   the victim of the beauty: *The Siege of Krishnapur*, p. 36.
56   I bravely make conversation: *The Rossallian, c.* 1953, 'Hazards of
       Holiday Tennis' by Seamus.
57   Girls and the fresh sea wind: *The Lung*, p. 46.

58   Puberty . . . It comes as: *A Girl in the Head*, p. 129.
58   It was he who lent: *The Lung*, p. 28.
58   It was all so unnatural: Ibid., p. 35.
59   I can still see us all: *A Girl in the Head*, pp. 204–5.
61   These days the mere sight: *Troubles*, p. 244.
62   You know, it smells so good: Ibid., p. 52.
63   very foreign, after all: Ibid., p. 59.
63   transfixed by sadness: Ibid., p. 216.
63   Almost twenty past five: *The Lung*, pp. 165–6.
63   D'you realise: *Troubles*, p. 310.
64   Why do other men: *The Lung*, p. 143.
64   had somehow imagined that the foyer: *A Girl in the Head*, p. 56.
64   That slight shock: Ibid., p. 144.
66   peering down at the water: *The Lung*, p. 69.

5 A Ballistic Missile

Interviews: Gary Arnott, Sue Bond, Ralph Burrows, Jill Cox, Roger
   Donald, Josephine Farrell, Richard Farrell, Robert Farrell, Revd
   Tom Farrell, Dr Elie Harar, Norman Ilett, Jack Kirwan, Brian
   Knox Peebles, Roger Murray, Prof. J.K.B. Nicholas, Brian Pearce,
   Hilary Pratt, John Spurling, Janet Watts. *Contemporary letter*:
   from Norman Man, Fire Marshall, Foundation Co. of Canada,
   Frobisher Bay, NWT (9.4.56). *Archives/private papers*: Farrell
   family; 'Living in the Arctic' by Alfred Copeland for Foundation
   Co. of Canada; Nuffield Orthopaedic Centre, Oxford (medical
   records); Brasenose College, Oxford; BBC archives ('The White-
   haired Novelist, Radio 3, 24.3.80). *Publications*: 'What's What',
   Cherwell (1956); 'A Personal Memoir' by Malcolm Dean (*The Hill
   Station* 1981). *JGF interviews*: Anon (1963); 'Writing in the Dark
   and Not a Detail Missed' by Caroline Moorehead (*The Times*
   9.9.78). *JGF dialogue from correspondence*: with Russell
   McCormmach (25.12.62). *JGF quotes*: 'Notebook' in *Oxford
   Opinion* (14.4.60 and 25.4.60).

page
68   An atomic war: *A Man from Elsewhere*, p. 49.
70   Streams of fire . . . the burning Majestic: *Troubles*, p. 443.
70   Now the fire . . . to its fiery heart: *The Singapore Grip*, p. 447.
74   The town had been pitch dark: *The Lung*, p. 12.
75   When I was an undergraduate: Ibid., p. 25.
77   Small muscles in his back: Ibid., p. 11.
78   I'm a python: Ibid., p. 24.
79   With some difficulty . . . was sweating.: Ibid., pp. 14, 20, 25, 27, 40.
79   Trees were drifting: Ibid., pp. 44–5.

6 In Human Affairs, Things Tend Inevitably to Go Wrong

Interviews: Gary Arnott, Sheilah Baird, Ralph Burrows, Jill Cox, Josephine Farrell, Richard Farrell, Robert Farrell, Tony Gould, Brian Knox Peebles, Roger Marshall, Prof. J.K.B. Nicholas, Brian Pearce, Stephen Wall, Yvonne Wall. *Letters*: Dr Alison Brady, The Welcome Museum. *Archives/private papers*: Farrell family; Brasenose College, Oxford; Nuffield Orthopaedic Centre, Oxford (medical records); BBC archives ('The White-haired Novelist', Radio 3, 24.3.80). *JGF dialogue from correspondence*: with Sarah Bond (16.6.68).

page
81 The nurse was standing . . . breathing faster: *The Lung*, pp. 48, 51, 54.
82 A touch of panic: Ibid., p. 64.
82 He pictured himself: Ibid., pp. 52–54.
82 A man in overalls: Ibid., pp. 63–66.
83 as horizontal and as petrified: Ibid., p. 66.
83 Nurse . . . for the love of God: Ibid., p. 87.
83 crimson, flashing darkness: Ibid., p. 67.
84 He began to sweat: Ibid., p. 71.
84 a sad ending: Ibid., p. 70.
84 among them a man, naked: Ibid., p. 84.
84 a prey to half-submerged fears: Ibid., p. 49.
84 His mind wearily attacked: Ibid., p. 77.
85 'Nurse, I need an amanuensis': Ibid., p. 84.
85 'I'm afraid the wine is only Australian burgundy': Ibid., p. 80.
86 One record programme: Ibid., pp. 108–9.
86 like a rare moth: Ibid., p. 73.
86 striped, dripping-fanged . . . lustre of the water: Ibid., p. 72.
87 Outside . . . the early sunshine: Ibid., p. 65.
88 'You know, it's difficult': Ibid., p. 71.
88 It seemed as if both his lungs: Ibid., p. 88.
89 Nothing at all was moving: Ibid., pp. 103, 108.
89 People drifted round the outskirts: Ibid., p. 108.
89 one scarlet streak of pain: Ibid.
89 It was wonderful: Ibid., p. 109.
89 All the objects in it: Ibid., pp. 109–10.
90 an elderly butterfly: Ibid., p. 57.
90 as dead as cooked hams: Ibid., p. 84.
90 The room was filling up: Ibid., pp. 123–4.
90 We'll take a cup of anguish: Ibid., p. 165.
90 with startled, sunken eyes: Ibid., p. 135.
91 locked tight, as immovably bent: Ibid., p. 145.
92 She . . . raised his arm again and pressed it: Ibid., pp. 119–20, 126.
92 the return to childhood was now complete: Ibid., p. 134.
93 'You look like the vamp . . .' She would feel sorry for him: Ibid., pp. 111–12.

93 It's all an illusion: Ibid., p. 97.
93 He thought of her growing up: Ibid., pp. 204–5.
94 bleeding slowly and peacefully . . . he could find a way: Ibid., p. 131.
95 The ward was cleaned, tidied: Ibid., p. 120.
95 boeuf à l'angoisse: Ibid., p. 118.
95 immense grey jungle: Ibid., p. 164.
96 staggered . . . with loose, swaying puppet-strides: Ibid., p. 136.
97 He was neither happy nor unhappy: Ibid., p. 199.
97 It was as if: Ibid., p. 185.
97 She took his overcoated arm: Ibid., pp. 183–185.
98 the best of us all: *The Siege of Krishnapur*, p. 312.
98 His past he now saw: Ibid., p. 74

7 The Beauty of the Cold Season

Interviews: Gary Arnott, Paul Barker, Pamela Bradley, Ralph Burrows, Jill Cox, Jill Davies, Phillip Davies, Roger Donald, Josephine Farrell, Richard Farrell, Robert Farrell, Revd Tom Farrell, Erwin Fleissner, Miriam Gross, Jan Hartman, Patricia Johnson, Jack Kirwan, Brian Knox Peebles, Russell McCormmach, Judy Miller, Terence Mitchell, Roger Murray, Prof. J.B.K Nicholas, Nevill Phillips, Hilary Pratt, Sally Sampson, Andrew Sinclair, Anthony Smith, Dermot Stokes, Molly Stokes, Dr A. Tansey, Stephen Wall, Yvonne Wall. *Letters*: Bob Cumming, Russell Meek, Dennis Potter, Calvin Trillin. *Archives/private papers*: Farrell Family; Nuffield Orthopaedic Centre, Oxford (medical files); *TCD – A College Miscellany* (November 1957); JGF papers (Trinity College, Dublin); Andrew Sinclair (notes). *Publications*: JGF obituary in *The Brazen Nose* (Vol. 27, 1993); backnumbers of *Isis* and *Oxford Opinion*, Bodleian Library; *My Friend Judas* by Andrew Sinclair (Faber & Faber 1959); 'As Does the Bishop' by John Spurling (*The Hill Station* 1981).

page
100 He was annoyed with himself: *Troubles*, pp. 14, 41.
100 Eternal Youth, First Love, Peace: *The Lung*, p. 41.
101 How beautiful . . . the glimmering colours: Ibid.
101 The blades of its petals: *A Girl in the Head*, pp. 80, 84.
103 Away into night and silence: *The Lung*, p.43.
103 'This isn't me': *A Girl in the Head*, p. 33.
103 He was isolated: Ibid., p. 156.
106 a city of effete embryo Hitlers: *The Lung*, p. 25.
106 sitting behind these same crumbling walls: Ibid.
106 I know every inch of every military base: 'Letter for Carola', *Isis*, 2 December 1959, pp. 16–18.
107 was something which had happened: *A Man from Elsewhere*, p. 24.
108 Magistrate's judgements were invariably pitiless: *The Siege of Krishnapur*, p. 14.

109   Have you ever ridden a bicycle: *A Girl in the Head*, p. 25.
109   He was unable to stop himself: Ibid., p. 71.
110   a screen of cheerful irony: *A Man from Elsewhere*, p. 63.
110   What he could never do was smile: *A Girl in the Head*, p. 87.
112   had been told that he had the talent: 'Letter for Carola', *Isis*, 2 December 1959, pp. 16–18.
115   down a long sunlit valley: *The Lung*, p. 19.
116   a bull in a bull-ring with its wonderful muscles: *A Girl in the Head*, p. 173.

8 Water Becoming Hard Ice

Interviews: David Caute, Jill Davies, Philip Davies, Roger Donald, Josephine Farrell, Robert Farrell, Erwin Fleissner, Sir Martin Gilbert, Brian Knox Peebles, Russell McCormmach, Dr James McCormack, Judy Miller, Brian Pearce, Hilary Pratt, Sally Sampson, Molly Stokes. *Letter*: Bob Cumming. *Archives/private papers*: Bob Cumming (diary, 1960); Farrell family; Sir Martin Gilbert (diary). *JGF contemporary account*: French journal (1960–62). *Publications*: *Wicklow People* (7.3.59, 2.5.59, 14.11.59); *Isis* and *Oxford Opinion* (Dec 1959; April and May 1960); *Irish Times* (28.7.60). *JGF dialogue from correspondence*: with Sarah Bond (27.6.68); with Norman Ilett (6.7.78); with Patsy Cumming (undated 1962).

page
120   strongest emotion I had ever experienced: *The Lung*, p. 70.
121   would cram on the brakes: *A Girl in the Head*: p. 146.
121   coarse-grained in black and white: *The Lung*, p. 138.
121   half buried in the sand: Ibid., p. 139.
122   'But of course . . . you can't do anything about': *A Girl in the Head*, p. 55.
122   'It's all my fault . . .' Nobody contradicted him: *The Lung*, p. 177.
122   He scrambled hastily: Ibid.
123   Nobody else seemed to pay any attention: *A Man from Elsewhere*, p. 39.
123   'What's the matter?': *The Lung*, p. 144.
125   a gifted young American: *The Singapore Grip*, p. 294.
127   'For God's sake get up': *The Lung*, p. 195.
128   The fact is . . . What a bastard that man is!: 'Letter for Carola', *Isis*, 2 December 1959, pp. 16–18.
129   My own imagined future . . . back on the road: 'Notebook' by James Farrell, *Oxford Opinion*, 25 April 1960.
130   Very few of us are stubborn enough: Ibid.
131   Peering into the pale . . . would heal themselves: *A Man from Elsewhere*, p. 154.
131   He had stood . . . that he could remember: *The Lung*, p. 149.
132   I sometimes feel that I'm made up: *A Girl in the Head*, p. 207.

133 The knowledge that they would soon: *The Singapore Grip*, pp. 317–18.

133 There is always a distinction: 'Notebook' by James Farrell, *Oxford Opinion*, 14 April 1960.

9 This Is the Kind of Life I Want

Interviews: Alan Cumming, Josephine Farrell, Hubert Hours, Nadege Lepra, Sally Sampson, John Spurling, Stephen Wall. *Letters*: Franz Beer, Patsy Cumming. *Archives/private papers*: Farrell family; JGF papers (Trinity College, Dublin); Lycée Chaptal (Mende); Lycée Dumont-d'Urville (Toulon); Rockefeller Archives Center (Harkness); English P.E.N. (commemorative JGF tape). *Publications*: *Irish Times* (July and November 1969); *Le Monde* and *Figaro* (1960–62); *The Gates of Ivory* by Margaret Drabble (Viking 1991). *JGF interview*: 'An Insight Job' by Malcolm Dean (Guardian 1.9.73). *JGF contemporary account*: French journal (1960–62). *JGF dialogue from correspondence*: with Patsy Cumming (6.10.61, 11.11.61, 21.2.62, 6.3.62, 28.3.62, 28.5.62, 2.6.62, 5.6.62, undated, 13.6.62, 16.6.62, 25.12.62, 18.2.63); with Russell McCormmach (25.12.62, 6.3.63); with Sarah Bond (16.6.68).

page
137 The explosions, the detention camps: *A Man from Elsewhere*, p. 49.
137 He wanted desperately to feel: Ibid., p. 144.
137 How was he to know?: Ibid., p. 165.
139 the whole object of a man's life: Ibid., p. 99.
140 cataclysm of the express: Ibid., p. 105.
142 It was as if he had been firmly sealed: Ibid., p. 166.
142 And the unbearable knowledge: *A Girl in the Head*, p. 120.

10 The Slow, Dangerous Ascent

Interviews: Gary Arnott, Paul Barker, Jonathan Clowes, Norma di Marco, Maureen Duffy, Josephine Farrell, 'Lucy Hughes', Jack Kirwan, Brian Knox Peebles, Rose Knox Peebles, Russell McCormmach, Bridget O'Toole, Brian Pearce, Michelle Pearce, Sally Sampson, John Spurling. *Archives/private papers*: JGF papers (Trinity College, Dublin); Rockefeller Archives Center (Harkness). *Publications*: Bookseller (24.8.63); *The Times Literary Supplement* (20.9.63); *Daily Telegraph* and *Observer* (September 1963). *JGF interviews*: Anon (1963); 'Writing in the Dark and Not a Detail Missed' by Caroline Moorehead (*The Times* 9.9.78); 'Epitaph for the Empire' by George Brock (*Observer* magazine 24.9.78). *JGF dialogue from correspondence*: with Patsy Cumming (28.3.62, 2.6.62, 13.6.62, 25.12.62, 18.2.63, 6.3.63, 12.11.63, 21.12.63); with Russell McCormmach (20.9.62, 25.12.62, 23.1.63, 6.3.63,

4.4.63, 25.8.63, 6.9.63, 21.12.63); with Sarah Bond (21.6.68); with Carol Drisko (15.10.68).

page
156   tasting his own destruction: *The Lung*, p. 54.
156   You reached a stage: Ibid., p. 68.
163   was standing naked and motionless: *A Girl in the Head*, p. 115.
164   magnificently baroque . . . a mink Dutch cap: Ibid., p. 206.
164   He could visualize a nightmare: Ibid., p. 97.
165   She was sometimes impatient: *Troubles*, pp. 247–9.
166   amused, paternal, indulgent: Ibid., p. 247.
168   'Hm, I told you' . . . quite enjoyable: Ibid., pp. 191,193.
168   he had only to close his eyes: Ibid., p. 355.

11 A Sea of Dark Feathers

Interviews: Gary Arnott, Jonathan Clowes, Beryl Dawson, Josephine Farrell, Tony Gould, Dr Elie Harar, Russell McCormmach, Reynir Oddson, Anna Simha, Dr Claude Simha, Andrew Sinclair, Stephen Wall. *Publications*: *Bookseller* (24.7.65, 23.10.65); 'As Does the Bishop', John Spurling (*The Hill Station* 1981); *Daily Telegraph* (28.10.65); *Guardian* (29.10.65); *Irish Times* (30.10.65). *Archives/private papers*: Farrell family; JGF papers (Trinity College, Dublin); Rockefeller Archives Center (Harkness); English P.E.N. (commemorative JGF tape). *JGF dialogue from correspondence*: with Russell McCormmach (6.9.63, 21.12.63, 21.12.64, 15.2.65, 16.3.65, 13.9.65, 19.11.65, 12.12.65); with Patsy Cumming (12.11.63).

page
173   The park sloped away gently: *The Lung*, p. 65.
173   a beautiful abstract painting: Ibid., p. 52.
182   I wonder if you've ever seen lizards: *A Girl in the Head*, p. 125.

12 A Nebulous Desire for Escape

Interviews: Gary Arnott, Jonathan Clowes, Jill Davies, Philip Davies, Norma di Marco, Maureen Duffy, Robert Farrell, Sandy Fuller, Russell McCormmach, Reynir Oddson, Michele Pearce, Hilary Pratt, Sally Sampson, Dr Claude Simha, Hilary Spurling, John Spurling, Tom Wakefield, Stephen Wall. *Letter*: Andrew Gemill. *Archives/private papers*: Farrell family; Rockefeller Archives Center (Harkness); JGF papers (Trinity College, Dublin); English P.E.N. (commemorative JGF tape); BBC archives ('The White-Haired Novelist', Radio 3, 24.3.80). *JGF interviews*: 'Grip of Empire' by Malcolm Dean (*Guardian* 13.9.78); 'Epitaph for the Empire' by George Brock (*Observer* magazine 24.9.78). *Publications*: *Wings of a Man's Life* by Gorley Putt (Claridge Press); 'A Personal

Memoir' by Malcolm Dean (*The Hill Station* 1981); 'Jim Farrell – A
Memoir' by John Spurling (*The Times Saturday Review* 11.4.81).
JGF dialogue from correspondence: with Russell McCormmach
(25.12.62, 21.12.63, 20.12.64, 15.2.65, 16.3.65, 30.5.65, 13.9.65,
19.11.65, 12.12.65, 7.2.66, 4.6.66, 10.7.66, 5.8.69); with Patsy
Cumming (13.6.62); with Bridget O'Toole (Dec 69).

page
187   I'd carried the luggage: *A Girl in the Head*, p. 143.
188   a theatre curtain would have been big enough: Ibid., pp. 105–6.
192   Imagination can only change things: Ibid., p. 173.
192   the cemetery of all initiative: Ibid., p. 35.
192   But there was another man: Ibid, p. 36.
193   unspeakable . . . a poseur and a layabout: Ibid., p. 107.
193   Once on his feet Boris realized: Ibid., p. 156.
195   And, you know, when I thought: Ibid., p. 122.
196   The hotel was largely patronized . . . blue flames: Ibid., p. 146.
196   All the white skeletons: Ibid., p. 52–3.
197   A nebulous desire for escape: Ibid., p. 164.
200   You know, life is really rather sad: Ibid., p. 223.

13 The Extreme Outer Edge of Endeavour

Interviews: Gary Arnott, Franz Beer, Kenneth A. Brown, Patricia Cum-
ming, Malcolm Dean, Elsie Donald, Roger Donald, Robert Down-
ie, Conor Farrington, Erwin Fleissner, John B. Fox, John Guare,
Paul Huxley, Altie Karper, Robert Kostrzewa, Russell McCorm-
mach, Patricia Moynagh, Gorley Putt, Michael Roemer, André
Shiffrin, Dyanne Simon, Roger Simon, Arnold Weinstein. *Letter*:
Bob Cumming. *Archives/private papers*: Farrell family; JGF papers
(Trinity College, Dublin); Rockefeller Archives Center (Harkness);
Bob Cumming (diary); Surf Hotel (Block Island). *Contemporary
letters*: Sandy Ellis–Yvonne Wall (13.9.66 and Dec 66). *Publica-
tions*: *Providence Journal* and *Evening Bulletin* (7.7.66); 'J.G.
Farrell' by Brigid Allen (*London Magazine* 1992); *Directory of
Commonwealth Fund Fellows and Harkness Fellows* (1925–1990);
Making Scenes by Robert Brustein (Random House NY 1981). *JGF
interviews*: 'Quandary of £5,000 Prizewinner' by David Brazil
(1973); 'Writing in the Dark and Not a Detail Missed' by Caroline
Moorehead (*The Times* 9.9.78). *JGF dialogue from correspondence*: with Brian Knox Peebles (5.11.66); with Russell McCormmach (22.9.66, 29.9.66, 16.11.66); with Carol Drisko (15.10.68,
2.12.68).

page
215   he, too, found himself in a situation: Unfinished story (NYC 1966/
       67), JGF papers in Trinity College, Dublin.
225   On his last day in Kilnalough: *Troubles*, p.446.

14 A Traveller through Unmapped Country

Interviews: Gary Arnott, Monika Beisner, Sarah Bond, Alastair Cooke, Malcolm Dean, Roger Donald, Hans Dorflinger, Carol Drisko, Robert Farrell, Sandy Fuller, Paul Huxley, Gorley Putt, Emily Read, Piers Paul Read. *Letters*: Bob Cumming, Sandy Fuller. *Archives/ private papers*: JGF papers (Trinity College, Dublin); Bob Cumming (diary entries 22.10.67 & 8.4.68); Sandy Fuller (US diary); Carol Drisko (diary); Rockefeller Archives Center (Harkness). *Publications*: 'At the End of the Line', *The Times Literary Supplement* (20.7.67); *Saigon Post* (2.10.75); *Vietnam War Almanac* by Harry L. Summers Jr. *Contemporary letter*: Carol Drisko–JGF (11.7.67). *JGF dialogue from correspondence*: with Carol Drisko (15.5.67, undated, 27.5.67, 29.5.67, 3.6.67, 15.7.67, 25.7.67 (pc), 1.8.67, 3.8.67 (pc), 15.8.67 (pc), 6.6.68, 15.10.68, 6.1.69); with Brian Knox Peebles (pc: 15.7.67); with Claude and Anna Simha (pc: 15.7.67); with G.M. Arthursen (30.8.67); with Russell McCormmach (29.8.67, Feb 68 (pc), 15.6.68, 5.8.69); with Sarah Bond (undated, 16.6.68, 26.7.68, 12.9.68, 12.10.68, 14.10.68).

page
242   He could go anywhere . . . Sarah would not be: *Troubles*, p.246.

15 Out into the Open Sea

Interviews: Gary Arnott, Paul Barker, Monika Beisner, Sarah Bond, Jonathan Clowes, Alan Cumming, Malcolm Dean, Norma di Marco, Diana Ditchfield, Carol Drisko, Josephine Farrell, Richard Farrell, Sandy Fuller, Francis King, Rose Knox Peebles, Derek Mahon, Russell McCormmach, Judy Miller, Bridget O'Toole, Brian Pearce, Piers Paul Read, Deborah Rogers, Dr Claude Simha, Hilary Spurling, John Spurling, Catherine Storr, Tom Wakefield, Stephen Wall. *Letter*: Alfred Brendel. *Archives/private papers*: Farrell family; JGF papers (Trinity College, Dublin). *Publications*: *Bookseller* (15.8.70, 15.5.71); A Personal Memoir' by Malcolm Dean and 'Things Fall Apart' by Margaret Drabble (*The Hill Station* 1981); 'Not a Crumb, Not a Wrinkle' by Bridget O'Toole (*Irish Studies* Autumn 1995). *JGF interviews*: 'Grip of Empire' by Malcolm Dean (*Guardian* 13.9.78), 'Epitaph for the Empire' by George Brock (*Observer* magazine 24.9.78). *JGF dialogue from correspondence*: with Sarah Bond (16.6.68, 25.6.68, 27.6.68, 4.7.68, 5.7.68, 12.7.68, 15.7.68, 7.8.68, 31.8.68, 5.10.68, 12.10.68, 14.10.68, 19.10.68, Sept 69, Nov/Dec 69 (undated), 28.9.70, 10.6.71); with Carol Drisko (24.6.68, 13.9.68, 15.10.68, 3.11.68, Feb 69, 10.1.69, 14.4.69, 9.5.69, 7.7.69, 14.7.69, 9.9.69, 24.11.69, 12.2.70, 28.5.70. 20.11.70); with Russell McCormmach (15.6.68, 5.9.68, 17.11.68, 22.1.69, 5.8.69,

9.9.69, 27.3.70, 29.5.70); with Bridget O'Toole (5.10.69, 21.10.69, 23.11.69, 3.12.69, 2.2.70, 9.10.70).

page
246 He wrote to her immediately: *Troubles*, pp. 250-1.
248 poignarded to death: Ibid, pp. 238, 254, 277.
251 he began to feel drowsy: Ibid., p. 396.
252 'So *that* was what she looked like': Ibid., p. 21.
252 After all, he was not a complete fool: Ibid., pp. 392-3.
253 after all, there is not so very much difference: Ibid., p. 78.
253 People are insubstantial: Ibid., p. 154.
254 And yes, it had been a bit hard: Ibid., p. 405.
255 Every now and then, however: Ibid., p. 169.
269 The years go by: *The Siege of Krishnapur*, p. 313.

16 A Foot Wedged in the Door of Eternity

Interviews: Shiv Chirimar, Malcolm Dean, Norma di Marco, Rose Knox Peebles, Michael Leonard, John Spurling, Catherine Storr, Dr Robin Stott, Stephen Wall. *Letters*: Bob Cumming, Robert Farrell. *Archives/private papers*: Bob Cumming (diary: 8.2.71); Farrell family; JGF Papers (Trinity College, Dublin). *Publication*: 'Indian Diary' by JGF (*The Hill Station*); 'Jim Farrell – A Memoir' by John Spurling (*The Times Saturday Review* 11.4.81); 'Not a Crumb, Not a Wrinkle' by Bridget O'Toole (*Irish Studies* Autumn 1995). *Contemporary letter*: Edmund Gibson-John Spurling (26.10.73). *JGF interviews*: 'An Insight Job' by Malcolm Dean (Guardian 1.9.73). 'Quandary of £5,000 Prizewinner' by David Brazil (1973). *JGF dialogue from correspondence*: with Sarah Bond (12.7.68, 7.8.68, 28.9.70, 31.1.71); with Carol Drisko (9.9.69, 1.2.71, 28.4.71, 26.10.71); with his parents (1.2.71, 11.2.71, 11.3.71, 5.4.71); with Russell McCormmach (27.3.70, 8.2.71); with Bridget O'Toole (23.11.69, 2.2.70, 25.1.71, 5.2.71, 15.2.71, 7.3.71, 17.3.71, 23.3.71); with John Spurling (17.2.71).

page
271 Bricks are undoubtedly: *The Siege of Krishnapur*, pp. 9–10.
273 What an advantage: Ibid., p. 169.
274 crowded with ladies and children: Ibid., pp. 92, 124.
277 What use is it if we bring the advantages: Ibid., p. 80.
278 What can be more distressing: Ibid., p. 49.
278 a sensual little angel: Ibid., p. 105.
278 the beauty of the cold season: Ibid., p. 20.
278 The infant . . . began to cry: Ibid., pp. 237–8.
287 Over there, beneath that group: Ibid., p. 171.
288 A lamp was burning: Ibid., p. 179.
289 Near a fireplace of marble: Ibid., p. 71.
290 Their way led past the Great Banyan: Ibid., p. 29.
290 Fleury . . . was fond of graveyards: Ibid., p. 36.

290 All the same, once he had spent: Ibid.
291 Fleury could see that Louise: Ibid., p. 40.
292 Fleury found . . . such an intricate mass: Ibid., p. 77.

17 In the Right Place at the Right Time

Interviews: Ian Angus, Vincent Banville, Paul Barker, Sarah Bond, Sue Bond, Kevin Brownlow, Sir Michael Caine, David Caute, Susannah Clapp, Jonathan Clowes, Alan Cumming,Malcolm Dean, Elsie Donald, Hans Dorflinger, Margaret Drabble, Carol Drisko, Maureen Duffy, Robert Farrell, Stephen Frears, Martyn Goff, James Hale, Philippa Harrison, Brian Knox Peebles, Rosemary Legge, Derek Mahon, Bridget O'Toole, Richard Rawlinson, Piers Paul Read, Deborah Rogers, Sally Sampson, Judy Scott-Fox, Andrew Sinclair, Christopher Sinclair-Stevenson, Hilary Spurling, John Spurling, Catherine Storr, Lavinia Trevor, Marina Warner, Janet Watts, Fred Zinnemann. *Letters*: Alan Bennett, Kevin Brownlow, Robin Denniston, Robert Farrell, Andrew Gemill, Karl Miller, Edna O'Brien, Ruth Prawer Jhabvala. *Archives/private papers*: BBC archives ('The White-Haired Novelist', Radio 3, 24.3.80); Farrell family; JGF papers (Trinity College, Dublin); English P.E.N. (commemorative JGF tape). *Publications*: *Sunday Times*, *Observer* (2.9.73); *The Times*, *Evening Standard*, *Irish Times* (29.11.73); *New Yorker* (18.11.74); *Bookseller* (15.9.73, 29.9.73, 8.12.73); *Prize Writing* by Martyn Goff; *The Gates of Ivory* by Margaret Drabble. *JGF interviews*: (1973): 'Quandary of £5000 prizewinner' by David Brazil, (1973); profile by Derek Mahon (*Vogue* June 1994); 'Grip of Empire' by Malcolm Dean (*Guardian* 13.9.78). *JGF dialogue from correspondence*: with Sarah Bond (10.6.71); with Carol Drisko (28.5.71, 4.8.71, 4.10.71, 26.10.71, 22.1.72, 27.2.72, 28.5.72); with his parents (27.1.74, 22.2.74, 15.5.74, 7.6.74, 11.10.74, 9.12.75); with Norman Ilett (23.9.74); with Russell McCormmach (8.8.74); with Catherine Peters (5.12.73); with Lavinia Trevor (30.3.73).

page
295 The Collector had become calm again: *The Siege of Krishnapur*, p. 215.
296 There's nothing one can actually *do*: *A Girl in the Head*, p. 144.
296 a cautious contempt: *The Siege of Krishnapur*, p. 301.
309 Perhaps, if one takes the long view: Ibid., p. 187.
314 He was like the ring-master: *Troubles*, p. 261.
320 Such was the reward for complacency: *The Siege of Krishnapur*, p. 15.

18 At Large in the Minefields

Interviews: Ian Angus, Brigid Allen, Gary Arnott, David Caute, Alan Cumming, John Curtis, Malcolm Dean, Diana Ditchfield, Elsie Donald, Roger Donald, Margaret Drabble, Josephine Farrell, Richard Farrell, Philip Haas, James Hale, Jan Hartman, Paul Huxley, Francis King, Rose Knox Peebles, Alison Lurie, Doreen Mahon, Patricia Moynagh, Bridget O'Toole, Nevill Phillips, Richard Rawlinson, Deborah Rogers, Dr Claude Simha, David Simpson, Hilary Spurling, Dr Robin Stott, Paul Theroux, Claire Tomalin, Shelby Tucker, Tom Wakefield, Yvonne Wall, Marina Warner, Janet Watts. *Letters*: Ruth Prawer Jhabvala, Lacy Wright. *Archives/ private papers*: John Curtis; Reading University (Bodley Head Editorial); Farrell family; JGF papers (Trinity College, Dublin); Claire Tomalin (diary 26.2.74-31.10.75); BBC archives ('The White-Haired Novelist', Radio 3, 24.3.80). *Publications*: 'Legacy of a Great Friendship' by Margaret Drabble in *People*, ed. Susan Hill (Chatto & Windus/Hogarth Press); *Decent Interval* by Frank Snepp (Allen Lane 1980); *The Fall of Saigon* by David Butler (Sphere Books 1986); 'Things Fall Apart' by Margaret Drabble and 'As Does the Bishop' by John Spurling (*The Hill Station* 1981); *New Statesman* (review by Timothy Mo 15.9.76). *JGF interviews*: 'Grip of Empire' by Malcolm Dean (*Guardian* 13.9.78); 'Epitaph for the Empire' by George Brock (*Observer* magazine 24.9.78); 'Writing in the Dark and Not a Detail Missed, by Caroline Moorehead (*The Times* 9.9.78). *JGF dialogue from correspondence*: with G.M. Arthursen (25.8.76, 19.2.78); with Carol Drisko (12.2.70); with his parents (6.1.75, 14.1.75, 29.1.75, 23.2.75, 6.3.75, 25.3.75, 31.3.75, 27.5.75, 23.10.75, 20.11.75); with Martin Gilbert (22.9.78); with Norman Ilett (12.4.78); with Russell McCormmach (8.8.74, 28.11.75); with Bridget O'Toole (25.11.74, 25.1.75, 9.7.77); with Claude Simha (6.1.75).

page
322 I was like a man who sees a breeze: *A Girl in the Head*, p. 145.
323 I loved her above all: Ibid., pp. 146–7.
324 How on earth could he disengage: *The Lung*, pp. 181–2.
325 The Collector admired pretty women: *The Siege of Krishnapur*, p. 27.
329 a jolting passage: *The Singapore Grip*, p. 80.
330 He found himself: Ibid., p. 456.
331 Strong nations . . . will always take advantage: Ibid., pp. 133–4, 141.
332 in human affairs things tend: Ibid., p. 306.
332 quite simply a gentleman: Ibid., pp. 72–3.
332 a tall, rather anxious-looking man: Ibid., p. 35.
332 The Major was a discreet: Ibid., p. 36.
332 'What's your name, son?': Ibid., p. 43.

333 Walter . . . pictured Mr Webb: Ibid., p. 17.
336 At [Matthew's] side: Ibid., p. 138.
336 How he loved the tropical: Ibid., p. 232.
337 more psychological than real: Ibid., p. 5.
337 The ranks of fat white pillars: Ibid., p. 30.
337 The insignia of the Federated Malay States Railway: Ibid., pp. 295–6.
337 Ehrendorf had the impression: Ibid., p. 296.
337 half closing your eyes and very vigorously: Ibid., pp. 298–9.
339 One, two, three butterflies: Ibid., p. 316.
339 remembered Saigon mornings: Ibid., p. 244.
344 Such was the swiftness: Ibid., p. 492.
345 Again the crowd pressed forward: Ibid., p. 517.
346 In the weeks, then months: Ibid., p. 595.
346 At long last they began to near: Ibid., p. 514.
348 a real pang of sorrow: Ibid., p. 77.
348 And slowly a peculiar feeling: Ibid., p. 429.
350 The starlight glints: Ibid., p. 224.

19 A Tiny Bit World-Weary

Interviews: Brigid Allen, Gary Arnott, Sheilah Baird, Monika Beisner, Susannah Clapp, David Caute, Alan Cumming, John Curtis, Malcolm Dean, Norma di Marco, Diana Ditchfield, Roger Donald, Hans Dorflinger, Margaret Drabble, Robert Farrell, Revd Tom Farrell, Sir Martin Gilbert, Philip Haas, Jan Hartman, Paul Huxley, Francis King, Jack Kirwan, Ann Kitz, Rose Knox Peebles, Suzanne Lowry, Alison Lurie, Derek Mahon, Patricia Moynagh, Jerry O'Mahony, Kathie Parrish, Robert Parrish, Brian Pearce, Hilary Pratt, Richard Rawlinson, David Simpson, Anthony Smith, Hilary Spurling, Dr Robin Stott, Carole Tucker, Stephen Wall, Yvonne Wall, Tom Wakefield, Marina Warner, Janet Watts. *Letters*: Irving Lazar, Bertrand Tavernier. *Archives/private papers*: JGF papers (Trinity College, Dublin); Farrell family; BBC archives ('The White-Haired Novelist', Radio 3, 24.3.80); English P.E.N. (commemorative JGF tape). *Publications*: 'As Does the Bishop' by John Spurling and 'A Personal Memoir' by Malcolm Dean (*The Hill Station* 1981); 'Not a Crumb, Not a Wrinkle' by Bridget O'Toole (*Irish Studies* Autumn 1995); *Growing Up in Hollywood* and *Hollywood Doesn't Live Here Anymore* by Robert Parrish, Little, Brown 1976, 1988; *Simla Past and Present* by Edward J. Buck (1904); *Bookseller* ('Critics' Crowner' by Quentin Oates, December 23 and 30, 1978). *JGF interviews*: 'Epitaph for the Empire' by George Brock (*Observer* magazine 24.9.78); 'Writing in the Dark and Not a Detail Missed' by Caroline Moorehead (*The Times* 9.9.78). *JGF dialogue from correspondence*: with John Curtis (2.6.78, 8.6.78); with his parents (7.11.75, 26.1.79, 29.1.79); with

Norman Ilett (12.4.78); with Jack Kirwan (22.5.78, 5.11.78, 7.2.79); with Bridget O'Toole (9.6.77, 8.7.77, 5.11.78, 25.1.79); with Claude and Anna Simha (5.12.77); with David Simpson (9.6.78); with Hilary Spurling (18.12.78).

page
357   extraordinarily moving: *The Singapore Grip*, p. 429.
358   a charming painting . . . newspaper: Ibid., p. 597.
359   Her delicate appearance: Ibid., p. 75
366   I was in the pulpit: *The Lung*, p. 206.
366   No, not plain exactly: *The Hill Station*, pp. 37,69.
366   This brave and independent way of thinking: Ibid., pp. 27, 101.
367   an attempt to distil some order: Ibid., p. 72.
367   an instinct that all things were one: Ibid., p. 73.
367   These happenings at a distant point: Ibid., p. 110.
367   He considered himself to be: Ibid.
368   A plump, bright-eyed fellow: Ibid., p. 13.
368   a handsome, powerfully built man: Ibid., p. 77.
368   The Bishop had taken McNab's hand: Ibid.
369   And so, there the Major had been: *The Singapore Grip*, p. 15.

20 A Place to Breathe

Interviews: Sheilah Baird, Michael Daly, Roger Donald, Josephine Farrell, Dr Elie Harar, Jack Kirwan, Ann Kitz, Alison Lurie, Patricia Moynagh, Jerry O'Mahony, Mary O'Mahony, Bridget O'Toole, Kathie Parrish, Robert Parrish, Hilary Pratt, Richard Rawlinson, Dr Claude Simha, David Simpson, Carole Tucker, Yvonne Wall. *Archives/private papers*: JGF papers (Trinity College, Dublin); Farrell family; English P.E.N. (commemorative JGF tape). *JGF dialogue from correspondence*: with G.M. Arthursen (18.7.79); with Ann Colville (17.5.79, Aug, 79); with Brian and Rose Knox Peebles (13.7.79); with Malcolm Dean (July 79); with his parents (29.3.79, 8.7.79, 18.7.79, 8.8.79); with Bridget O'Toole (19.5.79, 9.6.79, 22.7.79); with Bob Parrish (8.5.79, 6.7.69, 23.7.79, 9.8.79); with David Simpson (5.8.79); with Carole Tucker (18.5.79, 15.6.79, 13.7.79, 30.7.79).

page
380   The sun had risen: *Troubles*, pp. 377, 426–7.
383   It is always possible to rouse: *The Hill Station*, p. 126.
383   Romish rituals, dangerous all round: Ibid., p. 109.
385   How could I have forgotten?: *The Lung*, pp. 138–9, 174.
386   Are you worried that Simla: *The Hill Station*, p. 69.
386   A feeling of great peace: Ibid., p. 122.
390   The mob felt somewhat cheated: Ibid., p. 148.
392   a steady, interminable downpour: *Troubles*, p. 203.
394   'But I'm sure it's all a misunderstanding': *The Hill Station*, p. 151.

Epilogue

Interviews: Sheilah Baird, Monika Beisner, Pamela Bradley, Susannah Clapp, Jonathan Clowes, Michael Daly, Elsie Donald, Hans Dorflinger, Carol Drisko, Josephine Farrell, Richard Farrell, James Hale, Terry Johnson, James Kirwan, Brian Knox Peebles, Suzanne Lowry, Garda Lupton, Alison Lurie, Derek Mahon, Ann Mankowitz, Jerry O'Mahony, Liam O'Regan, Bridget O'Toole, Robert Parrish, Hilary Pratt, Michael Roemer, Dr Claude Simha, Andrew Sinclair, Dr Robin Stott, Paul Theroux, Claire Tomalin, Carole Tucker, Yvonne Wall. *Letters*: Timothy Mo, Dr Colm Quigley. *Archives/private papers*: Farrell Family; (Rockefeller Archives Centre (Harkness); Andrew Sinclair (notes); English P.E.N. (commemorative JGF tape). *Publications*: contemporary newspapers and obituaries (August and September 1979); 'Legacy of a Great Friendship' by Margaret Drabble from *People*, ed. Susan Hill (Chatto & Windus/Hogarth Press); *The Gates of Ivory* by Margaret Drabble (Viking 1991). *Contemporary letters*: Jo Farrell–Yvonne Wall (29.8.79); Sonia Orwell–Hilary Spurling (17.10.79); Dr F.D. Coakley–Coroner Dr Colm Quigley (17.9.79); Coroner's Verdict: Cork County (West) Bantry, 2 November 1979.

page
396   so eloquent, so succinct!: *The Siege of Krishnapur*, p. 36.

Index

Adler, Stella 209
Agerholm, Ms 91
Agra, India 281–2
Aitken, Gillon 298
Ajanta caves, India 293
Albany, The (pub), London 158, 159, 162, 190, 194, 199, 247
Albemarle, Countess of 199
Algerian War 137, 144–5
Allen, Brigid 322, 325, 344, 376
Ambler, Eric 361
Amis, Kingsley 201, 297
Amis, Martin 326
Anderson, Lindsay 361
Angus, Ian 321
Arnott, Gary: at Oxford 110; puts JGF up 151, 155, 187, 195; approves of JGF's callgirl 165; in New York 207; has JGF to stay 220, 221; offers to pay JGF's London Library subscription 328; gives JGF a send-off 377; JGF to 237, 263; mentioned 239, 258, 260, 331, 350, 396
Arthursen, G. M. (GMA) 42–3, 46–7, 49, 353
Arts Council grant 275
Ashby, Sir Eric 199
Author's and Writer's Who's Who 267

Baffin Bay: Distant Early Warning Line 67–72
Bainbridge, Beryl 304, 396; *The Dressmaker* 304; *Weekend with Claude* 191
Baird, Sheilah (*née* Russell) 9–10, 15, 22
Bangkok, Thailand 337, 338–9
Banville, John 304
Barker, Paul 260
Barker, Sally 260
Barry, Kevin 219
Beckett, Samuel 133; *Endgame* 212
Beecham, Sir Thomas 41
Beer, Claire 146, 147
Beer, Franz 146, 147, 207, 221, 222, 227
Beer, Marlis 222
Behan, Brendan 104, 110, 160, 184
Beiles, Sinclair 130

Beisner, Monika 327, 358
Bellow, Saul 175, 218, 268, 353; *Henderson the Rain King* 154
Benares, India 287–9
Bennett, Alan 315
Bentlif, Sally *see* Sampson, Sally
Berger, John xvii, 306, 307
Bergman, Ingmar: *The Seventh Seal* 250; *Through a Glass, Darkly* 156
Betelgeuse disaster 376
Bodley Head, The (publishers) 351, 352
Bombay, India 279–80, 293
Bond, Sarah: affair with JGF 238–40, 241, 245, 260; portrayed in *Troubles* 240, 248–9, 252–3, 261; meets JGF in New York 251, 252; last meeting with JGF 310; JGF to 248, 249–50, 253, 258–9
Bond, Sue (*née* Rogers) 305, 308, 317
Booker Prize: JGF xvii, 303–9, 310, 313, 334; Iris Murdoch 374–5
Bookseller 160, 184, 267, 302, 303, 308
Bowen, Elizabeth 265, 266, 350; *The Last September* 285
Braine, John 297
Brasenose College, Oxford 75; accepts JGF 49–50; JGF at 75–9, 102, 106–14, 123, 124, 126–31, 132, 133; lack of recognition of JGF 375
Brendel, Alfred 264
Bresson, Robert 314
Brewster, Kingman 208
British Museum/London Library 202, 253, 271, 328
Brook, Peter 209
Brown, Ken 210, 211; *The Brig* 210
Brown, Thomas Weildon 29, 30, 32
Browne, Peter 98, 198
Brustein, Norma 209
Brustein, Robert 208, 209, 210, 218–19
Bryan, Felicity 314
Buchan, John 75
Buchwald, Art 208, 361
Buck, Jules 315, 316

Burgess, Anthony 201, 257
Burgess, Peter 3, 395
Burroughs, William 111, 130, 146
Burrows, Ralph 76, 77, 79, 109–10
Butler, Richard Austen, Lord 306–7

Calcutta, India 19, 289–91
Caldicott, Pamela 103
Calvocoressi, Peter 309
Campbell, Patrick 40
Camus, Albert 140, 191; *La Peste* 271
Cao, Thé-Anh 341
Cape, Jonathan (publishers): and *A Girl in the
     Head* 200–1, 247; and *Troubles* 257, 259,
     262, 265, 274, 298
Carton, Tom 37, 38
Castlepark School, Dublin 59–65
Caute, David 152, 296, 318; *At Fever Pitch*
     128; *The Left in Europe since 1789* 206–7
Chaplin, Charlie 211; *City Lights* 360
Chaptal, Jean-Antoine 135
Charteris, Leslie 40, 58
Chatto and Windus (publishers) 147, 148, 152
Chekhov, Anton 207; *A Dull Story* 266
Child, Julia: *Mastering the Art of French
     Cooking* 234
Chirimar, Shiv 276–7, 290
Chisholm, John 93, 131–2
Chittagong, India 12, 16–19, 56
Clapp, Susannah 359, 376, 385
Clowes, Jonathan: signs up JGF 159; throws
     impromptu get-togethers 162; and *The
     Lung* 181–2, 183, 184; approves JGF's
     'greenhouse' 189; advises him on
     screenwriting 198; and *A Girl in the Head*
     200, 247; JGF leaves 256, 316–17; on JGF
     162, 200; mentioned 161, 177, 300, 302
Colegate, Isobel 304
Colville, Ann 3, 358, 374, 383–4, 385, 391;
     JGF to 386
Connolly, Cyril 234; *Enemies of Promise* 313
Conrad, Joseph xvi; *Heart of Darkness* 94;
     Nostromo 94
Cook, Robin 162, 238
Cooke, Alastair 237, 393–4
Coote, Captain John 2
Corgi (publishers) 184
Corso, Gregory 111
Cowdrey, Colin 75
Cox, Jill (*née* Kirwan) 53–4, 55, 92–3, 113–14,
     185, 395
Cumming, Alan 146, 305, 347
Cumming, Bob: with JGF at Oxford 110–11,
     129, 133; in Thailand 156; in North
     Carolina 207; JGF stays with 213, 229–30;
     with JGF in New York 240–1, 252;
     portrayed in *Troubles* 261; on JGF 111,
     113, 127, 133, 237, 276; mentioned 145,
     293
Cumming, Patricia (Patsy) 145–8, 149, 156,
     207; JGF to 157, 171

Curtis, John 4, 351, 352, 365, 389
Cyr, Ulric 222, 224

Daily Telegraph 19, 44, 160, 184, 303, 309,
     353, 398
Daily Worker 309
Daly, Jerry and Michael 382, 388, 395
David, Elizabeth 364, 390
Davies, Jill 119, 120, 188
Davies, Phillip 110, 114, 119, 120, 123, 124,
     188
Dawson, Janet 128, 129, 257
Deakin, F. W. D. 199
Dean, Malcolm: friendship with JGF 236, 259,
     261, 267, 309, 376; interviews him 266,
     302; on JGF 236, 314, 356; covers JGF's
     death 2, 3; portrayed in *Singapore Grip*
     332; mentioned 331, 336, 339, 370, 396
Dehra Dun, India 283–5
Deighton, Len 159, 160, 265
Delaney, Dick 69, 71, 336–7
Delbos, Dr 143–4
Delhi, India 282–3
Denniston, Robin 298, 301–2
Diem, President 341, 342
di Marco, Norma 248, 255, 263, 275, 364
Ditchfield, Diana (*née* Saville) 255, 260, 312,
     325, 327, 350
Don, Général André Tran van 341, 344, 346
Donald, Roger: with JGF at school 47–8; visits
     him in Ireland 59; with JGF in Connecticut
     72–3; visits him in hospital 93, 95; criticises
     his bicycle-riding 109; at Cambridge 111;
     on Spanish trip with JGF 114–15, 117;
     criticises his treatment of Judy Mitchell 119;
     in Ireland with JGF and Judy 119, 120; in
     New York 207; on JGF and women 324;
     unsatisfactory reunion with JGF 355–6; and
     'Swifty' Lazar 361–2
Donald, Elsie 4, 217–18, 318, 376
Dorflinger, Hans 236, 240, 313, 327, 358, 371
Dostoevsky, Fyodor 215, 241, 253, 297
Douglas, Kirk 361
Drabble, Margaret: friendship with JGF 311–12;
     and JGF's relationships with women 321–2,
     326; disapproves his entry into films 363;
     and JGF's death 4, 396, 399; portrays JGF
     in *The Gates of Ivory* 314, 326–7, 374,
     396; mentioned 364, 384
Drisko, Carol: affair with JGF 227–30, 234–6,
     237–8, 240–1, 245–6; visits JGF in London
     247; they meet in New York 252; supports
     JGF 258, 296–7; portrayed in *Troubles*
     261; last meeting with JGF 297; on his
     death 397; JGF to 231, 232–3, 242, 254,
     257, 262
Drought, Geoffrey 61, 63, 65
Dublin 35–7, 57, 104; Balholm 55–6, 100–1,
     183, 295, 370; Castlepark School 59–65;
     370; Dalkey Lodge 53–4, 370; The Gwanda
     36–8, 54, 55, 370

Duffy, Maureen 158, 159, 190, 191, 194, 199, 296

Einstein, Albert 68
Eisenstein, Sergei 192
Ellis, Sandy *see* Fuller, Sandy
Ellis, William Webb 75
English, Martha 4–5, 206, 212, 241
Eysselinck, Dr Walter 198

Faber & Faber 114
Faber Memorial Prize 236, 267, 311, 383
Falkus, Christopher 301
Farrell, Clare (niece) 368
Farrell, Frank (William Farrell's cousin) 65, 67, 72
Farrell, James G.: birth 21; christening 22; childhood 22–8; schooling 24, 28–33 (Terra Nova), 39–51 (Rossall); early writing 45–6, 48, 49, 54, 56; adolescence in Ireland 53–9; teaching post 59–65; Canada and the Arctic Circle 65–6, 67–72; America and return to England 72–4; at Brasenose, Oxford 75–9; struck down with polio 79–80, 81–98; convalescence in Ireland 99–104; meets Judy Mitchell 104–6, *see* Miller, Judy; back at Oxford 106–14; trip to Spain 115–20; first short story 128; teaches English in France 133–8 (Mende), 139–45, 147–8 (Toulon); starts novel 138–9, see A Man from Elsewhere (*below*); a year in London 151–69; success with *A Man from Elsewhere* 157–8; and Albany meetings 158, 159; approaches Clowes 159; relationship with callgirl 162–70, *see* 'Hughes, Lucy'; in Paris 171–8, and Morocco 178–83; writes *The Lung* (*see below*) 172; his 'greenhouse' in London 187–9; social life 189–90; becomes a Hutchinson reader 190–1; starts *A Girl in the Head* 191–2 (*see below*); affair with Sandy Ellis 193–5 (*see* Fuller, Sandy); moves to Notting Hill 195–6; awarded Harkness Fellowship 198–9, 205–6; at Yale Drama School 206, 208–16; moves to New York 212–15, 217–20; starts *Troubles* 218 (*see below*); on Block Island 222–5; meets Carol Drisko 227–8, *see* Drisko, Carol; on Lowry pilgrimage with Sandy Ellis 228–34; last weeks in America 236–42; completes *Troubles* in London 245–50, 253–5; a weekend in New York 250–2; moves to Knightsbridge 255–6; his new agent 256–7, *see* Rogers, Deborah; meets Bridget O'Toole 260, *see* O'Toole, Bridget; financial problems 262; moves again 263–4; Faber Prize 267, 298; a literary star over night 267; researches *The Siege of Krishnapur* 271–7 (*see below*); in India and Nepal 278–93; *Siege* published 298–303; wins Booker Prize xvii, 303–10, 313, 334; photographed by Snowdon 310; meets Margaret Drabble 311–12; ambitions for a film breakthrough 314–16, 319–20; women friends 321–7; French cycling holidays 328; starts *The Singapore Grip* 328–31 (*see below*); invites his parents to Albert Hall Prom 331–2; in Singapore and Thailand 334–44; back in London 346–7; deterioration in health 347–8; and the deaths of friends 348–50; and the publication of *Singapore Grip* 350–3; further affairs 355–60; further film deals mooted 360–2; writes screenplay 362–4; starts *The Hill Station* 365–8 (*see below*); moves to Ireland 369–78; sanctuary 379–84; enjoyment of fishing 384–5, 387–8, 392–3; last weeks 389–94; death xv, 1–6, 395, 396–8; funeral and memorial service 395–6
publications:
A Girl in the Head 23, 55, 58, 59, 64, 98, 100, 103, 109, 110, 116–17, 121, 122, 132, 140, 142–3, 145, 163, 164, 180, 182, 187, 188, 192–8, 200–1, 216, 217, 234, 247, 260, 262; reviews 228, 231, 233–4
The Hill Station 19, 66, 98, 100, 144, 365–9, 375, 383, 384, 386, 392–4
'Letter for Carola' 106–7, 128–9
The Lung 42, 43, 46, 50, 57, 58, 64, 66, 74, 75, 77, 79–80, 81–97, 100, 103, 106, 115, 120, 121, 122, 123, 127, 131, 171, 172–3, 175, 176, 178, 181, 182–4, 186, 192, 248, 366, 397; reviews 184–5
A Man from Elsewhere 39, 60, 107, 110, 122–3, 131, 138–9, 142, 146, 147, 148–9, 152–3, 154, 155, 157–8, 171, 173, 190; reviews 160–1
'Notebook' (*Oxford Opinion*) 129–30, 133, 231
The Siege of Krishnapur xv-xvi, xvii, 4, 24, 26, 27, 29, 41, 56, 66, 98, 108–9, 127, 135, 144, 163, 181, 271–8, 285–6, 285–93, 295, 297–302, 303–5, 309, 314, 315, 318, 319–20, 360–2, 389; reviews 302–3
The Singapore Grip xv, xvi, xvii, 12, 22, 27, 41, 125–6, 132–3, 256, 328–31, 332–4, 335–8, 339, 343–6, 347, 348–53, 356, 357, 358, 359, 367, 369, 375, 389, 398; reviews 353, 390
Troubles xv, xvi, 1, 13, 16, 24, 30, 31, 36, 37, 41–2, 43, 60–3, 70–1, 100, 125, 129, 137, 165, 166, 168, 188, 218–19, 221–2, 223, 225, 237, 238, 239–40, 242, 246, 248–9, 253–4, 257–66, 274, 297, 315, 362, 363, 380; reviews 266–7, 297, 303
Farrell, James T. (author) 4–5, 48, 160, 201, 234, 259, 370
Farrell, Josephine (*née* Russell) (mother): birth and early life in Ireland 12, 13–14; school 14; secretarial course 15; meets Bill 9–10, 15; marries in India 15–17; and his deafness 16; life in India 18, 19; pregnancy and

return to England 19–20; and JGF's birth
21, 22; on JGF 24, 28; in wartime
Southport 22–7; in Ireland 35–6, 38, 39,
55, 56; sends JGF a cake 71; visits him in
hospital 81, 84, 86; and JGF in Ireland 98,
99, 102; interest in roses 100; on *The Lung*
185; subsidises JGF 247, 385; wins New
York trip for JGF and Richard 250; in
Malta 263; returns to England 334, 350;
gives JGF furniture 376; visits him in
Ireland 384; and his death 3, 397; death xi
Farrell, Lindy (sister-in-law) 347
Farrell, Margaret (grandmother) 11, 16, 20
Farrell, May (aunt) 11, 377–8
Farrell, Michael (author): *Thy Tears Might
Cease* 160
Farrell, Richard (brother): birth 28; at Rossall
74; tennis with JGF 99, 100; in New York
with JGF 250, 251; helps on research for
Singapore Grip 331; and JGF's death 1, 3,
395, 396; mentioned 347
Farrell, Robert (brother): birth 19; and JGF 22,
24, 57; and his father 24–5; and evacuees
27; at school 28, 29, 30; at Trinity,
Dublin 48; emigrates to Canada 63, 65,
72; correspondence with JGF 161, 191;
JGF and Sandy stay with 232, 233–4;
visits JGF 315, 317; on JGF 50; mentioned
331, 371
Farrell, Thomas James (grandfather) 11, 20
Farrell, Tom (uncle) 11, 38
Farrell, Reverend Tom (cousin): sporting
triumphs 38–9, 74–5, 77, 78, 100, 109,
133; enters the church 309; portrayed in
Hill Station 39, 100, 368–9; conducts JGF's
memorial service 396
Farrell, William (father): early life 10–12; meets
Josephine 9–10; proposes 15; his deafness
16–17, 18; marriage in India 17; returns to
England 20; war work 22; relationship with
his sons 24–5, 26, 28; in Ireland 35, 37,
100; and JGF 39, 43, 55, 247; plays golf
56; visits JGF in hospital 81, 84; in Malta
263; helps JGF with his research 277; at the
Albert Hall 331, 367; returns to England
334, 350; worsening health 351, 371, 384;
and JGF 351, 372, 377, 385; and JGF's
death 3
Faulkner, William 199
Feiffer, Jules: *Little Murders* 208
Field, Michael 234–5
Fitzgerald, F. Scott 48, 143, 174
Fleissner, Erwin 110, 111, 112, 124, 125–6,
132, 207, 208, 252
Fleissner, Norma 207, 252
Fontana (publishers) 352
Ford, John 360
Forster, E. M. 214; *A Passage to India* 273
Fowles, John 201
Fox, John B. 206, 213–14, 241
Fraser, Antonia 311, 352

Frayn, Michael 4, 304
Frears, Stephen 315
Fuller, Sandy (*née* Ellis): affair with JGF 193–5,
197, 200, 203, 245–6; with JGF on Lowry
pilgrimage 212, 228–33; returns to England
234, 242

Garnett, David 304
Gascoigne, Bamber 304
Gaulle, Charles de 137, 144, 272
Gemill, Andrew 189, 194, 312–13
Gerhardie, William 351
Gibbon, Monk 133
Gibson, Sir Edmund 283–5, 332
Gide, André 136 175
Gilbert, (Sir) Martin 126–8, 277, 353, 371
Ginsberg, Allen 111
Godwin, Tony: publishes *Siege of Krishnapur*
298–9, 300, 302, 303, 306; and Deborah
Rogers 299–300, 317; and JGF 301, 308;
in New York 318, 319, 361; death 348,
349
Goff, Martyn 306, 307
Golding, William 75, 114
Gover, Tom 44–5, 46
Graham, Dr 10, 15, 16, 20
Greene, Graham 339, 375; *The Quiet American*
340
Gross, Miriam (*née* May) 114, 278
Guardian 2, 3, 185, 259, 266, 331, 359, 364
Guare, John 210, 211, 214
Guinness, Bryan (Lord Moyne) 133

Hale, James 298, 396
Hamish Hamilton (publishers) 298, 300, 312
Harar, Dr Elie 178–83, 379
Harcourt Brace Jovanovich 318, 361
Harkness Fellowships 5, 198–9, 205–6, 212,
218, 228, 236, 313
Harper and Row (publishers) 248, 265
Harrison, Philippa 319
Hartman, Jan 113
Harwood, Ronald 304
Heinemann (publishers) 311
Hemingway, Ernest 48, 65, 115, 116, 174, 265,
361; *The Sun Also Rises* 114
Hersey, John 208
Hillary, Sir Edmund 336
Hockney, David 260
Hodder and Stoughton (publishers) 298, 301
Holloway, David 398
Hours, Hubert 136
Howard, Frances 247
'Hughes, Lucy' (JGF's callgirl) 162–70, 246–7,
278, 324, 360, 396
Hughes, Richard xvi, 31, 239, 311, 331, 348
Hutchinson (publishers): publish *A Man from
Elsewhere* 155, 157–8, 161, 173; and *The
Lung* 182, 183–4; JGF becomes a reader
190–1, 193; *see also* Albany, The
Huxley, Paul 236, 323, 371

Ilett, Norman 44, 48–9, 78, 369
India: JGF's parents in 16–20; JFG in 275, 278–91, 292–3
Ionesco, Eugene 309; *The Seven Deadly Sins* 202
Ireland: the 'Troubles' 13–14; JGF in 120–1, 185–6, 196–7, 369–73, 379–94; *see also* Dublin; *Troubles* (*under* Farrell, J. G.)
Irish Times 133, 136, 184–5
Ironside, Dr 85
Isis: 'Letter for Carola' 106–7, 128–9

Jaipur, India 280–1
Jhabvala, Ruth Prawer 312
Joyce, James 69, 133, 147, 268; *Ulysses* 58

Kathmandu, Nepal 291–2
Kaufmann, Dr (maths master) 32
Kavanagh, Patrick 36
Kazan, Elia 208
Keating, Harry 293
Kent & Essex Courier 152
Kerr, Deborah 361
Khajuraho, India 292
Kilmartin, Terence 3, 307
King, Francis 267, 311, 325, 334, 378, 380
Kirwan, Hilary *see* Pratt, Hilary
Kirwan, Jack 54; at Trinity College, Dublin 63, 104; receives *Man from Elsewhere* 161; acts for JGF in house buying 373; on JGF 54, 57, 78, 102; and JGF's death 1, 395; JGF to 369–70, 372; mentioned 58, 59, 185
Kirwan, Jill *see* Cox, Jill
Kirwan, Valentine 54, 55, 56–7, 370
Knopf (publishers) 297
Knox Peebles, Brian 123, 124, 125, 130, 151–2, 158, 304–5, 309, 356; JGF to 167, 206–7, 208, 211, 230
Knox Peebles, Nina 278
Knox Peebles, Rose 152, 158, 322, 356
Koestler, Arthur 184
Korn, Ed 115
Kott, Jan 209
Kuala Lumpur 337–8, 342–3

Lala, Roshan 281
Lampedusa, Giuseppe di 144, 214; *The Leopard* 143, 237
Laulicht, David 342
Laulicht, Martine 342
Lawrence, Sir Henry 274
Lawson, Nigel 265
Lazar, Irving 'Swifty' 361, 362, 371, 389
Lean, David 211, 316, 319, 320, 360
Legge, Rosemary 301, 393
Lehmann, Rosamond 312
Leonard, Michael 276, 358
Lessing, Doris 159
Levin, Bernard 160, 333, 384
Lewis, Cecil Day 152

Listener 303
Literary Guild 352
Liverpool 11, 20, 26–8
London 203; JGF's homes: Egerton Gardens 263–4; Palace Gardens Terrace 187–8, 189; Pembridge Road 165, 189, 193, 247, 248; Pont Street Mews 255–6; Stanley House Hotel 195–6, 197, 245, 248
Loti, Pierre: *Pêcheur d'Islande* xvi–xvii, 136
Lowney, Ted 395
Lowry, Malcolm 113, 125, 175, 212, 221; JGF's pilgrimage 212, 229–33; *Hear Us O Lord from Heaven Thy Dwelling Place* 154; *Ultramarine* 115; *Under the Volcano* 113, 154, 190, 230, 231–2, 326, 333
Lowry, Suzanne 377
Lucknow, India 285–7
Lurie, Alison 268, 309, 321, 327, 364, 376
Lusitania, S. S. 13
Lusty, Robert 157

McCarthy, Mary 303, 305
McCormack, John 15
McCormmach, Russell: with JGF at Oxford 110, 111, 113; collaboration on filmscript 125; his manuscript 'a modern Faust' 145; *The Lung* dedicated to 186; visits JGF in London 186, 189; at University of Pennsylvania 207; with JGF in New York 219–20; introduced to Sarah 241; impressed by 'Lucy Hughes' 246–7; portrayed in *Troubles* 261; JGF to 153, 154, 155, 156, 158, 161, 162, 177, 183, 191, 192–3, 194, 196, 199, 200, 203, 207, 212, 228, 242, 259–60, 264, 279, 298, 316; mentioned 148, 161, 238
McDermott, Sean 219
MacGregor, Charles 274–5
MacGregor, Edward 274–5, 287
McKenna, Siobhan 57
Mackenzie, Clifton ('The Pie') 31, 99
McNair, Harry 40, 41, 47, 348
Mahon, Derek 268–9, 304, 310, 313, 314, 349, 396; *A Disused Shed in County Wexford* 311; *The Yellow Book* 401–2
Mahon, Doreen 349
Mankowitz, Wolf 372, 393
Mann, Thomas: *The Magic Mountain* 113, 136, 228
Manning, Olivia 214, 267, 269, 309, 311, 312, 351, 353, 359, 396; *The Balkan Trilogy* 312; *The Sum of Things* 398
Márquez, Gabriel García 312
Marriott, Oliver 250
Marshall, Roger 87, 110
Maschler, Tom 200–1, 257, 262, 298
Masters, John 273
Matthews, Sergeant-Major A. E. 31
Maugham, W. Somerset 143
Mauriac, François 130
Maurois, André 339

Mavor, Elizabeth 304
Mawdsley, Professor Ronald 76
Mawdsley, William ('Uncle Will') 22–3, 24
May, Miriam *see* Gross, Miriam
Mende, France 135–9
Merrick, David 361–2
Miller, Judy (*née* Mitchell): relationship with
    JGF 104–6, 113; Spanish holiday 114,
    119, 120; car crash and its effect on JGF
    121–4, 125, 129, 130–1, 132, 134, 141,
    185; travels to Australia 269–70;
    portrayed in *Siege of Krishanpur* 278;
    marriage 369
Miller, Karl 303, 304, 305, 306; (ed.) *Memoirs
    of Modern Scotland* 259
Minh, Général Dong Van 342, 345, 346
Mitchell, Judy *see* Miller, Judy
Mitchell, Molly *see* Stokes, Molly
Mitchell, Terence 105, 123
Mitchum, Robert 360, 362
Mo, Timothy 353, 399–400; *The Monkey King*
    382–3
Monsarrat, Nicholas 4, 265, 393
Morgan, Charles 75
Morocco, JGF in 178–83
Mountbatten, Lord Louis 5
Moynagh, Patricia 357–8, 374, 376, 391, 396
Muggeridge, Malcolm 268
Murdoch, Iris 160, 304, 305, 306, 375; *The
    Black Prince* 304; *The Sea, The Sea* 374–5
Murphy, John 306
Murray, Roger 77, 78
Murry, John Middleton 75
Musil, Robert 220, 221
Mussoorie, India 285, 366

Nabokov, Vladimir 191, 218; *Lolita* 113, 191;
    Speak, Memory 191
Naipaul, V.S. 312
Neave, Airey 379
Nepal 291–2
Nesbitt, Lynn 256
New Haven, Connecticut 206–12
New Society 260
New Statesman 160, 266, 303, 325, 353
New Yorker 4, 319
New York Times 319
Newman, Paul 208
Newsweek 319
Nicholas, Professor Barry 76, 88, 102
Nicol, Graham 157, 158, 159, 161, 178, 182,
    183, 190, 198, 247
Niesewand, Nonie 365

O'Brien, Edna 4, 268, 303, 305, 352
Observer 3, 160, 185, 266, 302, 307
O'Casey, Sean 133
O'Connor, Frank 36
O'Dell, Mr and Mrs 16, 17
O'Flaherty, Liam 36
Oliver, Stephen 363

O'Mahony, Jerry: sells cottage to JGF 372;
    friendship with JGF 381, 382, 384, 387,
    388, 389, 390, 391, 393; and JGF's death
    2, 3, 5, 6, 395, 398
O'Mahony, John 381
O'Mahony, Mary 381
Orwell, George 312; *Inside the Whale* 130
Orwell, Sonia 3–4, 267, 269, 312, 321, 330,
    350, 396
Osborne, John 315
O'Toole, Bridge: relationship with JGF 260–2,
    263, 264–5, 268–9, 283, 295–6, 324, 356,
    357, 385, 392; takes up lectureship at
    University of Ulster 266; portrayed in *Siege
    of Krishnapur* 278; works on *Siege*
    typescript 300–1; helps with research 331;
    in Cornwall with JGF 350; sends him a tin
    whistle 376; JGF to 279–80, 283, 309, 324,
    373, 381, 384, 391
O'Toole, Peter 315
Owen, Edward 29
Oxford 74, 106, 107, 111–12; Slade Hospital
    81–9; Vincents (sporting club) 77, 110;
    Woodstock Road 125; *see also* Brasenose
    College
Oxford Opinion: 'Notebook' 129–30, 133, 231

Paisley, Dr Ian 383
Pan (publishers) 256
Pantheon (publisher) 217
Paris, JGF in 145–6, 169–78, 264–5, 371, 377,
    379
Parker, Roy 61, 62
Parrish, Kathie 360, 361, 371–2, 378, 386, 396
Parrish, Robert (Bob): friendship with JGF 360–
    1; autobiography published 361;
    collaboration on screenplay with JGF 363;
    househunting in Ireland 371–2; visits JGF
    386; JGF to 388, 392, 393; at JGF's funeral
    396; mentioned 373, 377, 378
Pearce, Brian 75–6, 79, 88, 123, 124, 152, 263,
    371
Pearce, James 278
Peck, Gregory 361
Penguin Books 299, 309, 319, 389
Peters, A.D. 190
Peters, Catherine 262, 274, 298; JGF to 309
Philippe, Gérard 130
Phillips, Nevill 41, 43, 46, 106, 334
Pinter, Harold 311
Plant, Sergeant P. W. 31
Portlaoise prison, Ireland 38
Potter, Dennis 112, 304
Powell, Anthony 268; *A Dance to the Music of
    Time* 190, 268
Pratt, Amanda 388
Pratt, Hilary (*née* Kirwan): relationship with
    JGF 64, 65; and JGF's affair with Judy
    Mitchell 104, 119, 121, 123; embarrassed
    by visit from JGF 185–6, 359; and his
    return to Ireland 369, 370, 383, 386; visits

JGF 388; on JGF 57, 103; on his funeral 395
Pringle, Donald 60–1, 62, 65
Profumo affair 161, 162
Proust, Marcel 96, 102, 136, 143, 173, 174, 177, 215–16, 234, 328
Public Lending Rights campaign 296, 389
Putt, Gorley 199

Queen Elizabeth 74, 237, 241–2

Ranchi, S.S. 9, 10, 12
Range, Peter Ross 342
Rankin, Pat 57, 103, 105
Raven, Simon 160
Rawlinson, Richard 314
Read, Emily 236–7
Read, Piers Paul 236–7, 256, 267, 302, 304, 308; *The Junkers* 236
Remy, Pierre Jean 379
Rhys, Jean 4, 267–8
Riddell, Alan 193
Riefenstahl, Leni: *Olympiad* 211
Roberts, Dick 332, 365
Roberts, Mary 24
Robinson, Robert: book programme 347
Roemer, Michael 210, 211–12, 213, 215–16, 218, 220, 242, 273, 297, 397
Rogers, Deborah 256–8, 262, 298, 299–300, 306, 350, 389; on JGF 317–18
Rogers, Sue *see* Bond, Sue
Rossall School 32, 39–51, 74, 76, 106, 220, 348, 353
Rossallian, The 45, 46, 48, 49, 54, 56
Rossallians, Old 76, 78, 88, 100, 319
Roth, Philip 208
Rouse, Barbara Yvonne 92, 95, 97
Russell, Bertrand 68
Russell, Clara (*née* Miller) 13
Russell, Edith (*née* Miller) 13, 14, 15
Russell, George 12, 13
Russell, Harry 3, 13–14, 40, 383
Russell, Joseph 12
Russell, Robert Gordon Hall (Bob) 9, 12–15, 16, 35, 37, 38
Russell, Sheilah *see* Baird, Sheilah

Saigon 339–42, 344–6, 350
Sampson, Anthony 190, 319
Sampson, Sally (*née* Bentlif) 114, 115, 128, 190, 312, 319
Sartre, Jean-Paul 136, 138, 174, 250
Saville, Diana *see* Ditchfield, Diana
Saxonia, R.M.S. 65–6
Scott-Fox, Judy 316, 319
Secker and Warburg (publishers) 152, 155
Shabinska, Ita 115
Shackleton, Dr Robert 107–8, 127, 128–9, 260, 277, 375
Shakespeare and Company, Paris 130, 146, 147, 175

Shannon, Bill 259, 370
Shaw, Irwin 265, 361
Shawcross, William 364
Shepard, Sam 210
Shiffrin, André 111, 114, 217
Shone, Sir Robert 199
Sight and Sound 257
Simha, Anna 176, 264, 377
Simha, Claude: friendship with JGF 173–6, 177–8; portrayed in *Singapore Grip* 332; prescribes amphetamines 250; visited by JGF 264–5, 377; JGF to 231, 363; on JGF 177; on JGF's death 397
Simpson, David 2, 4, 384–5
Sinclair, Andrew 114, 115, 116, 117, 174, 309, 397; *The Breaking of Bumbo* 114; *My Friend Judas* 118
Sinclair-Stevenson, Christopher 312
Singapore, research in 335–7, 343
Slade Hospital, Oxford 81–9
Slaughter, Frank G. 184
Smith, Martyn 383
Snow, C.P. 265
Snowdon, Lord 310
Society of Authors 296, 347
Southport 22–8
Spain, JGF in 114, 115–20
Spark, Muriel: *Memento Mori* 214–15
Spectator 190, 259, 265
Spence, Jonathan 114, 115, 116
Spiegel, Sam 360
Spurling, Hilary 190; at *Spectator* 259, 265; tells JGF of Faber Prize 267; inspires JGF 365–6; chooses *Singapore Grip* as her book of the year 375; becomes Booker Prize judge 382; on JGF 195, 318; JGF to 201; and JGF's death 3, 4; on Olivia Manning 396
Spurling, John: friendship with JGF 189–90, 192, 194, 197, 203, 250, 309, 313, 364; introduces JGF to his uncle 283, 284; on JGF 189–90, 245, 247, 293; JGF to 255, 283–4; and JGF's death 3, 4
Spurling, Nat 328
Stevenson, Robert Louis: *Beach at Falesa* 362–4
Stokes, Anne 328
Stokes, Molly (*née* Mitchell) 105, 124
Storey, David 160, 303–4
Stott, Robin 277, 331, 397
Styron, William 208
Suez Crisis 101–2
Sunday Times 302, 309, 359
Symons, Julian 302
Synge, J.M.: *The Aran Islands* 5; *Playboy of the Western World* 57

Tansey, Alf 49, 100
Tavernier, Bertrand 362–3, 379, 393
Taylor, Frank 100
Teitelbaum, Irving 315
Terra Nova school, Cheshire 28–33, 313
Teusch, Bart 211

Theroux, Paul 327–8, 334, 375, 382
Thibault-Chambault, Professeur Jean 138, 139
Thieu, President 340, 345
Thody, Philip: *Albert Camus* 191
Time magazine 203, 319, 342, 390
Times, The 266, 328, 333, 352, 384
Times Literary Supplement 160, 185, 233, 266–7
Tolstoy, Count Lev 69, 173, 197, 329, 353; *War and Peace* 266
Tomalin, Claire 325–6, 376
Tomalin, Nicholas 325
Toone, W. P. 60
Toulon, France 139–40, 141–5, 147–9
Trevor, Lavinia 303, 376
Trevor, William 304
Trillin, Calvin 'Bud' 4, 115, 116, 117–18
Trueta, Professor 90, 99, 98
Tucker, Carole 374, 378, 385–6, 391–2

Unsworth, Barry 304

Van Allen, Jay 115
Van Briesgan, Christian 198, 228
Viceroy of India, S.S. 19
Vietnam 236, 296, 338–42, 344–6, 350
Vogue xvii, 310

Wakefield, Tom 197, 203, 250, 278, 305, 325
Waley, Arthur 357
Wall, Stephen 94, 96, 107, 132, 193, 334; JGF to 304, 356

Wall, Yvonne 107, 132, 348
Warner, Marina 352–3, 364
Watts, Janet 304, 359
Waugh, Auberon 112, 309
Weidenfeld, Sir George 302, 306, 308, 311
Weidenfeld and Nicolson: publish *Siege of Krishnapur* 298, 299, 300, 301–2, 303; publish *Singapore Grip* 351, 352–3, 375; mentioned 4, 357, 359
Weinstein, Arnold 209
White, Patrick 265, 353
Widerberg, Bo 363
Widmark, Richard 362
Wilby, Michael 308
Williams, Heathcote 250
Wilson, Angus 266
Wingfield Morris Hospital, Headington 89–98, 102
Winner, Michael 198
Wodehouse, P.G. 25, 67, 100, 317
Wolley, Clive Phillips 42
Wright, Lacy 338–9, 340–2, 345
Wright, Judith 355, 357, 358, 374
Writer's Guild 296

Yale 208; Drama School 198, 206, 208–16
Young, Reverend Carl 40, 50
Young, Dorothy 40–1
Young, Robert 210, 211

Zinnemann, Fred 315–16, 319–20

A NOTE ON THE TYPE

The text of this book is set in Linotype Sabon,
named after the type founder, Jacques Sabon. It
was designed by Jan Tschichold and jointly
developed by Linotype, Monotype and Stempel,
in response to a need for a typeface to be
available in identical form for mechanical hot
metal composition and hand composition using
foundry type.

Tschichold based his design for Sabon roman on
a fount engraved by Garamond, and Sabon italic
on a fount by Granjon. It was first used in 1966
and has proved an enduring modern classic.